A SCALAWAG IN GEORGIA

WILLIAM WARREN ROGERS JR.

A Scalawag in Georgia

RICHARD WHITELEY AND THE POLITICS OF RECONSTRUCTION

UNIVERSITY OF ILLINOIS PRESS
URBANA AND CHICAGO

Frontispiece: Richard Whiteley, circa 1871.
Courtesy of Billy McCoy.

Manufactured in the United States of America
C 5 4 3 2 1

∞ This book is printed on acid-free paper.

Library of Congress Cataloging-in-Publication Data
Rogers, William Warren, 1955–
A scalawag in Georgia : Richard Whiteley and the politics of Reconstruction / William Warren Rogers Jr.
p. cm.
Includes bibliographical references and index.
ISBN-13: 978-0-252-03160-1 (cloth : alk. paper)
ISBN-10: 0-252-03160-1 (cloth : alk. paper)
1. Whiteley, Richard H. (Richard Henry), 1830–1890. 2. Legislators—United States—Biography. 3. United States. Congress. House—Biography. 4. Reconstruction (U.S. history, 1865–1877)—Georgia. 5. Georgia—Politics and government—1865–1950. 6. Republican Party (Ga.)—Biography. 7. Irish Americans—Biography. 8. Pioneers—Colorado—Boulder—Biography. 9. Boulder (Colo.)—Biography.
I. Title.
E664.W612R64 2007
973.8092—dc22 [B] 2006029421

To the memory of

Richard L. Greaves and Bennett H. Wall

Contents

Illustrations

Acknowledgments

Various people made possible this book but none so much as my father, William Warren Rogers. He thought that a study of Richard H. Whiteley was possible and potentially important. Many advantages come with having a historian as a father, and I profited greatly from his advice, encouragement, and considerable editorial skills as the biography took shape. I am very grateful. This is not to discount my mother's contribution, because she has always been genuinely interested in my research. Lee Rogers, my wife, has followed Richard Whiteley's trail with me, and even helped with the research. She has in good spirits allowed me to combine vacation with research trips, and I thank her for that and much more. For advice on Whiteley as a lawyer, I have depended on two lawyers in the family, Katie Berry (my sister) and her husband, Jim Berry.

I am especially indebted to Juanita Whiddon, who considered making Richard Whiteley a dissertation subject. She generously gave me the topic and some of her early notes. Three colleagues of mine at Gainesville State College have been very helpful. Charles Karcher, head of the department, is extremely supportive of my scholarship, and has provided the financial means to make several research trips. Tom Burns has been generous with his time and helped me with formatting the manuscript. Jeff Pardue, a history colleague, has taken a interest in Whiteley's story and provided invaluable technological/computer knowhow. With good reason, Jeff may have wished our offices were not so close. Librarians Priscilla Rankin and Becky Webb have faithfully borrowed materials through the Interlibrary Loan Office. Rebecca Homan, the college archivist, has also made work easier. Those in the historical field who have made suggestions and offered much-appreciated support are Jonathan Bryant, Vernon Burton, Mike Denham, Lee Formwalt, Sally Hadden, Jim Lorence, Paul Pruitt, Bawa Singh, and David Ward. I extend a very special thank you to John Inscoe, at the University of Georgia, who has contributed greatly to this book.

At various archives, courthouses, and libraries, many people have provided assistance. At the Bainbridge College Library, Martha Mitchell did so, and at the Decatur County Courthouse in Bainbridge, circuit clerk Tripp Barwick was unfailingly solicitous and friendly. Frances Willis, administrative assistant to the mayor, at the Bainbridge City Hall, has been a helpful local source, and I thank Benny Brookship of Bainbridge for allowing me to look at private records in his possession. Suzanne F. Tubbs, vicar of St. John's Episcopal Church, permitted me to examine the St. John's Church records in Bainbridge. In nearby Albany, Georgia, C. S. Pritchett made available the diary of Nelson Tift. In Atlanta, the staff at the Georgia State Department of Archives in History were exceedingly helpful, and I especially thank archivists Gail DeLoach, Joanne Smalley, and Sally Moseley. I am indebted to the staffs at the Southern Historical Collection in Chapel Hill, North Carolina, and nearby, the Special Collections Department in the William Perkins Library at Duke University. I have been a regular patron at the Hargrett Rare Book and Manuscript Library at the University of Georgia. I thank the accommodating staff and especially Chuck Barber and Melissa Bush. Charles Reeves and other archivists at the Eastpoint, Georgia, branch of the National Archives provided aid, as did individuals at the National Archives. Kristen Wilhelm, archivist at the National Archive Center for Legislative Archives, especially exceeded the call of duty. So did Elizabeth Rybicki, analyst in American National Government at the Congressional Research Service. I feel very fortunate to be able to call on Peter Kraft in the capacity of cartographer.

David Hays, archivist at the University of Colorado at Boulder, directed me to various collections and sources. Very knowledgeable about Boulder's past, David has taken an appreciated and helpful interest in the project. The materials made available by the staff at the Carnegie Branch Library for Local History in Boulder also make this a better book. Those in Boulder whom I would like to thank further are Marti Anderson, Betsy Aspinwall, Joyce Davies, and Laurence Paddock. In Boulder, I interviewed Montford Whiteley, Richard Whiteley's grandson. Unfortunately, he has died since our meeting, but his daughter, Francie Whiteley, ably shoulders the mantle of family historian. Without the help of Billy McCoy, also a descendant, the picture of Whiteley would have been less complete.

This book is dedicated to Richard L. Greaves and Bennett H. Wall. In the 1970s I was fortunate to be a student of Richard Greaves, a member of the Department of History at Florida State University. Although his English history specialty is far from my field, Richard taught me a great deal about being a historian. As I found a place teaching and writing, I turned to him often, and Richard returned an interest and support that I will never forget. In Athens, Georgia, in the 1980s, I met Bennett Wall, the longstanding secretary treasurer of the Southern Historical Association. Ben was a historian, an influential teacher, and a student of history throughout his long and fine life. Beyond that, Dr. Wall was for me personally a great man whose friendship I cherished.

A SCALAWAG IN GEORGIA

Introduction

Richard Henry Whiteley participated directly in the epic events of nineteenth-century America. Arriving poor from Ireland in the 1830s, he and his family settled in Georgia. Whiteley climbed the textile factory ladder from "factory boy" to mill owner, and then became a lawyer. He served the Confederacy as an officer during the Civil War. As a Republican, Whiteley represented the Second District of Georgia in Congress from 1871 to 1875. He joined the American exodus west in 1877, moving to the recently designated state of Colorado. This biography concerns Whiteley's entire life but mainly concentrates on the Reconstruction years.[1]

Whiteley's political career spanned the period of Republican Party viability in Georgia and the South. Taking what was for a white Southerner an extremely unorthodox political course, he championed the freedpeople's interests after the war. Whiteley helped write the Republican-authored state constitution and served in Congress longer than any other Republican from Georgia. Republican power in the South rose and fell, and in keeping with the trend, so did that of Richard Whiteley. Ultimately, he and Georgia Republicans suffered virtual political extinction—the fate of Republicanism in all the southern states.

Whiteley described the years of Reconstruction as a time of "great moment and trial." The Civil War, though settling the sanctity of the Union, left other questions unanswered. The most critical was the civil status of the ex-slave. The First Military Reconstruction Act in 1867 and the Fourteenth Amendment answered that question. Blacks gained the right to vote and became United States citizens. Yet freedom in fact and freedom in name were different. Most southern whites (and much of the northern public) considered the ex-slaves unprepared for and unworthy of citizenship. In the South, where Reconstruction played out, the Republican racial ideology violated the dominant cultural mindset and shibboleths of white supremacy. Moreover, the newly formed Republican Party posed a major political threat to southern Democrats. Bitter and passionate opposition to Republicanism in the 1860s and 1870s was the consequence.

Whiteley's participation in this turbulent era imparts to his career a profound significance. That his legislative initiatives in Congress were often unsuccessful is irrelevant. So is the reality that he lost more congressional races than he won. Viewed in the context of Reconstruction, Whiteley's career reveals much about the postwar South. What circumstances accounted for the election of a white Republican from a Deep South congressional district? Once elected, could a man reviled as a traitorous scalawag and associated with the ex-slaves continue to hold office? Were his actions demonstrably Radical? The answers have bearing on the personal biography of Richard Whiteley but also contain larger implications for the South and the nation.

The political security and standing of Whiteley and the southern wing of the Republican Party were inevitably linked. If the party was to survive in the South, he and fellow Republicans would have to overcome staggering challenges. Republicans possessed no political heritage or tradition to draw upon, and formidable obstacles to the party's success existed. Blacks provided a natural Republican constituency, but tapping that potential posed difficulties, given white landlords' leverage over their black tenants. Attracting whites to the party was necessary if Republicans were to remain competitive, but white Southerners connected Republicanism with the recent enemy and black equality. How could the party achieve longevity when the wealth, property, and economic power in virtually every town, county, and city rested with the Democratic opposition? Some critics refused to concede to the Republican Party even the mantle of legitimacy. Political vigilantes, belonging to the Ku Klux Klan or other anti-Republican organizations, intimidated and murdered in the name of white supremacy. Vote-counting fraud did not begin or end with Reconstruction, but the scale of the political chicanery was enormous. The situation was unprecedented in the American political tradition.[2]

This was the world of Richard Whiteley. He ran for Congress five times between 1868 and 1876 (more than any other southern Republican during Reconstruction). Prospects of election or reelection were always tenuous. Recently enfranchised blacks, thousands strong, voted repeatedly for him. Whiteley represented their aspirations for a new and better life. Although freedpeople composed the rank and file of Whiteley's political army, he was for a time palatable to some whites. Whiteley managed to honor his Republican convictions and maintain a fragile coalition of moderate whites and freedpeople. As he precariously balanced appealing to blacks without alienating whites, and not driving off freedpeople by accommodating whites, the art of the politician came into clear focus, illuminating the dynamics of a grassroots Reconstruction election. What political survival for a Republican required in Georgia was often necessary in South Carolina, Louisiana, and throughout the South. It took a man of Richard Whiteley's skills to succeed, if only temporarily.

The term "Radical Reconstruction," frequently employed to describe the period following the war in the South, can be misleading. In the conventional sense, little was radical about Reconstruction. Private property was not confiscated, nor was there widespread or harsh political punishment. Yet seminal change occurred, and enfranchising the freedmen constituted the most radical aspect of congressional Reconstruction. Blacks voting the Republican ticket often changed the political guard in the South—on both local and state levels. Otto H. Olsen has written that the South represented the "testing ground" for the vision of Reconstruction architects. Whiteley's bailiwick, the Second Congressional District of Georgia, provides a point of instruction to evaluate the successes and failures of the Republican blueprint. More blacks than whites lived in the district, which was largely constituted from the state's plantation belt. What did Reconstruction mean to both races in this setting? Ted Tunnell in the Red River Parish in Louisiana has recently provided some answers; his biography of Marshall H. Twitchell offers telling insights, though Twitchell was a northern Republican who moved south. In a study examining six Texas counties, Randolph B. Campbell has recently shown the relationship between federal policy and its application on a local level. Through the eventful career of Richard Whiteley, this book looks at the forces at work in southwest Georgia.[3]

Until the 1950s and 1960s, Reconstruction was viewed as a tragic and benighted period. William A. Dunning of Columbia University and historians whom he inspired were partly responsible for the negative interpretation. The Dunning school indicted the period as a time of malfeasance and misgovernment, orchestrated by self-serving Republicans who curried favor with ignorant blacks. Redemption by the Democrats in the 1870s restored solvency, integrity, and morality to governments in Baton Rouge, Montgomery, Raleigh, and other southern capitals. Popular literature and even Hollywood perpetuated the Dunning view well into the twentieth century. According to this school of thought, the infamous scalawag emerges as a false prophet, an opportunist of the first order. Richard Whiteley and men like him were shown as despicable southern heretics. This one-dimensional view long remained the public perception. So pervasive were these assumptions that Allen W. Trelease in 1963 began his important article "Who Were the Scalawags?" by stating: "in the demonology of Reconstruction no reputation is blacker than that of the native white Republicans."[4]

By then, though, at least in academic circles, perceptions had begun to change. Beginning in the 1940s with David H. Donald's groundbreaking article "The Scalawag in Mississippi Reconstruction," southern white Republicans began to gain a more objective hearing. Donald emphasized an ideological continuum between prewar Whigs and postwar Republicans. Allen Trelease, though disputing the Whig influence, also offered a more positive view of southern Republicans. Sarah W. Wiggins calls the stereotype further into question in *The Scalawag in Alabama Politics,* published in 1970. James A. Bagget has recently provided an essential service in *The Scalawags: Southern Dissenters in the Civil War and Reconstruction.* Bagget's "collective biography" approach reveals wide differences among Republicans, their backgrounds, and what attracted them to the party. These and other studies have overturned the Dunning school and presented a more balanced view emphasizing the constructive achievements of Republican governments in the South. In proportion, the reputation of the southern Republican has undergone revision, and the nefarious Dunning archetype no longer dominates. Though hardly uncritical of the subject, this book continues that path of rehabilitation.[5]

1 *An Irishman in America*

The antecedents of Richard Henry Whiteley are found in County Down, in northern Ireland, where he was born on December 22, 1830. Richard's parents, Charles and Sarah Fullerton Whiteley, shared the very modest station of the vast majority of the Irish. On February 28, 1828, they had married in a Presbyterian Church in Garvagh, a small village in County Londonderry, another northern county. Except for his name, and that he fathered two more children by Sarah, little is known of Charles. He died of unknown causes sometime in the 1830s, leaving behind Sarah, then in her thirties, and three children, Richard, Eliza Jane, and Tomasina.[1]

The potato famine that began in the 1840s precipitated a massive flight of the Irish to America. Even so, the Irish had been immigrating to America well before that catastrophic event. Most came seeking a better life. Sarah Whiteley, poor and responsible for three children, aiming for a better future, joined the exodus. Sometime in the fall of 1837, the family of four set out on a steam-powered ship, heading across the Atlantic Ocean. Little was sure but their destination: Charleston, South Carolina. Sarah and her small children, having surely endured some discomfort during several weeks at sea, were relieved to reach America sometime in October. The family remained only briefly in Charleston. The hope of improving their situation that had apparently attracted Sarah to the new country led her to Augusta, Georgia.

Augusta, the seat of Richmond County and the second largest city in Georgia, lay 120 miles northwest of Charleston and was just across the Savannah River, which separates Georgia from South Carolina. About eight thousand people, evenly divided between blacks and whites, lived there. Georgia's founder, James Oglethorpe, had laid out the city; it boasted a handsome courthouse and the impressive Doric-style Medical College. James Silk Buckingham, visiting from England in 1839, found Augustans to be industrious people of "great intelligence, frankness, ease of manners, affability, and courtesy." In their leisure time, some attended the theater or turned out for visiting lecturers.[2]

Any cultural advantages Augusta offered were largely lost on the Whiteleys. The family was and remained poor. Even so, their new home provided opportunity and social advantages among the large number of Irish living there. The Whiteleys may have settled in the area known as "Dublin." Sarah became a dressmaker. By the end of 1839, she had been received as a member of the Presbyterian Church. In Augusta, Richard briefly attended school. In 1839 or 1840, he apprenticed as a "factory boy" at a textile factory outside Augusta.[3]

Although Georgia conformed to the antebellum Southern pattern of limited manufacturing, the textile mill industry grew in the 1830s and 1840s. Cotton was spun into cloth in Richmond County. At Bellview, about eight miles south of Augusta, John Schley had begun operating a textile factory in the mid-1830s on Butler's Creek. The workforce manufactured different types of cloth at the three-story wood and stone mill. Slaves and whites labored at Bellview, and among the workers were a number of poor Irish. Richard began working here at about the age of ten. He would have lived nearby in quarters probably provided by John Schley.

Richard was a slight, thin boy. He had a narrow face, and beneath his straight hair and brow, he looked at the world with dark eyes. Much of his adolescence was spent in a cotton factory. The boy could have been involved in any of the steps whereby cotton was manufactured into cloth. Whatever the exact nature of the tasks, he displayed aptitude and energy. Eventually, he became a weaver, operating a power loom that wove the yarn into fabric. A disciplined drive and keen intelligence, strong traits in the man he would be, were apparent at an early age.

John Schley noticed Richard. The Schleys were a prominent family (John's brother, William Schley, had been elected governor in 1837). An exceedingly compassionate and gregarious man, Schley was the judge of the Supreme Court of the Middle Circuit. Acquaintances admired him for his kindness and generosity. Judge Schley lived outside Augusta, near the Bellview mill, and often supervised operations. He seems to have recognized Richard's potential. Schley extended various opportunities to the boy and became something of a surrogate father.[4]

How much contact Richard had with his mother and his sisters is not known. Sarah continued her seamstress work in nearby Augusta. She shared a cultural identity with the numerous Irish. Among them was John O'Neil, a dyer, with whom Sarah began spending time. They married on November 8, 1846, in Augusta. What Richard thought of his stepfather is not known. All that is certain is that at Bellview, Richard maintained the long hours associated with textile labor. As a grown man, he would speak of the lessons to be learned by facing adversity early in life. Those experiences taught him about work and perseverance. Nonetheless, it is likely that during these hard years at Bellview, the young apprentice could not appreciate such theoretical and deferred awards.

Richard was sixteen years old when John Schley died suddenly, at age sixty-two, at his country home, on May 26, 1847. Richard was one of many who mourned a man described by the *Augusta Daily Constitutionalist* as "joyous and social in his temper, remarkably amiable and affectionate in his disposition."[5] Richard had benefited from another quality mentioned by one eulogist: Schley's "overflowing charities." No doubt John Schley profoundly influenced Richard during these formative years. By example, the unpretentious aristocrat likely contributed to the formation of the open and friendly man he became. Schley introduced Richard to the science of textiles, a business he came to understand and profit from, and to the law, which he eventually claimed as a career. The personal interest the mill owner and judge had shown in him was not forgotten. Richard felt indebted enough to give one of his sons the middle name of Schley.[6]

The death of John Schley seems to have been the event that caused young Whiteley to leave Augusta. Sometime in the late 1840s, he moved to Greensborough, the seat of Greene County, with a population of approximately six hundred people, some sixty miles west of Augusta, in middle Georgia. John Cunningham and Henry Merrill had established the Greensborough Manufacturing Company in 1845, and workers produced cloth at the steam-powered mill. Richard became a weaver at the company.

At some point, probably in Greensborough, he met Margaret Eliza Devine. Her parents, Archibald and Mary A. Devine, had immigrated to Georgia from Ireland sometime in the 1840s, and by the end of the decade lived in Greensborough. Some evidence indicates that Archibald Devine had been an Episcopalian minister. In 1850, though, he was supporting five children as a clerk in Greene County. Margaret, as she was known, was the oldest. She, too, had been born in Ireland. How she and Richard met is not known, but no class barriers (hers was a humble background also) complicated their romance. William Bryan, a local deacon, married them on November 29, 1849. Richard was nearing his twenty-first birthday, and Margaret was between fifteen and seventeen. In 1850, the newly married couple lived in a home near her parents, and Richard worked at the nearby Greensborough factory. They shared an Irish background, little money, and soon, a child. Charles Fullerton, named for Richard's father, was born on Christmas Day of 1850.[7]

The couple did not reside in Greensborough long. Years later, an acquaintance would note "the marked spirit of enterprise characteristic" of Richard Whiteley. Restless in Greensborough, and seeking a better life, he moved a few miles north to Clarke County, where John White, an Irishman, had established in the 1830s a cotton mill on the north fork of the Oconee River. What became known as the Georgia Factory was five miles south of the county seat of Athens (and less than thirty miles north of Greensborough). Richard, Margaret, and Charles probably lived in the mill village White had built for his workers. Employment at the Georgia Factory, at least for a time, met Whiteley's expectations. In 1851, the first year he appears on the Clarke County tax rolls, Whiteley owned no land or assets. He had accumulated $110 in assets by the next year, and in 1853 claimed property valued at $500. That was not an inconsiderable sum. Acquisition of a slave in 1854 signaled his rising economic stature. A level of financial stability had been achieved. That was important for someone who had arrived impoverished from Ireland. It was also significant because the Whiteley family was growing.

Women of childbearing age in the nineteenth century were often pregnant. Margaret, who eventually gave birth to ten children, was no exception. Charles had been born on Christmas Day, 1850, and Montford Schley would be born on September 1, 1859. In between, Margaret gave birth to George, Tomasina, William, and possibly another infant. By 1860 she would be the mother of four children, ranging in age from one to nine. A high mortality rate among newborns and children was also characteristic of the time. Five of the children born to Richard and Margaret Whiteley died in infancy or childhood.[8]

For Richard Whiteley, eager for success and acceptance, it was important to become a United States citizen. He did so in 1854. Immigrants could become naturalized at any point after arriving in the United States. A court of record granted citizenship. Applicants petitioned for citizenship, and one or more witnesses usually attested to the petitioner's character. Naturalization also involved swearing a loyalty oath in a court of law. In most instances, citizenship was conveyed perfunctorily. In his application, Whiteley wrote of coming to Georgia in 1837 and of his deferred hopes of becoming a United States citizen. He pointed to a record of good conduct.

On Wednesday morning, February 8, 1854, Whiteley appeared in Clarke County Superior Court in Athens, probably dressed in his best clothes. No taller than five and a half feet, at twenty-four Whiteley had reached his adult height. James C. Wilson and Nathaniel Richardson, both acquaintances, attested to his character and law-abiding nature. Whiteley then raised his right hand and, renouncing loyalty to the "reigning queen of Great Britain," swore allegiance to the United States. As time had passed, the Irish accent had become less distinct. Whiteley sounded like an American, and after the ceremony he was one.[9]

Later that year, or in 1855, the Whiteleys moved again. Decatur County, in extreme southwest Georgia, was the destination. Bainbridge, the small county seat, lay about 240 miles west of Savannah. Only fifty miles separated the town from Tallahassee, the small and unprepossessing capital of Florida. Decatur County was a flat, hot, almost tropical area, served by the Flint River, which flowed diagonally across the county. Approximately the same number of slaves as whites lived in the region, which was wedded to agriculture. In terms of value of farms and livestock, acres of cotton under cultivation, bushels of corn raised, and other agricultural measurements, this county, named for Commodore Stephen Decatur, was one of the top producers in the state. Hardwoods and pines rose to great heights, magnolias and sycamores thrived, fruit trees yielded peaches, figs, and oranges. Some 5,985 whites, 5,624 slaves, and 13 free persons of color lived in the county by 1860. With its density of slaves, and cotton firmly entrenched as king, the Whiteleys' new home was representative of the plantation South.

Ira W. Sanborn was responsible for Whiteley leaving the employment of John White and the Georgia Factory. A native of New Hampshire, Sanborn had come to Decatur County in the 1830s. He established two gristmills, a tannery, and cigar and shoe factories in the area. Near Faceville, a village some twelve miles southwest of Bainbridge, he built Eastabatchee, or Sanborn's Factory, in 1856. Utilizing the power generated by a creek that emptied into the Flint River, workers began manufacturing cloth there. How Sanborn and Whiteley became acquainted is not known, but probably the entrepreneur lured Whiteley from Georgia Factory with the promise of an advanced position and financial rewards.[10]

Whiteley did not regret settling in Decatur County. The family apparently lived near the rural factory in a rented home or possibly in a residence provided by Sanborn. At the textile factory, where kersey and cotton yarn were produced, Whiteley acted in a supervisory role. Sanborn's assurances of a prosperous future were not unwarranted. The family's financial position continued to improve. Whiteley owned $1,500 of property in 1855, over $2,000 by 1856, and $2,300 by 1857.[11]

Whiteley made different impressions on people, but it was hard not to notice his intellect, ability, and Irish warmth. Moving forward with sureness and purpose, he soon acquired part ownership in a textile factory. In 1857, ending his association with Ira Sanborn, he established, with several local men, the Bainbridge Manufacturing Company. On the Flint River, a mile and a half north of Bainbridge, the owners began construction on a three-story cotton mill. Production was underway at the factory by 1858. Workers made sheetings, kersey, osnaburgs, and shirtings, and the Bainbridge Manufacturing Company soon advertised to planters and merchants "negro kerseys at low figures."[12] Profits came from the outset, and the workforce sometimes struggled to keep up with demands. With merited pride, the *Bainbridge Southern Georgian* favorably compared the factory to "institutions of the like kind in the North."[13] Archibald Curry, William Williams, and Whiteley served as the directors of the company. Whiteley was also the company's agent. Meeting on February 2, 1859, at the company office, the directors increased the company's capital stock, because the demand in southwestern and northwestern Florida had grown. Whiteley and his fellow directors displayed southern patriotism befitting the times by advertising "our enterprise being Southern in its conception, and thoroughly Southern in all the elements of its formation."[14] Whiteley, moving with alacrity and the ease of manner that always served him well, solicited and received subscriptions for the increased capitalization. He promised to meet any inquiries with "prompt attention." The enterprise continued its profitable operations.[15]

Late in the 1850s, after Whiteley severed his connection to the Sanborn Factory, the family presumably moved to Bainbridge, where they seem to have continued their practice of renting. About a thousand residents lived in the county seat, named to honor Commodore William Bainbridge of War of 1812 fame. At least every other person was black, and even though a few free blacks resided in Bainbridge, the vast majority of Africans were slaves. The town, situated on a bluff of the Flint River, was laid out in squares. Dirt streets were the rule, and they were often shaded by impressive live oak trees. A two-story brick courthouse, finished in 1855, dominated the square, and, as a visitor observed, "attracts the notice of the stranger." Various businesses surrounded the courthouse, filling out a town square of wood and more recently constructed brick buildings. Some children attended school, and construction of a Female College began in 1860. Residents made their way to the Baptist,

Methodist, or Presbyterian churches on Sunday. They turned for information to the *Bainbridge Argus* and the *Bainbridge Southern Georgian.* Anxious for more progress, residents began a campaign to attract the Atlantic and Gulf Railroad, which at that time terminated thirty-five miles to the east in Thomasville.[16]

People in Bainbridge associated Richard Whiteley first with the Bainbridge Manufacturing Company but soon knew him as a lawyer. He quickly became a well-known and increasingly influential man. By 1860, with $5,000 in assets, he was also financially successful. He owned two slaves by now, a thirty-year-old black woman and a seven-year-old girl, possibly her daughter. Whiteley soon joined the local chapter of the Masons. These were years of intellectual development. Although he had been denied a formal grade school education, let alone the opportunity of college, he continued independent study. Having driven himself to achieve a level of financial stability, he pursued knowledge with similar resolve. He read newspapers, journals, and ancient and modern history. One person familiar with him during these years described a regimen of self-improvement that was carried out "by persistent application, between the regular work hours."[17] Another added, "his studies, with but little exception, were pursued without the aid of a teacher."[18] Both at the Sanborn Factory or the Bainbridge Manufacturing Company, Whiteley also taught, and he formed "a debating club of greasy factory boys." The debating exercise, with its obligatory give-and-take, suited his nature. Whiteley also considered the exchange of competing ideas healthy. He would never be short of ideas.[19]

Margaret Whiteley became one of the most gracious and well-liked women in Bainbridge. Keeping a home, and raising her young children, occupied her. As a woman of means and social standing, her devotion to family, faith, and charity became clear. She was a devout Episcopalian, and though no Episcopalian church existed in Bainbridge, a small number of members worshiped privately. Just as her husband found his place, in a different way, so did Margaret.

Whiteley's association in the hierarchy of the textile business brought him financial comfort but, ultimately, not professional contentment. In the late 1850s, not yet thirty, he decided to become a lawyer. In some form John Schley, judge of the Supreme Court of the Middle Circuit, had first exposed him to law, or the magistrate at least made an impression on the boy. Perhaps Whiteley was pursuing a long-held desire. An acquaintance noted that he had begun reading the English jurist Blackstone at the age of fifteen. Whiteley also was aware of the financial profitability of being a successful attorney. Quite possibly, he desired a more public forum. For whatever reason, or combination of reasons, he began late in the 1850s to prepare to become an attorney.

Practicing law in Georgia required passing an oral exam administered in one of the state's superior courts. Like other aspiring lawyers, Whiteley may have prepared by "reading law" with a local attorney. It was necessary to become familiar with various fields: equity and equity pleading, criminal law and penal code, and the Code of Georgia and Statutes were among them. Whiteley applied himself with the diligence he seemed to bring to everything. Reading at night, even as he represented the Bainbridge Manufacturing Company during the day, Whiteley studied. He passed the examination, almost certainly administered at the Decatur County courthouse, sometime early in 1860. About the same time, Whiteley ended his relationship with the Bainbridge Manufacturing Company and began practicing law.

About a dozen men belonged to the Decatur County bar. Their styles and effectiveness varied. Some made emotional appeals, relying on florid oratory, dramatic presentations, and biblical injunctions. Others pitched didactic logic to juries sitting in judgment. The best lawyers understood the nuances of human nature and the art of persuasion. Jurisprudence was ideally an objective science. Even so, jurors and judges were subject to the foibles and prejudices of humankind. Whiteley began developing his own style. It was not long before he began making a name for himself.

Twice each year, the usual lull at the Decatur County courthouse at Bainbridge was broken when Superior Court opened. In 1860, on October 22, Richard Sims, George W. Hines, William H. Crawford, William O. Fleming, Daniel H. McGill, and others assembled for "court week." Adhering to time-honored practice, Judge Alexander A. Allen sounded the gavel and called court to order. Over the next few days, cases were opened, decided, continued, and sometimes dismissed. Hugh M. King, a local lawyer, asked Whiteley to represent him in a suit involving a debt owed him. The young barrister did so successfully. On the eve of the Civil War, Whiteley, at thirty, was a man of increasing stature and, as the events of that year proved, a person of local political importance.[20]

The most momentous presidential election in the country's history would take place in 1860. Nothing less than the fate of the Union depended on the outcome. The fact of slavery increasingly divided the nation by the 1850s. Attacks on slavery and Southerners were met by adamant defenses of the peculiar institution. The differences between the sections widened during the decade. Pro- and antislavery forces clashed in undeclared war in 1856–57 in the Kansas Territory. When the abolitionist John Brown attacked an arsenal at Harpers Ferry, Virginia, in 1859 and was executed, he died a martyr in the view of some Northerners. His activities and political creed repulsed a bitter South.

Sweeping anti-slavery sentiment gave rise to the Republican Party. Advocates of the newly formed party pledged their intention to keep slavery out of the territories. For some Republicans, that represented a first step toward abolishing slavery. Southerners came to believe that a Republican president would do the northern abolitionists' bidding. The so-called fire-eaters claimed that protecting the region's interests and institutions justified secession. Their fears of an increasingly powerful and hostile antislavery political majority gained resonance. Secession had been the radical proposition of a relative few in 1850. By 1860, though, in the view of a determined majority, if a Republican was to be elected president, leaving the Union would seem more necessary than drastic. If that course was taken, war would likely follow. Military companies formed across the South. The bonds of the Union had frayed.[21]

The sectional debate received hearings in state legislatures, election contests, and local gathering points across the South. Theories and opinions were rendered brilliantly, illogically, often emotionally, but rarely sparingly. The rhetoric and the printed word in Bainbridge were no exception. In this highly charged atmosphere the *Bainbridge Southern Georgian* editorialized that the South had "everything to fear, at the hands of the existing political organizations of the non-slaveholding states."[22] The martial spirit evidenced throughout the South was obvious. The Bainbridge Fusiliers had first appeared in full uniform in October 1858. Participants in a courthouse debate in March 1859 argued the question "Are the signs of the times unfavorable to the perpetuity of the Union?" Following John Brown's assault on Harpers Ferry that October, many answered affirmatively.[23]

Whiteley watched the deteriorating national scene closely, considering the consequences for the country, and himself personally. Questions regarding the South's course interested him mightily, the sign of a personal interest in politics and public life that he never lost. Having become a Democrat at some point, and taking an instinctive liking to politics, he participated in the local debate as Georgia's place in the Union became more precarious. Taking a moderate stance, Whiteley thought the fire-eaters were extreme and secession was an alternative of last resort. At a political meeting at the courthouse on December 3, 1859, he spoke of "the great Democrat Party of Decatur." Whiteley disagreed, though, with most of that party's local partisans, who insisted on definitive protection of slavery in the western territories. Early on, Stephen Douglas, senator from Illinois, seemed to be the candidate of the moderate Southern Democrat in the upcoming presidential election. Whiteley lent his support to Douglas. His approach was intelligent, rational, and at odds with the more hotheaded alternatives others proposed. But this moderation should not be understood as greater than it was; a future Confederate officer, Whiteley faulted the southern fire-eater, but he had contempt for the furious abolitionist.[24]

At Charleston, Democrats met in April to nominate a candidate. Stephen Douglas was the favorite. His position on slavery's expansion—abiding by the territorial residents' decision—was not strong enough for more demanding Southern elements. Delegates from eight southern states (including most, but not all, of the Georgia delegates) left the convention in protest. Those who remained decided to meet in Baltimore in June, and the party nominated Stephen Douglas. Unreconciled Democrats, meeting at Baltimore later that month, nominated John C. Breckinridge. As a reaction to the sectional crisis, the Constitutional Union Party formed and turned to John Bell. Meanwhile, at Chicago, the Republicans made Abraham Lincoln their standard-bearer.

Aroused residents of Bainbridge considered the situation. Several weeks after the Charleston convention, and before the Democrats met at Baltimore, Decatur County Democrats convened at the courthouse on May 26. Well aware that Douglas would prevail at Baltimore, the majority opposed any Georgia delegates attending the convention. A Committee of Five, to which Whiteley belonged, drafted a report commending the delegates who had left Charleston and recommended that no delegates be sent from Georgia to the Baltimore convention. Whiteley alone dissented. This small but confident man stood and read a report that placed him firmly in the Douglas column. Lines were drawn for and against Douglas. Those opposing sending delegates to Baltimore prevailed by a vote of sixteen to nine. Whiteley participated in the debate, in which the *Bainbridge Southern Georgian* reported "some close sparring was done." A strong indication of the man he was, and would remain, was clear. Whiteley maintained and stated his convictions despite their unpopularity. Something else was apparent. He liked politics and did not shy away from conflict.

Later in the year, in November, Abraham Lincoln carried every free state but one and won the presidency. The Republican's election triggered conventions across the South at which delegates considered the resort to secession. Ordinances of secession passed over the next three months in South Carolina, Alabama, Mississippi, Florida, Georgia, Louisiana, and Texas. In February, at Montgomery, Alabama, the Confederate States of America was formed. President Jefferson Davis and Vice-President Alexander Stephens were inaugurated. In March 1861, in his inaugural address, Lincoln firmly stated that the right of secession did not exist. He also reaffirmed that federal troops would remain in southern forts. War seemed more likely than at any previous point. Early in April, when the Lincoln administration sent ships to resupply the garrison at Fort Sumter in Charleston harbor, southern forces opened fire, and the Civil War began.[25]

Whiteley's fears of secession leading to war had come true. He faced the decision that thousands of other male Southerners confronted in the spring of 1861. Would he volunteer and join the Confederate Army? Once secession was a fact, the question posed no dilemma. His actions during the sectional crisis had been temperate and were directed against those southern groups he believed were intent on breaking up the Union. A minority of his fellow Southerners had thought and behaved the same way. Yet, after secession and with the outset of the war, most considered serving the Confederacy their duty. Whiteley certainly did so, and he may have believed that the Lincoln administration had forced the war. Defending the South from the northern aggressor, Whiteley thought, had become necessary. As a slaveowner, regardless of his future Republican ties, he may also have fought to preserve the institution of slavery and a southern way of life. After all, he owned two African Americans, and though his relationship with them cannot be known, he certainly did not repudiate slavery. Although officially an American since 1854, by the Civil War he considered himself more specifically a Southerner. Now thirty-one, Whiteley made preparations to leave the comforts of life in Bainbridge and Decatur County for the field of battle.

Impending conflict, much as in many southern settings, added immediacy to military organizational efforts that had been underway for some time in Decatur County. The Bainbridge Independents (formerly the Bainbridge Fusiliers) had formed late in the 1850s. Its members enthusiastically joined the First Georgia Infantry Regiment, which left for war in the spring. Whiteley enlisted with the second company raised in Decatur County, Hardee's Rifles, established in 1860 or early 1861. Hugh King, the prominent lawyer, was most responsible for forming the company. King served as captain of the company, which was named for William J. Hardee, a Georgian and author of the influential *Rifle and Light Infantry Tactics.* Whiteley was also instrumental in raising the company, which originally had about seventy members, and he became its first sergeant. Like other companies in the South, Hardee's Rifles drilled, paraded, and generally prepared; Sergeant Whiteley played a significant role. By May, he was confident of progress, and he described Hardee's Rifles as a "hardy and well-behaved company, and ready and able to do good service." Perhaps because of his past in textile manufacturing, he further noted that the soldiers were smartly uniformed in Georgia kerseys.[26]

In the first months of 1861, Whiteley made final plans before leaving for the war; he suspended his law practice indefinitely and said goodbye to friends. Much harder was leaving Margaret, and their children, Charles, Montford, George, and Tomasina. In March 1860, William, only two, had died after a short illness. By 1861, Margaret was again pregnant. With the apprehension of any departing soldier for war, Whiteley left home knowing he might not return.

Duty for Hardee's Rifles began that spring. As Company H, Hardee's Rifles was mustered into the Fifth Georgia Infantry Regiment, which formed at Macon on May 11, 1861, and was composed of about ten companies. Colonel John K. Jackson of Augusta commanded. On the evening of May 14, the Fifth Georgia Infantry Regiment left Macon by railroad. Acting as the spokesman for Hardee's Rifles, Whiteley penned a short note to the editor of the *Macon Daily Telegraph* just before departing. He testified to the soldiers' commitment. Intending the letter to be published, he gratefully wrote that the company "entertain a lovely sense of the many pleasing reminiscences of our sojourn among the citizens of Macon."

Orders directed the Fifth Georgia Infantry to Pensacola, where they joined the forming command of Brigadier General Braxton Bragg. Across the bay, Union troops held Fort Pickens. Southern reinforcements continued to arrive, and by September, some six thousand Confederate troops were in the vicinity. Expectations of an early clash of arms fizzled, and a tedious routine set in for some of the Confederacy's earliest volunteers.

Whiteley adjusted to the life of a soldier. The Fifth Georgia Infantry remained in Florida for the second half of 1861. Confederate soldiers elected their regimental officers. Whiteley's standing was reflected in his election as lieutenant in June. As an officer, he enjoyed privileges others did not. In August, granted leave for fifteen days, Lieutenant Whiteley returned to Bainbridge to see his new son. Several weeks earlier, in July, Margaret had given birth to Richard Henry Whiteley.

This uneventful period in Florida was interrupted early in 1862, when Bragg left Pensacola for northern Mississippi with approximately ten thousand troops. John Jackson, promoted to brigadier general, was placed in command of the brigade to which the Fifth Georgia Infantry belonged, which departed to join the Army of Mississippi. Organizing troops in eastern Tennessee and moving them on to Corinth, Mississippi, was part of Jackson's responsibility. Encounters with the federal foe in 1862 would offer a sharp contrast to the Florida inactivity for Lieutenant Whiteley.[27]

Leaving Florida was not the only change. Whiteley's service with the Fifth Georgia Regiment soon ended, and at some point early in 1862 he became connected to the Second Georgia Sharpshooters Battalion, commanded by Major J. J. Cox. Battalions were somewhat smaller than regiments—usually composed of about five companies—but identical in every other way. What apparently precipitated Whiteley's severance from the Fifth Georgia Regiment was the expiration of the one-year enlistment period of some members of Hardee's Rifles. Some reenlisted with Company A, which Whiteley organized. In January 1862, he was elected the company's captain. The Second Georgia Sharpshooters Battalion (as did the Fifth Georgia Regiment) remained part of John Jackson's brigade. Captain Whiteley soon had some procedural questions for Samuel Cooper, the Confederate adjutant and inspector general. Writing from Cumberland Gap, Tennessee, on March 12, Whiteley explained that he had organized a company of reenlisted men out of the Fifth Georgia Infantry. The soldiers were transferred to "my command," and Whiteley wanted to know if the company roll had reached Richmond authorities. The responsibilities of Captain Whiteley were many.

Solidifying the South's western holdings caused Confederate authorities to concentrate troops at Corinth, Mississippi, early in 1862, and General Albert S. Johnston took command of the newly formed Army of Mississippi. At Shiloh, on April 6–7, a bloody but inconclusive engagement was fought with federal forces. Johnson's successor, Braxton Bragg, led an unsuccessful invasion of Kentucky later in 1862. It ended with the major battles of Perryville (October 8) and Murfreesboro as the year concluded. During the winter of 1863, what was now called the Army of Tennessee remained in the vicinity of Tullahoma, between Murfreesboro and Chattanooga. As part of Jackson's Brigade, Whiteley and the Second Georgia Sharpshooters Battalion fought at Shiloh, Perryville, and Murfreesboro. Whiteley commanded Company A at each. There were no engagements of any significance in which officers were not killed. Captain Whiteley gained an appreciation of what it was like to face combat. On the last day of 1862, at Murfreesboro, he and the Georgia Sharpshooters were under heavy fire for three hours.

Whiteley's service to the Confederacy was not limited to field activities. Late in 1862, he helped muster cavalry near Chattanooga. He also served as a judge advocate on various occasions. A judge advocate presided over trials involving soldiers charged with crimes and sentenced those found guilty to hard labor, dismissal, confinement, or even death. Confederate authorities appointed men who were lawyers or judges to these positions. Whiteley was a natural choice.[28]

In the spring of 1863, Whiteley was promoted to major. Brigadier General Jackson, among others, recognized his abilities. Writing to Adjutant and Inspector General Cooper from Chattanooga on June 1, 1863, Jackson confided that Whiteley's obvious competence precluded him from taking the examination sometimes required. Major J. J. Cox had been promoted, and Whiteley became the ranking officer of the Second Georgia Sharpshooters Battalion. With characteristic confidence, Major Whiteley soon wrote of "the battalion which I have the honor to command." As the war entered its third year, Whiteley understood that fighting with the Army of Tennessee would continue indefinitely.[29]

The lackluster record of the Army of Tennessee contrasted with the brilliance achieved by the Army of Northern Virginia under General Robert E. Lee. Outright success continued in 1863 to elude the Army of Tennessee during the Chattanooga–Chickamauga–Missionary Ridge campaign. On September 19–20, the largest engagement took place at Chickamauga, northeast of Chattanooga. Federal lines broke, but Union disaster was averted by the determined stand of troops under General George H. Thomas. Confederates claimed victory at Chickamauga, but Union armies soon gained the upper hand in Tennessee. General Ulysses S. Grant's strategies forced the Army of Tennessee, under the much-criticized Bragg, to abandon Lookout Mountain and Missionary Ridge, and any hopes of retaking Chattanooga.

It became Major Whiteley's responsibility to file a report summarizing the participation of the Second Georgia Sharpshooters Battalion at Chickamauga. He described the first day's involvement and how the battalion had taken its position on the extreme right of the line of battle and had faced enemy fire for several hours—"during which time the officers and men," Whiteley reported, "illustrated in an eminent degree those soldierly qualities for which Georgians have become so justly celebrated." Advancing with Jackson's Brigade, the battalion helped drive the enemy back, capturing horses and artillery. Whiteley and his men slept on the field of battle that night. On the next day at Chickamauga, September 20, Jackson's Brigade charged over a hundred yards of open area and forced the enemy's retreat. That was accomplished, Whiteley wrote, "in most gallant style, the entire command passing the open space at a run and, with a shout, striking such consternation to the foe that they fled." Over the course of two days at Chickamauga, Whiteley assessed the changing battlefield situation and accordingly issued orders. His adjutant delivered these directives to other officers, and Whiteley acknowledged: "I am indebted for his cool and fearless conduct in the transmission of orders." Major Whiteley was becoming accustomed to giving orders.

Just as combat in Tennessee had characterized 1863, fighting in Georgia occupied the Army of Tennessee in 1864. Joseph E. Johnston had replaced Bragg as the army's commander. A much larger Union army, led by General William T. Sherman, steadily moved toward Atlanta through north Georgia in the spring and summer of 1864. At various places—Resaca, New Hope Church, Kennesaw Mountain, and elsewhere—thousands clashed, and casualties mounted. The replacement of Johnston with John Bell Hood as the Army of Tennessee commander preceded the fall of Atlanta early in September. Following defeats at Franklin and Nashville, Tennessee, early in the year, the Army of Tennessee attempted to regroup under General Joseph Johnston. Near Durham Station, North Carolina, on April 26, Johnston surrendered that once imposing force to General Sherman. Two weeks earlier, Lee had met Grant at Appomattox Courthouse. The short life of the Confederate States of America was over.

Following the movements of the Second Georgia Sharpshooters Battalion in these final months is difficult. The battalion continued to fight with the Army of Tennessee, but when Brigadier General Jackson was transferred the summer of 1864, the battalion became part of a brigade commanded by Brigadier General States R. Gist. At various Georgia settings, Major Whiteley directed the Georgia Sharpshooters during the defense of Atlanta. The battalion contributed to Confederate victory at Kennesaw Mountain on June 27, and on September 1 participated in the southern defeat at Jonesboro. The Georgia Sharpshooters were furloughed late in 1864 or early 1865, but Whiteley reorganized them in Augusta, Georgia, and soon rejoined the Army of Tennessee. When the army was surrendered, Major Whiteley and the battalion were among the approximately twenty-one thousand men laying down their arms.[30]

Whiteley spoke later of a "long and bloody war." He had invested four years of his life in the Confederacy, enduring the privations of field life, including grueling marches, heat, cold, and disease. In November 1863, shoulder problems forced him into either the Floyd House or Ocmulgee Hospital in Macon.[31] His experience was diverse. He recruited soldiers, commanded troops in battle, and sat in judgment of them as judge advocate on Confederate military courts. That Whiteley served ably with the Fifth Georgia Infantry Regiment and the Second Georgia Sharpshooters Battalion is indicated from his steady rise in rank. Men under him later praised their officer for never allowing a soldier to be placed in the pillory, paraded in humiliating style before others, or punished in a degrading way. One man, who knew Whiteley well, observed "there was something about him that drew men irresistibly to him." These intangible qualities were evident during the war. Whiteley was comfortable leading. Soldiers serving under him recognized a sureness, confidence, and intelligence that inspired their trust. Later, in another arena, the political battlefield, these traits were equally obvious. He would be known for the rest of his life as Major Whiteley.

In May, Richard Whiteley was paroled in North Carolina. It was a war-weary man who reached Bainbridge sometime in the spring of 1865. Whiteley had rarely seen Margaret or their children during the last four years. Yet he counted himself fortunate. As with all southern places of any size, many who had left Bainbridge for war did not return. John W. Evans, a fellow lawyer, was killed at Petersburg leading soldiers under his command. Others from Bainbridge fell to Union bullets or succumbed to disease at distant places.

The year 1865 was a personal marking point. Twenty-eight years had passed since Whiteley had arrived in America with his mother and sisters. If Whiteley's life in the new country had followed the pattern of most Irish immigrants, he would have worked almost constantly to achieve a minimum standard of living. Yet he rose from factory boy to textile factory owner, moving from Augusta to Greensborough, then Athens, and finally settling at Bainbridge. Whiteley mastered law, and performed ably as a Confederate officer. Always, he pursued opportunity and seized it. The most improbable turn in Richard Whiteley's career, though, was yet to be made.[32]

2 *An Avowed Republican*

Southerners faced devastating physical and psychological circumstances following the Civil War. The South sustained approximately 350,000 casualties in a thoroughly lost cause. Some cities lay in ruins. Farming implements had been destroyed, stock had been carried off, fences were down, and money was scarce. The capital invested in four million slaves was irretrievably lost. Reviving agriculture offered the most fundamental variable in the regeneration equation. Some blacks made labor arrangements with their white landlords. Under the impression the United States government was to give them land, others hesitated to make contracts. Circumstances combined to extend the continuum of misery.

The postwar malaise inevitably affected Bainbridge and Decatur County. Although neither the town nor southwest Georgia had suffered much wartime destruction, residents confronted extreme adversity. As one Bainbridge resident testified, "the war left us impoverished." Some whites and blacks agreed to labor terms in 1865. Some freedpeople, enjoying the elixir of freedom, did not honor their contracts. As for landholders, they often underpaid, deceived, and badly provided for the ex-slaves. Blacks remained the poorest of the poor. Whites prayed for better times in the Baptist, Methodist, or Presbyterian churches. A shell of an old building lacking windows or doors served as a house of worship for the freedpeople. Agriculture was the linchpin of what passed for prosperity in rural Decatur County, but because of its languishing state, little progress was evident. A smallpox epidemic late in 1865 exacerbated the general misery and suffering. Some of the afflicted were treated in the unfinished Female College at the town's edge.[1]

Times were not as hard for the Whiteleys. Despite the loss of his two slaves, freed under unknown circumstances, Whiteley did not suffer as large slaveholders did from emancipation. In 1862, he had paid James Griffin $1500 in cash for a home in Bainbridge. It was one of Bainbridge's finer homes, located south of the courthouse, and on Evans Street. The home no longer stands, and there is no picture of the residence, but references to the "mansion" provide some indication of the home Whiteley returned to in 1865. Here he and Margaret resumed their lives as husband and wife. Their children were central to that life. Charles, the oldest, was fifteen in 1865. Montie, as Montford was called, was six when his father's Confederate service ended, and Richard had reached the age of four. Although the family had increased with Richard's birth in the war's first year, its size was to be tragically diminished. Little William had died in 1860, and sometime in the 1860s, George and Tomasina, the Whiteley's second and third children, died of unknown causes. Mary Devine, Margaret's mother, was also part of the family in Bainbridge. Margaret's father had died at some point, and her mother had moved to Bainbridge, though she did not live at the Evans Street home. What became of Whiteley's mother (one of his sisters eventually settled in Arkansas) is not known.[2]

For a man such as Whiteley, intelligent, hard-working, and ambitious, thirty-five years old when the war ended, success was almost inevitable. The war had merely delayed his rise. He looked forward to resuming the practice of law. At least by 1866, Whiteley was consulting with clients in what was called Sanborn's New Building. His office was on the second floor of the two-story structure, which was located on Broughton Street. Broughton ran alongside and south of the courthouse. A small-town lawyer dealt largely with debt disputes, land titles, and trust estates. The construction of wills also often concerned Whiteley. In easy reach, in all likelihood, were past volumes of the *Georgia Compilation* and *Digests and Laws,* the recently adopted *Georgia Code,* and the very essential *Blackstone's Commentaries on the Laws of England.* Whiteley could cross Broughton Street to the courthouse, where in the years ahead, he became a familiar figure.

A measure of his local standing was his election in December 1865 to the City Council. The spreading smallpox epidemic immediately challenged all the councilmen. On December 9, the first time the new City Council met, Whiteley proposed consulting local doctors about the best course of action. Four days later, when the aldermen reconvened, Whiteley introduced an ordinance aimed at containing the disease. As 1865 neared an end, Willis M. Russell, editor of the *Bainbridge Argus,* noted: "Major Whiteley is a man of no ordinary ability."[3]

Whiteley and other southerners speculated about the consequences of military defeat. Troops remained in the South, and the ex-Confederacy was divided into districts as the war ended. Following the assassination of Abraham Lincoln, Andrew Johnson became president. In May 1865, Johnson provided some direction when he established civil governments aimed at bringing the South back into the Union quickly. He appointed a provisional governor in each ex-Confederate state and required that a constitutional convention be called and that the delegates abolish slavery, repudiate war debts, and renounce secession. Johnson also issued a general pardon to former Confederates who took an oath of allegiance. Rapid restoration to the Union seemed possible.

The events and timetable in Georgia resembled that of other southern states. James Johnson, who had opposed secession, became provisional governor in June, and in October, voters elected delegates to the constitutional convention at Milledgeville. Later that month, they fulfilled the president's specifications. Anticipating the establishment of a state government, the delegates set November 15 as the date for electing a governor and legislature. Taking an oath of allegiance was required in order to vote. United States soldiers often administered the oath. Sometime that summer, Whiteley and hundreds of others in Decatur County took the oath of loyalty.[4]

Whiteley's stature in the community became increasingly apparent. As a local Democrat, he sought a seat in the state senate for the first time in 1865. A group of influential local men publicly requested in writing (a common practice) that he run for the senate from the Eighth District. Decatur, and nearby Miller, and Mitchell counties formed the senate district. Isaac E. Bower, a respected Bainbridge lawyer and judge, and over twenty years older than Whiteley, provided the opposition.

Whiteley accepted the nomination in a letter published in the *Bainbridge Argus.* He laid out what served as a platform. The candidate admitted: "we failed to establish the right of a state to dissolve her connection with the Federal Union." The conflict vindicated, Whiteley concluded, the founding fathers' intention of constructing an indivisible Union. Just as that principle had been upheld, Whiteley cautioned against violating another axiom established by the constitutional fathers. He warned about "the powers of the General Government . . . to steal upon us." State sovereignty remained an honorable principle. Whiteley was proud but not defiant. "Let our sufferings increase our wisdom," he mused philosophically, and then, more pointedly, "and our wisdom protect our rights."

The editor of the *Bainbridge Argus* immediately endorsed Whiteley. That the candidate had risen from the underclass partly measured the man. Whiteley's efforts at self-improvement, *Argus* editor Willis Russell further decided, had prepared him for public office, and "few men of his age have taken more pains to cultivate his gifts." The *Argus* noted that Whiteley's modest, unaffected demeanor made him "universally popular among all classes of the community." Service to the Confederacy also recommended the candidate. Russell concluded that the senate district "will be fortunate in securing the services of one so well qualified to represent it."[5]

Little of a substantial nature probably divided Bower and Whiteley. It is doubtful that Whiteley said anything during the campaign that anticipated any special empathy for the freedpeople. At this point, according to a Bainbridge contemporary, the lawyer was "a warm supporter of the conservative cause."[6] His vision of a postbellum South was anything but color blind, and he endorsed no blueprint for a social revolution. On Election Day, November 15, a majority of voters in Decatur County cast ballots for Whiteley. Yet Bower gained majorities in Miller and Mitchell counties and won the election by an unknown margin. On the basis of Whiteley's performance, the *Argus* predicted for him "a successful and bright future as a politician."[7]

Georgians elected Charles J. Jenkins governor in the November election, and the legislature convened in December. In Georgia and throughout the ex-Confederacy the requirements of President Johnson were met. The state legislature ratified the Thirteenth Amendment and, anticipating readmission, elected Alexander H. Stephens and Herschel V. Johnson to the U.S. Senate.

Although the South's course in 1865 satisfied the president, congressional Republicans held serious doubts. There were shades and hues of Republicanism, but at least in the broadest sense, the party favored making the freedpeople full citizens. Recent developments alarmed Republicans. Southerners had elected former high-ranking Confederate officials to Congress, legislatures had passed discriminatory Black Codes, and some states had hedged at abolishing slavery. Moreover, Congressional Republicans doubted Johnson's commitment to the freedpeople. In December 1865, when the Thirty-ninth Congress convened, Republicans blocked the South's admission. Instead, the Joint Committee on Reconstruction was established to investigate conditions there. An extended period of uncertainty lay ahead.

White Southerners wished for a quick restoration to the Union. Acceptance of Andrew Johnson's terms had been easily accomplished. It became clear, though, that what Republicans contemplated violated white Southerners' sense of what should and should not be. A region wedded to the racial assumptions of slavery passionately opposed elevating the ex-slaves beyond a station of emancipation. Attempts to force more rights for the freedpeople caused extreme bitterness across the South.

In 1865 Congress created the Bureau of Refugees, Freedmen and Abandoned Lands, commonly known as the Freedmen's Bureau, and by 1866 it was established in the South. Facilitating the transition from slavery to freedom was the Bureau's most basic purpose. Doing so involved supervising labor contracts, educating the ex-slaves, and providing food and clothing. Freedmen's Bureau officials soon began their duties throughout Georgia.[8]

In southwest Georgia, where the state's largest concentration of freedpeople lived, the Bureau became a powerful and controversial force. There was much delicate work to accomplish in an area where conflict often characterized labor relations between white landlords and their black tenants. The most deeply etched theme concerned the freedpeople's vulnerability and exploitation by the white population. An objective observer in several southwestern counties concluded that efforts were made to force the freedpeople into "a semi-serf condition."[9] In 1866, Robert R. Terrell, a Decatur County resident, became the local Freedmen's Bureau agent. Terrell believed that the irresponsibility of many blacks was matched by the imperious attitude of some white landlords. He soon wrote a Bureau official in nearby Thomasville: "I have decided I have no more right to arrest a *freedman* for quiting his employer than I have to arrest a white man for the same offense."[10]

The people of Bainbridge faced continuing economic struggles throughout 1866. John Sharon, who operated the Sharon Hotel, was fortunate if he made expenses from month to month. Some commodities could be purchased at the Empire Dry Goods Store, but few whites and almost no blacks could afford them. That its proprietor accepted cotton and produce for exchange provided telling commentary. Not surprisingly, when a visiting brass band entertained one October night, few paying customers attended. A few federal soldiers were stationed at Bainbridge. Taking lumber from the abandoned Female College, they constructed some crude shelters and settled in at Bainbridge post. Begun before the war, and once bright with promise, the neglected and deteriorating brick structure was a metaphor for local conditions.

Richard Whiteley remained a visible public man. As a city councilman, he attended the regular meetings at City Hall, serving on the Ways and Means, Streets, Cemetery, By-Laws, and Ordinances committees. At one point, at a meeting in November, Whiteley introduced an ordinance requiring all males between the ages of eighteen and thirty-five to enroll for fire duty. Maintaining that it was "customary in other cities," the councilman asked the city marshal to ring the fire bell constantly until "the fire is on the decrease."[11]

What best indicated Whiteley's public-spiritedness were his efforts in a campaign to bring a railroad to Bainbridge. The Atlantic and Gulf Railroad stretched from Savannah to Thomasville, the county seat of Thomas County, located thirty-five miles east of Bainbridge. Plans for extending the railroad west from Thomasville predated the war. At a public courthouse meeting on November 13, 1866, citizens considered the proposition that Bainbridge take stock in the railroad. When Whiteley presented the benefits of bringing the railroad to Bainbridge, townspeople weighed the councilman's words. A resolution was passed that acknowledged that the "interests of our city, as well as its future prosperity," depended on linking with the railroad. By January 1867, with Bainbridge committed to buying stock, Whiteley was one of ten men appointed by the mayor to solicit subscriptions to pay for the bonds. Soon a sum of $100,000 had been raised in subscriptions. Whiteley and two aldermen drafted a letter to the president of the Atlantic and Gulf Railroad stating that Bainbridge had raised the necessary subscriptions and urging the line's early extension.[12]

Whiteley was present in January 1867 when Judge David A. Vason convened Superior Court. The neophyte lawyer took part in over fifty cases during the four-day term. About this time, he began representing Mary E. Adams, a widow who had encountered difficulty gaining title to land left to her. With Whiteley's counsel, the first steps were taken. In another instance, he attempted to gain alimony payments for a woman named Milly Blausett. For the later years of his career, some of what Whiteley said in court remains, but there is no record for this early period. Some surviving interrogatory testimony (formal written questions) provides at least a sense of style.

In one instance, involving litigation in Bainbridge between Isaac Grass and William C. Subers, Whiteley played a central part. Subers was a jeweler, and Grass sold dry goods, leather, tobacco, and liquor from a store they shared on the Bainbridge courthouse square. On October 14,

1865, Subers had left for lunch, and Grass soon followed. In their absence, a thief or thieves entered a rear door and stole watches belonging to Subers. Subers blamed Grass for not locking the back door and sued him for negligence. Whiteley represented Grass. Understanding that Grass would respond negatively, Whiteley asked him whether an agreement existed "as to either watching over and taking care of the goods of the other in their absence." Fixing culpability was also the purpose of the question "Was not the back of store open to be approached by any one who desired so to do?" Once Whiteley established opportunity, he even provided suspects. Federal soldiers, stationed locally, were in and out of the store that October day. No jury in southwestern Georgia would consider Union soldiers above theft.[13]

Earlier in the textile business, and later in the field of journalism and even western mining operations, Whiteley proved himself a man of sound business instincts. In postbellum Georgia he displayed that talent in acquiring land. It was easy for a man of some means to do so in this land-poor region. Less than a year after the war, acting with two other local men, Whiteley bought fifty acres of land on the public road leading from Bainbridge to Albany. Acting independently, Whiteley paid $100 for 250 acres of land early in 1867. In February, he was high bidder at a courthouse auction for about 250 more acres. Maybe not immediately, but eventually, he believed the land would translate into wealth, and Richard Whiteley desired that. He continued to buy land, eventually even identifying himself as "a planter."[14]

Some vitality was returning to Bainbridge by 1867. Every other day, a steamboat arrived at the wharf with goods from the Gulf port of Apalachicola, Florida, two hundred miles to the south. Even so, as one visitor stated, business was "exceedingly dull." In May, a revival at the Methodist Church "won the hearts of saints and sinners." Outside of prayer, residents took hope from the approaching Atlantic and Gulf Railroad. Construction was well underway by summer, and a visitor commented: "the whole population seems to be enthroned with the railroad question." The opening of the Atlantic and Gulf line to Bainbridge on December 16, 1867, was an event of great local significance. Major Whiteley, a firm exponent of commerce and progress, was undoubtedly one of the townspeople present at the commemoration of that event.[15]

There were different ways to measure progress. Blacks began to attend a freedpeople's school, and many enthusiastically pursued education. Efforts to educate the ex-slaves, the vast majority of whom were illiterate, had begun. In Bainbridge, as elsewhere in the South, some whites opposed the experiment. Among other objections, they feared the educated blacks would become less tractable, or that politically minded teachers would instill in the ex-slaves objectionable political ideas. Other whites supported black education, especially Benjamin F. Bruton, who began efforts to acquire a lot on which to build a school. Charles W. Robbins, a Union army veteran, began in 1867 instructing local blacks at a Freedmen's Bureau school. Robbins boarded at the Sharon Hotel because no one would rent a room to him. Although taunted as a "Yankee," the teacher continued his efforts at what some whites called the "nigger school."[16] Robbins soon wrote "of the hatred which exists towards any man whose object is the enlightenment of the colored race."[17] Under the aegis of the American Missionary Association (AMA), William L. Clark, white like Robbins and a Massachusetts native, arrived that Thanksgiving with two female teachers and opened another school. The AMA representatives were soon providing educational and Christian instruction to freedpeople in a house overlooking the Flint River. In a letter to northern acquaintances, Clark described the area's primeval beauty but noted the teachers' ostracism, and that "the white people do not come near us."[18] That included William H. Allen, principal of the Bainbridge Male and Female Academy, who, Clark stated, "hates a Yankee from the very bottom of his soul."[19]

In the meantime, the long period of uncertainty as to what Reconstruction would constitute was nearing an end. The Joint Committee on Reconstruction reached its conclusions in the spring of 1866. The committee advocated ratification of the pending Fourteenth Amendment. It defined citizenship and extended federal protection to ex-slaves by guaranteeing to all American citizens "due process of law" and "equal protection of the laws." Although not explicitly requiring black enfranchisement, the amendment provided for reduction of a state's congressional representation if all males of voting age were not allowed to vote. The amendment also barred from holding office ex-Confederates who had sworn to uphold the Constitution before the war but violated that oath by serving the Confederacy. Every Southern legislature (with the exception of Tennessee) rejected ratification. The Fourteenth Amendment became the pivotal issue in the midterm elections of 1866.

Republicans increased their majorities in Congress in those elections and seized total control of Reconstruction. Moving to implement their ideas of a new South, they passed, over President Johnson's veto, the First Military Reconstruction Act in early March 1867. This legislation divided the South into five military districts, and a general commanded each. Steps for the South's readmission were laid out. Each state was required to draft a constitution enfranchising the freedmen and to submit it for approval. If a majority of registered voters favored ratification, a state government could be established. Then ratification of the Fourteenth Amendment assured readmission. Until then, each state faced an indefinite period of provisional government, and the military and Johnson-appointed civil governments awkwardly overlapped. Congressional or Radical Reconstruction soon commenced. Johnson and his Reconstruction ideas had been repudiated.

The Republican Party became established in the South in 1867. Whites from the North, pejoratively referred to as carpetbaggers, and some native whites, anathematized as scalawags, led the party. Freedmen made up the rank and file and largely accounted for Republican political strength. Identifying Republicanism with Lincoln and Emancipation, blacks enthusiastically converted to the party. The Union League, organized locally throughout the South, acclimated freedmen to politics, and more specifically, Republicanism. Blacks walking (often long distances) to political meetings became a common sight across the South. So it was that a party that did not exist in the South before the war grew rapidly there afterward.[20]

As the political differences between the president and congressional Republicans widened, Republicanism spread to Georgia. Recognition of the freedpeople's new rights and the necessity of bringing Georgia back into the Union accounted for the formation of the state Republican Party. Unionists, former Whigs, recently arrived Northerners (bringing their Republican affiliation with them) and at least some ex-Democrats directed the party. Joseph E. Brown, former governor of Georgia in the 1850s, was the recruit with the highest profile. On a grassroots level, throughout the state, the Union League assembled the freedmen. At Atlanta, on July 4, 1867, the state Republican Party took official form. Foster Blodgett, former mayor of Augusta and a wartime Unionist, presided over the gathering. State Republicans advocated following the congressional guidelines and bringing Georgia back into the Union.[21]

Although some whites did affiliate with the Republican Party, the great majority did not. Like their counterparts throughout the South, Georgia whites opposed the vision of the Republican Reconstruction architects. Southerners did not dispute slavery's end, but neither did emancipation alter their certainty of blacks' inherent inferiority. The vast majority considered granting full citizenship rights to four million ex-slaves an unconscionable act. That a black man could cast an intelligent ballot defied southern conventional thinking. Writing from Atlanta, a *New York Times* journalist captured this perspective. "The elevation of political equality with the white race of millions of negroes . . . untutored, unintelligent and unlettered," he observed, represented "startling changes" for even the most temperate and least prejudiced. At the same time, a specific class of whites was prevented from holding office by the Fourteenth Amendment and was disfranchised by the Reconstruction Act. The Republican blueprint seemed clear to white Southerners. Radical Republicans were bent on elevating the black man to a place he was not ready for, even as they demoted and punished ex-Confederates. Bitter resistance followed.[22]

Georgia Democrats (often referred to as Conservatives) did not propose an alternative conception of a reconfigured South, but virulent exception to the Republican master plan bound them ideologically. Democrats settled on a strategy of obstruction. The electorate would decide between October 29 and November 2, 1867, whether to hold a constitutional convention. Since the First Military Reconstruction Act required that a majority of registered voters approve such a convention, Conservatives intended to frustrate Republican plans by registering to vote and then boycotting the polls. If the call for a convention failed, so did the cause of congressional Republicans.

Georgia belonged to the Third Military District, and General John Pope made his headquarters at Atlanta. The state was divided into forty-four registration districts, and during the spring and summer over ninety-five thousand whites and ninety-three thousand blacks registered. Delegates to the constitutional convention (assuming the question carried) stood for election at the same time.

As was done throughout Georgia, Decatur County residents registered in the summer and fall of 1867. Decatur, Miller, and Mitchell counties formed the Eighth District. Hundreds of whites and blacks took the oath of loyalty and became registered voters. In keeping with Democratic strategy, most whites who registered had no intention of casting a ballot. Freedmen eagerly anticipated voting for the first time. Just over eleven hundred blacks and slightly more than a thousand whites registered in Decatur County.[23]

Richard Whiteley had watched as Reconstruction crystallized. He ultimately came to consider President Johnson and Democrats to be intransigent and their plans to be detrimental to the South and the country. As he later reflected, "the first duty of the Southern people was to unconditionally and in good faith accept the results of the war." That meant granting that "secession was rebellion" and working to "enfranchise and protect the late slaves." Nothing indicates that Whiteley the slaveowner ever seriously questioned the legitimacy of the peculiar institution. Neither did he operate under any illusions after the war. He recognized that the race emerging from bondage was illiterate, without material possessions, and lacking experience in living as free men and women. It was a white man's world and would remain so. Yet, if given the opportunity, Whiteley believed blacks could make contributions. Freedom and justice were the rights of the ex-slaves, and with the enlightening consequences of education and individual application, he optimistically viewed the race's future. A vital interest in the South's future also framed his shift to Republicanism. Georgia could not regain any economic footing until she returned to the Union. It was the alternative of cooperation, rather than continued obstruction, that Whiteley felt Georgia and the defeated South must follow. Just as he had faulted the vituperative secessionist, Whiteley took issue with those calling for continued southern defiance.[24] Defending his unusual political tack, Whiteley later explained: "in the one course I could see reasonable prospect for the peace and prosperity of all; in the other, nothing but pride satisfied at the expense of our material interests and prospects." Such was the ethos that caused him to abandon one party and move in another direction.[25]

As it became clear in 1867 what Democrats rejected and what congressional Republicans demanded, the faltering Democrat staked his ground. He first did so in a series of articles published in the *Bainbridge Southern Guardian* that he entitled "On the Situation." Although no copies exist, it may be assumed that Whiteley wrote in terms of fairness for the freedmen and the advantages of the South's restoration to the Union. These essays were not the manifestoes of a Radical Republican. Even so, as one observer later commented, Whiteley's position "plainly pointed to the stand which he was soon to take." His conversion to Republicanism, an act no white Southerner made without considerable deliberation, was undoubtedly a gradual process. That evolution, though, was complete by the summer of 1867. He had become—defiantly, controversially, and incongruently—a scalawag.[26]

Whiteley's Republicanism was demonstrated in various ways. On July 16, 1867, Whiteley took the required oath of allegiance to the United States. Doing so made him eligible to participate in the constitutional referendum. Unlike the large majority of whites, the ex-Democrat intended to vote for a constitutional convention. His relationship with Charles Robbins—cooperative at least—further indicated a point of view. Robbins had been teaching blacks locally. Applying to become a Freedmen's Bureau agent in Decatur County, the man who had served in a Rhode Island regiment during the war expressed "special and deep interest in the welfare of the colored race." Robbins invited authorities to seek corroboration from Richard Whiteley. About that same time, in the fall of 1867, Whiteley intervened in behalf of two AMA teachers. Arriving in Bainbridge in November, the women could find no one to rent them a place to live. Until a place could be found, Whiteley proposed they board at the Sharon Hotel.[27] These were the acts of a man whom one Bainbridge resident later said was "from the first . . . an avowed Republican" and who practiced a "straightforward and unchangeable policy."[28]

The course Whiteley pursued was extraordinary and unorthodox. He was not the only local white in Bainbridge taking that step, however. Benjamin Bruton, a prosperous commission merchant and well-respected citizen, made the same decision. So did John J. Higdon, a merchant. As for Benjamin F. Powell, conventionality had never been his hallmark. His domestic arrangement (he lived with a black woman by whom he had four children) had not prevented citizens from electing him to several legislative terms before the war. Now Powell affiliated with the Republican Party.

In the future years of Reconstruction, the freedmen voted the Republican ticket in Decatur County. As was the case across the South, where large numbers of blacks lived, the Republican Party gained instant political traction. Sweeping change came to Whiteley's southwest Georgia. A Union League chapter formed in Decatur County, and hundreds of blacks joined. Judge Glenn, formerly a bondsman, used what he termed the "emancipation" as a point of reference. Isiah Williams was also influential. As had thousands of other ex-slaves, the gray-headed freedman had defiantly changed his slave surname: Isiah Sanborn became Isiah Williams. Adam N. Bruton, a slave for the first forty years of his life, preached to local blacks. His personal catechism included a strong Republican faith. Randall Kinney, a blacksmith, also spread the Republican word. Alexander J. Nicholson, a grocer, commanded respect and soon would become a Republican legislator. These men raised the political and economic consciousness of their fellow blacks. They also became political allies of Richard Whiteley.[29]

Major Whiteley campaigned as a Republican for the first time in the fall of 1867. He had recently been nominated by the Republicans of the Eighth District (formed by Decatur, Miller, and Mitchell counties) to serve as a convention delegate should there be a constitutional convention. In the weeks before the election, Whiteley made the case for himself as a delegate and more generally for the convention. He reminded the ex-slaves of their debt to the party of Lincoln and the promise of the Fourteenth Amendment. He also told the black man to expect justice before the law and fair treatment from his landlord. Such was the message at Camilla, Mitchell County's seat of government, and Colquitt, county seat of Miller, and at smaller venues in the district. A Bainbridge acquaintance soon concluded that Whiteley "fully understands the art of winning the confidence of the negro." He also appealed to whites. Returning to the Union was in Georgia's interest, Whiteley emphasized, and by rejecting the congressional plan, residents risked harsh punishment. Like most other Georgia Republicans favoring a convention, Whiteley must have promised that a new constitution would provide debt relief and a homestead exemption for the poor. Speaking to crowds of various sizes, he assured, it was the Republican Party that offered personal economic salvation and a revived Georgia. Whoever the audience, and wherever in the three counties, Whiteley spoke well and persuasively.[30]

Over 102,000 of the 188,000 registered state voters recorded their support for a constitutional convention over the five-day voting period between October 29 and November 2. The Democratic boycott strategy failed. Approving the convention was one step toward statehood. Framing a constitution was another. Five weeks later, delegates were to begin deliberations in Atlanta.

Whiteley would be present. In Decatur County, blacks cast the vast majority of the 997 ballots for holding a constitutional convention. Nobody voted against doing so. Opponents had abstained as planned. Whiteley, John Higdon, and Benjamin Powell were elected as convention delegates from the Eighth District. Building the future required repudiating the past, and though Major Whiteley had fought for an Old South, a New South was emerging. Whiteley planned to help facilitate that in Georgia. In other southern states, men like him, promoting economic development and elevating blacks to a constitutional plateau that did not include social equality, were active, too. Richard Whiteley packed his bags for Atlanta.[31]

3 *The Only Freedman's Lawyer in the Place*

Bound for the Georgia constitutional convention, Whiteley departed from the Atlantic and Gulf railroad depot at Bainbridge in early December 1867. The 180-mile trip took him almost due north to Atlanta. The city had rapidly rebuilt since the destruction caused by General William Tecumseh Sherman's federal army. About thirty thousand residents lived in Atlanta, which the convention delegates would soon designate as the state capital. Most delegates lodged at one of several hotels. Whiteley probably registered at the National Hotel, a congregating point where guests enjoyed a "table that has always been bountifully supplied." Others took rooms at the United States Hotel, whose name indicated that its proprietor was either an old-line Unionist or a reconstructed Rebel. The delegates met at City Hall. In this remnant of old Atlanta (the building had survived the city's burning) a new course would be chartered. Whiteley realized the importance of this historical moment, and was cognizant of the opportunity to positively shape the future, but also the perils of missteps.

Constitutional conventions were held in nine southern states between November 1867 and May 1868. As elsewhere, white Southerners composed the majority of the 169 delegates gathered at Atlanta. Approximately thirty-five blacks took part, and about a dozen men with recent northern ties contributed. Republicans overwhelmingly dominated the convention because the Democrats, or Conservatives, had not participated in the recent referendum. Future leaders of the state Republican

Party were present, including Amos T. Akerman, Foster Blodgett, John E. Bryant, Rufus B. Bullock, and Benjamin Conley. Whiteley was relatively unknown, but that was about to change.[1]

Beginning in early December and continuing into March, the delegates deliberated in a confining room at City Hall that barely served the purpose. Acquainting himself with Republicans, black and white, Whiteley settled in behind a pine desk on the morning of December 9. He and others drew what comfort they could from a single wood-burning stove. Long narrow windows behind the president's chair were poorly covered by differing shades of green calico. Newspaper reporters occupied desks at the rear. A *New York Herald* correspondent's appraisal of the room as "small and shabby" was not unfair.

Foster Blodgett, the Republican State Central Committee chairman, addressed the delegates when the convention opened. He reflected on slavery's passing and spoke of restoring prosperity. In the weeks ahead, delegates constructed the constitution section by section. Committees offered reports on their assignments; the convention collectively considered, debated, and often amended these reports before incorporating them into the constitution.[2]

Whiteley's became a familiar voice. On the floor and behind the scenes he contributed significantly. The committees met and drafted the articles; in hotel rooms, and other places, delegates attempted to influence others. Whiteley circulated widely, maintaining a high profile throughout, and made a name for himself. When a colleague proposed extending each daily session, Whiteley objected that more was accomplished off the floor than on it. After some observation, a journalist pronounced him "earnest in all his acts."[3] Some considered him too earnest. Noting that Whiteley spoke sometimes for trivial reasons, a *New York Times* journalist commented that he would make a motion to change the Lord's Prayer. Another reporter intended no compliment by mentioning that Whiteley was "very great on suggestions."[4]

Introducing a resolution calling for the repeal of the cotton tax caused him to rise from his seat on December 13. Between 1862 and 1868, and especially since the war, the government had taxed raw cotton. Across the South, vocal opponents contended that the tax was unconstitutional since the South was not represented in Congress. Payment of the cotton tax increased southern hardships. Whiteley declared that the successful cultivation of cotton was "essential to the prosperity of the people." Eliminating the tax, he said, was vital to "restoring the prosperity of the people of Georgia."[5]

Following a Christmas recess, the delegates confronted a question bearing more relevance to Reconstruction than constitution making. In 1862, Congress had passed a law forcing office-holders to swear that they had not borne arms against or supported a cause hostile to the United States. This so-called test oath prevented thousands of Southerners from serving in many public offices, including county ordinary (probate judge) and postmaster. Republicans protested in Louisiana, the Carolinas, Virginia, and other states when men who could not honestly take the test oath occupied public office. The situation was no different in Georgia, and George W. Asburn, a delegate, proposed removing such office-holders from office. Contentious debate followed.

On January 11, Whiteley offered an amendment calling for a more selective housecleaning. Like Ashburn, he declared that only loyal men should occupy public offices. Yet Whiteley proposed stripping office only from those who were "seriously retarding the work of reconstruction" and "insidiously using their influence against the restoration of Georgia." In his view, the test oath was too comprehensive because it excluded men "who honestly regret the past." To act in the spirit of magnanimity, rather than punitively, he thought, would best serve Georgia and Republicanism. As an act of "justice to the friends of restoration," Whiteley recommended waiving the oath for loyal citizens supporting "the return of the state under the basis of the Reconstruction Acts." Delegates agreed and ten days later voted to accept the resolutions framed by Whiteley and send them to the president and Congress.[6]

The issue of providing financial help for the destitute received much attention. Thousands of Georgians had fallen into debt during (and often because of) the war. Property had been destroyed, and depreciation of real estate exacerbated conditions. Money remained scarce, and bankruptcy threatened. Postbellum economic realities often made repaying debts impossible. After considerable disagreement, delegates dismissed debts incurred in contracts entered into before June 1, 1865. A homestead exemption, widely debated, was also passed, mainly for the benefit of the underclass. The homestead clause written into the constitution placed some private property beyond the reach of creditors. These were among the most important and controversial acts of the convention.

Whiteley joined the coalition supporting debt relief and the homestead. Less than a week after the convention opened, he proposed a homestead exemption preventing levying against a home for debt. As the debt relief debate continued on the morning of February 5, Whiteley spoke in favor of striking previous financial obligations. Exactly what he said is not known, but at one point the Decatur County delegate asked "Why raise the argument of protection for the creditor?"[7] Whether it was reflection of his personal past or not, Whiteley felt compassion for the poor throughout his life. That sentiment was manifested in various ways. Aside from his support of debt relief and a homestead exemption, he took the floor on January 15 and advocated abolishment of imprisonment for debt. The terms of the report of the Committee on the Bill of Rights reduced the likelihood of (without eliminating) imprisonment for debt. An individual could usually pay his bail before the war, Whiteley explained, but recent impoverishment frequently made meeting obligations impossible. The Republican asked the delegates if they could consciously incarcerate "the very head of a family?" Citing historical precedent, Whiteley urged his colleagues to follow the lead of other states and end the practice. "In strict harmony with the progress of the age," he forcefully declared, "imprisonment for debt should be abolished." Delegates voted minutes later to do so.[8]

Educating the freedpeople was central to Republican ideology and fundamental to making the ex-slave a contributing citizen. In Georgia, as other southern states, Republicans established a public school system, providing for "common schools" that were basic to the framework of free and universal public education. On March 5, from the floor, Whiteley urged establishing common schools "at the earliest moment practicable."[9]

By then, the constitution was nearing completion. The most dramatic changes in Georgia's sixth constitution had to do with race. An expanded Bill of Rights incorporated the language of the Fourteenth Amendment. As Congress had demanded, the constitution gave black males the right to vote. Whites as well as blacks profited from the establishment of the first public school system in the state. The state judiciary was simplified, punishment for debt abolished, and other overdue reforms instituted. What the document did not do was also significant. In five other southern states, Republican delegates drafted constitutions that disfranchised some white residents or imposed some political restrictions, causing extreme bitterness. Republicans in Georgia did not do so. Whiteley had reminded delegates at one point: "we came here to make an advance in government." The constitution represented that, in his judgment.

If the electorate ratified the constitution, Georgia would return to the Union. In April, when Georgians decided the fate of the constitution, they would also vote for a slate of state officials. Republicans had intended to nominate a gubernatorial candidate and other officials at a separate nominating convention. Yet, influenced by Foster Blodgett, chairman of the State Central Committee, the delegates suspended their deliberations on March 7 and nominated a Republican state ticket. The maneuver strengthened the gubernatorial chances of Rufus Bullock, a delegate and a man favored by Blodgett. The change in plans weakened the prospects of Henry P. Farrow, who was considered the favorite candidate but was not a delegate. A number of delegates resented Blodgett's interference, and sharp division resulted.

As with so much of the convention, Whiteley played a prominent role in the disagreement. He supported Farrow, a former supporter of Stephen Douglas and a reluctant Confederate. On March 7, a Saturday, when the delegates became a nominating convention, Whiteley was appointed chair of the committee that drafted nominating guidelines. A committee majority report proposed basing the gubernatorial nomination on the votes of a simple majority of delegates. Whiteley and Henry K. McCay, submitting a minority report, contended that two-thirds of the delegates' support should be necessary. They represented the faction loyal to Henry Farrow. If a nominee could muster only a bare majority among Republican delegates, Whiteley asked, how effective a candidate would he be? Delegates decidedly rejected the motion, which would have substituted the minority for the majority report, and Bullock gained the nomination.[10]

Whiteley's stature, though he had been unable to deny Bullock the nomination, was obvious. Meeting in separate caucuses that afternoon, Republicans nominated a candidate in each of the seven congressional districts for the Fortieth Congress. Second District delegates unanimously nominated Richard Whiteley. The Bainbridge lawyer's abilities were clear. Quite possibly, so was his ambition. No one, though, doubted his Republican principles. Several days later, formally thanking the delegates in writing, Whiteley pointed to a "restored, strengthened and perpetuated . . . Union." In the reconfigured nation, he insisted that an equitable place for the freedpeople must be made. "Should it be the pleasure of the people to endorse your action by my election," the candidate vowed with classic humility, "I will be found unwavering in the advocacy of equal justice and equal rights to all men." Whiteley clearly endorsed these principles. Considered in another perspective, the words revealed something else. Whiteley desired office, maneuvered for it, and was determined to go to Washington as a congressman.[11]

Several days later, on March 11, the convention adjourned. Georgians would vote for or against ratifying the constitution between April 20 and April 23. Whiteley had three months earlier arrived in Atlanta as a little-known Republican from Decatur County. He left the city well recognized and the congressional nominee of the Second District.

Georgia Democrats, who had opposed holding a convention, began a campaign aimed at blocking the constitution's ratification. The financial cost, objectionable features of the proposed document, and the possibility that Congress could change the constitution accounted for the opposition. Acknowledging, though, that the constitution might be approved and Georgia readmitted, Democrats nominated a slate of state candidates. John B. Gordon, a former Confederate general, was the gubernatorial candidate. Democrats also selected candidates for Congress in each district.

Whiteley's opponent was chosen when Second District Democrats held their nominating convention on March 31, at Albany, the Dougherty County seat, forty miles northwest of Bainbridge on the Flint River. Delegates gathered at the courthouse and nominated Nelson Tift. After moving from Connecticut to the South in the 1830s, Tift had figured prominently in Albany's founding. He went into the mercantile business, married, and in the years that followed served as an Inferior Court justice, militia colonel, editor of the *Albany Patriot,* railroad developer, and state representative. Elevating his name further was his financing of the construction of what became Tift's Bridge, finished in 1858—a 930-foot bridge that conveniently spanned the Flint River at Albany. Tift's acclimation to the South had also included owning slaves. He did not enlist in the southern army, but he and his brother, Asa, sold large amounts of beef and pork to the Confederacy from their packinghouse and made other contributions. His efforts for Southern independence also included promoting the construction of ironclad ships. In 1868, at fifty-eight years of age, Tift had various business interests, but he was primarily a cotton commission and warehouse merchant. He was very devout, a teetotaler, and a vegetarian. As the campaign illustrated, Nelson Tift was also a committed foe of Republicanism.[12]

The nomination of candidates signaled the outset of the campaign. So did escalating political violence. The murder of George Ashburn, a Republican who had recently returned from the constitutional convention in Columbus, gained much attention. Late on the night of March 30, several men entered the room Ashburn rented and shot and killed him.

The assailants belonged to the Ku Klux Klan. That organization, which originated in Tennessee, dated from the period just after the war. Originally an apolitical and largely fraternal order, the Klan changed in purpose and size following the advent of congressional or Radical Reconstruction. The Klan was merely the largest of the violently anti-Republican organizations that formed across the South, for example, the

Nelson Tift. Courtesy of Hargrett Rare Book and Manuscript Library, University of Georgia Libraries.

Knights of the White Camellia in Louisiana and the Young Men's Democratic Clubs of Florida. Whatever their affiliation, maintaining absolute white supremacy was their political creed. Doing so often meant intimidating and brutalizing Republicans. Klansmen usually struck at night, often in disguise, and acted without mercy. Blacks were most frequently the targets. Ashburns's murder offered a foreboding hint of the violence that became endemic to Reconstruction. State legislatures passed laws designed to combat the nightriders, and the federal government would do so later. Even so, violence remained a fact of Reconstruction politics. This was certainly so in southwest Georgia.[13]

The Second District was one of seven congressional districts drawn by the constitutional convention. Twenty-two counties of varying size and population composed the sprawling area. Florida provided the southern border, and the Chattahoochee River separated the district from Alabama to the west. Pine and hardwood forests and cotton and corn fields covered the rural district. There were no cities, but Albany and Americus were sizeable towns. Bainbridge, Blakely, Cuthbert, and Dawson were places

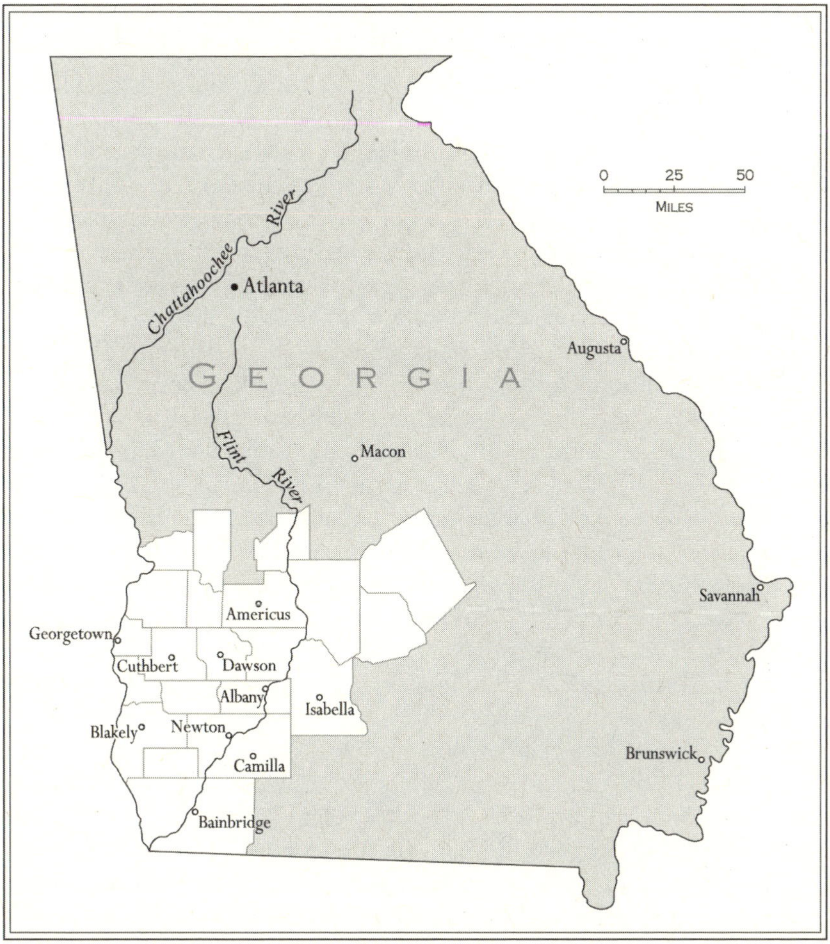

Map of Second Congressional District, Georgia, 1868.

of importance. Speaking at crossroads, churches, courthouse squares, and elsewhere in the six weeks ahead, Tift and Whiteley made the region a political battleground. The South Western Railroad and the South Georgia and Florida Railroad transported the candidates to some destinations. Sometimes they took a steamboat up or down the Flint River. Traveling overland by carriage was required to reach voters at less convenient places.

Neither Tift nor Whiteley was sure of victory or resigned to defeat. The vast majority of whites supported Tift. Democrats bitterly associated Republicanism with black equality, political proscription, and the recent enemy. Whiteley inherited strong allegiance among the freedpeople. Blacks' identification with Republicanism—the party of emancipation and citizenship—was seemingly inviolate. These political realities did not prevent Tift from seeking black votes or Whiteley asking for the allegiance of whites.

Demographic logic favored Whiteley. Over 106,000 blacks and 77,000 whites lived in the county district. Some counties were potentially staunch Republican strongholds. Four times as many blacks (9,424) as whites (2,092) resided in Dougherty County. Stewart County was the home of 9,100 freedpeople and only 5,104 whites. Blacks also composed large majorities in Baker, Lee, Macon, and Sumter counties.[14]

Whiteley knew that other considerations skewed any laws of mathematical probability. The local power structure in each county supported Tift. Every newspaper (there were no Republican newspapers) in the district endorsed the Democrat. Landlords might dismiss their black tenants or make other economic reprisals if they voted Republican. Some freedmen accepted money, whisky, clothes, and other bribes. Also beyond his control, Whiteley realized, was the effect that threatened and real violence would have on Republican voters.

A pattern of intimidation, replicated in other southern areas of Republican strength, was by 1868 quite clear in Georgia's Second Congressional District. In Decatur County, mistaking a school gathering for a Union League meeting, whites had broken up the meeting and threatened to cut the throats of any who acted with the League. Andrew Clark, a Freedmen's Bureau official in nearby Baker County, cited increasing attacks on blacks since voter registration had begun. He noted threats aimed at him and reported: "I am in the worst section of Georgia."[15] Freedmen's Bureau agent C. C. Hicks issued a strong statement from Albany. He noted the intention of whites to destroy the Union League by force and the utter lack of respect for the United States government, and concluded: "*if any place* is in need of *martial* law this is one."[16] In another Second District setting, Randolph County, a Republican attributed shots fired at another Republican "to the Ku Klux Klan, which has been organized recently in this place."[17]

In March, against this backdrop, Whiteley began campaigning. Sometimes speaking from prepared notes and at other times extemporaneously, he sounded the Republican call to arms. He promoted himself and the constitution. At Dawson, the seat of Terrell County, he addressed a large black and white audience on April 13. He explained how the homestead exemption protected a family's land. Elaborating on debt help, Whiteley described the promise of a fresh start for those who owed money. Blacks cheered his favorable references to their rights and recent citizenship status. In a more elemental sense, freedpeople wanted to own land, and they sought equal treatment before the law and the opportunities equated with freedom. Whiteley told the black man what he had a right to expect as a free man. And the ex-slaves, from the outset, listened to Richard Whiteley. "His clear demonstrative way of talking," one local white observed, "adds greatly to his popularity among them [blacks]."[18]

Since Democratic editors rarely quoted Republicans, and no Second District Republican newspapers existed, exactly what Whiteley said is rarely part of the public record. Some idea of it may be inferred from how Democrats reacted to him. At one campaign stop, a political foe described Whiteley as a "renegade" who had betrayed his Confederate past and "the rights and interests of his own color." More bluntly, the *Cuthbert Appeal* denigrated "Scalawag Whiteley, nigger candidate for Congress." These judgments and epithets, though, were too facile. In 1868, and in the future, Whiteley also worked hard to gain white support. He understood that in the short and long run, neither he nor the Republican Party could rely almost exclusively on black votes. It was incumbent on him and Republicans anywhere in the South to make Republicanism respectable. In the Second District of Georgia, doing so involved promoting political amnesty and the debt relief and homestead clauses of the constitution. In a more expansive sense, he urged ratification of the constitution as leading to a return to the Union and prosperity.[19]

Tift, like most Georgia Democrats, opposed ratifying the constitution. Between April 9 and April 11, Tift traveled from Georgetown to Cuthbert, and then to the small village of Fort Gaines on the Chattahoochee River. On April 10, at Cuthbert, the seat of Randolph County, Tift did not let an uncomfortable cold prevent him from denouncing the proposed constitution. Listeners heard him label the relief clause a "swindle" and fault the homestead plan. His emphasis was much the same at Bainbridge on April 15.[20]

A paternalistic outlook allowed Tift to refer sincerely to "our colored friends." He attempted to persuade blacks that Democrats were "their only real friends." Republican politicians, Tift exhorted repeatedly, merely used them for selfish reasons. As Democrats in Arkansas, North Carolina, and other southern states argued, he contended that blacks were best served by looking for direction to "the white people of the South, among whom they are raised."[21] At Cuthbert, Tift warned freedmen to be "beware of the seductive arts" of white Republicans. The candidate informed his audience that blacks elsewhere were setting up Democratic clubs. He proposed that Cuthbert freedmen do the same. When Tift asked for a show of interest, about twenty blacks raised their hands. The Democrat implicitly endorsed black suffrage by seeking the freedmen's support. The truth was something else. Having to ask for their vote was, to Tift, a regrettable necessity. He kept private (at least in front of blacks) his dismay concerning the death of slavery.

With this campaign, Whiteley began to build a network of Republican supporters in the Second District that would serve him well in the years ahead. Some were white, others were black. Philip Joiner, an ex-slave, had represented Dougherty County at the constitutional convention. He would have spoken highly of Whiteley during the campaign. Efforts in behalf of Whiteley were often channeled through the Union Leagues, which existed in most counties. Prominent Republicans in the Second District told blacks that Democrats favored limiting their freedom and even reviving slavery. During the election, the indoctrination continued, as freedmen were sometimes marched, with their ballot or ticket in hand, to the polls.[22]

A voter in Second District cast his ballot or ticket at any one of the twenty-two courthouses in the district. Except in presidential elections, where federal law required that all votes be cast on the same day, Georgia Reconstruction elections took place over several days. That allowed those in the rural areas of the county time to travel to the polls and vote. An individual voted by handing his ticket to an election official at the polls. Balloting, though, was not conducted secretly (until later, with the adoption of the Australian ballot) and an individual's preference was common knowledge. At Isabella, in Worth County, at Americus, the Sumter County seat, and at any Second District place of voting, the election procedure was supposed to be uniform. That was often not the case, however.[23]

Two weeks before the election, William Clark, of the AMA at Bainbridge, writing to Captain William White, the Freedmen's Bureau official in Thomasville, mentioned the "excitement" caused by the campaign and advised White to send a few soldiers to Bainbridge for precautionary reasons. In Reconstruction Georgia, as elsewhere in the South, soldiers often oversaw elections because of the volatile circumstances. Clark observed: "the opposition is going to vote *this* time," but he predicted that Whiteley would easily carry Decatur County. A similar situation existed at Albany, where Republicans pled with authorities for troops. As the election approached, soldiers took up positions in the Second District.[24]

Whiteley campaigned strenuously until the campaign closed. Sometime over the three-day voting period of April 20–23, he cast his ballot at the Decatur County courthouse. Nelson Tift did likewise at Albany. And it was there that the Democrat learned of his victory. Tift triumphed in fourteen of the twenty-two counties and gained 12,890 votes. He ran well in the predominantly white counties, and also registered majorities in seven of fourteen counties where blacks outnumbered whites. In Bainbridge, Whiteley received the news of his defeat. He carried Decatur and seven other counties and received 11,736 votes in a losing cause.

The contest confirmed Whiteley's fears concerning intimidation and fraud. In Cuthbert, William B. Dixson, a white Republican, declared that blacks were "forced to vote against their will." The Randolph County grocer stated that "wealth & intellect were also used to the extreme point."[25] Immediately to the west of Randolph, in Stewart County, there was trouble at the county seat of Lumpkin. Witnesses claimed that the soldiers were "bought off." Some soldiers became drunk, threatened blacks, and even tore up Republican ballots. Almost twice as many blacks as whites lived in Stewart County, but Tift gained two hundred more votes than Whiteley. Equally improbable, in Sumter County, where two of every three people were black, Tift claimed a slight majority. Over one thousand blacks lived in Quitman County, but Whiteley only received six votes there. These results defied all political logic and probability.[26]

How far the situation could degenerate was seen in Bainbridge. Soldiers were not stationed there, but Sheriff Samuel W. Patterson had deputized several whites and blacks for election duty. One of them was William J. Brannon, a local young white man. On Monday and Tuesday, blacks and whites voted without incident at the courthouse. Wednesday was more eventful. Jabez Donalson, a young black standing in line outside the courthouse, was waiting to cast a Republican ballot when Brannon approached him. Brannon offered Donalson crackers and whisky not to vote. Overhearing him, Isiah Williams, an outspoken black Republican, urged Donalson to "hold fast my son to the ticket you have." Brannon and Williams exchanged strong words and then began fighting. Brannon pulled his pistol and shot Williams. Falling to the ground, the freedman died within minutes.[27]

Whiteley considered the results with anger and the certain understanding that the contest represented something far short of an exercise in political democracy. Accepting defeat, on this occasion, was Whiteley's only recourse. At least, the election of Rufus Bullock as governor, Republican control of the legislature, and the ratification of the constitution provided some consolation. His long-deferred hope of Georgia's return to the Union was approaching realization. In June 1868, Congress passed the Omnibus Bill that admitted Georgia and five other states to the Union. Meeting in July at Atlanta, legislators ratified the Fourteenth Amendment, and Bullock took the inaugural oath on July 22. Whiteley was young, and so was the Republican Party in Georgia. He envisioned a strong Republican organization and, not incidentally, an important role for himself in the future. Even so, for the rest of his life, Whiteley maintained that he would have defeated Nelson Tift in a fair election. At a slightly later point in his career, writing to an ally about political fraud, he declared: "put it down at the first and it will be forced to show its monstrous form under circumstances that will shame it into silence on the one hand in defeat on the other." Defeat in 1868 taught Whiteley a lesson he did not forget. Following another election, twenty months in the future, that would become clear.[28]

Whiteley probably welcomed returning to a certain routine after three months in Atlanta and another month campaigning. Although helping construct a constitution and conducting a congressional campaign inevitably drew him from his legal practice, he remained a committed lawyer. He began most days by walking or riding the short distance from his Evans Street home to the Sanborn Building on Broughton Street. He often represented blacks. While the scales of justice were weighted against the poor and women, no segment of society faced the discrimination experienced by ex-slaves in the South. Whiteley's Georgia offered graphic evidence. The recently adopted constitution allowed blacks to sit on juries, but in practice relatively few were allowed to do so. Undercurrents of racism mocked the ideal of jurisprudential objectivity. As one Freedmen's Bureau agent in nearby Albany decided, the ex-slaves' "chances for obtaining justice hereafter in the civil or criminal courts of this section of country will be deplorably poor."[29]

Whiteley took strong exception to the circumstances. In at least one instance, he accepted the task of prosecuting a white man who killed a freedman. On February 16, 1868, following a dispute over shares of a crop and strong words, Thomas E. Speight shot and killed Lindsey Wells outside Bainbridge. Speight was white and Wells was black. William Clark, recently appointed Freedmen's Bureau agent in Decatur County, wrote Captain William White of the Freedmen's Bureau in Thomasville and explained his difficulty in finding a lawyer to prosecute Speight. The army officer advised prevailing on Whiteley to take the case once he returned from the constitutional convention in Atlanta. The Republican lawyer agreed to do so.[30]

William Clark, affiliated with the AMA, who had moved from Malden, Massachusetts, to Bainbridge the previous Thanksgiving, had joined the unofficial army of those who came South after the war to give blacks religious and educational guidance. Clark's experiences were much like those of many others connected to the AMA. He and two women composed a teaching corps that met with instant ostracism. Clark soon wrote an AMA colleague of the "unfriendly feeling" whites exhibited toward them.[31] In Georgia, he described the situation to the highest ranking Freedmen's Bureau official in the state, Colonel Caleb C. Sibley. He informed Georgia's assistant commissioner: "Yankees and 'Blue Legs,' radicals and negroes are cursed heartily." Early in 1868, Clark became the Freedmen's Bureau agent at Bainbridge. Arbitrating between blacks and whites in labor contract disagreements, the Republican Clark usually (but not always) sided with the freedpeople. He remained an object of extreme resentment among whites.[32]

Whiteley met Clark soon after Clark moved to Bainbridge. Party kinship and loyalty promoted cooperation among the finite number of local Republicans, but there could have been little personal closeness between Clark and Whiteley. Clark was pious, unctuously principled, and seems to have been a man of reserved New England temperament. Whiteley was less constrained by the word of God, essentially pragmatic, and eminently sociable. Clark was an outsider, sure to leave Bainbridge, and not overly worried with what local whites thought of him. Continued acceptance in the community where he and his family had spent the last ten years was important to Whiteley.

As the Freedmen's Bureau agent, Clark often referred blacks to Whiteley for legal consultation. The circumstances of a local (but unknown) freedman are illustrative. A sharecropper, he raised cotton on rented land, and in the fall of 1867 he had sent his crop to market; he had then not been paid for the cotton when rent was demanded. The landlord confiscated the freedman's corn and fodder, leaving him without feed for his hogs or cattle. Unwilling to ride his weak and unfed horse, the freedman walked twenty-five miles to Bainbridge and consulted Clark. Realizing he was helpless to intervene, Clark thought of calling on Whiteley. Only

Whiteley's absence in Atlanta at the constitutional convention prevented Clark from directing this man to him. In another case, Clark urged freedman Henry Clay to have Whiteley represent him; a local white man had shot at him. In still another instance, Robert Wright, a freedman, related how his landlord had violated their labor agreement and had assaulted him with a board. As usual, Clark advised Wright to consult Whiteley. The resolutions of all of these cases are not known. A grand jury refused to indict Thomas Speight in the shooting of Lindsey Wells. Even so, the instances verify Clark's estimation of Whiteley as "the only freedman's lawyer in the place."[33]

Clark also depended on the Republican lawyer for legal advice. In April 1868, thirty-nine local whites signed a petition asking for Clark's removal as the Freedmen's Bureau agent. Enlisting the aid of five local lawyers, they accused Clark of unjustly levying against citizens' property and favoring freedpeople over whites in labor contract disputes. Whiteley alone represented Clark. He was instrumental in seeing that nothing came of the weak and legally groundless charges. In the court of public opinion, Clark remained guilty among whites. Nor did others overlook that Whiteley had acted in behalf of the much-detested Yankee educator and Bureau agent.

Whiteley played no direct role but took much interest in the most controversial trial to take place that year. William Brannon, who had shot to death Isiah Williams during the previous April election, was tried before a military commission. Such trials, sometimes held in the South during Reconstruction in political cases, were by nature controversial. For over ten days in June, six United States army officers heard testimony at the courthouse before the judge advocate Campbell Dallas Emory. Despite conflicting testimony from whites and blacks, a clear case of murder emerged. On June 24, Judge Advocate Emory pronounced Brannon guilty of voluntary manslaughter and sentenced him to twenty years in the state penitentiary at Milledgeville. Outraged whites in Decatur County soon circulated another petition. Over 260 residents protested that Brannon had acted in self-defense and should have been tried in a civilian rather than military court.[34]

Whiteley believed justice had been served, and he did not sign the petition, which was addressed to President Johnson. On the June morning that Brannon's conviction was announced, he and William Clark talked with each other. Their conversation, probably much like many others, concerned political animosity in Decatur County. As serious as the situation was, Whiteley told Clark he considered Decatur "the best governed county in the district." That was faint praise to Clark. A few troops remained bivouacked outside of town, and Clark believed, with some justification, they should be kept there. In November, William Brannon was released early from prison, and he returned to Bainbridge. Numerous friends met him at the depot. Bainbridge remained a town of festering political unrest.[35]

Republican affiliation usually assured extreme ostracism in the Reconstruction South, but many in Bainbridge overlooked or minimized Whiteley's apostasy. He was a man of wealth and standing and was personally well liked. Whiteley's temperate voice also provided him with some protection. He did not advocate land confiscation, indiscriminate racial mixing, or political punishment of ex-Confederates. One local citizen described him as a "moderate man and . . . opposed to the extremists and their policy." In part, Whiteley framed the racial changes he did advocate in terms of economic advancement for both races. Whites also favorably noted advice that he gave local freedpeople in Bainbridge. He urged the ex-slaves to honor their labor contracts. The gospel of Victorian values that Whiteley preached to freedpeople—industry, temperance, and responsibility—gave him credibility among whites. When he spoke of biracial cooperation in the interests of Georgia's greater welfare, the words rang true. If the cloak of respectability did not fit Richard Whiteley seamlessly, he wore it comfortably. How long he could do so remained to be seen.[36]

4 *A Representative Man of New Georgia*

From his imposing home, or possibly his busy law office, Richard Whiteley wrote grandiosely of "the great work of restoration."[1] He was guardedly optimistic about the future of the freedpeople and of race relations. Also in an idealistic vein, he noted: "we are in a new era." Slavery, he pointed out, "exists no more, and with its past must be left the prejudices it engendered."[2] Yet, on a local level throughout the South, the promise of that new era would go begging unless committed public officials accepted and respected the changes. When the Red River Parish was created in Louisiana, Governor Henry Clay Warmouth appointed Republican officials for partisan reasons. Such commonplace moves merely represented political realities. In Decatur County, Whiteley did his part to make sure that Republicans controlled office. Local Republicans had won all the county offices in the April 1868 elections. Joel Johnson assumed the duties of ordinary (probate judge) for Decatur County that summer. Another white Republican, John C. Blount, became tax assessor, and Thomas J. Jeter served as the county tax collector. Whiteley acted as a surety for each.

The Republican lawyer contributed in a different way to the installment of a Republican sheriff. Heil B. Waugh had defeated Samuel Patterson in the April election. Yet the incumbent Democrat maintained that Waugh had not carried out proper office bond procedure and refused to step down. As late as October 1868, Patterson defiantly remained in office. Waugh turned to Whiteley for legal aid. Whiteley recognized Patterson for what he was, an unreconstructed individual who had wielded his powers as sheriff politically and against Republicans and freedpeople, and worked out the legal groundwork that enabled the sheriff-elect to assume office.[3]

Whiteley also took a new office. Governor Bullock nominated him as solicitor general of the Southwestern Judicial District. Sixteen judicial districts existed in Georgia, and a solicitor general represented the state in each. Acting in a prosecutorial role, the solicitor general worked to indict and convict defendants in Superior Court. The state senate confirmed Whiteley in July. Both his legal training and Republican affiliation accounted for the appointment. The position represented a professional advancement and was financially rewarding. Relying exclusively on the practice of law was, if the experiences of fellow lawyer Alexander Allen were representative, not advisable. Complaining to his brother of financial difficulties, the Bainbridge lawyer attested: "I do my full share of all the law business but there is very little to do." Whiteley was not blind to another consideration when he accepted the solicitor generalship. The position offered him the chance to become acquainted with more Second District residents. That could clearly benefit a man with political aspirations.[4]

Baker, Calhoun, Decatur, Dougherty, Mitchell, and Worth counties composed the Southwestern Judicial District. Whiteley followed a circuit that took him to the county seats of Newton, Morgan, Bainbridge, Albany, Camilla, and Isabella. When Superior Court met, at each town, Whiteley was present. Decatur County grand jurors succinctly defined the duties of the solicitor general. The most fundamental included punishing "bad men" so others "will feel they cannot with impunity violate the law." Having both defended and prosecuted felons, Whiteley understood the connotations of "bad men." He soon gained greater insights into the dark side of human nature.[5]

Southwest Georgia was neither more nor less crime-ridden than other areas of the state. That fact could be construed as an affirmation of law and order. Solicitor general Whiteley encountered similar criminal behavior from county to county between 1868 and 1871. Those committing offenses in Dougherty County did so with the same motivations as those in Worth County: anger, revenge, avarice, or lust. In moments of fury, some culprits acted impulsively; others proceeded with care and guile. Crime transcended gender, class, and race lines, and perpetrators operated in the dark of night or broad daylight. Males belonging to the lower economic ranks provided the profile most often confronted. As Whiteley considered his duties, he would have remembered that the solicitor general must do "justice to the state, as well as the accused." Although he considered a man or woman innocent until proved otherwise, he extended every effort to substantiate their guilt.

Whiteley could always assume when he reached the next courthouse that a lengthy docket had accumulated since his last visit. Offenses ranged from the relatively innocuous to the gravely serious. He dealt with alleged vagrants, usurists, and thieves, and bigamists and adulteresses who stood accused of moral turpitude; it was rare that a murder case was not adjudicated. As Superior Court opened, Whiteley familiarized himself with individual cases. That required working with the county sheriff, marshaling evidence, and lining up witnesses. Swearing in both the grand and petit jurors fell to him. Whiteley often presented evidence to the grand jury that might or might not result in an indictment. If a true bill was brought, he read the indictment at the arraignment and asked the defendant how he or she pleaded. A jury trial might follow. Whiteley could act with a local lawyer or handle the case independently. Sometimes he took no part in the trial. The solicitor general, during the week or two of Superior Court, was indispensable to the proceedings. Whiteley, a man who relished the law, legal tradition, and a courtroom atmosphere, must have coveted the office.[6]

Neither did the solicitor generalship prevent Whiteley from participating in politics. He became involved in the presidential campaign of 1868. When Republicans gathered at Philadelphia in May and nominated Ulysses S. Grant, Whiteley, having been selected as a delegate to the convention at the Republican convention back in March, was present. He soon belonged to the Executive Committee of the Central Grant Club for Georgia, which promoted the Republican nominee and his running mate, Schuyler Colfax. The campaign provided Whiteley with an opportunity to spread the Republican gospel and help build the young party in Georgia. At the same time, he intended to further establish his credentials as a prominent state Republican.

Campaigning for Grant brought Whiteley on July 28 to a Republican rally in Macon, a large town of about eight thousand residents 130 miles northeast of Bainbridge. A crowd that may have reached seven thousand (mostly blacks) assembled in a grove near Rose Hill Cemetery. Jefferson F. Long, a former slave and merchant-tailor in Macon, introduced Whiteley, who was the first Republican notable to speak. One witness believed his "forcible and patriotic" remarks had a "telling effect." Several Republican speakers followed, and resolutions were adopted pledging support to the Grant-Colfax ticket. Setting and defining the issues, Whiteley had done his part. Jason Clarke Swayze, the Republican editor of the *American Union* in Macon, complimented Whiteley's performance, writing that his speech "would do good service in pamphlet form as a campaign document."[7]

Several weeks later, in further service to his party, Whiteley traveled to Atlanta to attend the meeting of the Republican State Central Committee, chaired by Foster Blodgett. Whiteley and three other Second District Republicans joined that committee when it met on August 18. Republican activities demanded his attention a week and a half later, when Second District Republicans met at Albany on August 29 to nominate a candidate for the Forty-first Congress. Whiteley did not seek the nomination, but, befitting his stature as a party leader, he spoke to the convention. Second District Republicans nominated William P. Pierce, a captain with a Union cavalry regiment from Kentucky who had moved to Georgia and begun planting cotton in 1865. He had more recently been a Freedmen's Bureau agent in Lee and Terrell counties. Nelson Tift, the incumbent, was renominated by district Democrats.

Whiteley probably continued to campaign for Grant during the fall, but he was far less enthusiastic about William Pierce. Pierce had sought the Second District nomination when Whiteley had run the previous April. For whatever reason, rather than endorsing Whiteley, Pierce had told blacks that the nominee did not deserve their support, condemning him as a "Rebel" who had fought to keep them slaves. Not a man to forget a political slight, Whiteley now refused to support Pierce as congressional candidate.[8]

The Democrats had met in New York and nominated Horatio Seymour for president. Francis P. Blair was chosen as the New York governor's running mate. The party platform denounced Reconstruction, and Blair called in even harsher terms for the overthrow of Republican governments in the South and the elimination of blacks from politics.

The stark differences between the two parties contributed to what was arguably the most violent presidential election in the nation's history. The Ku Klux Klan and other organizations terrorized southern Republicans. Two Republican legislators were murdered in South Carolina. Black Belt Klansmen in Alabama committed crimes only exceeded by their Invisible Empire brothers in the Tennessee Valley of that state. Numerous parishes in Louisiana became one-sided battlegrounds. The highest profile crime of this sort in Arkansas, but by no means the only one, involved the assassination of a Republican congressman. Allen Trelease, the most authoritative Klan historian, contends that nightriders played a large role in eight southern states during this election, including Georgia. Violence and ballot box fraud destroyed any semblance of a fair contest there. A conservative estimate by the Freedmen's Bureau in Georgia listed 31 killings, 43 shootings, and 55 beatings during the political canvas.[9]

Some of the worst violence took place in the Second District. At Camilla, a small village about fifty miles northeast of Bainbridge, shooting and chaos resulted when whites refused to allow freedpeople to hold a political rally on September 19. At least nine blacks were killed and more wounded, and the so-called Camilla Riot gained national attention. Events there represented only the most sensational episode of violence in the Second District. In Early County, near Blakely, a black Republican who was organizing a Grant and Colfax Club was abducted and shot to death. Philip Joiner, the former slave and outspoken Republican, provided political leadership for Dougherty County freedpeople. Whites armed with shotguns and pistols made it clear, Joiner maintained, that "it was their country and they was going to rule it."[10] In nearby Cuthbert, contemplating the defiance of some whites, a Freedmen's Bureau agent declared: "this portion of the South is in a state of quasi rebellion against all authority, except such as is agreeable to them."[11]

Whiteley regretted these circumstances and also the course of events in Decatur County. After midnight, on August 27, about a half dozen men took Adam Ganey, a black man, from his home, led him into the woods, and whipped him. Recent attempts to form Democratic Clubs among blacks had failed, and William Clark speculated that Ganey's assailants aimed to intimidate politically minded freedpeople. The chances of bringing Ganey's assailants to justice were as remote as apprehending those who attacked the freedman Basil Weaver on the night of October 13. A party of men roused Weaver from bed, forced a bag over his head, roughly escorted him into the woods, and administered a whipping. William Clark expressed the situation well when he observed: "nearly the entire community would not approve or would not advise violence in any form." Having said as much, the Freedmen's Bureau agent continued: "but their sentiments and conversation are such as to encourage and influence the more lawless spirits."[12]

The election in Georgia was a Republican debacle: Horatio Seymour received 102,000 votes to Grant's 57,000. Some twenty-five thousand more Republican ballots had been cast for Rufus Bullock in the recent April election. In some counties where Republicans had done well in that contest, the fall-off challenged credulity. The Republican vote in

Columbia County dropped from 1,222 to a single vote. Eleven counties reported no Republican votes. Democrats won most of the seven congressional seats, including the Second District, where Nelson Tift easily defeated William Pierce.

Whiteley took satisfaction in Grant's election. Southern votes played a major part in that victory. In the ex-Confederacy, where the Republican Party had not existed during the last presidential election, Grant had carried every state but Georgia and Louisiana. In another sense, the incredible violence in Georgia and elsewhere reinforced Whiteley's understanding of the virulent opposition to Republicanism and the impossibility of guaranteeing a fair and uneventful election in Georgia. That was a sobering reflection, considering his hopes for a political future.[13]

In the meantime, the path of Reconstruction in Georgia had taken an unforeseen turn. In September, two months before the election, Democratic (and some Republican) legislators expelled twenty-nine black legislators from the General Assembly. Although the recently adopted state constitution did not explicitly provide that blacks could hold office, removing the legislators violated at least the spirit of Reconstruction. Democrats who had finished second replaced the black legislators. This provoked great protest from Governor Bullock and most state Republicans. So did the fact that many Democrats sitting in the legislature could not take the test oath. The expulsion of blacks who should have kept their seats and the installation of Democrats who could not take the test oath caused consternation in Washington. Under the circumstances, Georgia's representatives were not seated when the Forty-first Congress opened in March 1869. As a result, the state, suddenly unreconstructed, returned to a state of limbo outside the Union.

Just as Klansmen's activities and vote-counting chicanery outraged Whiteley, so did the expulsion of the legislators. He was present on February 15, 1869, when some state Republicans met at City Hall in Atlanta, and he joined their Committee on Resolutions, which submitted resolutions calling for reseating the black legislators and evicting legislators proscribed by the Fourteenth Amendment or unable to take the test oath. In March, the Republican State Central Committee met at Atlanta, and Whiteley was appointed to another term.[14]

He remained the most prominent Republican in southwest Georgia. Under the circumstances, it was natural that Joseph J. Christie, the Republican probate judge in Miller County, facing a political dilemma, would write to him. Miller bordered Decatur County to the north, and from the neighboring town of Colquitt, Christie asked if Whiteley could help Charles H. Vann. The probate judge described Vann as deserving because of his Republican loyalties and his personal situation: poor, crippled, and trying to support a family. Whiteley sympathized, and realized that what Christie advised was true, that the party would benefit if Miller County residents understood that the Republicans looked after the disadvantaged. Several days later, replying from Bainbridge, Whiteley advised making Vann a notary republic, reasoning: "he is one of us and a good man." Christie had mentioned that Republicans were in local positions of power. Whiteley encouraged him to "run a stiff line and do not dread the consequence . . . the enemy are on their backs and keep them there."[15]

Tending to political matters, practicing law, and carrying out his solicitor general duties consumed Whiteley's time. Lawyers from Albany, Bainbridge, Macon, Newton, and Thomasville were present when Judge James M. Clark convened Superior Court at Bainbridge in April 1869. Whiteley fulfilled his responsibilities as solicitor general. Several weeks later, when Mitchell County Superior Court opened at Camilla, Whiteley attended. In the second-floor courtroom of the Dougherty County courthouse, Judge Clark called court to order at Albany late in June. A week or so later, after justice was served, or possibly denied in some instances, Dougherty County grand jurors extended thanks to solicitor Whiteley "for his polite attention to this body."[16]

As the solicitor general, Whiteley gained an even clearer understanding of black vulnerabilities. In Baker County, a white foreman had cut a black woman across the forehead, seriously hurting her. When Freedmen's Bureau agent William Clark visited Baker County, the poor and homeless woman approached him in desperate need of help. Also in Baker County, Clark heard of a white boy who without provocation had struck a black boy, causing him to lose his sight. Mindful of both Whiteley's empathy for the freedpeople and his power as solicitor general to do something about such crimes, Clark informed a Freedmen's Bureau official: "I reported both cases to Major Whiteley." From various corners, frequently Republican in outlook, Whiteley received requests for help.[17]

The responsibilities of the solicitor generalship contributed to Whiteley's decision to take on a law partner. John E. Donalson became his associate early in 1869. Donalson had been born in Bainbridge into a respected and old Decatur County family. The Civil War interrupted his education at the University of North Carolina; he served in the Confederate Army and following the conflict resumed his studies at the University of Georgia, including the study of law. Returning to Bainbridge, he soon became Whiteley's partner. Noting the new partnership, the *Bainbridge Argus* acknowledged "Major Whiteley's abilities as a lawyer" and described

Donalson as "a young man of the highest order of talent." The firm of Whiteley and Donalson advertised a willingness to practice in thirteen southwest counties. That Donalson was a Democrat posed no problems. Whiteley dropped political differences when professional business and financial profit were involved.[18]

In 1869, Richard and Margaret Whiteley would mark twenty years of marriage. Although his unconventional course had made him enemies, Margaret did not share any of that notoriety. She was a model of etiquette and decorum and instilled in their children the importance of honesty, generosity, responsibility, and, not least of all, faith. As a leading lady in the community, she donated a "magnificent cake" when the Oak City Hook and Ladder Company had a picnic on June 16, 1869. The appreciative firemen responded with three cheers.[19] The staff of newly established newspaper the *Bainbridge Southern Sun* mentioned Margaret's gift of seven gallons of lemonade and "different kinds of elegant cake in proportion." This was the woman who would later present their son Richard on his birthday with a copy of *The Poetical Works of Henry Wadsworth Longfellow.* Those who knew her also realized that Margaret was a strong woman who held fixed opinions as to right and wrong and who believed that punishment for error must be accepted as dutiful penance.[20]

The family became bigger as 1869 opened; Margaret Hortense was born thirteen days into the year. With three boys, the family welcomed the girl they called Hortense, and sometimes Maggie. More than ever was the assistance needed of a white servant named Eliza Williams, who lived with the family in their large Evans Street home. In 1869, Richard was seven and Montford, or Montie, was nine, and both were enrolled at Bainbridge Male and Female Institute. That fall, Charles, the oldest Whiteley child, entered the College of New Jersey (later Princeton University), becoming one of the first (if not the first) young man from Bainbridge to attend that fine college. Charles would be in and out of Bainbridge for the next few years. At one point, organizing a local baseball team, he and a teammate announced: "we greatly need something of the kind to exercise our limbs."[21]

As the 1860s drew to a close, Bainbridge was slowly emerging from its postwar economic blight. When Bill Lake's Circus arrived, large numbers of whites and blacks "invested their greenbacks freely to see it."[22] The extension of the Atlantic and Gulf Railroad had provided a boost to commerce. At least twelve different merchants sold dry goods and groceries. Casper Lewis attempted to live up to his motto of "quick sales and small profits."[23] On West Street, running east of the courthouse, a customer might buy a saddle from Noel Gainey, consult with dressmaker

M. J. Reynolds, or, if necessary, make arrangements with E. J. Henderson for a casket. William Brannon, having returned early from his imprisonment for killing Isiah Williams, ran the Exchange Saloon, which was arranged as tastefully "as any we have seen this side of New York."[24] Some citizens emphasized the social graces, and at the Dancing School, students gained instruction in the "graceful movements of the body and all fashionable dances of the day."[25] Construction on several fine homes, notably on Shotwell Street, was also underway. Noting various improvements, the *Bainbridge Southern Sun* boasted: "there is nothing to prevent Bainbridge from being one of the first cities of Georgia."

A new log schoolhouse for the freedpeople, begun under the auspices of the AMA and the Freedmen's Bureau, rose during the first months of 1869 in Bainbridge. The completed building was the scene of activity on March 4, when prayer, singing, and white and black speakers consecrated Whittier School. Ceremonies closed with the singing of "America." The school, named for New England abolitionist John Greenleaf Whittier, became the center of black education locally. Whiteley was in all likelihood one of the speakers on March 4. He became a consistent supporter of the Whittier School.[26]

Whiteley also took satisfaction in developments regarding Georgia statehood. Georgia was the last state remaining outside the Union when the Forty-first Congress reconvened in the final month of 1869. In his opening remarks to Congress, President Grant urged Georgia's readmission, and it was accomplished under Republican conditions. Congress immediately passed legislation that forced a reorganized Georgia legislature to reseat the black legislators and remove the white legislators who were unable to take the test oath. Readmission further required adopting the Fifteenth Amendment, which enfranchised the freedmen. Until then Georgia was remanded to military control, and Bullock became provisional governor by legislation passed on December 22, 1869. The action represented a victory for Bullock and was welcomed by most state Republicans, including Richard Whiteley. He looked forward to the black legislators' reinstatement, the exile of the Democratic impostors, and Georgia's return to the Union.

Within weeks, in January 1870, the legislature met. Over twenty Democrats who were unable to take the test oath were forced from the legislature. The expelled black legislators were reseated. The reorganized and Republican controlled legislature reratified the Fourteenth and then ratified the Fifteenth Amendment that January.

Anticipated readmission raised the question of who would represent Georgia in Congress. A year and a half earlier, in July 1868, the legislature had elected Joshua Hill and Horace Virgil Milton Miller to the Senate. Hill was a Republican, and Miller, an ex-Whig, defied political categorization; he had accepted the Republican Reconstruction plan. Neither Hill nor Miller had been seated because Georgia had been denied representation. As 1870 opened and readmission approached, Bullock and Republicans favored electing new senators with sounder party credentials. Hill and Miller, the argument went, could not legally represent the state because the legislature that had elected them was tainted by members who were unable to take the test oath.[27]

Meeting in January 1870, the reorganized legislature declared Hill and Miller's previous election invalid. Who would represent Georgia in the Senate was uncertain, but because Republicans controlled the legislature, his political affiliation was a given. Amos Akerman, Foster Blodgett, Henry Farrow, Josiah R. Parrott, and others were mentioned. The *Atlanta Constitution* declared: "the senatorial aspirants are crowding up to the rack."

Richard Whiteley was one of them. Intelligent and likeable, he was well regarded in state party circles. His Republican resume included helping draft the state constitution, running for Congress, campaigning for Grant, and serving on the Republican State Central Committee. His political moderation and his identification with the South further recommended him. Although born in Ireland, he was perceived as a Southerner and could not be tarred as a carpetbagger. A move undertaken in Whiteley's behalf, either generated by him or others, was soon underway. Well aware of what might develop, he went to Atlanta.[28]

In January and February, maneuvering for advantage openly and sometimes more discreetly, various state Republicans attempted to position themselves for the Senate. Whiteley must have done so. Little else, except that he and his supporters were successful, can be stated with certainty about these efforts. On the evening of February 14, when Republicans caucused at Schofield's Hall on Peachtree Street, Whiteley was nominated. Although Whiteley's acceptance remarks have not survived, he must have thanked fellow Republicans for their confidence in him. Josiah Parrott, former president of the constitutional convention, spoke that night at the caucus. He reminded listeners of the important services that Whiteley had performed as delegate to the constitutional convention. Parrott praised the nominee that night as "a young man of great merit" and declared: "there is no brighter mind nor better Republican in Georgia than this little man from Decatur." Henry Farrow was the other nominee.

Farrow and Whiteley's nomination was tantamount to election, because Republicans claimed a legislative majority. Farrow would replace Joshua Hill, whose term did not expire until 1873. Whiteley, the junior senator, would serve out the term of H. V. M. Miller (as he was generally known), which ended in 1871. Over the course of the next two days, in the legislature, Farrow and Whiteley were perfunctorily elected.[29] Whiteley received 110 of the 111 votes cast by the participating legislators (Democrats protested by not voting), and the *Atlanta Daily New Era* praised him as "a representative man of New [*sic*]Georgia."[30]

In early 1870, not even forty years old, Richard Whiteley was poised to become a United States senator. If the man whose legislative experience consisted of but several months as a constitutional delegate was apprehensive, he did not seem to betray any doubts. Anxious to join the Senate, Whiteley left Atlanta immediately for Washington.

Some uncertainty tempered his expectations. Hill and Miller maintained that they had been legally elected and refused to concede their Senate seats. Congress would ultimately decide which set of senators had the best claim. Arriving on the night of February 17, 1870, Whiteley and Farrow took private lodgings at a house on C Street near the National Hotel. Whiteley, characteristically, went to work making influential allies. A correspondent soon reported that both he and Farrow were "in communication with men of influence daily." None was potentially as important as the president. At the White House, within the next few days, Grant made clear to Whiteley and Farrow in a brief meeting that determining who represented Georgia in the Senate was the responsibility of Congress.

Both Whiteley and Farrow were no doubt present on February 22 when Senator William M. Stewart of Nevada presented their credentials to the Senate. Credentials stated an individual's name, when and to what office he was elected, and by what authority. Senator Charles Drake objected that Farrow and Whiteley's credentials had not been properly certified to the president of the Senate. Stewart considered the objections specious, but he withdrew their credentials. In the meantime, Farrow and Whiteley remained at their C Street lodgings.

Various controversies meant that Congress confirmed none of the four senatorial aspirants that spring. The recent expulsion of the Republicans from the state legislature caused controversy in Washington. So did the so-called prolongation controversy. Legislators served two-year terms, and elections were scheduled for the fall of 1870 in Georgia. Citing the black legislators' absence for fifteen months, Bullock advised prolonging the sitting legislature and postponing the scheduled state elections. Doing so, a decision ostensibly based on fairness, served his purpose of extending Republican legislative control for two more years. Differences of opinion in Washington further delayed Georgia's return to the Union.[31]

Unsure of his Senate prospects, Whiteley returned to Bainbridge in March after several weeks in Washington. In response to inquiring acquaintances, whose opinions were divided, Whiteley did not waver. He and Farrow, the well-known lawyer reiterated, had been elected by the only legitimate legislature. Whiteley's status was the subject of public discussion. Over the next few years, the *Bainbridge Southern Sun* would be edited by several men, most prominently John R. Hayes and Robert W. Johnston. Both were on friendly terms with Whiteley. If a Republican had to be sent, the somewhat independent-minded *Southern Sun* conceded that Whiteley was the best possible choice. The editors noted his moderate brand of Republicanism and his personal integrity, and added: "we must give him credit for, as we know him to be, a gentleman and a man of decided ability."[32] The staunchly Democratic *Bainbridge Argus* differed sharply, dismissing the notion of Whiteley sitting in the Senate as "simply ridiculous and absurd." In the meantime, Whiteley would not have corrected anyone who referred to him as Senator.[33]

Whiteley remained in Bainbridge during most of 1870. On May 5, he addressed local freedpeople at a picnic near the Flint River where blacks gathered for food, society, and oratory. He gave, according to the *Bainbridge Southern Sun,* "a good, sensible talk, avoiding the subject of politics altogether." Whiteley traveled later that month to Andersonville in nearby Sumter County. About thirteen thousand Union soldiers had died at the notorious prison, their deaths caused by a lack of supplies and general neglect. On May 30, recently designated Memorial Day, Whiteley attended a ceremony at which the graves of former Andersonville prisoners were decorated. His participation represented the act of a man moved by the tragedy but also that of a Republican, for few Democrats attended. Governor Bullock and the grand chaplain of the Grand Army of the Republic spoke at the thoroughly Republican event. Whiteley listened with approval.[34]

Back in Bainbridge, local freedpeople often climbed the stairs to Whiteley's second-floor office in the Sanborn Building. They consulted with him on any number of topics, often with questions concerning labor relations, politics, and making a living. A few blacks owned land, but, as elsewhere in the South, freedpeople remained in virtual economic bondage to their white landlords. Hopes of a land grant from the government had vanished. Not surprisingly, a black debating club would soon debate the merits of tenant farming as opposed to sharecropping. Whiteley encouraged freedpeople and in any number of ways acted as their ally.

In the theoretical future, Whiteley might be seated in the Senate. In the certain present, he was a lawyer and solicitor general. In June 1870, when Superior Court met in Dougherty County, lawyers from Camilla, Macon, Americus, and elsewhere joined those assembled at the brick courthouse. Whiteley was there. Defendants were charged with larceny, seduction, stabbing, burglary, and bigamy, and Nathan Braxwell, a freedman, stood accused of murder. Whiteley's successful prosecution of Braxwell and others prompted the *Albany News* to note: "Solicitor Whiteley is conducting the state's business efficiently." The Democratic newspaper, facetiously alluding to Whiteley's disputed status as a United States senator, further noted: "we failed to discover any decided improvement in his personal appearance, his dignity, or ability, in consequence of his Senatorial career."[35]

An informed Decatur County citizen listed several necessary traits for a solicitor general. That included being "a man of nerve." Whiteley was that. Those who knew him also realized that he longed to return to politics.[36] That he would do so in the United States Senate was becoming less likely. By the summer of 1870, six months had passed since Whiteley had apparently been elected to the Senate. On July 15, just before the Forty-first Congress recessed, the Georgia bill passed. It allowed the state's long-deferred return but did not provide for extending the legislature. That same day, Senator William Stewart asked that Farrow and Whiteley's credentials be placed on the table until the next session. Congress adjourned later that day, not to meet until December. If ever carried out, the seating of Whiteley and Farrow would have to wait.

Prolonging the legislature and avoiding elections remained at issue in the Georgia legislature. All Democrats opposed as unconstitutional Bullock's plan postponing elections. So did many prominent state Republicans, such as Amos Akerman and Henry Farrow. Whiteley also made his opinion public. Writing from Atlanta on August 2, six legislators asked Whiteley about his views regarding prolongation.

Whiteley replied in a public letter within the week from Bainbridge. He reasoned that "law and justice" required holding elections when the state constitution provided for them. Two-year terms, he affirmed, were mandated by the constitution. Justice was aborted when the people were denied "a right held sacred by free men." Any other reasoning was tortured. As for extending the legislature, "I confess I have not the ingenuity to devise even a plausible legal reason for doing so." Maintaining that Republicans were the truest exponents of democracy, Whiteley contended that skipping elections repudiated party principles. The stakes were high for the young Republican Party in Georgia. Whiteley argued that thousands of Georgians loyal to the Union could affiliate with a moderate Republican Party. Prohibiting elections alienated these elements. In a concluding paragraph he declared: "moderate republicanism is the best guarantee for National Union and prosperity."

The prolongation controversy ended several days later. On August 11, the Georgia House rejected a bill extending the legislators' term without an election. As the state constitution specified, elections would take place in the two-year interval as scheduled. The legislature set the election dates for December 20–22, 1870.[37]

Within the next week, Whiteley, writing to Henry Farrow from Bainbridge, noted the split that prolongation had caused in state Republican ranks and asked if the party could be "harmonized" and whether "concert of action" could be achieved before the upcoming election. Whiteley added: "I am anxious to know what task is proposed to enable us to weather the storm." Referring to his open letter to the legislators, Whiteley proposed that Republicans forge an alliance with Union men. Republicans and moderate Democrats could unite over principles of loyalty to the United States Constitution and the "rights of the colored race." As it was, "I need not tell you that the chances are against us in the election." Whiteley and Farrow had forged a friendship and a political alliance, and in the future, each would help the other.[38]

Whiteley had by then decided, or soon would do so, to run for Congress. The circumstances that accounted for that decision were that in December 1870, when the final session of the Forty-first Congress convened, Georgia would be eligible for representation. Whiteley might join the United States Senate then. Yet, since he had been elected to the short term, and the Forty-first Congress would close in March 1871, this Senate term would be short. Whiteley contemplated a different route to Washington. A full term as congressman appealed to him much more. In December 1870, Georgians would elect representatives for the final session of the Forty-first and all of the Forty-second Congress. Whiteley hoped to become at that time the Second District's congressman.

At Atlanta, when Foster Blodgett convened the State Central Republican Committee on September 14–15, 1870, the congressional elections were the most crucial item on the agenda. The committee determined that Republicans in each of the seven districts should designate a nominee in separate conventions on October 5. Whiteley did not attend the meeting. Writing the day after the Atlanta gathering, he informed Henry Farrow, "I would have been glad to have been present." Responsibilities as solicitor general prevented him from attending. As matters stood, he advised: "I leave on the fall circuit tomorrow, and shall be busy until it is over." Whiteley also realized that it might be his last circuit.[39]

5 *Whiteley versus Tift: A Sequel*

Since the first three months of 1870, when Mississippi, Virginia, and Texas were readmitted to the Union, Georgia had stood alone as the only ex-Confederate state not to have returned. Yet the state's jagged odyssey back was nearing completion. In December, elections would be held in the seven congressional districts and candidates elected to serve for the short duration of the Forty-first Congress; they would then take their place in the Forty-second Congress. A decision involving the hanging question as to who should represent Georgia in the Senate was also imminent. These circumstances had enormous consequences for Richard Whiteley.

On October 5, 1870, Second District Republicans would convene at Albany to nominate a congressional candidate. Whiteley expected to be selected. That he had abandoned his Senate aspirations and was seeking the congressional nomination was common knowledge. In a recent letter to Henry Farrow, Whiteley had mentioned opposition from a Republican whom he identified only as Jones. Whiteley speculated that Jones was angry with him for opposing an extension of the legislature. Whiteley confided: "I suppose his move is a punishment for not following blindly the Atlanta Ring as my nomination was conceded by him and others previous to the prolongations issue." As matters stood, Whiteley promised to "keep my eye on Jones."[1]

Neither Jones nor anybody else provided significant opposition. In the weeks before the convention, Republicans met across the Second District and designated convention delegates. Some counties sent representatives to Albany who were already pledged to a candidate; other delegates were uncommitted. An unidentified Dougherty County resident, endorsing Whiteley in a letter to the *Macon American Union,* reasoned that a successful candidate must appeal to some whites and all the freedmen. As solicitor general, Whiteley had "mingled freely" with a wide cross-section and commanded political appeal among white moderates.[2]

The choice among Democrats was also clear-cut. Second District Democrats scheduled their nominating convention for September 21 at Albany. In the weeks before the convention, Nelson Tift emerged as the prohibitive favorite. Tift claimed the odd distinction of having defeated two Republicans in one year for a congressional seat. In April 1868, he had beaten Whiteley and taken a place in the Fortieth Congress. That September his defeat of William Pierce had sent him to the Forty-first Congress. Yet, because Georgia had lost representation in Congress, Tift had actually served little time in Washington. He had recently reinforced his standing among state Democrats by circulating a questionnaire regarding the political situation in Georgia. Respondents (almost all Democrats) testified to good order, and Tift's much-cited questionnaire contradicted Republican representations of intimidation and political persecution.

Support emerged in Americus, where the *Weekly Sumter Republican* endorsed and thanked Tift for his efforts when "the heel of the military despot was then upon our necks."[3] Eleven days before the convention, at Isabella, Worth County Democrats also endorsed the apparent nominee. In Terrell County, at Dawson, support was recorded for Council B. Wooten. A former Confederate officer, Wooton was presently a state senator and resident of Dawson.

The fact that Albany was centrally located in the Second District and was its largest town recommended it to both Republicans and Democrats. Delegates could come overland, arrive by railroad, or take a steamer up the Flint River. About four thousand people, equally divided between blacks and whites, lived in Albany. It was a place of wide streets and well-finished brick buildings of one, two, and even three stories. Numerous chinaberry trees dotted the business district. A two-story brick courthouse, surrounded by a fence, was the town landmark. Visitors often stayed at the comfortably appointed Albany House.

At the courthouse, Democrats assembled on the morning of September 21. Men of various occupations and backgrounds were present, but William Styles, a black delegate from Sumter County, seemed the most incongruous. All obstacles to Nelson Tift's nomination were removed when Council Wooten withdrew his name from consideration. The delegates nominated Tift, Albany's most prominent citizen, by acclamation. Accepting the offer, Tift invited all to join what he envisioned as a crusade for Democratic restoration. This was the man who had recently issued an address to Georgians pointing to the "devilish malignity" of the political opposition and their "evil motives."[4]

Two weeks later, on October 5, about forty Republican delegates representing fourteen counties assembled at the Dougherty County courthouse. At this convention, whites and blacks were almost equally present. Whiteley had promised Henry Farrow, "I will look after the 2nd Dist."[5] If doing so meant building support for his nomination, Whiteley had succeeded. The delegates nominated him, the most prominent Republican in the district, by acclamation. He thanked the convention and expounded on the promise of the recent amendments. He affirmed the "equal rights of all people," declaring that "the law was all powerful and would protect all alike," and praised the Thirteenth, Fourteenth, and Fifteenth Amendments.[6] He also added a word of caution, warning against large and rowdy meetings, where strong drink contributed to irresponsible behavior and provoked criticism. Speaking in a "spirited and convincing manner," Whiteley urged Republicans to organize.[7]

Both candidates campaigned widely during the next few weeks. In an early public announcement outlining his appearances, Tift concluded, "I invite my opponent, Major Whiteley, to meet me and discuss the questions." At Camilla, the seat of Mitchell County, and at Isabella, the seat of Worth County, Tift and Whiteley sparred in debate. More often, both men independently crisscrossed the Second District.[8]

Tift spoke on November 12 at Cuthbert to whites and blacks who had gathered at the courthouse grounds. He attributed misguided policy and corruption on the national and state levels to "Radical villainy." As he spoke, a small marching band appeared, and though the loud music diverted some, Tift quickly regained his audience. He continued a dissection of "every joint and fibre of the radical carcass." Tift made it clear that anyone associated with the Republican Party, and that included Richard Whiteley, was inimical to the country's interest.[9]

At Bainbridge the following Saturday, Tift blasted the Republicans without any interruptions. A general suspension of business and fair weather boded well. From behind a makeshift podium on the courthouse square, he denounced the Grant regime for funneling land to railroad "rings" and sanctioning a high tariff. Closer to home, Tift mentioned scandals connected to the governor and "showed up Bullock and his clan in all their hideous deformity." Tift refrained from criticizing Whiteley in his hometown but expressed regret that his opponent was not present to debate.[10]

As Republicans waged an uphill battle for respect and success throughout the South, men of the so-called scalawag ilk were passionately denounced as traitors to their region and race. Whiteley refused to be defined by the political opposition. In fact, fashioning a political battle plan in Georgia's Second District, he built a coalition that included whites. Some were ex-Whigs, never enamored with the Democratic Party, and attracted by Republican promises of economic development. In a region of chronic poverty, he converted other whites by portraying the Republican Party as the natural home of the common man and pointed to the debt relief and homestead measures sponsored by the party. He also vigorously championed political amnesty for ex-Confederates. In 1870, five years since the last shots of the war had been fired, thousands of Southerners could not hold office because of the limits imposed by the Fourteenth Amendment. Striking these disabilities was Whiteley's unequivocal cry. Any one of these considerations could attract some white support. Robert M. Johnston, a prominent Bainbridge Democrat, made public his intention to vote for Whiteley. Others like him, upstanding men in the Second District, did likewise.

Even so, it was to the black man that Whiteley most clearly addressed himself. "The blackest African," Whiteley had stated when he accepted the nomination at Albany, possessed "all the rights of the American citizen." That concept was basic to his political creed. Campaigning in the Reconstruction South before black audiences involved affirming their political rights, demanding reasonable economic treatment, and declaring strongly for a fair hearing in judicial courts. Whiteley did so enthusiastically and categorically. Freedpeople's churches became centers of political activity for the newly enfranchised. Speaking from a black church's pulpit, near the town of Dawson, Whiteley took full political advantage when a crowd gathered for services.[11] At Bainbridge, he spoke at a meeting to select a county slate of Republican candidates on Saturday, November 10. Benjamin Powell (white) and Adam Bruton (black) were nominated for the legislature. One witness noted Whiteley's egalitarian message and dismissed his remarks as "thoroughly Radical." Blacks with a different mindset, in his audience that day, and on many other occasions, were stirred by Whiteley's words.[12]

In Decatur County, where there were more black than white voters, Whiteley figured to run strongly. That could also be generally assumed in other counties where blacks formed a majority. Five hundred freedmen belonged to the Calhoun County Republican Club, and in Early County, four hundred blacks composed a similar organization. Whiteley also had reason for confidence in Sumter County. The races were so

African Americans living in Thomas County, Georgia, whom Whiteley represented. Courtesy of Georgia State Department of Archives and History, Atlanta; pho. 175, Vanishing Georgia Collection, Georgia Archives Small Print Collection, box 15, no. 10, Georgia Archives.

polarized politically that the Democratic editor of the *Americus Weekly Sumter Republican* doubted appeals to blacks. Editor Charles W. Hancock thought that freedpeople were "thoroughly under the control of the few white Radicals in our midst . . . and they cannot be disconcerted by public speeches."

While his Republican foe asked for white votes, Tift wooed the freedpeople. He told blacks at Americus that white Republicans were exerting a control over them that was worse than slavery. At the Sumter County seat, Tift compared "slavery of the body" favorably to "slavery of the head and heart."[13] He asked freedpeople to resist the party straitjacket being fitted for them by Union League manipulators. At Cuthbert, Tift admitted that some whites had mistreated blacks. Yet he pointed out that many freedpeople who had worked for him had neglected their duties. Just as Tift hoped blacks would not dismiss his candidacy because of a few whites' behavior, he had not turned on the other freedpeople he employed. Tift made a special point of addressing the freedpeople at Bainbridge. Well aware that some blacks connected the Democratic Party to slavery, he reassured them of their permanent freedom. Oath-binding Union League promises to vote Republican were incompatible with freedom, Tift argued. One observer decided that the Democrat was making a "decided impression" among the "better class" of freedpeople.[14]

Tift labored at a severe disadvantage among the freedpeople, however. At Cuthbert, he spoke from the courthouse steps; whites congregated on the right and blacks on the left. The segregated arrangement indicated a physical and philosophical line of demarcation. An ex-slave's demur that day was also revealing. He had listened (not without some resentment) as Tift talked of fair treatment for blacks. Given an opportunity to speak, this freedman argued that blacks could never support a Democrat and pointed to systematic mistreatment. In a personal context, he recalled how he had been beaten and defrauded by his white employer. Other blacks at Cuthbert and across the Second District had experienced or knew of similar instances. Freedpeople fundamentally did not trust Democrats.

The campaign over Georgia's Second District turned into an extended political brawl. Allies of both men, acting as supernumeraries, often swerved from the letter of the truth and sometimes did so dramatically. On occasion, Whiteley and Tift debated, and the partisanship was heated but apparently not overtly personal. After a debate at Isabella early in December, one witness contrasted the lackluster effort by Whiteley to the effectiveness of Tift. He concluded: "there is not a white Radical in Worth County." The estimate of the Republican's lack of support among whites was more accurate than the evaluation of Whiteley's debating skills. Objectivity was not a hallmark of either side.[15]

Violence flared. Louis A. Guild, a white, Massachusetts-born physician who lived in Calhoun County, supported Whiteley. Writing from the county seat of Morgan in late November, Guild maintained: "there is a set of lawless cutthroat Democrats . . . who will do anything to prevent the freedmen from exercising their political views." He referred to the situation in Baker, Calhoun, and Early counties. Guild had personally received several threatening letters from the Ku Klux Klan. "Notwithstanding all this," the Republican predicted, "I shall be able to carry the district largely for Maj. Whiteley."[16] One week before the election, whites in Baker County abducted a freedman from the field where he was working, took him to the edge of the Flint River, and whipped him severely, as pistol-wielding whites looked on. Minnie Hanson, the AMA schoolteacher at Newton, wrote privately "the people here said they would wade knee deep in blood before Niggers should represent Baker

Co." As did Republican candidates elsewhere in the South, Whiteley realized that real and threatened violence could deter a critical number of freedmen from participating. Nelson Tift, whose much-cited questionnaire had reputedly absolved Georgia whites of political crimes, would never admit to any significant violence. The facts, though, contradicted his and other Democrats' disavowals.[17]

In December, as the campaign neared a conclusion, both candidates pushed on with an added sense of immediacy. Whiteley did not let his solicitor general's duties detain him. When Superior Court opened in Dougherty County early in December, the *Albany News* reported "Mr. Solicitor Whiteley was not in attendance" and wryly commented: "whether he is out among the suffragers or gone to Washington to take his seat in the Senate, we are not advised." In fact, Whiteley was furiously campaigning. At Dawson, in Terrell County, he appealed specifically for white votes. To remove an individual's Fourteenth Amendment political disabilities required an act of Congress. Calling into question Tift's commitment, Whiteley informed the audience that his opponent had managed to have only three people's political disabilities struck.[18]

Between December 20 and December 22, taking advantage of a three-day election period, Second District blacks and whites cast their ballot. All of the voting was done in the respective county courthouses. In Bainbridge, where Whiteley voted, cool weather made the demand for "ginger cakes brisk." In sharp contrast to his previous run for Congress (when Isiah Williams had been murdered), the election passed quietly there. It snowed at Cuthbert, where a few blacks, braving the catcalls of fellow freedmen, voted for Tift. The election also took place without complications at Fort Gaines, Camilla, and most other places.[19]

The situation elsewhere was much more eventful. At Newton, the county seat of Baker, whites tore up Republican ballots. One particularly determined Democrat, declaring that he "would die before Republicans were elected," positioned himself in the courthouse lobby and confiscated Republican ballots. On the final day, when most blacks attempted to vote, many were denied entrance to the Newton courthouse. Democrats bought some black votes for fifty cents each, and other freedmen went home without casting a ballot. Republicans alerted military authorities at Newton but were informed that the soldiers' narrowly circumscribed duties were limited to putting down political uprisings. The judgment of Minnie Hanson was correct; from Newton, she reported that "the election passed off with all the unfairness and duplicity that could [be] practiced."[20]

At Americus, in the northern reaches of the district, some whites were equally determined that Republicans would not vote. William

McCoy, a local black man, distributed Republican ballots to the freedmen from a table near the courthouse yard. After repeated threats from whites, the former bondsman took down his table and abandoned his courthouse post. Some Democrats chased a visiting Republican through the streets. The situation worsened on the election's last day. That Thursday morning, December 22, an altercation broke out when some whites crowded the voting grounds. Several blacks were hurt, and others were prevented from voting.

Over twenty-seven thousand residents participated in three days of voting across the twenty-two-county district. An initial ballot count indicated that Nelson Tift had beaten Whiteley by about five hundred votes. The Democrat had unofficially carried thirteen counties, and Whiteley had won six. Tift prevailed in Chattahoochee, Clay, Dooly, Early, Marion, Miller, Mitchell, Pulaski, Quitman, Sumter, Terrell, Wilcox, and Worth counties. Whiteley won in Decatur, Dougherty, Lee, Macon, Stewart, and Webster counties but failed to carry a single county with a white plurality, and lost six counties where blacks outnumbered whites.

In the meantime, secretary of state David G. Cotting faced an uncertain task as he tabulated the votes in the Second District. Baker County returns were listed as "irregular" because the tally sheets and other documents connected to the election had not been returned to the secretary of state's office. Theft of a ballot box accounted for the lack of final results in Calhoun County. In Randolph County, 620 voters marked their ballots improperly, and all the returns were struck. David Cotting did not count the ballots in these three counties—Baker, Calhoun, and Randolph. Reports of fraud and violence elsewhere also seemed to taint Tift's apparent victory. Even so, unofficially, Tift had 13,921 votes, and Whiteley 13,437.[21]

Once again, as in 1868, Whiteley faced defeat. Yet he did not concede. Instead, learning of some of the election disturbances, Whiteley traveled to Atlanta very soon after the voting period and appealed to Governor Bullock. He described an egregious and profound miscarriage of the democratic election process. He cited circumstances in Calhoun County, and the stolen ballot box, which he claimed cost him 350 votes. According to his adamant summation of events, even less attention to fairness had been paid in Sumter County; he contended that Democrats had intimidated blacks at Americus and that ballot box tampering had further skewed a true count. In Sumter County, where twice as many blacks as whites lived, he pointed out that Tift had claimed an unlikely 734-vote majority. Whiteley attributed Tift's showing there to "outrageous conduct." Real justice, the candidate informed Bullock, demanded that the executive declare him the winner. The governor listened sympathetically.[22]

A ten-week-long dispute ensued, involving both congressional candidates, the state attorney general, the governor, and, ultimately, Congress. The Georgia Code and a recently passed state law provided regulations for elections and the procedure for declaring a victor in congressional contests. In each county, five election managers (three picked by the governor and two by the county ordinary) tabulated the votes, signed the returns, and sent them to the secretary of state. He tabulated the votes in each county and gave the governor his compilations. In turn, the governor issued an election certificate to the candidate with the most votes. A certificate served as the congressman-elect's credentials, and was presented to Congress before he was sworn into office. Circumstances in the Second District complicated a normally uncomplicated procedure. In this election, voters expressed their preference just days before Christmas, and a winner was not declared until mid-February.

David Cotting received the returns from the Second District within days of the election. By January 10, he had given a copy of the tabulated votes to Bullock. The results in eighteen of the twenty-two counties were unremarkable. Cotting explained the irregularities in Baker, Calhoun, and Randolph counties and why the votes had not been counted. Cotting also called the governor's attention to Sumter County, where two election managers had since the election filed statements taking issue with the returns' accuracy. Cotting counted the Sumter County votes but noted that the returns were officially "protested." He totaled 13,921 votes for Tift and 13,437 for Whiteley. Overall, Cotting informed Bullock, he could not "judge whether the irregularities amounted to such illegality as would suffice for the rejection of the returns." That was up to the governor to determine.[23]

Bullock considered the allegations concerning the election at Americus especially crucial. David Barwald and Dennis Shepard, election managers at the Sumter County seat, swore affidavits disputing the tabulated vote. Barwald was white, and Shepard was black. Both were Republicans. The two men stated that hostile and unruly whites had prevented a fair election at Americus. In affidavits taken on January 6–7, 1871, they contended that Republican ballots had been removed from the ballot boxes. Barwald and Shepard considered the election a "farce." Bullock became convinced that this was true.[24]

In the meantime, Nelson Tift dismissed the allegations and made plans to take a seat in the Forty-first Congress. If he outwardly expressed confidence, Tift also understood that Whiteley had powerful Republican allies who controlled the election confirmation process. He first had to collect the certificate of election, and on January 10 at Albany, Tift boarded a train for Atlanta. Soon after arriving, he heard speculation that Bullock was balking at issuing him the certificate. On Wednesday afternoon, January 11, he and several other congressmen-elect presented themselves to the governor. Marion Bethune, William P. Price, Archibald T. MacIntrye, and Pierce M. B. Young were all commissioned. Tift's fears were confirmed. Explaining to Tift that complicating circumstances required further examination, Bullock did not give him a certificate.

Tift and Bullock met several times over the next two weeks. The increasingly frustrated Democrat tried to impress on the governor his constitutional responsibility: awarding the certificate to the person with the greatest number of votes. Tift earnestly pointed out that Secretary of State Cotting's returns indicated that he had a five-hundred-vote majority. Bullock countered that another interpretation of the results indicated that Whiteley had won. The governor considered problems in Baker, Calhoun, and Sumter counties. As Tift waited in Atlanta, the other six congressmen were seated in Washington. In a faithfully kept diary, Tift recorded developments. "I mentioned the importance of time to myself and my constituents" he wrote of his interview with Bullock, and "the simplicity of the question which he had to decide." Bullock did not consider the answer simple.[25]

Angry about what he began to view as a partisan conspiracy, Tift remained impatiently in Atlanta. He wrote in his diary: "I am told that a few extreme Radicals here have brought all their power to be against me." A week passed before he learned anything definite. Late on the afternoon of January 18, Bullock informed Tift of his intention to issue the certificate to Whiteley. Tift reiterated that the returns were prima facie evidence of the election and gave him a comfortable majority. Acceding to the Democrat's request, Bullock agreed to withhold the certificate. He would ask three members of the Georgia Supreme Court to review the case immediately and offer their unofficial opinion.

The controversy took another turn when Chief Justice O. A. Lochrane cited a judicial conflict of interest and declined. Lochrane advised Bullock to have the state attorney general, Henry Farrow, examine the situation. At the time, Farrow was in Washington because a decision regarding the longstanding dispute over the Georgia Senate question was imminent. Seating either Farrow and Whiteley, or Joshua Hill and H. V. M. Miller, was necessary because the Forty-first Congress had reconvened in December 1870, and the Georgia Senate seats were vacant.

Writing to Farrow in Washington on January 24, Bullock asked him to provide an official opinion. The governor promised to commission the candidate whom Farrow declared the legitimate winner. Bullock sent related election papers and documents to Farrow, strangely enough, by Nelson Tift, who left for Washington by train on January 25. A month had passed since the election.[26]

Several weeks after Whiteley personally made his case to Governor Bullock, he returned to Bainbridge, and then, because the Senate question was nearing resolution, traveled to Washington. Whiteley's was a unique and possibly unprecedented position as 1871 opened. He might be seated in the United States Senate, but it was also conceivable that a place would be made for him across the rotunda in the House. To learn his fate, and help shape it, Whiteley was in Washington by the middle of January. He roomed with Farrow at the National Hotel.

Who would represent Georgia in the Senate would be settled before the dispute in the Second Congressional District dispute. Determining the answer was an early item of business in the Forty-first Congress. The Senate Judiciary Committee considered a basic question. Were Joshua Hill and H. V. M. Miller, elected by the legislature in 1868, the legitimate senators? Or did Richard Whiteley and Henry Farrow, elected by the reorganized legislature in February 1870, have the better claim?

A divided Judiciary Committee issued majority and minority reports on January 24, 1871. Lyman Trumbull, the Illinois Republican who had defied the party line and voted against removing Andrew Johnson from office, presented the majority opinion, which contended that the state legislature organized in July 1868 had been qualified to elect Hill and Miller. Forcing the black members from the assembly had not tainted the validity of their election. William Stewart authored the minority opinion. Because some of the legislators could not take the test oath, the Nevada Republican countered, it was a "pretended legislature" without the "power to elect a clerk or sergeant-at-arms," and certainly not two United States senators. The dictates of a legal legislature, organized in 1870, should be observed. That meant seating Farrow and Whiteley.

Between January 30 and February 1, the senators considered the Judiciary Committee report, committee members spoke, and discussion continued at length. Most crucially, Senator Stewart offered a substitute resolution calling for seating Farrow and Whiteley. Nineteen senators favored doing so, and thirty-six opposed. The Senate accepted the majority report. On the next day, February 1, Joshua Hill took the oath of office, and H. V. M. Miller did so later that month.[27]

Whiteley did not despair. Earlier in January, when the Judiciary Committee had been deliberating, the four contesting Senate candidates had been given an opportunity to make their case before the committee. Whiteley did not even attend the meeting. He had months earlier decided that a full congressional term was much preferable to a short stint in the Senate. (Miller only served eight days before the Forty-first Congress and his term expired.) If he and Farrow were seated in the Senate, Whiteley had planned to resign and contend for a place in the House.

A strong sense of Whiteley's frame of mind was revealed in a letter he wrote from Washington on January 19. Jason Clarke Swayze, the Republican editor of the *Macon American Union*, had written to him regarding the disputed election. In Whiteley's reply, he outlined his position in much the same terms in which he had presented it to Bullock. "The mystery about the election in the 2nd dist. is easily explained," he began. Whiteley charged that Democrats engaged in "violence and fraud." He mentioned the stolen ballot box in Calhoun County and "bad conduct elsewhere." The situation at Americus, Whiteley informed Swayze, most blatantly violated the expression of the popular will. In Sumter County, Tift had been awarded a majority of over seven hundred votes, but Whiteley indignantly maintained that a true count would have resulted in a one-thousand-vote Republican margin. He declared: "the truth is the governor should take the bull by the horns and refuse to issue the certificate to Tift and then force him to make the contest against me."[28]

Meanwhile, Tift had arrived in Washington and checked into the Ebbit House on January 27. He visited Farrow and Whiteley the next morning at the National Hotel. Farrow agreed to begin considering the case. No doubt Tift questioned his impartiality. Farrow and Whiteley were friends, political allies, and now roommates in Washington.

The two House aspirants, one more confidently than the other, waited through the final days of January for Farrow's decision. Tift consulted with various Washington politicians. Among them was Henry L. Dawes, the Massachusetts Republican who would later sponsor important Indian legislation. Dawes reacted by stating he "would as soon steal a neighbor's sheep as to keep a man out of Congress as Bullock was."[29] On January 30, after sounding out some congressmen at the Capitol, Tift recorded in his diary: "they all think Gov. Bullock is acting badly and hope I will get my seat."[30]

Although some shared Tift's indignation, it was Farrow's opinion that mattered. Tift again called on Farrow at the National Hotel on the evening of February 1. Only Whiteley was present. He informed Tift that Farrow was working on the opinion and would finish the next day. Tift inferred from their meeting and conversation at the National Hotel (which must have been awkward) that his Republican opponent already knew the outcome. "Judging from his appearance," Tift wrote later that evening of Whiteley, "he expects or knows it will be against me and in his favor."[31]

Tift's intuition was correct. Writing the governor from Washington on February 2, Farrow recommended commissioning Whiteley. The attorney general concluded that the incomplete results in Baker, Calhoun, and Randolph counties would not alter the outcome. That made the Sumter County returns all-important. Tift had received 1,972 votes and Whiteley 1,238 there. Farrow drew heavily on the affidavits of David Barwald and Dennis Shepherd. Both election managers, the attorney general contended, signed the returns only because they were "menaced and threatened with death if they did not." The law required three managers to sign the election returns. Because Barwald and Shepherd had done so under "duress," Farrow concluded, their compliance meant nothing. Without the requisite number of signatures, Farrow determined that the Sumter County returns were not "regular and legal" and could not be counted. That meant that Tift lost his 734-vote plurality over Whiteley in Sumter County. The new total gave Whiteley 12,179 votes and Tift 11,949. Having made this determination, Farrow reported that Whiteley had 240 more "regular and legal" votes than Tift. The attorney general advised Bullock: "I would most respectfully advise your excellency to carry out your original purpose of issuing the certificate to R. H. Whiteley."[32]

Tift and Whiteley learned of the decision immediately. Whiteley must have felt relief and vindication. It is less likely that he was surprised. Neither was Tift. Anticipating the decision, the Democrat had made up his mind to contest the election. Tift telegraphed his brother in Albany: "Farrow decides against me—I appeal to Congress." Doing so required submitting a memorial to Congress making known that intention. It then devolved to the Committee on Elections to investigate the election (usually taking testimony) and make a recommendation to the House. Within the week, on February 4, John Kerr, an Indiana Democrat, introduced Tift's memorial.[33]

Acting on Farrow's opinion, Bullock issued Whiteley the certificate of election early in February. Whiteley resigned as solicitor general on February 6. Writing from Washington, he informed Bullock: "I have the honor to tender you my resignation as Solicitor General." Only the presentation of his credentials to Congress remained.[34]

Whiteley probably paid special care to his appearance as he dressed on February 9. He would take the oath of office later that day. His morning would have involved taking a carriage from the National Hotel six blocks up Pennsylvania Avenue to the Capitol. The swearing-in ceremony provided the first order of business that Thursday. Minutes after Congress convened at noon, the Wisconsin congressman Halbert E. Paine rose and stated that he had Whiteley's credentials and moved that he be sworn in. As Whiteley looked on, Pierce Young, a Georgia Democrat, challenged: "I must object to swearing in Mr. Whiteley." Young volunteered to explain why, but Paine refused to yield, and Whiteley's credentials were read. Paine then deferred to the Philadelphia Democrat Samuel J. Randall, who belonged to the Committee on Elections; Randall acknowledged that the election's outcome remained in doubt. Even so, precedent and form required that Whiteley be sworn in. Not honoring his credentials would "send us to sea without either rudder or compass." If an injustice was being done, Randall believed the Committee on Elections could decide that in the future. Undeterred, Young gained the floor and urged his colleagues to wait a few days because a committee decision was imminent. The Illinois Democrat Albert G. Burr, who belonged to the Committee on Elections, disagreed, stating "I have not had an opportunity to look at one line of the evidence in this case." Burr explained that "when a man presents himself with a certificate in due form he should be sworn in." Minutes later, in an unrecorded vote, the House approved Paine's motion. Whiteley presented himself and, repeating the words of House Speaker James G. Blaine, took the oath of office. Congressman Whiteley then made his way to a seat. It was only a few steps, but, considered in another sense, the route there had been long, circuitous, and controversial. At least for the moment, Richard Whiteley was triumphant.[35]

Whether Whiteley kept the seat would depend on the Committee on Elections. A subcommittee of three, composed of George M. Brooks, George W. McCrary, and Samuel Randall, took the case under consideration. Brooks and McCrary were Republicans, and Randall was a Democrat. Tift and Whiteley met with them several times in the next three weeks as the Forty-first Congress neared its end. On March 3, the final day of the term, chairman George Brooks of Massachusetts reported that the Committee on Elections had not had time to consider the Tift-Whiteley case. Until the committee could act, Brooks and the committee recommended providing Tift with $500 in compensation for expenses incurred contesting the election. Later that day, when the Forty-first Congress closed, Whiteley was sitting in the House. How long he would do so remained an open question.

After spending all of February lobbying in Washington, Tift, frustrated, returned to Georgia. He soon decided against challenging Whiteley's right to a seat in the Forty-second Congress. Writing a public letter from Albany on March 21, Tift bowed before the "injustices of the radical majority." He considered it fruitless to continue the battle, since Republicans controlled Congress. He remained bitter and certain that he had been the victim of a partisan conspiracy.[36]

Nelson Tift was right in believing that political considerations had figured prominently in the outcome. Bullock was predisposed to support Whiteley. So was Henry Farrow, whom Pierce Young accurately described as "the intimate friend of Mr. Whiteley." An objective verdict from Whiteley's friend, fellow Republican, and National Hotel roommate was unlikely. Farrow did not give any credence to the Democratic version of events at Americus. Tift had arranged for Solomon B. Council and Andrew J. Williams, two of the election managers at Americus, to give affidavits. Both Democrats disputed the narrative of intimidation and ballot box tampering that Barwald and Shepard had described. Even granting fraud in Sumter County, the governor's course is hard to justify. Tift's fundamental argument—that the secretary of state's returns incontrovertibly proved he had more votes than Whiteley—should have been irrefutable. Issuing him the certificate was the correct decision, and contesting the election should have been Whiteley's option. In denying Tift the election certificate, Bullock took liberties with precedent, the state constitution, and the Georgia Code.[37]

Whiteley was sure justice had been done. In a private (and surely terse) conversation in Washington on February 24, Tift told Whiteley: "I have thought hard of you for taking a seat to which you are not entitled by law." He added: "you know that the returns show that I am elected." Whiteley countered that he had been legally elected. Otherwise, the congressman informed Tift, he would not have taken the seat.[38] Whiteley sincerely believed that more ballots had been cast for him. Issuing a certificate of election to Tift, he wrote to Jason Clarke Swayze, would mean that "fraud and villainy will be *encouraged* because it will be allowed to *win.*"[39] Charges of political cronyism did not disturb him. Democrats gave no quarter, and he certainly would not. Rationalization was easy for Whiteley. The opposition cheated and intimidated, and retribution was his and the Republican Party's. This was the man who had referred recently to Democrats as "the enemy," gloated that they "are on their backs," and resolutely counseled "keep them there." He felt no guilt. Whiteley was sure he would make a better congressman than Tift and would represent the future of Georgia rather than its past. The Forty-second Congress was about to convene, and Congressman Whiteley, elected legitimately or not, had work to do.[40]

6 *Congressman Whiteley*

In 1871, the year Richard Whiteley joined Congress, he was forty-one years old. A short, thin man, with a narrow face, he was described as "very wiry looking." He was dark-eyed and had brown hair and wore a thick mustache. Few would describe him as handsome. He had long since lost his Irish accent, and, as one observer noted, "to hear the major talk you would set him down as emphatically a Southern man." Whiteley enjoyed the pleasantries of society and, true to his Irish heritage, was not averse to taking a drink. His was a gentlemanly bearing, and he dressed the part—often wearing the dark hat and suit common to men of his class. Georgia's only Irish-born congressman was a person of good cheer and a kind word, and even political enemies admitted his amiability. Whiteley could also be dogmatic and sly and, as the future would reveal, no paragon of virtue.[1]

Washington was a city of broad avenues, gaslights, and public buildings. About one hundred thousand people lived there, but the population and level of activity increased dramatically when Congress was in session. Pennsylvania Avenue ran through the heart of the city and connected the White House and Capitol. Carriages and pedestrians crowded other well-traveled streets. The most important hotels—the National, Metropolitan, and Willard—were on Pennsylvania Avenue. A sense of history having been made, history in the making, and more history to be made permeated the city. Although the grand sense of the past loomed, it was the present that concerned many. Some of those who came to Washington, and would sit with Whiteley, did so out of a sense of public service. Brilliance, dedication to country, and the common good emanated from

Congressman Richard Whiteley, circa 1872. Courtesy of Library of Congress.

the nation's capital. So did unbridled ambition, deceit, and self-interest. Washington offered fame, importance, wealth, and, for some, disgrace. Above all, taking the admirable with the sordid, the national capital was a city of power and a place where "nobody thinks or talks of anything else but politics."[2]

Activity was centered at the Capitol, where congressmen and senators congregated, joined by a multitude of lobbyists, office-seekers, and the curious. Slightly fewer than 250 men assembled in the large House chamber on the south side of the Capitol. Congressmen sat at handsome desks that rose in ascending amphitheater-like fashion. James G. Blaine, the Speaker of the House, presided over proceedings from a marble desk at the front of the room. Full-length portraits of George Washington and Lafayette flanked him on both sides. By the time Whiteley was seated, a fresco depicting the 1781 siege at Yorktown, Virginia, had been completed on one wall. A beautifully painted ceiling enclosed the gas-lit chamber.

What transpired on the House floor often seemed dissonant with the elegant setting, surprising the naive gallery observer. Parliamentary procedure governed, but House members' deportment could be less than exemplary. Quite oblivious to the most impassioned orator, congressmen placed their feet on desks, read newspapers, tended to correspondence, and talked among themselves. Those who listened strained to do so over what one witness described as "a perfect din [that] seems to pervade the House." Congressmen taking the floor often yelled to be heard across the hall. Interruptions and insults were common, despite the competent hand of Speaker Blaine, who held the power of recognition and issued final opinion on rules and practice. One onlooker wrote amazedly of the "Babel of confusion." Into this Byzantine world Richard Whiteley made his way.[3]

His seating, in early February 1871, marked a Reconstruction milestone. Georgia was the final state to return to the Union, and he was the last congressman from the state to be sworn in. On February 9, when Whiteley took the oath of office, it was the first time the South had been fully represented in the House since before the Civil War. Reconstruction issues had dominated congressional consideration since the war ended. Ratification of the Fifteenth Amendment, achieved in 1870, offered the latest indication of the Republican Party's interest in the ex-slave. Increasingly, questions peculiar to the South were discussed less, and the tariff, currency, and other issues took center stage.

Like the vast majority of representatives, Whiteley labored rather anonymously. A congressman's duties were generally prosaic, and the mundane rather than the dramatic dominated. Casting an informed vote on various questions required familiarity and study. Every congressman sat on at least one standing committee; placing men in patronage offices could be absorbing; keeping up with correspondence posed the most constant responsibility. Thomas J. Speer, a fellow Republican congressman from Georgia, concluded: "no man should be sent here who is not able to employ from one to six competent clerks." That was not total hyperbole.[4] What Whiteley referred to as "the press of business" was steady and sometimes consuming.[5]

The farmer who lived in Hawkinsville, the Fort Gaines merchant, and anyone from the remotest Second District crossroads considered Whiteley their most direct liaison to government. How a congressman met (or failed to meet) constituents' needs formed a large measure of his effectiveness. It also had a direct bearing on whether he returned to the next Congress. Whiteley understood and acted on that reality.

He had little time to do much during the Forty-first Congress, because less than a month remained before adjournment when he took his seat. On February 13, four days after taking the oath of office, Whiteley petitioned Congress on behalf of eight Lee County residents. He asked for the removal of their Fourteenth Amendment political disabilities. The nation's newest congressman considered the Lee County residents to be "honestly attached to the government of the United States" and deserving of full citizenship privileges.[6]

Serving constituents was accomplished on and off the House floor. One of Whiteley's first acts involved circulating public documents in the Second District. Government pamphlets and books, often dealing with practical agricultural knowledge, had not been systematically distributed in the hinterland of southwest Georgia. In a letter to Benjamin F. Bell, Whiteley expressed his desire for a change. He informed the probate judge of Sumter County that making the information available was "demanded by the very nature of the trust to me confided." Whiteley promised to have a complete set of documents sent to officials in each county.[7]

He began recruiting a candidate for the Naval Academy at Annapolis, Maryland, during his first spring in Washington. A cadet could be nominated annually from each congressional district, but nobody had represented southwest Georgia at the academy since before the war. Whiteley outlined the requirements for aspiring cadets/midshipmen in a public letter that circulated in the Second District. Prerequisites included passing a physical examination that challenged even the "well formed" and those "of robust constitution." An additional quality, presumably more difficult to quantify, included "good moral character."[8]

Other correspondence was more private. Writing to Governor Bullock in February, Whiteley warned Bullock against appointing William

Sims to succeed him as solicitor general. The man who had held that office for over two years well understood its critical importance. Several individuals had recommended the Bainbridge lawyer to Bullock. Whiteley informed the executive that he was familiar with Sims "personally and professionally." He advised Bullock of unspecified harmful political consequences. Neither did Whiteley consider the Democrat suitable in other respects. "He is totally *unfit* for the discharge of the duties of office," Whiteley continued, "both to *education, legal knowledge* and *professional experience.*" Whiteley had apparently commended another individual to Bullock. He closed on a strained note. "In recommending a worthy and efficient person for the appointment & giving you the benefit of my *personal* knowledge as to the other," the congressman concluded, "I have discharged my duty and here my connection with the matter shall cease."[9]

On March 3, 1871, the last day of the Forty-first Congress, Whiteley received some unwelcome attention. The Judiciary Committee had determined that the recently seated Georgia congressmen should be paid one year's salary of $5,000. Samuel Randall, who belonged to the Committee on Elections and had been sympathetic to Nelson Tift's position, asked that an exception be made in Whiteley's case. In the final hours of Congress, for proceedings had carried over well into the night, Randall objected that Whiteley had already received $5,000 in expenses from the Senate contingent fund for contesting the Senate seat. Several minutes of debate followed. "It is a fact well known to us all that Mr. Whiteley has received a large sum of money," Randall persisted, "and I protest against the House paying him as a sitting member for the time which he has already received pay." Among others, Benjamin F. Butler of Massachusetts argued that the House was obligated to compensate Whiteley. The scrutiny must have made the very new congressman somewhat uncomfortable. The outcome suited him, though. Minutes later, the House voted to accept the Judiciary Committee decision, and Whiteley counted himself $5,000 richer.[10]

The day after the Forty-first Congress closed, on March 4, the Forty-second opened. Republicans continued their control of both the House and Senate. Whiteley had plenty of company among southern Republicans. More Republicans than Democrats represented the former Confederacy, which was entitled to fifty seats. A shared sense of the burden that any southern Republican congressman bore accounted for a sense of collective identity, as well as of precarious political security. As Speaker of the House James G. Blaine observed, all southern Republicans were "doomed to a hopeless struggle against the influence, the tradition, the hatred of large majority of the white men of the South." Congressmen drew for their seat assignments. Whiteley claimed seat 47W, a well-located vantage point on the western side of the hall, centrally positioned, on the fourth row, and fairly close to the Speaker's chair. James A. Garfield of Ohio sat to Whiteley's immediate left.

Seven congressmen and two senators composed the Georgia delegation. Joshua Hill had been seated in January, and would be reelected in 1873. Another Democrat succeeded H. V. M. Miller. Dudley M. DuBose, Archibald MacIntrye, William Price, and Pierce Young, all Democrats, represented Georgia in the House. Whiteley's fellow Republicans were John S. Bigby and Thomas Speer.

Speer represented the Fourth Congressional District. A Barnesville attorney and a native Georgian, he had known Whiteley at least since the constitutional convention, when they had served as delegates together. They became personal friends and political allies. Speer was a verbose and likeable man. Well over six feet tall, he towered over Whiteley. John Bigby, a former Superior Court judge, had also served with Whiteley at the convention. The Third District representative lived in Newnan. As Georgia Republicans, Bigby, Speer, and Whiteley shared many concerns.[11]

One of the most crucial questions, relevant to all southern Republicans, was that of federal protection of Republicans in the South. Discussion of legislation that would bring the power of the federal government to bear on nightriders was a frequent topic during Reconstruction congresses. In May 1870, Congress had passed the First Enforcement Act, but crimes against Republicans of a political nature remained commonplace. The worst recent violence had taken place in the Carolinas. Over eighty representatives argued for and against the Ku Klux Klan bill. The legislation made it a federal offense to "conspire together, or go in disguise upon the public highway" and allowed the president to suspend the writ of habeas corpus. Democrats objected that prevailing peace made the legislation unnecessary. Moreover, the contemplated law represented an unconstitutional extension of federal jurisdiction and an infringement on state authority. On April 6, dividing on party lines, the House approved the enforcement legislation, and Grant soon signed the Ku Klux Klan Act.[12]

Support for the law had been agreed on at a joint Republican caucus. Like other southern congressmen, Whiteley did not need to be convinced. He could recite a litany of brutal acts directed at Republicans in the Second District and Georgia. As he would attest in a future letter to the United States attorney general, "it is all important that every effort be put forth to show to all that protection is the right of the citizen and that this is a real truth not a simple theory." He voted for the Ku Klux Klan bill.[13]

If strong measures were needed to counter nightriders, Whiteley favored extending amnesty to others. He regretted that Southerners loyal to the United States could not seek office because of the disabilities of the Fourteenth Amendment. He also realized the political capital to be made among whites back home. Any southern Republican could stand that. On March 20, Whiteley introduced legislation striking the political disabilities from several Second District citizens.

Economic issues of national importance did not receive much attention during the session, although the Tariff of 1872 did pass. It represented the first significant reduction of duties since before the war. As before the conflict, the South remained firmly antiprotectionist. A majority of Republican and Democratic legislators supported the Tariff of 1872. Economic questions in Congress often blurred party lines, as Terry Seip has shown in his study of southern congressmen and economic questions during Reconstruction, accentuating southern Republican and Democratic likenesses rather than differences. Whiteley offered no exception. He voted with a large southern majority for reducing the tariff.[14]

Making decisions that involved federal office-holding positions greatly concerned Whiteley. In Georgia, or any state, the party in power controlled federal jobs. These positions offered employment with the Post Office, the Internal Revenue Department, the Treasury Department, and other government agencies. The biggest single source of patronage in Georgia was the Customs Office at Savannah. Congressmen and senators often used the patronage offices at their disposal to reward individuals. Therein lay the problem. The main criteria for office—party loyalty—did not always make for the most competent civil servant. Even so, when Whiteley came to Congress, civil service reform lay in the future. As one observer noted during the year Whiteley took office, "fitness for the position is the last quality demanded of an aspirant to a public office."[15]

Whiteley largely determined who held various federal positions in the Second District. He could influence who occupied the postmastership at Camilla and who was employed as a postal route agent on the Atlantic and Gulf Railroad. The congressman based what he did or failed to do for an individual on various considerations. A close association with the Republican Party was the most critical prerequisite. As Whiteley informed an office-seeker, "you in common with all who have labored under harness will find in me a zealous supporter." An individual's competence and financial needs might be important. Race could be determinative. Whiteley favored promoting blacks to office who could prove themselves and, correspondingly, their race. How the appointment played politically in the Second District or Georgia might also be of concern. As a general rule, Whiteley supported Southerners over Republicans who had arrived from the North. Making Republicanism legitimate in the South depended on having upstanding natives representing the party. He understood that a Republican Party based on largely black votes, in the South or in Georgia, could not indefinitely stand. Without question, the opportunity to hold a federal office attracted some southern white men of influence to the Republican ranks.[16]

Campaigns to promote, maintain, and remove office-holders in Georgia seemed almost consuming for Whiteley at times. He acted shrewdly, with calculation, often deftly. He maneuvered, extending and withholding his influence, and by wielding the patronage at his disposal, he gathered allies in the Second District. He also made enemies. He became the consummate man of influence. In the years ahead, Whiteley worked, as he said, to make sure Georgia received "her due share of the Federal offices." Doing so benefited the state, the Republican Party, and, not incidentally, Richard Whiteley.[17]

Jason Clarke Swayze was among the first Whiteley attempted to help. Swayze had moved to Georgia from New York in 1860 and had been sympathetic to the Union during the war, after which he became a Freedmen's Bureau agent in Georgia. By 1871 he was editing a Republican newspaper, the Macon *American Union.* Swayze wanted the postmastership at Macon, and he turned to Whiteley early in 1871. "Since I wrote you last touching on the Macon Post Office," Whiteley replied in March, "I have talked with several of our friends regarding your interests." Elijah J. Bond, he informed Swayze, was in line for the postmastership. Yet Whiteley asked Swayze to consider pursuing Bond's vacated position as an assistant assessor with the Internal Revenue Department: "While this may not be what you want it will aid you very much and I hope it will not be unacceptable."[18]

Competition for offices was keen. Appealing to the commissioner of revenue in March, Whiteley endorsed Elijah Raiford for a position in Georgia with the Internal Revenue Department. Raiford lived in the Second District in Chattahoochee County. Congressman Thomas Speer backed Henry S. Glover, who received the appointment. Speer wrote that this "greatly chagrins and mortifies Whiteley."[19] Senator Joshua Hill and Congressman John Bigby took part in another skirmish among Republicans. Speer observed: "Whiteley wants Bell of Sumter County and Bigby wants Hunt of Houston Co.[,] and who Hill desires Hell only knows."[20]

Competition for offices contributed to the factionalism that plagued the state Republican Party. The battle over the office of collector of customs of the Port of Savannah, a powerful position, provides a classic illustration. Thomas P. Robb had served as collector since 1869. An Illinois native, Robb had resided in Savannah since Union troops had occupied the city. Some Georgia Republicans charged that Robb compromised Republicanism and too often favored northern Republicans with office. Allegations of fraud plagued his tenure as collector. By 1871, numerous state Republicans were calling for the removal of Robb and for replacing him with James S. Atkins, a native Georgian and Atlanta lawyer.

Whiteley entered the fray. At face value, he preferred that a Southerner be collector. Moreover, Whiteley also had some reservations about Robb. In that first spring in Washington, he confidentially advised treasury secretary George Boutwell that Atkins would be welcomed "by all Republicans" and that replacing Robb could "strengthen and unify the party in and beyond the limits of the first congressional district of Ga." Fellow state congressmen Bigby and Speer signed the note. Robb also had his defenders. The situation at Savannah continued to divide Republicans.[21]

On April 20, 1871, the short first session of the Forty-second Congress ended. Whiteley's brief tenure (he had been seated on February 9) could be measured in weeks. His public record was short and generally uncontroversial. Whiteley's private behavior, though, offered a stark contrast. At some point in the first months of 1871, he became involved in an illicit relationship with a young woman named Catherine Carmody, the daughter of Patrick and Mary Carmody, an Irish-born couple of very modest means. She was about eighteen. How she and Whiteley met, like almost everything about their relationship, is not known. It is certain though, that by the time Congress recessed, Catherine was carrying his child.[22]

Whiteley returned to Bainbridge in late April. Over three months had passed since he had seen Margaret, who was pregnant again (giving him the highly dubious distinction of having two women pregnant by him at the same time). He had missed his children, Richard, Montford, and Hortense. On Sunday morning, April 22, Whiteley stepped down from the train at the Bainbridge depot. A fine homecoming at the Evans Street home would have been in order that Sunday.

Congressman Whiteley, as he would now often be addressed, was soon circulating locally. Noting his return, the *Bainbridge Argus* reported: "the Major is in fine health." In all likelihood, four days later on April 26, Whiteley attended ceremonies marking Confederate Memorial Day, at which his law partner, John Donalson, invoked the sacrifices of local soldiers for the late Confederacy. Whiteley saw nothing incongruous in his Confederate past and his present Republican status. He fully approved of his wife's connection to the Ladies' Lee Monument Committee of Richmond. Robert E. Lee had died the previous October, and the organization had formed to solicit money for erecting a monument in that city. Margaret and two other women in Bainbridge collected subscriptions for that cause.[23]

Several weeks after returning, on the morning of May 16, 1871, the Whiteleys and about forty other Bainbridge residents boarded the steamer *Atlanta* and traveled on it down the Flint River to the Gulf port town of Appalachicola, Florida, about two hundred miles to the south. The excursionists enjoyed dancing and the scenery as the *Atlanta* moved down the tawny-colored waters of first the Flint and then the Appalachicola rivers, reaching Appalachicola late that night. A walk around the small village, music and dancing, and a trip out to St. George Island (where the party collected shells) were among the next day's activities. Whiteley chose on the return trip between two activities: more dancing or shooting at alligators. Toward the end of the three-day outing, the sociable congressman helped draft resolutions thanking the steamer's crew for their hospitality. Most also agreed that more wine was in order, and Whiteley seconded that motion. He hardly seemed the shunned and ostracized scalawag.

A hot summer was unremarkable in southwest Georgia. What distinguished the summer of 1871 for the Whiteleys were various family developments. Margaret gave birth to the couple's last child, Zena Agar Whiteley, on July 25. The family attended a wedding several weeks later. Having left the College of New Jersey after his sophomore year, Charles Whiteley that fall began studying law at Columbian College (later George Washington University) in Washington, D.C. At some point, he had met and fallen in love with Josephine Blake Peyton. With both families in attendance, they married in Washington, D.C., on August 22. Congressman Whiteley, knowledgeable of the city, surely would have shown his family around the nation's capital.

Even granting his moral lapses, Richard Whiteley would have described himself as a properly God-fearing man. The previous year the Episcopal bishop of the diocese had administered the rite of confirmation to him in Bainbridge. It was Margaret, though, who most fervently embraced Christianity, and she and other local Episcopalians longed for a church in Bainbridge. As it was, Rector C. A. Arnold conducted services at various places. That fall, on November 19, 1871, Arnold baptized Hortense and Zena.[24]

In the present and the future, when Whiteley was not in Washington, he practiced law, and he could be found at his Sanborn Building office across from the courthouse. The firm of Whiteley and Donalson retained its solid reputation. Their services, at least according to the Savannah commission merchant William H. Stark, did not come cheaply. When Whiteley and Donalson acted on his behalf, Stark protested: "they charge a most unreasonable fee."[25] Whiteley and Donalson represented Burchard, Wilson and Company, a New York business that dealt in "fancy goods." Not without some difficulty, they managed to collect from Malichi M. Cohen, a Bainbridge merchant, the balance of a sum owed the New York company. Donalson explained: "Cohen has given us considerable trouble making this collection and we have therefore charged you the full rate." That summer, Whiteley and Donalson were engaged by a resident of New Bedford, Massachusetts, in another claim case against a resident of Decatur County.[26]

Whiteley continued to buy land. With John Donalson, he had purchased fifteen hundred acres in August 1870; in September of the next year, he paid $1100 for 275 more acres. Other changes included improvements to the family's Evans Street home. It would soon be noted that Whiteley "has made several handsome additions to his residence."[27]

He could have taken some satisfaction from advancements locally. He knew most of the blacks in Bainbridge and the county. Men like Adam Bruton confirmed his faith in the possibilities for the black race. Bruton had vigorously studied American history and arithmetic and had been elected to the state legislature in 1870. Although Whiteley regarded the services at the black Methodist and Baptist churches as frenzied, he nonetheless considered religion ameliorative. A black debating club had formed, and freedpeople staged festivals that summer and fall to raise funds for a brass band and a church bell. Yet Whiteley also realized that progress was extremely incremental. Freedom had not translated into any discernable economic security. Blacks remained impoverished, landless, and, largely because of these circumstances, beholden to whites. Lizzie Parsons observed: "I do not see how many live at all."[28]

Whiteley befriended Parsons. Recently arrived from New York, the AMA teacher instructed blacks at Whittier School. At the outset, no one would rent to her, and Parsons boarded at the Sharon Hotel and gamely bore the hotel expense and the long walk to school. Both her predicament and the efforts she made on the freedpeople's behalf gained Whiteley's attention and sympathy. He rented Parsons a small two-room house near the school. On May 1, within days of returning from Washington, he visited Whittier School. From her remote southern outpost, Parsons corresponded with Erastus M. Craveth, an AMA field secretary headquartered in New York. She described Whiteley as a man who "is very kind to me, and I go to him when I need some advise or aid."[29] She mentioned Whiteley's visit on May 1, and wrote: "I have full faith in him, and his influence and interest are with us."[30]

Whiteley returned to the school on the evening of September 18, 1871, when several prominent citizens, including him, gave speeches. He commended the AMA. The *Bainbridge Argus* judged Whiteley's remarks "calculated to create excitement in the easily inflamed minds" of the black audience. The *Argus* faulted him for delivering a political speech and decided the effort was "in bad taste."[31] Whiteley immediately responded in a letter to the *Argus.* "I am surprised to learn," he defiantly stated, "that recounting the good deeds of a Christian Association can be tortured into a political harangue." What was wrong with crediting the AMA? he asked. He considered it correct to pay some homage to those educators, and concluded acerbically: "I have yet to learn that I will be serving my race and country, by teaching the colored people ingratitude."[32]

Whiteley also maintained ties with his white constituency. Later in 1871, he traveled to Blakely when Superior Court convened. Why he made the thirty-five-mile carriage trip seemed clear to the *Early County News:* his aim was "making the acquaintance of our citizens." Whiteley desired their acquaintance, and in the future, their vote.[33]

Congressional duties were never far removed. That summer, Whiteley received a letter from Alvin B. Clark, a native Kentuckian who had served in the Union Army, had moved to Georgia in 1866, and now lived in Thomasville. He hoped to become the assessor of internal revenue of the First District at Savannah. Clark apprised Whiteley of the post and asked for his endorsement. The congressman replied that Senator Joshua Hill controlled the appointment. In deference to Hill and accepted protocol, Whiteley declined to interfere "in any matter outside of my own district." Whiteley explained to Clark that he favored local Republicans settling on a candidate. After all, they knew better than anyone what "the masses want." Without their input, he worried, "I do not see how we are to have a party."[34]

Whiteley also heard from John Bryant, who had moved from Maine to Augusta after the war and became a powerful state Republican. Yet he then broke with Governor Bullock and other prominent state Republicans and became, at least for a time, the naive instrument of Georgia Democrats. Among other acts, Bryant's outspoken opposition to seating Farrow and Whiteley in the Senate gained him extreme Republican criticism.

Even so, Bryant advocated party principles, and in 1870 he was editing in Augusta the *Georgia Republican.* Bryant's efforts at replacing Edwin Belcher as the assessor of internal revenue for the Third District led him to write to Whiteley. The congressman had ample reason to dislike Bryant. Nor did Whiteley wish to have Belcher, a black man, removed from his position. As it was, freedmen held few significant offices in Georgia. Bryant anticipated the possible hesitancy. "If you do not wish to ask for the removal of Belcher," he asked, "will you not write to the commissioner that, if Mr. Belcher is removed, you recommend my appointment." Whiteley's relations with Bryant remained lukewarm. Belcher continued as assessor.[35]

Whiteley understood that his political future was tied to the good standing of the state Republican Party. That was not a reassuring fact by 1871. The Bullock administration was increasingly accused of mismanagement and corruption. The name of Hannibal I. Kimball, a friend of Bullock, had become synonymous with graft. Some charged that the governor gave his entrepreneurial-minded ally preferential treatment. When Kimball's railroad plan, based on state bonds, failed, Bullock was partly blamed. Circumstances surrounding the leasing of Kimball's Opera House in Atlanta further called the governor's integrity into question. The state leased the Opera House for use as the capitol because the city hall was inadequate. Financial irregularities (an unmentioned Kimball House mortgage of $60,000) reflected poorly on Bullock, who had supported the lease. As the superintendent of the state-owned Western & Atlantic Railroad, Foster Blodgett, chair of the Republican State Central Committee, was charged with misuse of funds in a scandal involving the railroad. Again Bullock suffered by implication.

Against this backdrop, a movement was undertaken to repudiate Bullock and Blodgett. Many influential men, friends of Whiteley, joined the secretly organized "State Council of the National Guard." Its aim was to reorganize the state party or, as secretary John Bryant hoped, to "rescue the party from these corrupt men who have disgraced it."[36]

Whiteley had lost confidence in Bullock also. He blamed the governor for exposing the young and vulnerable state Republican Party to criticism just as the party struggled for a political hold. In an earlier letter to Henry Farrow, Whiteley had written of "the blunders of the State Administration."[37] Bullock's disgrace reflected poorly on Georgia Republicans and provided grist for the Democratic mill. Yet Whiteley objected in principle to secret political societies and resisted joining the State Council of the National Guard. In September, Bryant wrote that

Whiteley was balking but that various Republicans were "at work upon him and expect to overcome 'his scruples.'"[38]

Whiteley's resistance soon did not matter. Bullock resigned that fall. Some had openly speculated that he might be removed from office when the legislature (controlled by Democrats) convened in November 1871. On October 23, a week before the legislature met, Bullock resigned, and he soon left the state. Benjamin Conley, a longtime resident of Augusta and the Republican president of the senate, was sworn in as governor within the week.

Whiteley might have hoped for better circumstances surrounding Conley's ascension, but the changing of the political guard pleased him. He liked and respected Conley, with whom he had served at the constitutional convention. Conley was a gentleman, identified with Georgia, and was politically moderate. He epitomized the type of man who reflected well on Georgia Republicanism. Unlike Bullock, about whom Whiteley had mixed feelings, Conley was not a lightning rod for controversy. Writing from Bainbridge on November 7, 1871, Whiteley congratulated the newly installed governor. In a disparaging reference to Bullock, Whiteley said he regretted that Conley's assumption of office "did not sooner occur." Whiteley expressed a desire "to talk with you in reference to matters in this part of the State before I go to Washington." He promised to visit soon. For the present, Whiteley advised against appointing solicitor generals for the southwestern or Albany judicial circuits. As the situation stood, "bad appointments have been made in each," and "a change should be for the better."

A short gubernatorial tenure (seventy-five days) prevented Conley from making many appointments of any kind. Democrats controlled the legislature, and they immediately forced a special election to fill Bullock's unexpired term. The disgraced Bullock administration discredited Conley and Republicanism. Georgia Republicans did not even nominate a candidate. Protests that the election was invalid did not make it so, and James M. Smith was easily elected on December 19. Smith was inaugurated on January 12, 1872, and Democrats reclaimed the governor's office.[39]

Meanwhile, Whiteley had returned to Washington, as the Forty-second Congress had reconvened in December 1871. The trip by railroad north through the Carolinas and crossing into Virginia took two days. As he approached Washington on the second day, the sight of the Capitol dome would have greeted the weary congressman, before the train crossed the Long Bridge over the Potomac River. He would spend the first half of 1872 in Washington.

Whiteley never bought a home in the Washington area but boarded at places of various size and comfort. Sometimes Margaret and, presumably, some of their children were with him. This time, Whiteley soon settled into a rented place, probably a hotel, at 464 C Street. He later resided on D Street, at an Indiana Avenue brownstone apartment, and finally at the National Hotel on Pennsylvania Avenue.[40]

Whiteley's typical day can be approximated. General business brought him to Capitol Hill in the morning, although the House did not convene until noon. People needed to see him on business, committees met, and correspondence always awaited. House proceedings dominated the afternoon and sometimes stretched into the night. On some evenings, he may have joined others at the larger hotels, such as the Willard, where food, drink, and political conversation were the staples. When Margaret was in Washington, they likely attended the theater, receptions, and parties together. From the outset, the eminently sociable congressman enjoyed life in Washington.

Neither did he always let his marriage check his pleasure. Just weeks after his return, on January 25, 1872, Catherine Carmody gave birth to Catherine Cecilia. Margaret knew, or soon became aware, of her husband's infidelity. How, when, and where she learned of his betrayal is purely speculative. Her reaction, though it cannot be documented, is much more certain: as an upright Episcopalian, she condemned the misconduct. Nonetheless, their marriage—whatever the immediate strain and resulting scar—survived the episode. How much or little he saw of his daughter Catherine Cecilia afterward is not known.[41]

Whiteley was in his seat on December 4, 1871, the first day of the Forty-second Congress. An inventory of legislative proposals bearing on the Second District and Georgia had accumulated since Congress last met. Near the top of Whiteley's priorities was gaining federal funding for improving the navigability of the Flint, Chattahoochee, and Apalachicola rivers, which drained southwest Georgia. Originating in northeast Georgia, the Chattahoochee flowed past Atlanta and ran southwestwardly until it reached Columbus. It then turned sharply south, forming the border of Georgia and Alabama. The Flint, beginning in the vicinity of Albany, flowed southwest past Bainbridge, and continued south. The confluence of the two rivers at Chattahoochee, Florida, formed the Apalachicola River, which emptied into the Gulf at Apalachicola.

These rivers' limited navigability compromised the natural advantages they offered. Various obstructions—drift logs, snags, rocks, boat wrecks, even piles driven by Confederate authorities during the war—seriously impeded trade and commerce on the tri-river system. Except for a recent survey begun on the Chattahoochee River, Whiteley objected that the rivers had been "totally overlooked." He intended to redress that neglect. A week into the session, on December 11, he introduced a bill continuing the surveying work on the Chattahoochee and funding the surveying of the Apalachicola and Flint. Whiteley viewed surveying the Appalachicola and Flint as a first and incremental step that anticipated future funding. Without a survey, he noted, "not a dollar could be appropriated for their improvement." The Committee on Commerce took the bill under consideration.[42]

It was a functional congressman, not a Radical ideologue, who worked to restore political privileges. Early in the new year, on January 18, 1872, Whiteley asked colleagues to lift the political restrictions on Herschel Johnson, the former running mate of Stephen Douglas in 1860. Among the strongest foes of secession in Georgia, Johnson had served in the Confederate senate during the war. Whiteley praised him as a "consistent Union man." After reciting Johnson's credentials, he concluded: "can I say more and need I say more to secure the passage of this bill by the House?" Congress honored his request and removed Johnson's penalties.[43]

On several occasions Whiteley introduced bills on behalf of other Georgians petitioning for removal of political disabilities. Most bills regarding amnesty were introduced on Mondays. What took place on February 26, a Monday, was especially noteworthy. That day Whiteley introduced a bill striking the disabilities of about two hundred Georgians from over forty Georgia counties. Almost simultaneously, other southern Republicans attached their amnesty requests to the bill. Intending to expedite the wearisome ritual that slowed proceedings, Speaker Blaine signaled his approval. Neither did Whiteley object. He acquiesced from the floor: "Very well; if all want to combine, let it go." The clerk's desk quickly filled with amendments, and the disabilities of presumably hundreds were lifted.

The necessity of submitting individual bills for pardoning the politically disabled ended for the most part with the passage of the Amnesty Act later in the session. That legislation, which became law with strong bipartisan backing, removed the Fourteenth Amendment restrictions that had prevented a class of Southerners from holding office. Whiteley joined the entire Georgia congressional delegation and voted for the Amnesty Act.[44]

Although common ground with Democrats existed, there could be no mistaking on which side of the aisle Whiteley sat. Even as he praised Herschel Johnson to colleagues as "high-toned," Whiteley added: "when I say that for one opposed to the Republican party I say a great deal." Whiteley's efforts regarding the Union prisoner-of-war camp at Andersonville, Georgia, indicated his point of view. In May 1870 he had attended the decoration ceremony at the former site of the infamous prison. He now offered a bill that transferred some condemned cannons to the national cemetery at Andersonville. Later in the session, he presented a petition of some Georgians requesting the erection of a monument to buried federal soldiers there. These were the acts of a man who believed in consecrating a tragic episode in a tragic war. Many Democrats in southwest Georgia did not share Whiteley's sense of urgency.[45]

Other initiatives exhibited a distinct Republican indoctrination. Early in the session, on December 18, 1871, Whiteley offered a bill establishing another district federal judge, attorney, and marshal in Georgia. As it was, duties in both the northern and southern districts of the state fell to these officials. Violators of postal and revenue laws had traditionally occupied the attention of the district attorney and federal marshals. Bringing political outlaws to justice had challenged them more recently. Whiteley's reasoning was obvious. More officials would facilitate the arrest and trial (a fitful and inadequate procedure in Georgia) of those who were violently anti-Republican. He also introduced two bills on January 22 that reflected the concerns of a southern Republican who was well aware of political realities. One established a role for poll supervisors in some circumstances during congressional elections. After introducing that measure, without sitting down, he proposed another providing for the preservation of ballots and documents connected to elections. Both bills were referred to the Judiciary Committee.

A measure Whiteley introduced only two days into the session clearly revealed his Republican credentials. On December 2, 1871, he offered a bill designed to guarantee one of the most fundamental Republican principles: the right of freedmen to vote. That was compromised in Georgia by a poll tax, which had the practical effect of disfranchising thousands of blacks. Applied retroactively by the time the Forty-second Congress met, the poll tax amounted to several dollars. An inability or unwillingness to pay that sum meant that thousands, mostly poor blacks, would not vote. Whiteley's proposal required the enforcement of the Fourteenth Amendment's second section, which required reducing the representation in Congress of states that disfranchised eligible voters. Whiteley believed Georgia's poll tax was in direct contravention of the amendment. In February 1872, he wrote to Benjamin Conley "I am at work on the tax matter," informing the ex-governor of his intention to "make an argument before the House."[46]

Whiteley composed this argument carefully, with purpose, and as a devout Republican. He maintained: "the history of partisan legislation furnishes no bolder attempt to ignore the rights of the poor and friendless." The poll tax forced an unfair burden on the laborer who made $150 annually and attempted to support "a large family of helpless children." Poor whites often forfeited the suffrage, but three times as many blacks were adversely affected. He attributed the tax to the Democratic legislature's "zeal for a white man's government." After all, "slavery though dead in law, yet lives in the spirit of a dominant race." As a Republican, Whiteley's sense of racial justice was violated. As a politician, the poll tax threatened his political survival. He completed the final draft by the middle of March.[47]

On Saturday, March 16, when Whiteley entered the House chamber, he may have been apprehensive. He intended to speak at length from the floor for the first time. As the day progressed, debate concerned topics as wide-ranging as the inhumanity of Chinese coolie labor and river improvements in Wisconsin. Most consuming, however, was the tariff duty question. When the time arrived at which Whiteley had planned to speak, rather than doing so, he yielded to William D. Kelly, a Pennsylvania Republican, who asked to offer "an immediate rejoinder" to the free trade argument just presented. Under the circumstances, Whiteley consented, explaining: "the gentleman from Pennsylvania desires to reply and in order to afford him that opportunity, I will ask that my remarks be printed without delivering them." His maiden speech would have to wait. So would removing the poll tax—for ninety-three years.[48]

Patronage questions demanded attention during the long session. In January 1872, Moses H. Hale, an official at the Treasury Department at Savannah, appealed to Whiteley from there. The collector of customs at Saint Mary's had recently resigned, and Hale recommended Joseph Shepard to Whiteley as "a good Republican." John D. Pope stepped down in February as United States attorney of Georgia. With Whiteley's support, Henry Farrow succeeded him. He convinced Bigby and Speer to back Farrow. They signed the endorsement of Farrow, penned by Whiteley, which was sent to the United States attorney general for Georgia, George Williams.[49]

The longstanding controversy at the Savannah Customs House reached a resolution. Pending indictments in federal court for embezzlement and other alleged transgressions increased the outcry for the resignation of collector of customs Thomas Robb. Whiteley's opinion of Robb had not changed. Replacing him with James Atkins, Whiteley pointed out to treasury secretary George Boutwell, was of critical political importance. Whiteley considered Atkins "the only man I know whose appointment to the place will insure efficiency in the discharge of the duties of the office and harmony." In an unmistakable reference to Republican differences in Georgia, Whiteley added "how greatly we need the latter you are no doubt fully advised" and concluded: "Atkins is the man for the place."[50] Whiteley was certain that Robb was not. Thomas Robb resigned the collectorship under pressure, and James Atkins replaced him. In February 1872, writing to ex-governor Benjamin Conley to inform him of the situation, Whiteley speculated "the change at Savannah will benefit us" and maintained that he considered other alterations overdue, adding: "we will not stop there if my advise is heeded." He closed with an expression of the hope to "yet have peace in Ga."[51]

By April, several months had passed since Whiteley's introduction of legislation appropriating money for Georgia river improvements. Requests of that nature were granted (or not granted) by the Committee on Commerce and were usually included in a comprehensive river and harbors appropriations bill that typically passed near the end of the session. Following up on April 2, 1872, Whiteley called from the House floor for the secretary of war to "at once" furnish his colleagues with materials relating to the river surveys. His diligence was rewarded. The major river and harbors bill (H.R. 2208) that passed early in June included funding for the Appalachicola, Chattahoochee, and Flint rivers.[52]

The Forty-second Congress recessed on June 10. Whiteley had failed to attract great praise, scorn, or, in fact, much attention during the six months' session. He did, though, continue to act on the behalf of Second District and Georgia residents. On February 29, moments after the daily prayer was offered, Whiteley opened House proceedings with the statement "I hold in my hand a memorial." The memorial, authored by the state legislature, called for reimbursing Georgians for the cotton taxed between 1865 and 1867 (Congress had repealed the tax in 1868).[53] In this and subsequent sessions, Whiteley worked to improve postal services in the Second District. He would write: "few things more intimately concern the people than the workings of the postal system." The establishment of a postal road from Bainbridge to Steam Mill (in rural Decatur County) was due to him. These and other acts did not go unnoticed in Georgia. The *Albany News*, no friend of Whiteley, commended him for having the political restrictions on some thirty Second District whites removed.[54]

Whiteley also spoke, acted, and voted as a partisan Republican. If largely symbolic, his efforts at memorializing the deceased prisoners at Andersonville were important. That Whiteley's speech condemning the poll tax was consigned to obscurity in the pages of the *Congressional Appendix* does not detract from its power. The words remained. He vividly referred to "political slavery" and past Democratic attempts "to unite the whites against the colored voters." Whiteley unflinchingly condemned the proscriptive tax for ignoring "the rights of the poor and friendless" in the interest of an "oligarchy" and at the expense of "freedom and justice for all men."[55] Congress had created the Joint Select Committee to Inquire into the Condition of Affairs in the Insurrectionary States, which took testimony from members of both parties and races over several months. James Atkins, the candidate of some to replace Thomas Robb as collector of customs, was among those who testified. He judged that the passions created by the war were diminishing, "but I confess they are not doing so as rapidly as I would like to see them." Richard Whiteley was also, at best, cautiously optimistic. He realized that extreme elements in the South, Georgia, and certainly the Second District refused to recognize the legitimacy of Republicanism.[56]

On June 16, 1872, Whiteley, with Margaret, returned to Bainbridge. He had not been home for six months. Exaggerating and mocking black vernacular, the *Bainbridge Democrat,* which had recently replaced the *Bainbridge Argus,* noted Whiteley's return by stating that the "trooly loil" welcomed him. Benjamin Russell, the newspaper's editor (no relation to Willis Russell) became a vicious critic of Whiteley.[57] Nonetheless, Whiteley could expect a warm homecoming from blacks and whites. Many Democrats continued to overlook their likeable friend's political affiliation. A couple of months later, on September 5, the Whiteleys hosted a party at their home at which the principal guests were friends of Montie, Richard, and Hortense. A representative of the *Bainbridge Southern Sun* pronounced the dinner "nothing short of splendid." Margaret proved "a charming hostess," and her husband "industriously plied himself to the task of entertaining his guests." The *Sun* further observed: "the Major never looked better in his life, and in fact we believe he improves with age." That was fortunate, in view of the severe political test he faced in the campaign ahead.[58]

7 *A Wily and Able Man*

The presidential election of 1872 was underway by the time Whiteley returned to Georgia. At Philadelphia, early in June, Republicans renominated Ulysses Grant. Henry Wilson of Massachusetts became his running mate. The nomination of Grant on the first ballot belied Republican dissension. The unfolding narrative of how Republicans had accepted stock in the Union Pacific Railroad Company's construction company, the Credit Mobilier, reflected poorly on the administration. A combination of groups—civil service reformers, low tariff proponents, and some general critics of Grant—refused to accept the nominee. These elements formed the Liberal Republican Party. At Cincinnati, on May 1, the Liberal Republicans nominated New York's Horace Greeley and B. Gratz Brown of Missouri as his running mate. Holding their national convention at Baltimore in July, the Democrats threw their support to Greeley in a desperate attempt to defeat Grant.[1]

Throughout the South, Democrats accepted the Liberal Republican nominee with difficulty. The editor of the *New York Tribune* had been an outspoken critic of slavery and the Democratic Party. Yet Greeley favored amnesty for ex-Confederates and ending congressional interference in the South. Among other acts Southerners appreciated, Greeley had signed Jefferson Davis's bail bond. Some Southern Democrats considered him preferable to Grant, but other so-called straight-out Democrats refused to back Greeley. Georgia Democrats met in their state convention on July 24 in Atlanta and renominated James Smith for governor. With less enthusiasm, they endorsed the Greeley-Brown ticket.

Also in Atlanta, on August 21, Republicans held their state convention. Dawson A. Walker, a former justice of the Georgia Supreme Court, was nominated for governor. Republicans passed resolutions criticizing the legislature, pointing out the poll tax requirement, and registered their approval of the Grant-Wilson ticket. Few leading Georgia Republicans made common cause with the Liberal Republicans.

As he had four years earlier in 1868, Whiteley endorsed Grant, and he was present at the convention. He had represented the Second District on the Republican State Central Committee since 1869, and when the committee was reorganized in Atlanta, he became one of its fourteen members-at-large.

He realized that Republicans confronted an unpromising situation. In the South, the rising trajectory of the Republican Party had been slowed, and as measured in numbers of legislators, governors, congressmen, the party was losing strength. Uniquely adverse circumstances faced Georgia Republicans. The legacy of the Bullock administration was one of disgrace. Foster Blodgett, his reputation undermined by scandal, had resigned as chairman of the State Central Committee, and after gaining a controversial pardon from Governor Benjamin Conley, had left the state. Henry Farrow succeeded Blodgett as chairman of the State Central Committee. Farrow admitted publicly that "the shameful administration of Governor Bullock has driven thousands of the best men in the State out of our party." Factionalism further weakened the Republican cause. Democrats controlled the legislature, the governorship, and state patronage. Joseph Brown, governor of Georgia before the war, had earlier lent credibility to Republicanism by joining the party. His widely publicized return to Democratic ranks in 1872 was indicative of political trends. The *Atlanta New Era,* the most influential Republican newspaper, had ceased publication, and fewer than five Republican newspapers existed in the state.[2] It was with reason that Whiteley had recently written dubiously of "our success in 72."[3]

In the face of disillusionment and defections, Whiteley firmly maintained his Republican convictions. Joel R. Griffin, a former slaveowner and Confederate officer who edited a Republican newspaper in Fort Valley, a small town in the middle of Georgia, admitted to Benjamin Conley that many former Republicans had drifted into the Democratic ranks. "I do not know anyone," he informed Conley, "but Hon. R. H. Whiteley of our section who dares say from the stump with myself he is a Republican and attempts to make converts."[4] In September, Benjamin Brimberry and M. A. Marshall wrote Frederick Douglass from their southwest Georgia town of Camilla. They noted how the poll tax disenfranchised blacks, and asked the nation's most recognized black man to help raise money to pay poor blacks' poll taxes. Brimberry and Marshall also wanted to put funds toward establishing a Grant-Wilson newspaper in southwest Georgia. "Our representative, Hon. R. H. Whiteley, is giving us his influence in the matter," they informed Douglass.[5]

Having arrived from Washington in June, Whiteley scheduled several speaking engagements. Making his own case for reelection and that of Ulysses Grant was the object. A largely black audience gathered at a grove near the Flint River for barbecue and oratory on July 13. Recalling his recent time in Washington, Whiteley told blacks that he had fought for "equal rights," but reminded them that the battle had not been won. Praise of Grant and criticism of Greeley formed part of the hour-long presentation. A witness concluded that Whiteley intended "to get up an enthusiasm among his colored supporters," and judging from the "howlings of his faithful constituents," he believed the congressman had succeeded.

The promised land was theirs. So said Whiteley to Dougherty County freedpeople when he appeared at the Albany courthouse on August 9. Whiteley again lauded Grant and the Republican Party for serving the ex-slaves' interests. Well aware of the effect of biblical imagery on his audience, Whiteley compared Grant to Moses. Other advice had nothing to do with politics. Whiteley prevailed on the freedpeople to attend to their crops, and, as he often did, admonished them to be personally responsible and upright.

He returned to Albany three weeks later when Second District Republicans held their convention. Whiteley's renomination was never in doubt. The incumbent's ability and obvious strength in southwest Georgia discouraged any challenger. On August 31, at the Dougherty County seat, the delegates unanimously nominated him on the first ballot. Gaining renomination had been a perfunctory exercise.

Reelection was something quite different. Winning a congressional race as a southern Republican involved battling the forces of wealth and power. Victory meant overcoming the influence of landlords who often exerted economic pressure on their black tenants and nightriders who terrorized the freedpeople. The stigma of Radicalism among whites was forbidding. Even if all these essentials were accomplished or minimized, there was another variable. Would the ballots be fairly counted? Charles Hays, a fellow Republican congressman, understood the situation from his vantage point in west Alabama. In 1872, a largely black constituency would reelect him. Robert W. Flournoy, a Mississippi scalawag, hoped to gain election to Congress that year. A former slaveholder who more recently had passionately advocated black rights, Flournoy would be unable to overcome obstacles. If the circumstances of Flournoy, Hays, Whiteley, and others differed in detail, the pattern and problems were much the same for Republican candidates throughout the ex-Confederacy.[6]

The recent reconfiguration of the congressional districts added to Whiteley's burden. Reapportionment had increased Georgia's representation in Washington to nine congressmen, and the legislature had redrawn the congressional districts. The Second District had been reduced from twenty-two to seventeen counties; ten counties where Whiteley had previously sought votes no longer belonged to it. Five other counties—Berrien, Brooks, Colquitt, Lowndes, and Thomas—had been attached to the district. Thomas, Brooks, and Lowndes bordered Florida, and Berrien and Colquitt were just to the north. In geographical terms, the Second District had lost territory to the north and gained size in the south. Whiteley considered the demographic alterations more important. About thirty thousand more blacks than whites lived in the former Second District. Some sixty-eight thousand blacks and fifty-eight thousand whites resided in the reconstituted district. The political ramifications seemed obvious to Benjamin Russell, editor of the *Bainbridge Democrat.* Having joined a Georgia regiment as a drummer boy and eventually been incarcerated as a Confederate prisoner-of-war at Johnson's Island, Ohio, Russell was one of Bainbridge's most unreconstructed citizens. Happily ruminating about the consequences of the "new order of things," he predicted: "Whiteley has made his last visit to Washington."[7]

Favorable Democratic prospects drew the interest of several candidates in the Second Congressional District nomination race. The editor of the *Quitman Banner* stated: "there is no scarcity of aspirants for Congressional honors." In Terrell County, F. M. Harper, a state representative, claimed support. William Fleming, a Bainbridge lawyer, received considerable attention. Gilbert J. Wright, the mayor of Albany, also gained serious consideration. It seemed possible that Nelson Tift might pick up the Democratic mantle. The prospect of gaining the seat he was convinced Whiteley had stolen from him two years earlier tempted him. Urged to do so, Tift declined to seek the nomination actively but agreed to run if drafted.[8]

Whiteley soon learned who the opposition would be. Democrats representing each of the seventeen counties were present when their convention opened at the Dougherty County courthouse on September 4. The reading of a public letter from Nelson Tift was one of the first acts.

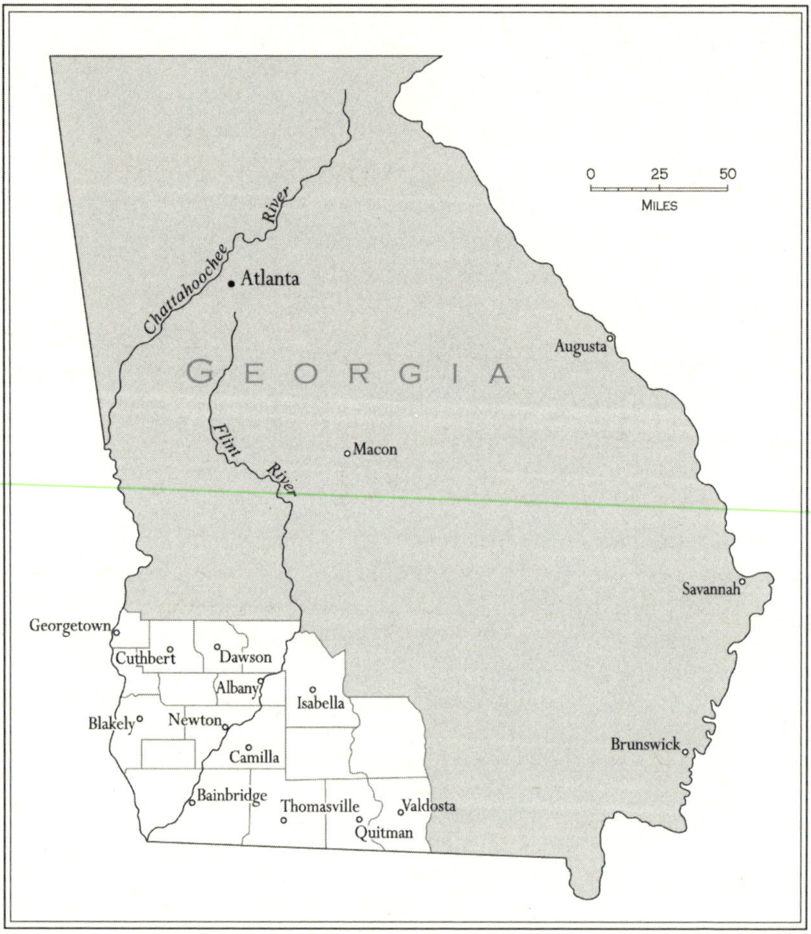

Map of Second Congressional District, Georgia, 1872.

The district's best known Democrat remained bitter, making reference to the "fraud and perjury" that had kept him out of the Forty-first and Forty-second Congresses. Apparently, however, Tift was not interested in joining the Forty-third. He withdrew from consideration. The delegates considered Gilbert Wright, William Fleming, F. M. Harper, and Archibald McIntrye. Wright received the nomination on the eighth ballot.[9]

Gilbert Wright practiced law in Albany where he lived with his wife and two daughters. Forty-seven years old, he claimed an impressive military record: he had served with the Georgia First Regular Volunteers during the Mexican War, and his opposition to secession had not prevented him from fighting for the Confederacy. He began a gallant Confederate career as an officer with T. R. R. Cobb's Cavalry Legion, and his meritorious service (he was wounded twice) had made for advancing rank as a lieutenant, captain, major, colonel, and brigadier general. Wright had been Albany's mayor for five years after the war. Aspiring to higher office, he now sought a seat in Congress. It was his stated intention to "redeem the district from Radical rule."[10]

The lionization of the Democrat and the Republican's vilification began immediately in the newspapers of the overwhelmingly Democratic district. Among his other qualities, the *Albany News* proclaimed Wright "a zealous supporter of the right."[11] And there was virtual Democratic unanimity as to Whiteley's unsuitability. The *Cuthbert Appeal* called for a "united effort to carry the district over the Whiteley Radical faction."[12] Only their relative fierceness in denouncing Whiteley differentiated Democratic newspapers. The *Dawson Journal* emphasized the importance of repudiating the man who "prefers the company of the negro in the short watches of the night."[13]

Heaping animus on Whiteley might help the Democratic cause, but Wright had to make his own case. A tall and portly man, Wright was neither a bad nor a brilliant politician. He spoke forthrightly, frankly, and, though no orator, usually held his audience's attention. One listener described Wright as a "plain, forcible speaker" who could be "argumentative, and at times eloquent."[14] Wright campaigned from September to late October. In between, traveling by railroad, steamboat, and carriage, he spoke in all seventeen counties. Successive days in late September took him to Fort Gaines, Blakely, Cuthbert, Georgetown, Dawson, and elsewhere. The pace and requirements challenged even an ex-soldier accustomed to a different kind of campaigning. Wright later concluded from his experiences that "it is no child's play to canvas."[15]

At Quitman, the seat of Brooks County, on September 16, Wright favorably contrasted Greeley's record with that of Grant. Two days later, having made the eastward trek via the Atlantic and Gulf Railroad, he addressed a large crowd at Bainbridge. Admitting to limited speaking skills, he pledged to state simple facts; this mainly involved denouncing the graft-ridden Grant administration. A Greeley presidency, pledged to civil service reform, could chase "the robbers out of office." That evening some young local men serenaded Wright at the Sharon Hotel. There were no black voices among the impromptu choir.[16]

At Bainbridge, Wright refrained from harshly attacking Whiteley. Confessing that he had never met Whiteley, he wondered how any white man could be such a "renegade." Wright exercised less restraint several weeks later at Newton on October 5. In that Baker County setting near the banks of the Flint River, Wright sharply criticized the "wily scalawag" with "an artistic admixture of sarcasm, irony, and ridicule."[17]

As had Nelson Tift, Wright made repeated overtures to the freedpeople. Promising them fair economic treatment formed the basis of his message. He took the stock Democratic approach. Republicans were opportunists, intent on self-promotion, and seeking the black man's vote but not delivering anything in return. After listening to Wright at Dawson, one observer wrote: "the General did not forget that they [blacks] were a part of the voting population." Even so, freedpeople remained skeptical about Democratic promises.[18]

Blacks who made common cause with Democrats faced intense ostracism. The Union League had died out, but Republican clubs had formed, and served much the same purpose. A Randolph County Democrat described "secret meetings" where the freedpeople were "drilled and their fears of slavery and the overseer's whips . . . kept alive."[19]

Whiteley, as he campaigned over territory both familiar and not so familiar, reacquainted himself with some constituents and forged new connections with others. Making an impression was especially necessary in at least four of the five counties recently added to the district: Brooks, Colquitt, Lowndes, and Thomas. In Berrien, the fifth county, 90 percent of the population was white, and his appeal was limited.

Whiteley relied on the political clubs and on the leading black and white Republicans in a given county. Writing to an ally in September, Whiteley informed him of "too much work on my hands" and asked for help, since "we have no time to delay." Moses Knight, a former slave, presided when Brooks County Republicans met at Quitman on August 10. Philip Joiner, the black politician, remained a crucial liaison in Dougherty County. Writing from Mitchell County, a worried Democrat likened Republican efforts to military precision.[20]

Whiteley once again made a strong case to the freedpeople. He warned ex-slaves at Albany that Democrats favored consigning freedpeople to Fiddler's Green—a place somewhere between heaven and hell. As he constructed the analogy, blacks would be quasi citizens lacking full constitutional rights. At a Randolph County meeting he made a similar argument, and blacks were "listening and applauding."[21] One critic noted Whiteley's close fraternization with blacks at Dawson, and blamed him for "abominable principles instilled into the minds of ignorant negroes."[22] With the courthouse as his backdrop at Blakely, Whiteley spoke to a largely black audience. A Democrat there dismissed Whiteley's "illogical tirade to the negroes." A more objective witness could have countered that Whiteley offered the freedpeople a source of self-worth and hope.[23]

The incumbent chose a different emphasis when significant numbers of whites were present. Sounding very unlike the Radical Republican some pictured him as, he recited a litany of services he had performed in Washington. He spoke of his work gaining federal funds for river improvements, efforts to improve postal service, and the decreasing numbers of those who were politically disabled. This self-portrait was of a responsive representative who served district interests. At Cuthbert, one observer decided that Whiteley "scarcely noticed" the freedpeople and "seemed to labor to attain to respectability with the whites."[24] Whiteley delivered generally the same message at Bainbridge. The *Bainbridge Sun,* renamed but still far less politically outspoken than the *Bainbridge Democrat,* decided that what Whiteley said was "very moderate and characteristic of the man" and concluded that he "gave no advice nor laid down any proposition that was not entirely allowable under the rule of political warfare."[25]

He devoted considerable attention to Decatur County. More freedpeople lived there than in any other county in the district, and he continued to command allegiance among a significant number of whites there. Here he called the vast majority of voters by their first names, warmly shook hands, and asked knowledgeably about their families. County Republicans met in Whiteley's Sanborn Building office on September 14 and nominated a slate of legislative candidates. Alexander Nicholson (black) and Benjamin Brimberry and Thomas A. Swearingen (both white) were selected. As the *Bainbridge Sun* declared, "the Maj. composed the ticket." Late in September, campaigning on successive days in Decatur, Whiteley spoke at Attapulgus, Harrell, Lime Sink, Bainbridge, and, after a Sunday break, Rock Pond. He advertised for "a large attendance of the people" and invited "both white and colored."[26]

Walking a political tightrope was not accomplished without attracting criticism. Whiteley's friendly relationship with Jason Clarke Swayze, the editor of the *Macon American Union,* had ended by 1872. Swayze joined the Liberal Republicans and supported Horace Greeley. One indication of his desertion of the regular Republican Party was a denunciation of Whiteley he published in the *Macon American Union.* An extremely shrill and controversial man who easily made enemies, with a pronounced reputation for excessive rhetoric, Swayze charged Whiteley with failing to do anything for the freedpeople he represented in Washington. Back in Georgia, Whiteley represented himself differently to "ignorant negro voters to tune them up to vote for him again."[27]

On October 2, a month before the congressional elections, Georgians reelected Governor James Smith. He defeated Dawson Walker by over sixty thousand votes, and Democrats practically swept the legislative seats. The poll tax contributed to a light black turnout. Political violence was not as serious as in the past, but problems persisted. Although both parties shared the blame for a riot at Macon on Election Day, the Democrats were more culpable. Trouble also occurred at Savannah and various other places.

Results in the Second District likely discouraged Whiteley. Some 9,300 Democratic votes had been recorded, and just 6,500 Republican ballots were cast. The same mix of voters would return to the polls in a month. The *Cuthbert Appeal* seized on the verdict and pronounced Whiteley's defeat "beyond doubt."[28]

He continued to project strength and confidence from makeshift podiums at crossroad gatherings or courthouse square engagements. He praised Grant and spoke of their shared Republicanism. After hearing Whiteley's overtures to the freedpeople at Camilla, a disgusted Democratic observer referred to him as a "worthy disciple of Grant."[29] In Terrell County, Whiteley reminded blacks that Grant was responsible for their freedom. Convincing the black man that he and the Republican Party had their interests at heart was not Whiteley's most critical task. More precisely, it was making sure that the black sharecropper in Lowndes County, or his counterpart anywhere in the district, actually voted. Some Democrats continued to use vigorous persuading, bribery, economic coercion, and sometimes violence to discourage blacks from participating. Three weeks before the election, a troubled Whiteley urged a friend "go to work and don't delay."[30]

The astute politician also capitalized on the problems Horace Greeley presented his opponent: the Liberal Republican was an awkward albatross for Wright and any southern Democratic candidate. One Democrat reluctantly described Grant as merely "the greater of two evils." Other "straight-outs" simply refused to support Greeley. Whiteley made a difficult decision a little harder: he denounced Greeley at every opportunity. He decided to circulate a handbill picturing Greeley at an earlier point in his career gloating over southern misfortunes, correctly calculating that criticizing Greeley would keep Democrats from the polls and cut into Wright's support.[31]

On Election Day, November 5, Whiteley won one of the closest congressional elections in Georgia history, receiving fewer than a hundred more votes than his opponent in an election in which over nineteen thousand were cast. Whiteley received 9,616 votes and Wright 9,530.

Substantial majorities in the three largest counties—Decatur, Dougherty, and Thomas—provided the margin of victory. The incumbent triumphed in both Decatur and Dougherty by over five hundred votes. In Thomas County, 1,637 citizens voted for Whiteley, and less than half that number cast ballots for Wright. The Democrat made up considerable ground in overwhelmingly white Berrien County, where he received 444 votes to Whiteley's 4. In most counties, the race was competitive. In Lowndes, 1,242 voters participated, and Wright gained a majority of eight. Only 77 ballots separated the antagonists in Randolph County, where 1,779 were tallied.

How and why Whiteley won is clear. Supervising federal election officials, who were not present at the state election, accounted for a stronger showing among blacks. In the Second District, some three thousand more Republican ballots were cast than in the gubernatorial contest. The number of Democratic votes remained roughly the same from the October to the November election. Apathetic toward Greeley, many Democrats simply did not vote. Wright later despaired over the difficulties of campaigning in a presidential election year "with no candidate in the field to aid you in bringing the voters to the polls." On the other hand, blacks eagerly turned out for Grant, and Whiteley was the beneficiary.[32]

Whiteley also campaigned hard and effectively among blacks and whites, taking full advantage of his incumbency and exploiting the weaknesses of his opponent. He could point to a record of service to all Second District residents. Although freedpeople cast the vast majority of ballots for Whiteley, he could not have won the election without attracting some white voters. They perceived him as a reasonable and effective congressman. If some whites voted for him, more felt no compelling reason to vote against him, and simply did not participate in the election. Jason Clarke Swayze had charged that Whiteley deceived blacks and used his influence more for whites. He took exception to a candidate who "swears fealty to the negro in attic rooms with the door locked, and claims fellowship with Democrats by daylight and in public."[33] There was at least a patina of truth to that assertion. Yet what Swayze condemned as insincerity, and others attributed to guile, Whiteley simply viewed as political self-preservation. He was a master of pragmatic gamesmanship and the art of survival. The *Bainbridge Sun* knew Whiteley well and accurately summed him up, describing him as "a wily and able man" who would "leave no expedient untried to secure his election." Gilbert Wright would have defeated any lesser candidate.[34]

Besides his own reelection, which Whiteley had been extremely worried about, other results pleased him. Republicanism fared better than expected in Georgia. Although Greeley carried Georgia, with seventy-six thousand votes to Grant's total of sixty-two thousand, the margin of defeat was respectable. Two other Republicans would join Whiteley in the Forty-third Congress. The outcome encouraged a demoralized party that had been decimated in the October state election.

However personally relieved about his reelection, Whiteley realized that Republicanism continued to inspire fierce hatred. In the recent southern elections, violence had been a fact, even if less pronounced than previously. When Congress reconvened in December, Grant would note in his annual message that "reckless and daring men . . . have committed deeds of blood and violence."[35] That was so in Georgia. Over twenty whites were charged with violating the Enforcement Act for their actions during what was called the Macon Riot. What took place there represented only the most flagrant example of continued political troubles. Within a week of the gubernatorial election, United States attorney Henry Farrow had telegraphed United States attorney general George H. Williams about serious difficulties. He maintained that "gross violations of the Enforcement Act were perpetuated at the election in this state."[36]

Whiteley shared Farrow's concerns and outrage. Just days after his reelection, Whiteley also reiterated to Attorney General Williams the severity of the situation. Protesting from Bainbridge, Whiteley wrote: "I take the liberty of calling your attention to the necessity for a prompt and vigorous prosecution of violators of the law in this state." He asked that Henry Farrow be given more professional support. In Whiteley's estimation, "the means at the disposal of the district attorney are not equal to the emergency." Drawing on his "personal knowledge," he laid out problems and possible solutions. He advocated establishing and placing at Farrow's disposal a detection force capable of acting swiftly. Even if arrested, he pointed out, offenders all too often were acquitted by fellow whites. A move in the right direction involved excluding "criminals or their sympathizers" from the jury rolls. Farrow must have more power, Whiteley averred, to "make the law a living reality." In Georgia, and elsewhere in the South, "it is all important that every effort be put forth to show to all that protection is the right of the citizen and that this is a real truth not a simple theory."[37]

On Sunday evening, December 1, Whiteley left Bainbridge for Washington. Only ninety-two working days remained in the Forty-second Congress when House Speaker James Blaine sounded the gavel on December 2, 1872. Although Whiteley introduced only two bills and a resolution, the session was personally eventful. He spoke for the first time at length from the floor. Several struggles for patronage offices required attention.

Before Congress closed, Whiteley also found himself the object of attacks that threatened his expulsion from office.

What was termed the "gay season" was in full swing when Whiteley returned to Washington.[38] As 1873 opened, an observer noted that the nation's capital had no rival for receptions, balls, and dinners. The president periodically hosted formal State Dinners. Whiteley became the first Georgian since before the war to be invited to one of these dinners. On the evening of January 2, 1873, he enjoyed what was described as a "gorgeous dinner" at the White House.[39]

Whiteley inevitably drew the attention of the *Atlanta Herald*'s correspondent in Washington. Legislation offered by Georgia congressmen, patronage struggles, scandal, and rumor formed the stock in trade of "Specks" (the reporter's pseudonym). Despite political differences, "Specks" developed a respect for Whiteley and soon judged him "keen, shrewd, and quick-witted." In Washington, in matters effecting Georgia, Whiteley was clearly a central figure and a man to be reckoned with.[40]

Whiteley came to be associated with what was pejoratively referred to as the "Georgia Ring." The term "ring," which denoted self-serving collusion and corruption was most commonly associated with the graft of William M. Tweed in New York City. Such organizations often made office and patronage appointment decisions. Henry Farrow, in and out of Washington, figured prominently in the Georgia Ring. So did another Republican, James C. Freeman, who had been elected to the Forty-third Congress and had come to Washington during the final session of the Forty-second largely for the purpose of influencing patronage appointments. What most clearly revealed concert of action among these Republicans and inspired the "ring" epithet was their influence in assigning patronage. According to at least one detractor, the Georgia Ring represented "a regular Federal office brokerage in Washington." Struggles over postmasterships at Atlanta, Macon, and Savannah illustrated the Ring at work and Whiteley's influence.[41]

At the beginning of 1873 Elijah Bond was the Republican postmaster at Macon. Edwin Belcher, the Third District's assessor with the Internal Revenue Department in Georgia, hoped to replace him. A black man, born free in South Carolina and educated in the North, Belcher had served with a Massachusetts regiment during the war. He moved to Georgia after the war and had been the Third District's assessor since 1869. He counted Senator Charles Sumner among his allies. Whiteley also admired Belcher, whom he described as a "competent and representative man of the colored race in our state." Calling on United States postmaster John A. J. Cresswell in early March, Whiteley, Farrow, and several other

Republicans asked him to make Belcher postmaster of Macon.[42] Weeks of maneuvering followed. Jefferson Long, the prominent black Republican who lived in Macon, objected that Belcher was a resident of Augusta and should not become Macon's postmaster. Long considered Belcher an outsider and "one of Whiteley's carpetbaggers."[43] Whiteley's hand in the battle was evident. A Macon newspaper blamed the nefarious Georgia Ring and, more specifically, concluded: "Whiteley's fugleman must be awarded."

As in Macon, the postmasterships at Atlanta and Savannah lay outside the Second District, but Whiteley had his own ideas about filling them. The Georgia Ring supported John G. Clark at Savannah and James L. Dunning at Atlanta. Other men had their supporters, and Whiteley went to work.[44]

Whiteley sometimes acted for those seeking positions in Georgia and on other occasions threw his influence against them. John F. Quarles, a black Republican from Augusta who had recently delivered a seconding speech for Henry Wilson as the vice-presidential candidate at the Republican nominating convention, sought Whiteley's support. Anxious for a diplomatic appointment, Quarles asked Whiteley to endorse him as American consul to Belgium. Whiteley complied and described Quarles to Grant as "one of the most promising and worthy young men of his race in our State or in the South." Quarles soon became the consul to the Spanish island of Minorca.[45]

Whiteley deeply regretted the death of Thomas Speer, his fellow Republican from Georgia, who died at his Barnesville home on August 18. On February 20, Whiteley addressed the House as one of five congressmen who eulogized Speer. Whiteley had lost a friend and a political ally. "I have known him intimately in both the public and private walks of life," he told his colleagues. He described a man who had offered freedpeople "legal and political equality." Ignoring "calumny, intolerance, and proscription," Speer had won Whiteley's commendation for acting on the truth that "the great basis of restoration was equality of rights." Whiteley's words also provided insight into his own political course since the war. He reflected on the relationship of the races. When the war ended, held back by centuries of slavery, black men were poor, ignorant, and accustomed to serving as "mere machines . . . to do their masters' bidding." Most Southern whites, regrettably, refused to recognize the legal and political equality of the ex-slaves. Whiteley had chosen otherwise and recognized "a new era of freedom." So had his deceased friend, and Whiteley praised Thomas Speer for his humanity.[46]

In the meantime, Whiteley confronted several challenges to his reputation for integrity. Allegations circulated that he, Freeman, and Farrow had sold their influence to office-seekers. Unspecified enemies claimed that Whiteley had received $400 from an unnamed Georgia official who wanted to maintain his postmastership. Whiteley pledged to resign if it was proved that he had taken money from an office-seeker. A postmaster general's inquiry exonerated the Georgia Republicans.

About the same time, in what was suddenly becoming for him an uncomfortable session, Whiteley faced other allegations. Another unidentified source claimed that the Irishman was not a naturalized American citizen and therefore was unable to sit in Congress. The charges, which circulated in Georgia newspapers, gave the *Atlanta Constitution* an opportunity to feign outrage and jibe "Good Heavens! How much nearer a negro do they want a man to be."[47] Whiteley soon wrote Benjamin Conley; "there is no truth in the report that I am an alien. . . . I was nationalized in 1854 and have my papers in my desk before me." The false charges came to nothing.[48]

The short session of Congress concluded in early March; that did not end congressman Whiteley's work. For several weeks after Congress recessed, the Senate deliberated in special executive session and finished uncompleted business. At this time, various appointments (such as the postmasterships) were made. Whiteley delayed his departure for Washington until the status of various office appointments was known.

Momentum for both Elijah Bond and Edwin Belcher for the Macon postmastership shifted before the Senate confirmed Belcher late in March. A skeptical *Macon Enterprise* noted: "our people are not used to having negro officials in their midst." Whiteley knew these changes were unwelcome to some, but he insisted they were needed in Macon and, for that matter, should be implemented in Richmond, Charlottesville, Little Rock, and any other southern town or city.[49] About the same time, to Whiteley's satisfaction, John Dunning and John Clark were confirmed at Atlanta and Savannah. Whiteley had done his part to make that so. In the estimation of "Specks" he was a "splendid 'log-roller,'" and it was an appropriate description. Whiteley took satisfaction in these patronage victories, and with his reputation intact, he put the session's work behind him.

Whiteley and his wife returned to Bainbridge on April 1, 1873. Practicing law, presiding as the head of a family of six, and never-ending congressional duties concerned him for the rest of the year.[50]

8 *The Prince Wire-Worker*

Whiteley spent the second half of 1873 in Bainbridge. Although he and sometimes Margaret (and possibly the children) were often in Washington, the family maintained a sense of continuity in Georgia. Richard was twelve, Montie had turned fourteen, and both continued to attend the Bainbridge Male and Female Institute. When "Master Montie" fell off a wagon and broke his arm that year, the *Bainbridge Democrat* noted the mishap. Hortense and Zena, neither of whom was even five years old, stayed closer to home. The summer offered occasions for celebration and grief. Charles graduated from the law school at Columbian College in June, and the *Bainbridge Sun* predicted for him a "brilliant future."[1] Several weeks later, on July 10, Margaret's sixty-three year-old mother, Mary Devine, died after a lingering and painful illness. Friends joined the "bereaved relatives" at the cemetery for her burial.

Margaret Whiteley welcomed the construction that had begun late in 1871 on an Episcopalian church. The work had stalled, though, and she endorsed the *Bainbridge Sun's* admonition to her fellow parishioners: sponsor a benefit and raise funds for completing the church. In 1872, Episcopalians had observed Easter in the courthouse. The price of procrastination became apparent on September 19, 1873, when a tornado swept through Bainbridge, and high winds destroyed the unfinished structure.[2]

Bainbridge and southwest Georgia had only begun to escape the postbellum economic blight when the Panic of 1873 struck. Unemployment and plummeting agricultural prices shook the economy for the next several years, during the nation's worst depression yet. Residents of southwest Georgia faced the same difficulties that others encountered throughout the South.

Bainbridge residents endured various hardships. In 1868, building on the work of the constitutional convention, the legislature had passed the Homestead Law, which allowed for $1,000 personal property and $2,000 real estate exemptions for debt. Now a recent Georgia State Supreme Court decision declaring the Homestead Law unconstitutional increased burdens. Its repeal allowed countless executions for debts contracted before and during the war. The fallout in Decatur County was tremendous. "People hereabouts are seemingly trying to cut each other's throats," according to the *Bainbridge Democrat,* which predicted: "if something is not done to relieve people, this part of the country is 'gone-up.'" Some talked of leaving Bainbridge. A new life out west beckoned. Not many left, but the situation did not improve in the short term. The unfinished and languishing brick Female College building on the town's edge offered a constant reminder of hopes deferred.[3]

Congressman Whiteley attempted to provide explanations, advice, and hope. In a public letter of May 2, he addressed the crisis created by the repeal. Whiteley noted "the indiscriminate levy of executions" and "the alarm of the people who are so unfortunate as to be in debt." Whiteley referred the public to a bankruptcy law passed by Congress in 1867 that sheltered some. At least, he informed constituents, they were "not yet at the mercy of creditors."[4]

Whiteley continued to represent clients in various local courts. When Mayor George W. Lewis fined Lewis Robb, a mulatto barber, for disturbing the peace, he engaged Whiteley for appeal purposes. His efforts on Robb's behalf dominated much of a June court day but changed nothing. After Allen Gore forced J. L. Butler to surrender an outstanding debt on a rural road that summer, Whiteley prosecuted him for highway robbery; William Fleming defended Gore in August. Following "able and exhaustive" arguments from both lawyers, Magistrate Daniel McGill ruled for Butler. Judge McGill decided against Whiteley in another case heard that August. Two freedmen, Sam Greene and Primus Munnerly, had been arrested for breaking into a local merchant's store. Whiteley's argument failed to dissuade the judge from setting a $500 bond and committing Green and Munnerly to jail until Superior Court met.[5]

It was impossible to entirely separate practicing law from politics. Whiteley remained the favored lawyer of local freedpeople. Blacks often did not receive justice in courts. Well aware of inherent unfairness, Whiteley utilized his abilities to represent the freedpeople, at least slightly ameliorating the situation. He did so often with little or no compensation. When Lizzie Parsons, who had taught at the Whittier School since 1870, was threatened by a levy at the school that spring, Whiteley agreed to represent the school. Parsons soon described the congressman to a northern acquaintance as "a good friend." Whittier School remained open, and the situation was settled to her satisfaction.[6]

That summer, he handled the prosecution in a case with strong racial overtones. In Bainbridge, as throughout Georgia and the South entirely, the life of a freedperson was valued less than that of a white person. The circumstances of a man like Tom Warren were representative. Warren, a freedman, worked for James Wilson, a white man who owned a plantation about ten miles outside Bainbridge. On August 12, when the two argued over whether an unnamed black woman should wash clothes for the Wilson family, Wilson shot and killed Warren. Whiteley avidly pursued judicial retribution for Warren's death. In a larger sense, he acted for the dignity of blacks throughout the South. In the quickly forthcoming commitment trial, Whiteley chiefly composed the prosecution, and four attorneys represented Wilson. Whether Warren had provoked Wilson formed the crux of the question. The trial lasted several days and drew great interest. On August 18, in a charged atmosphere, Whiteley delivered closing remarks. Judging from the reaction of Benjamin Russell's *Bainbridge Democrat,* Whiteley probably attributed Warren's death to a pattern of mistreatment directed at blacks. Russell charged Whiteley with making a political speech "in the guise of a lawyer, prosecuting a case." The *Democrat* called the remarks "inflammatory and incendiary" and condemned Whiteley for "one of the most outrageous and unscrupulous partisan efforts ever delivered by a Radical politician, even on the stump." The verdict concerning the guilt or innocence of James Wilson is unknown. It is certain that, at least among some whites, the congressman further confirmed their low estimation of him. Just as surely, among blacks, he reinforced their high regard and loyalties.[7]

Whiteley also attracted unfavorable attention outside Bainbridge. Writing to Benjamin Conley in July, a Republican critic objected that "the patronage of the state and especially this District has been used to build up the fortunes of the Hon. R. H. Whiteley." The congressman's power was unquestioned, final, and, according to the writer, bad for the state Republican Party. He asked Conley: "how can any movement be made to organize to work; when every office holder in the District has to wait to hear what Whiteley says."

Without identifying the author, Conley immediately apprised Whiteley of the accusations. The former governor warned Whiteley of his "supposed friends" and recorded his personal "disgust at the petty jealousies and backbiting of your Republican allies." Conley also recalled "my lamented friend Speer" and touched on his past correspondence with the deceased congressman. "I have still some old foggy notions," wrote Conley, promising to keep Whiteley informed of them. The ex-governor could not resist making one proposal immediately: unless something was done to remove the poll tax, Conley predicted the Republicans would never elect another congressman. He asked Whiteley to "ponder this matter."[8]

Whiteley refuted the accusations within days. "I have no schemes to carry out, pets to reward, or enemies to punish," he informed Conley. He maintained that he had awarded patronage to individuals only after discussions with local Republicans. Whiteley indignantly denied basing decisions on any personal friendship and said he would only appoint someone "because he deserved appointment as a *Republican.*" He further declared: "I have done *nothing* for the man but *everything* for the cause." As for hindering party efforts, "I am not knowingly in the way of any one in my own district or any other. Nor have I any control of the actions of any one here or elsewhere hence I cannot see how I am in the way of organizations working." Whiteley did not ask Conley to identify the third party but attributed the accusations to a simple fact: when he placed the party's welfare over an individual's interest, enemies inevitably were made. If that constituted impeding Republican activities in the Second District, "than I shall remain so until I lose my self respect and conclude to be the slave of others." Whiteley promised to "fight it out on that line independent of all jealousies or personal interests." Making patronage appointments, by the definition of the process, inevitably caused division. If Whiteley's defense was somewhat self-righteous, his critic's judgments could have resulted from any number of misconceptions and prejudices.[9]

Whiteley represented the Second District, but he was far from representative. Land holdings and personal assets made him a wealthy man. When an attractive business and political opportunity presented itself in the summer of 1873, he acted decisively and bought the *Bainbridge Sun.* Residents had read the weekly newspaper since 1869, when it was the *Southern Sun;* it had been renamed the *Sun* in 1872. Passing through the hands of several men during its lifetime, the paper was at best moderately successful. The most recent change of hands had taken place at the beginning of 1873, when Robert Johnston had sold his interest in the paper to John Hayes. Under Hayes the *Sun* took a Republican tack. Yet the newspaper had, by any standard—quality of print, content, advertising—seriously deteriorated. Half way into 1873, Hayes admitted: "we have had a pretty hard road to travel."[10] That was an understatement. The newspaper was failing. Whiteley considered the *Bainbridge Sun* "not even readable." In early August, he paid $280 for the newspaper's printing press, type, and various accoutrements at a sheriff's sale.[11]

The congressman envisioned promoting himself and Republicanism through the newspaper. He intended to spread party news, disseminate Republican views editorially, and, as an embattled politician, reply to critics. The only Republican journal in the Second District would challenge the monolithic Democratic press. His objectives were not solely political. Whiteley wanted the *Sun* to become the best source of news for local residents. Not incidentally, for a man extremely interested in making money, Whiteley planned to turn a profit. The Sun Publishing Company was formed. His decision, like much of what Whiteley did, was unconventional, and many would consider ill advised.

Whiteley faced an imposing undertaking. A white and Democratic audience bought, read, and importantly, advertised in the newspaper. Would they patronize a Republican journal? A high illiteracy rate and a lack of money to buy the paper, as with any Southern Republican newspaper, limited the readership among the freedpeople. As Richard W. Abbott, the historian of Republican Reconstruction newspapers in the South, has observed, "in the best of circumstances, Republican editors faced problems finding subscribers in the South." These circumstances meant that only about twenty Republican newspapers existed in Georgia, and usually for short periods, while there were at least 130 Democratic journals. Auguring further against the *Sun*'s success was the strength of the *Bainbridge Democrat.* The established newspaper enjoyed a healthy circulation, advertising revenues, and an editor, Benjamin Russell, well experienced in the journalism business.[12]

None of these considerations unduly discouraged Whiteley as he began his enterprise with all the skill, diligence, and determination he seemed to bring to everything. He kept the newspaper's weekly format but altered almost everything else. He moved the publication day from Saturday to Wednesday, and he relocated the newspaper's office to the second floor of the Sanborn Building, near his and John Donalson's office. He assumed the title "political editor."[13] Assembling writing and managerial talent, he hired Robert Johnston, who had published and helped edit the *Sun.* Whiteley persuaded the self-described "journeyman printer," who was a Democrat, to return to the *Sun* as the publisher. Johnston's presence was important. John Hayes, covering local events, became the "city editor."[14]

The printing press began rolling early in September, and Whiteley immediately addressed the public in the *Sun*'s columns. Acknowledging the newspaper's serious limitations, he cautioned against rushing to judgment because "the present edition was gotten up with old, worn out material, and a limited supply at that." Even so, Whiteley noted marked improvements and, complimenting Robert Johnston, said, "it is clearly demonstrated that our Publisher is wide-awake and knows his business." He also understood that matters of the physical press, the print, even those working for the paper would be less crucial than another test: clearing the hurdle of respectability or legitimacy among Democratic whites. All Republican editors faced that dilemma. Whiteley's carefully chosen words point to his understanding of that reality and of his local standing. Well aware of inevitable preconceptions, Georgia's most recent editor urged: "take the *Sun*; read it; and judge us by what we say and do, not what is said of us."[15]

The newspaper reading population noticed a stunning and rapid transformation. Various features were added, local coverage increased, and the print became much more presentable. Within weeks the newspaper boasted: "the *Sun* is daily increasing its popularity." Agents distributed the newspaper in Albany, Camilla, Cuthbert, Quitman, Thomasville, and Valdosta. Republican editors sometimes gave newspapers to blacks. It was certainly in Whiteley's interest to do so.[16]

Behind the scenes, Whiteley tapped into available financial support. Edward McPherson, the clerk of the House of Representatives, held the legal power to distribute federal printing patronage to two newspapers in each state. The selected newspapers were paid to print government laws, treaties, and other official business. A strong Republican, McPherson awarded these printing contracts to Republican newspapers. Wasting no time, Whiteley wrote him from Bainbridge in September and asked that the *Bainbridge Sun* be designated one of the two newspapers in Georgia. He cited recently incurred expenses for putting the *Bainbridge Sun* "in proper trim." Moreover, help was needed, because "the opposition are doing all they can to prevent my success by appeals to the prejudices etc. of the whites." McPherson complied, and the federal advertisements were running by early 1874. Whiteley had acted with alacrity to see to it that the wheels of patronage politics had been thoroughly greased.[17]

The editorial page offered Whiteley a convenient forum and reflected the moderate philosophy of its proprietor. He continued his efforts at disassociating Republicanism and Radicalism. An early editorial he penned linked Republicanism with Whig antecedents. He recalled Whig endorsements of a national bank system, tariff protection, and internal improvements. These concepts, he maintained, represented the "cardinal principles" of the Republican Party. Comparing the Whig and Republican parties, the *Sun*'s editor asked: "Is not that which is a virtue in the dead, commendable in the living?"[18] No mistake could be made, however tempered the point of view, about the editor's Republican perspective. In keeping with the *Sun*'s changing face, the masthead soon read "The Constitution As Amended—The Union As Restored."[19]

The existence of a Republican paper in Bainbridge was a philosophical affront to Benjamin Russell. Almost thirty years old in 1873, Russell had become the editor of the *Bainbridge Democrat* by early 1872. He loathed Whiteley and Republicanism. The *Sun* also directly threatened the profit and life of the *Bainbridge Democrat.* Referring to speculation that the resurgent *Sun* might drive his paper out of business, Russell defiantly stated otherwise. He took issue with *Sun* editorials and attacked Whiteley personally. The *Democrat* condemned the "thorough Radical sheet" and "that sneaking, snivelling demagogue . . . who from week to week writes his sentiments." Whiteley seems to have had no greater local enemy.[20]

The *Sun*'s editor did not reply in kind. Whiteley maintained a higher standard and avoided such sulphuric terms. In one response to a *Democrat* assault, he charted a different course. Whiteley identified reason, argument, wit, and sarcasm as tools of the journalist, "but never scurrility, abuse or blackguardism." The *Sun* became the most visible Republican symbol in southwest Georgia, and one of the few party newspapers in the state. Agents began promoting the newspaper outside the Second District in Americus, Macon, and several hundred miles away at Augusta and Savannah. At a time when Republican newspapers were folding in the South, in southwest Georgia, Richard Whiteley was constructing a powerful party organ and, not incidentally, a fine newspaper.[21]

Nothing indicated the *Sun*'s health so well as advertising by local merchants. Many Southern merchants philosophically opposed to Republicanism refused to advertise in Republican newspapers. Whiteley's experience was different. Publisher Johnston observed: "a majority of the business men of this city have been quite liberal in their use of printer's ink."[22] In Quitman, fifty-five miles to the east, a Democratic editor noted an alarming development. "Two-thirds of the merchants of Bainbridge must be Radicals," the *Quitman Banner* lamented, and through their advertising "support Whiteley's blasphemous and social equality organ."[23] The *Sun* cost the *Bainbridge Democrat* considerable advertising revenue. By September, Benjamin Russell felt compelled to pledge: "a Democratic paper can, will, and SHALL live in Bainbridge." The next month, he put the *Democrat* up for sale. Whiteley returned Russell's enmity, and held him and the *Democrat* responsible for inciting violence against Republicans. He would have welcomed a change in stewardship at the *Democrat*.[24]

The people of Bainbridge carried on as usual in the late summer and fall of 1873. The first cotton bale was brought to town in August, and rural blacks were soon arriving with their cotton and "converting it into national currency."[25] The Thespian Corps continued rehearsals for the farce *Good For Nothing, Nan.* Local blacks organized a fire company. The *Democrat* decided that "Bainbridge is a good place after all. People get tired of her, and swear 'she's going down,' and 'go west' in sheer disgust. But they haven't been away long . . . and back they come." What nobody foresaw that fall was a yellow fever epidemic.[26]

The sudden death of four residents on Sunday, October 19, signaled the beginning. At least fifteen residents were dead by the month's end. Merchants closed their stores, and business as usual all but ceased for the remainder of October and much of November. Hundreds of residents fled Bainbridge, adopting any mode, departing as fast as possible, ignoring the cost. Mayor George Lewis, who heroically comforted the sick, also came down with yellow fever and died. Appealing for aid, acting mayor Daniel J. G. McNair addressed himself to "the Christian World" in requesting outside help.

Whiteley likely sent Margaret and their children to a place of safety. He remained behind. Attempting to bring out the *Sun* apparently occupied him. Since most of the printers had left town, the *Sun* only promised readers "some sort of a sheet." Whiteley also helped with relief efforts. Julius Steininger, a local merchant, had left for the safety of Savannah. Writing Whiteley from there in mid-November, Steininger sent him over $250 for the needy; he had collected the money from "the Jews" in that city. Whiteley turned the donation over to the Relief Committee of Bainbridge.[27]

Whiteley's decision to remain in the deserted epidemic town soon had personal consequences: he contracted yellow fever. Only then did he leave for treatment in Savannah. By early December, his condition had improved, and with the danger over, he returned to Bainbridge. The *Sun* reported he was "rapidly convalescing." Some friends, including the prominent Benjamin Bruton, were less fortunate. Isaac Bower, who had defeated Whiteley for the state senate back in 1865, was another victim. About fifty people died in the worst tragedy in the town's history.[28]

Whiteley was recovering in Bainbridge when the Forty-third Congress opened in early December 1873. Henry Farrow was among those who missed Whiteley in Washington. Writing to him at Bainbridge in

December and noting his struggle with yellow fever, Farrow wished Whiteley a speedy return to Washington after the holidays. More than the congressman's health concerned him. Farrow stood accused of fiscal mismanagement (if not fraud) in his operation of his office as the United States attorney general in Georgia. His removal was possible. Reminding Whiteley of the charges of influence-peddling that had been brought against them the previous spring, Farrow mentioned the inquiry that had "gloriously vindicated us." He informed Whiteley that the present allegations represented a continuation of those partisan misrepresentations. Expecting him back in Washington, Farrow asked Whiteley to speak in his behalf to United States attorney general, George Williams.[29]

Whiteley did not wait until he returned to Washington. Writing to Williams from Bainbridge in mid-December, he emphatically maintained: "a more unfortunate move in Georgia could not be made than to remove Col. Farrow." Explaining he had been ill, Whiteley asked the attorney general not to make any decision until they could speak. Once Williams was informed of the true situation in Georgia, Whiteley wrote, "I am fully satisfied . . . you will fully concur in this opinion." Farrow survived the threat.[30]

Whiteley gradually regained his strength. Various affairs had to be put in order before leaving for Washington. That included, for the soon-to-be-absentee editor, making arrangements for the *Bainbridge Sun.* He took considerable pride in its renaissance, and he planned to contribute editorials from Washington. In early January, a newspaper spokesman announced: "we shall endeavor to prevent the *Sun* losing any of its attractions during the editor's absence."[31]

Georgia's Second District congressman was present when the Forty-third Congress reconvened on January 5, 1874. Just after noon, after the chaplain delivered prayer, and the journal of the last working day (December 19) was read, Whiteley presented himself, repeated the oath of office, and took his seat. Representatives had drawn for their seats when Congress had convened several weeks earlier. Thomas Haucks, who covered the Washington beat for the *Atlanta Constitution,* anticipating Whiteley's late appearance and poor seat, speculated that the Republican would need "a spy glass, a speaking trumpet, and an ear trumpet, if he wished to see, hear, and be heard." That was not a great exaggeration, as it turned out. Located on the western edge of the House, seat 94W was virtually parallel to the Speaker and indisputably one of the worst in the chamber.[32] John R. Lynch, a mulatto from Mississippi and the only self-proclaimed "photographer" in Congress, sat next to Whiteley. Their proximity offered a kind of historical serendipity.

Six Democrats and three Republicans composed the Georgia state delegation. James Freeman (and eventually Andrew W. Sloan) joined Whiteley in the Republican ranks. Whiteley was the senior but not the most recognized Georgia congressman. Alexander Stephens, the former vice-president of the Confederacy, claimed that distinction: he had been elected to Congress the previous November. Amid much attention, the somewhat infirm Stephens had settled in at the National Hotel.[33]

As it had since the war's close, the Republican Party controlled Congress. Yet the most pressing question as 1874 opened did not respect party lines. The so-called Salary-Grab scandal demanded immediate attention. At the close of the Forty-second Congress in March 1873, its members had raised their salaries, and the increase (from $5,000 to $7,500 for representatives) had been made retroactive to the Forty-second Congress. The public bitterly protested the "salary grab," and the fallout was tremendous throughout the country. On January 13, by an overwhelming margin, congressmen restored their salary to $5,000.

Whiteley had voted for the raise in the spring of 1873. Early in 1874, with characteristic independence, he defiantly cast one of only twenty-five votes against repeal. It seems unlikely, given his wealth, that Whiteley based his decision on personal financial needs. More probably, he agreed with Alexander Stephens, who, supported by a crutch, in his first House speech had justified the increase as necessary to attract the best minds to public service. Other congressmen felt similarly but feared political repercussions of opposing repeal. Whiteley doggedly supported the controversial raise.

The public also demanded some relief from the continuing depression. The situation turned Congress's attention to currency questions. Southern representatives, irrespective of party, generally voted together on currency issues and believed more circulating money was in the region's interest. Increasing the money supply made borrowing easier for farmers and facilitated debt repayment. A major piece of legislation (H.R. 1572) provided for increasing bank note circulation and also a gradual method of specie resumption. The bill passed in altered form. Inflationary forces staved off resumption, which would contract the currency. They also turned back attempts by anti-inflationists to retire greenbacks as bank notes increased. The single most important piece of currency legislation, though, was the Inflation Bill, which increased greenbacks and bank notes. Whiteley consistently voted the soft money line and, along with many other Southerners, was disappointed when Grant vetoed the Inflation Bill.[34]

His efforts on behalf of Thomas Hardeman, chairman of the Democratic State Central Committee, were also decidedly nonpartisan. The Amnesty Act of 1872 did not pardon all Southerners, and Hardeman, who lived in Macon, was the most visibly proscribed Georgian. He was alleged to have been most responsible for the election riot at Macon in 1872. Earlier, however, Hardeman had counseled fellow Democrats to cooperate, end their inflammatory denunciations of Republicans, and treat blacks with consideration. After Whiteley asked colleagues to remove Hardeman's disabilities, "Specks" noted that "Mr. Whiteley had taken Tom Hardeman in hand." The House consented on March 17, the Senate concurred, and Grant signed the bill within weeks. Whiteley considered Hardeman worthy of pardon. He was also well aware of the benefits of currying favor with Democrats.[35]

Whiteley served the Second District in different ways. Responding to the concern of some constituents from Albany, he inquired of agriculture commissioner Frederick Watts as to the adaptability in Georgia of the so-called fever tree (*Eucalyptus globuler*), a plant that absorbed moisture and counteracted the conditions associated with various fevers. The wrenching memory of yellow fever remained vivid.

Writing to Henry Farrow in January, Whiteley suggested that he come to Washington. Farrow replied that his United States attorney's duties kept him from doing so. At least, he optimistically reported, progress was underway in Georgia. Farrow pointed to his work integrating federal juries and replacing Ku Klux Klan sympathizers with loyal men in that pool. It all constituted "the greatest revolution in Georgia," and "I tell you, my friend, this change is a wonderful one."[36]

Whiteley considered the "revolution" far from complete. He remained certain of election fraudulence in Georgia. On February 16, he introduced a bill that established new standards for holding congressional elections. In the main, he recommended saving the ballots, lists of voters, tally sheets, and other papers connected to congressional elections for a specified period of time. The Judiciary Committee took the measure under consideration.

Whiteley needed to look no further for confirmation concerning fraud than the previous congressional election in Georgia's First District. Morgan Rawls, a Democrat, had apparently defeated Andrew Sloan. The Republican charged that fraud had altered the true result, and he contested the election. The Committee on Elections investigated and recommended removing Rawls and seating Sloan. Charges and countercharges followed in the House in March. Whiteley took a special interest when the controversy was settled on March 24. Rawls asked to address the House that day. Whether Sloan should also be given the opportunity was taken under consideration. Whiteley suggested that both men be allowed to speak for thirty minutes. After Rawls and Sloan spoke, the House voted 135 to 74 to accept the Committee on Election's recommendation. With some satisfaction, Whiteley immediately escorted Sloan down the House's main aisle, and the Republican took the oath of office.[37]

Henry O. Flipper, the son of Georgia slaves, had become in 1873 the first black to enter West Point Academy. Although some opposed Flipper's admission, Whiteley promoted military career opportunities for blacks. He advertised an open cadetship from the Second District at both West Point and Annapolis. Whiteley marked the day of examination, and noted that the competition "will be open to any youth white or colored."[38]

The representative of the Second District remained a strong ally or a formidable foe in the never-ending patronage struggles. He lost and won battles during the session's first few months. When Sam Bard attempted to replace James Dunning as the Atlanta postmaster, Whiteley spared no effort to deny him the office. Although a Republican, the former editor of the *Atlanta New Era* had alienated many in the state party by turning very early on Governor Bullock. Whiteley flatly considered Bard a political traitor. Assessing the Atlanta postmastership, "Specks" thought Bard's chances would have been better if "Whiteley had remained at home with the yellow fever a little while longer." The *Atlanta Herald* journalist noted that Whiteley possessed the "brains, the dash and the nerve to make a strong fight." Yet Grant supported Bard. The picture cleared slightly when Dunning died suddenly. Bitterly unreconciled to Bard, Whiteley argued against him on February 21, before the Post Offices and Post Roads Committee of the Senate. Nonetheless, early in March, Bard gained confirmation.[39]

Whiteley supported Benjamin Bell's attempt to replace David Barwald as postmaster at Americus. Both Barwald and Bell were Sumter County Republicans. In 1870, when Henry Farrow had recommended seating Whiteley over Nelson Tift, he had done so largely on the basis of an affidavit from Barwald (an election manager) alleging fraud. Since then, though, Barwald had provoked Whiteley by stating that blacks should not sit on juries. One observer theorized that Whiteley opposed Barwald because "he does not love the colored man."[40] As with the Atlanta postmastership, the controversy wound slowly to a resolution. On April 10, Whiteley strongly advanced Bell's credentials before the Senate Committee on Post Offices and Post Roads. The committee decided in Bell's favor five days later. Wiring Bell immediately from Washington at 5:20 P.M. on April 15, he triumphantly telegraphed: "you are confirmed postmaster."[41]

The office was Bell's, but the victory was Whiteley's, and Republican principle had prevailed. It remained for "Specks" to conclude: "Whiteley is the master of the situation."[42]

Benjamin Conley soon congratulated the congressman for winning "the Bell fight." Conley had hopes of replacing Henry Prince as the postmaster in Augusta or a recently vacated position in Georgia with the Internal Revenue Department. The former governor asked Whiteley for his support. Possibly trying flattery, he quoted "Specks," "who says that you are the 'brains of the Georgia delegation.'" Whiteley was highly intelligent, unsparing in the patronage wars, and sometimes ruthless, and the combination made him a powerful man. Conley could reasonably expect a favorable outcome when he added: "put your shoulder to the wheel . . . to help a needy friend."[43]

Whiteley was glad to do so. Foster Blodgett, former chairman of the Republican State Central Committee, had recently written Whiteley in Conley's behalf. Whiteley replied by promising to "do all I can for him." Yet powerful enemies opposed Conley, and Whiteley lamented, "I consider it a shame but have no power to control their acts." Mentioning his fellow Republican congressmen from Georgia, Whiteley further informed Blodgett: "Sloan is against him & Freeman is afraid to act: such is Georgia of today. What she will be tommorrow I can't tell." At least, Whiteley seemed never afraid to act.[44]

He did not fail to do so when Grant nominated Lafayette McLaws as collector of internal revenue for the First District. A former Confederate general, McLaws had attended West Point with Grant, and the president liked and respected the Georgia Democrat. By nominating McLaws, Grant confounded political practice and angered state Republicans, and Whiteley considered awarding McLaws the coveted position a serious mistake. This was no time or place for personal considerations, magnanimity, or, in Whiteley's partisan mind, quarter for Georgia Democrats. Aside from party considerations, Whiteley opposed removing A. W. Wilson, a reliable Republican and the present collector. Whiteley and other Georgia Republicans protested to Grant. The president persisted, and the Senate Finance Committee confirmed McLaws late in April. A quid pro quo was involved. Whiteley met with Grant, presumably in his office suite on the second floor of the White House, where Grant conducted most business. As "Specks" learned, "Whiteley saw the president, and they had a quiet talk over Georgia matters." In return for accepting McLaws, Grant compromised on another unknown point. The *Atlanta Herald's* correspondent reported: "Whiteley wanted something, and, in my opinion, got it."[45]

Whiteley also helped his eldest son. He and his wife, Josephine, lived in Washington with a recently born baby, and Charles took a position with the second auditor's office in the Treasury Department. Charles hoped to move South; he suffered from a serious kidney ailment, and Washington physicians recommended a warmer climate. With entree provided by his father, Charles met with Grant at the White House on March 24 and inquired about a federal office in the South. His father, Charles told the president, did not want to be perceived as having gained an audience for his son. Grant replied: "father need have nothing to do with it." The president recommended a position at the Savannah Custom House.

Acting on his father's advice, Charles wrote Amos Akerman, a former United States attorney general, at his residence in Cartersville, Georgia, and requested a letter of recommendation. Charles informed Akerman of his situation and said that his father, not wanting to intervene directly, "feels a delicacy about appearing in the matter himself."[46] Although careful sometimes about appearances, Whiteley could also abandon his disinterested pose. He seems to have abandoned any scruples the next month, for David Porter, who held a position with the Custom House in Savannah, became aware that "Whiteley wants his son to have my place" and, fearful that Whiteley would use his influence, came to Washington in April to save his job.[47]

Filial devotion accounted for Whiteley's efforts in behalf of Charles; he promoted others for office out of a sense of Republican kinship. Race considerations figured in the case of Tom Beard, whose status as a freedman caused Whiteley to have him appointed as the route agent/postal clerk with the Georgia Railroad. Writing to Benjamin Conley, Whiteley explained: "I put Beard forward believing that he was a good man . . . and that his *race* ought to be represented on the road."[48]

Enemies could resent but not dispute the fact of the congressman's power. Thomas Haucks of the *Atlanta Constitution* complained that Whiteley "holds the rod over the Republicans of Georgia and they dare not oppose his wishes."[49] Benjamin Conley, hoping to become the postmaster at Augusta, arrived in Washington on January 22 and soon sought out Whiteley. Contemplating his chances of securing the Americus postmastership, Benjamin Bell knew he had a strong proponent in Washington. David Barwald, the incumbent postmaster, realized the threat of the congressman working against him. As the fight over the Americus postmaster position continued, a Republican predicted: "Mr. Whiteley will have his own way."[50] Parker W. Perry, an Internal Revenue Department employee, provided more testament. In regard to an appointment, Perry asked Whiteley to "fix the whole thing up, at once." He knew the congressman could do that.[51] It was left to "Specks" to crown Whiteley "the prince wire-worker of the Republican delegation."[52]

Whiteley used his influence in different ways. Mayor Edward C. Anderson of Savannah came to Washington in April hoping to help gain appropriations for Savannah River improvements. On the night of April 9, at Alexander Stephens's National Hotel room, Whiteley and several other Georgia congressmen caucused to settle on a strategy. Whiteley agreed to hand out commercial statistical tables on the Republican side of the House. The next morning, on the floor, the well-connected representative introduced Mayor Anderson to various congressmen.

Whiteley evinced an even keener interest in the rivers serving the Second District. His earlier efforts in the Forty-second Congress had resulted in surveys of the Apalachicola, Chattahoochee, and Flint rivers. Acting on the recommendations of the Corps of Engineers, Whiteley asked in January 1874 for funding for the improvements that had been suggested by those who had carried out the surveys. He did not give up when the House Committee on Commerce failed to report the bill favorably. Several months later, when a delegation came to Washington from Columbus seeking appropriations for the Chattahoochee River, he made common cause. The Chattahoochee, the longest river in Georgia, ran through Columbus. Whiteley met with the four visitors at the National Hotel on the morning of May 2. Omar D. Conger, chairman of the House Committee on Commerce, and Phillip Cook, the Democrat who represented the Third Congressional District of Georgia, were also present. Whiteley impressed Alfred R. Calhoun—a Democrat, the editor of the *Columbus Enquirer,* and part of the Georgia delegation. He found Whiteley knowledgeable, influential, and an invaluable ally. Having heard a great deal about him from his opponents, Calhoun soon praised Whiteley and admitted: "I very foolishly permitted myself to think him a very different man from what he turned out to be on close inspection."[53]

Whiteley further demonstrated his commitment within the week. Maybe at his brownstone apartment on Indiana Street, or at his House desk, Whiteley began composing a speech outlining the need for federal financial underwriting. He planned to argue for increasing the "development of the section I have the honor in part to represent." At issue in Georgia, besides the Chattahoochee, were the Apalachicola and Flint Rivers. Drawing on the recent Corps of Engineers surveys of the tributaries, Whiteley began with the Apalachicola River. Obstructions placed there by Confederate authorities had altered the true course of the river, creating an awkward detour and impeding transportation. Removing snags, loose rocks, and steamer wrecks constituted the brunt of the task at the Chattahoochee. Rock shoals hindered navigability on the Flint, and deepening the channel promised significant results. Serious problems on all three rivers slowed commerce and jeopardized the safety of cargo and crew. Fifteen steamers had been wrecked, he noted, and he planned to invoke the government's duty to protect life and property. Some sunken ships, as abandoned wrecks, further worked against navigation. "We are aware it is urged that now is an unpropitious hour to enter upon the work of improvement," Whiteley admitted as he neared the speech draft's conclusion. Yet, he reasoned, "we answer, no hour is unpropitious for a great and paternal Government to commence to make secure the life and property of her citizens."

Sometime before Friday, May 8, he put the finishing touches on the speech, apparently planning to speak on that day. Once again, though, as when he had planned to denounce the poll tax, special circumstances intervened. When proceedings carried over well into the night, at nearly ten o'clock, Whiteley rose and asked that the speech be printed in the *Congressional Record.* The House then immediately adjourned. That Whiteley never delivered the speech was a fact of little significance. Congressmen did not usually listen to speeches, and few were concerned with a subject as personally irrelevant as river improvements in Georgia. Far more important, Whiteley lined up and built support off the floor. He seems to have gained critical allies on the Committee on Commerce, and none was as important as the Michigan representative Omar Conger, the chairman of the committee; he praised Whiteley's efforts to the visiting delegation from Columbus. The comprehensive River and Harbor Bill that passed the next month contained $40,000 for the Georgia tributaries.[54]

In the *Columbus Enquirer,* Alfred Calhoun soon commended Whiteley for his efforts. Aware that some faulted Whiteley politically, Calhoun declared it unfair to "think him truckling or dishonest, while all must acknowledge his ability." Calhoun decided that Columbus was "under many obligations to Major Whiteley."[55] "Specks" noted Whiteley's printed speech with approval. "If a Radical is to be sent" from the Second District, he maintained, "no better man could be selected."[56]

In June, as Congress neared recess, Whiteley helped Georgia gain more pork-barrel funding. Atlanta had been recently designated a "port of delivery," and building a customhouse became necessary. How much money would be appropriated for that purpose was at issue. On June 18, Congressman Phillip Cook tried but failed to gain an appropriation of $250,000. Whiteley rose from the obscure recess of seat 94W the next day and asked that the rules be suspended and the money appropriated. Attempting to delay consideration, the Ohio representative James Garfield requested that the House recess for thirty minutes, and frankly stated his opposition to constructing any more public buildings at federal government expense. A few procedural points were raised, but Speaker James Blaine clarified that Whiteley had the floor, and Whiteley declared: "I insist on my motion to suspend the rules." Minutes later, the bill passed the House, the Senate concurred within the week, and funding was established for the customhouse building. Whiteley received a rare favorable mention in the *Atlanta Constitution*.[57]

Whiteley and Democrats were at wide variance on other subjects. Nothing drew lines with so much finality as the Civil Rights Bill. By accepted practice, less than law, blacks sat in inferior places at theaters and on railroad cars and were often denied admittance altogether to public inns and restaurants. The Forty-second Congress had considered various measures to break down segregating barriers that the constitutional amendments and the Civil Rights Act of 1866 had done nothing about. The recent death of Charles Sumner, the Massachusetts senator most identified with the cause, created a sense of urgency. A proposed statute guaranteed equal access to accommodations in private hotels, theaters, restaurants, railroads, and steamboats and provided as well for the integration of public schools and cemeteries. Consideration of this statute sparked emotional debate across the country, and nowhere were denunciations as shrill as in the South. The bill cleared the Senate in May. In the House, there was less support, and some southern Republicans feared opening the subject before the off-year elections. Less than a month remained in Congress, and the civil rights measure never reached the House floor.[58]

On May 25, when supporters came closest to suspending the rules and forcing a vote in the House, many southern congressmen sidestepped the controversy. Whiteley did not. That Tuesday, when the reading clerk alphabetically moved down the congressional roll and reached Whiteley, he firmly answered "aye." He was the only Georgia congressman to do so. Fellow Republicans James Freeman and Andrew Sloan did not vote. "Spucks" gauged the magnitude of the moment and observed: "Freeman and Sloan are very weak-kneed, and shallow in their faith," but "Whiteley takes the pill at a single swallow and smiles as he gulps it." It would be the most controversial vote of his congressional career.[59]

Whiteley voted for the Civil Rights Bill with some trepidation. Having carefully cultivated support among whites in the Second District, he did not dismiss the many letters Democrats wrote him in Washington opposing the legislation. He considered the upcoming election and how supporting the measure opened him to charges of Radicalism. Underestimating the passionate racism of Second District whites was a mistake that could be politically catastrophic. Whiteley, conversely, may also have worried how his opposition to the bill might be received by district Republicans. Blacks in Atlanta, Savannah, and the Second District resented second-class treatment. Some Republicans had recently criticized him for not doing enough for the freedpeople (see chapter 9). In his public explanation, Whiteley simply honored his political philosophy. He had based his action on the conviction that blacks should be allowed to ride on first-class railroad cars, engage a hotel room, and expect what he termed "public rights." Summarizing his overall voting record in Congress, Whiteley explained that it was his intention "to keep pace with . . . the great changes which have been brought about by the action of emancipation, and to illustrate by my votes that Georgia accepts the status of freedom in good faith." Doing so meant supporting the Civil Rights Bill.[60]

What became notoriously known in Georgia as "Whiteley's Election Bill" pointed further to partisan differences. The legislation Whiteley had introduced early in the year concerning congressional elections emerged from the Judiciary Committee in June. Amendments in committee made the proposed statute more far-reaching than the original bill, which in essence required maintaining for a time the ballots, a list of those who voted, and tally sheets. In revised form, commissioned federal supervisors (required by law to be present at federal elections) were required to count the votes along with the state managers. Another amendment required that deputy marshals be stationed at the polls. In instances where voters lived considerable distances from precincts, the bill allowed the creation of a convenient precinct. The proposed legislation that New York Republican Lyman Tremain praised in the House on June 17 for promoting "an honest and fair election" Democrat Charles A. Eldredge of Wisconsin condemned for "the destruction of the states, and placing them utterly in the control of Federal power." An attempt to bring the bill up for a vote, as with the Civil Rights Bill, required suspending the rules. Whiteley regretted its bare failure. He did not participate in the floor debate but voted for suspending the rules, and was on record as advocating the controversial measure.[61]

The second session of the Forty-third Congress closed a week later, and Whiteley immediately left Washington, returning to Bainbridge on June 29. It had been six months since he had been in Decatur County, spent a night at the family home, or, presumably, seen some family members for any length of time. High on his list were overdue meetings with clients, conversing with his law partner John Donalson, and greeting his numerous friends. Among other concerns, he turned his attention to the *Bainbridge Sun.* In an editorial entitled "Home Again," Whiteley admitted that congressional business had prevented him from contributing to the *Sun.* Nonetheless, the newspaper had flourished, and he thanked his anonymous stand-in, "a gentleman of the city, whose modesty alone keeps his name from the public." Whiteley promised readers that the editorial policy of the paper would continue to appeal "to all who value a bold defense of Republican measures and men." That summer, Charles Whiteley, having temporarily given up on federal office, joined the staff of the *Bainbridge Sun,* becoming the newspaper's business manager.[62]

Several weeks later, on Thursday evening, September 3, 1874, Richard and Margaret Whiteley hosted a party at their home. Many whites attended the gathering. The *Sun* noted that guests enjoyed dancing and a supper prepared by the "incomparable lady of the house."[63] Offering a toast, though, fell to the genial congressman. Benjamin Russell of the *Bainbridge Democrat* chose not to emphasize the entertainments. He labeled Whiteley a "miserable demagogue" and noted the "unblushing impudence" of a man who would vote for a Civil Rights Bill and then extend to whites "the hospitalities of his mansion." Whiteley was accustomed to extreme language from Russell. The invective foretold what lay ahead for Whiteley as he sought reelection.[64]

9 *The Scalawag Whiteley Will Be Driven into Obscurity*

Ten years after Appomattox, the debate over the Civil Rights Bill pointed to the unresolved questions regarding the relationship between the races. In the South, where most blacks lived and the region was most affected, custom, tradition, and sometimes legal statutes separated the races on a daily basis. Blacks were not allowed to ride on first class railroad cars. Whites and blacks attended different schools, worshiped usually at their own churches, and, when they died, were buried in different cemeteries. Critics held that the Civil Rights Bill was unworkable, unnatural, and, in the minds of most white Southerners, even immoral. Its defeat in the last weeks of Congress did not close the debate. In the 1874 off-year election, the question dominated political discussions, especially in the South.

Six years earlier, during the presidential election of 1868, the Republican and Democratic parties were in stark contrast. When Grant defeated Greeley in 1872, with the New Departure Democrats taking a more moderate racial position, differences over race had narrowed. Now, during the midterm elections of 1874, condemnation of the pending civil rights legislation plainly raised racial passions. In the South, the political polarization was most evident. Horace V. Redfield, a journalist with the *Cincinnati Commercial*, traveled in the South that summer. He noted the opposition to the Civil Rights Bill, which "was feared by Southern-born men almost as much as death itself."[1]

Heightened political emotions contributed to a sharp increase in violence toward southern Republicans. Beatings, whippings, shootings, and general intimidation recalled earlier Klan activities. Those belonging to the newly inaugurated White Leagues, other organizations, or no group at all resorted to nightriding. The Reconstruction historian William Gillette aptly describes a new terror that had replaced the largely defunct Ku Klux Klan, and "a crescendo of violence." In the Second Congressional District of Georgia, where differences imbued the election with a searing intensity, politics took on an Armageddon quality.[2]

Until Richard Whiteley supported the Civil Rights Bill, numerous white constituents had viewed him as a productive congressman. A Bainbridge acquaintance, signing himself "An Old Line Whig," noted Whiteley's service favorably. He admitted "we began to feel like he was kin to us—at least second cousin."[3] Others in the district thought similarly. Whiteley destroyed that relationship overnight when he supported civil rights. The *Early County News* granted the congressman "the credit that may be due him for anything he has done for the good of the people of the district"; but now, "had he done a thousand fold more than he has, it could not atone for . . . his efforts to procure the passage of the civil rights bill." Such reasoning reflected the outlook of many Second District whites.[4]

An angry white population, Whiteley fully realized, threatened his reelection. He also worried in the spring and summer of 1874 about Republican opposition. Paradoxically, even as he forfeited white allegiances, Whiteley saw his dedication to blacks questioned. Some Republicans considered him too attentive to white Democrats. In regard to the freedpeople, critics claimed, Whiteley seemed far more interested in their vote than their welfare. William Clark, formerly an ally, maintained that Whiteley "does not occupy the advanced high ground that he should with regard to their [blacks'] wants." Republican detractors also charged that the congressman had awarded patronage offices to undeserving men and that several appointees did not even live in the district. At Albany on July 22, the Republicans would nominate someone, and Whiteley could not be sure he would be named.[5]

The dissent was centered in Albany. Charles Arnold, chairman of the Republican Executive Committee in the Second District and Albany's postmaster, directed the opposition. He had become disillusioned with the man who he decided was not a "good Republican." Arnold recruited opposition in the spring and summer of 1874, working with his brother-in-law, Isaac N. Wiseman, in Dougherty County to bring Whiteley down. Charles Wessolowski, a man of Prussian extraction who had taken an active role in county Republican politics and was the Dougherty County clerk of the Superior Court, also hoped to deny Whiteley the nomination. Even the black politician Philip Joiner, another former ally of Whiteley, joined the cabal.[6]

Whiteley's foes in Dougherty County threw their support to Frank F. Putney. A New Hampshire native who had moved to Dougherty County in 1865, he bought a plantation several miles south of Albany, and became a planter, a merchant, and, after the war, a Republican. Putney represented Dougherty County in the state legislature in 1871–72. Thirty-four years old in 1874, Putney had for unknown reasons opposed Whiteley's nomination in the past. Henry Farrow, chairman of the Republican State Central Committee, visited Albany in April. Inferring that Farrow wanted to replace Whiteley, Carey W. Styles, editor of the *Albany News*, remarked: "it is intimated that Whiteley is to be left out in the cold." The rising Putney seemed to be the alternative, and the *News* labeled him the "coming man."[7]

William Clark also considered challenging Whiteley. After coming to Georgia from Massachusetts in 1867, establishing the AMA School at Bainbridge, and serving as the Freedmen's Bureau agent for Decatur County (see chapter 3), Clark had moved to Thomasville in 1869 and had been elected to the state senate. Writing to AMA field secretary Erastus Craveth in New York, Clark called Whiteley's political convictions into question. Whiteley "ignores carpetbaggers," Clark related, and the freedpeople believe he "does as little for them as he dares and as much for whites as he can." Clark further blamed Whiteley for passing over some needy black and white Republicans for patronage offices and appointing "rebel friends." Nor could Clark respect a man who opposed repealing the recent congressional pay raise. Clark entertained no illusions. He described Whiteley to Craveth as a "fine speaker," a "lawyer of ability," and admittedly "successful in what he undertakes." Ownership of the *Bainbridge Sun* added to the incumbent's advantages. As for campaign funds, Whiteley could call on his considerable resources; and "I hear too that he proposes to spend it freely to secure his reelection."[8]

An undercurrent of dissatisfaction with the incumbent congressman was obvious. Opposition to Whiteley built in the spring while he was in Washington. In May, noting rumblings, the *Bainbridge Sun* reported that a few Dougherty and Thomas County Republicans were "casting about for a more suitable person." Although hardly objective, the *Sun* pointed to "falsehoods and misrepresentations" and condemned those who were taking "advantage of Whiteley's absence to hold secret caucus."

One such meeting was held at Albany on May 25, when about a dozen Republicans met and considered the upcoming election. Philip Joiner and two other Dougherty County Republicans attended. William Clark made the trip from Thomasville. Republicans from Baker, Calhoun, and Mitchell counties increased the attendance. Frank Putney was apparently not present. Both opposition and support for Whiteley were voiced. Since the deliberations remained secret, at the motion of Clark, it is impossible to know anything further of this meeting.[9]

Efforts to block Whiteley's renomination took different forms. Henry Singleton, a Dougherty County Republican, offered $100 a month to James A. Jackson, a Cuthbert resident who figured prominently in local Republican politics, and promised to meet his expenses if Jackson worked for Putney and against Whiteley. A Calhoun County Republican stalwart noted: "bitter, scandalous reports circulated, at great expense, pains and labor, to induce his [Whiteley's] friends to discard him." Another Whiteley loyalist mentioned the efforts of Philip Joiner and Isaac Wiseman in Mitchell County "to sow discord among our people."[10]

By June, William Clark had decided to seek the Republican nomination. He and Frank Putney had reached an understanding based on their shared opposition to Whiteley. If Putney gained significant support in the northern counties of the district, the Dougherty County Republican promised to withdraw (presumably at the Albany convention) in favor of Clark. The Thomasville Republican realized that he and Putney still faced long odds. Communicating with Erastus Craveth a month before the nominating convention, Clark was cautious: "the prospect is not bad but might be much better." He complained of a lack of money for campaigning and admitted: "Whiteley is rich and is to use money."[11] Several days later, he reiterated that he was "troubled for money . . . can only hope that my opponents suffer as I do—but that cannot be."[12] Clark's efforts to gain the nomination involved attacking the incumbent. He did so unabashedly and publicly. The *Thomasville Times* soon reported that Clark was "going for Whiteley with gloves off."[13]

The establishment of the *Albany Republican* provided more evidence of dissent. Charles Arnold was the editor, and Clark had a financial interest in the newspaper, which began circulating in June. Its purpose seemed clear and succinct to one Dougherty County Democrat. After perusing it, he decided the newspaper stood for taking the black man's money, social equality, and "Whiteley to get out."[14] Clark soon informed Craveth: "we are running a paper at Albany and it is doing us good."[15]

Some of what was said of the incumbent was valid. Whiteley had supported the salary increase even after the large majority of his colleagues had voted to rescind the raise. He had his own criteria for making patronage choices, and differences of opinion with others were unavoidable. For instance, he did not conceal his preference for southern whites over northern men. Wary of alienating whites, he had also been solicitous of Democrats. The inverse conclusion, that he had failed blacks, was false. Whiteley did play both sides, but not at the expense of surrendering his Republican principles. Detractors enjoyed a luxury Whiteley did not. They did not face reelection in a district where the overwhelming power of the white establishment was aligned against Republicanism and Republicans.

Whiteley followed developments from Washington. He knew both Clark and Putney. Between 1867 and 1869, when Clark had been in Bainbridge, Whiteley had had frequent contact with the teacher and Freedmen's Bureau agent. Whiteley had with Putney, at best, a working relationship based on a shared Republicanism. Whiteley publicly reacted to his attackers by making reference in the *Sun* to the "unholy ambition" of some, but he did not single out Putney and Clark by name. He felt betrayed, greatly angered, and politically endangered, and privately he surely chose words with far less restraint. He also moved quickly to check the challenge. In all likelihood, he orchestrated the public campaign of support that soon began.

One of the first to defend Whiteley in word and deed was Henry Farrow. The United States attorney general of Georgia soon reacted to the *Albany News*'s assumption that his recent visit to Albany indicated dissatisfaction with Whiteley. In a letter to Judge Thomas F. Hampton of Bainbridge, a Republican friend of Whiteley, Farrow branded as "absolutely untrue" that "remarkably strange report." In the correspondence, published in the *Sun*, Farrow explained that he had made the trip in his capacity as chairman of the Republican State Central Committee. "Not only does the political course of Mr. Whiteley meet with my warmest endorsement," Farrow insisted, "but there exists between us the most cordial personal friendship."

Other letters endorsing Whiteley and attacking his critics began appearing in the *Bainbridge Sun*. Louis M. Pleasant, a mulatto who lived in Dougherty County, writing to the *Sun* in May, singled out Charles Arnold specifically and opposition to Whiteley generally, faulting those "poisoning the minds of colored men."[16] Charles Arnold had temporarily convinced James Jackson of Whiteley's unsuitability. Reassessing the situation, the Cuthbert resident defiantly wrote: "I consider you, Mr. Arnold, the grand sachem of this movement." Jackson described Arnold and Isaac Wiseman as selfish men who resented Whiteley because he had passed over their friends for office. He alluded to "Major Whiteley's past record and what he has done for the colored people." C. H. Norris, who also lived in Randolph County, considered Whiteley "an able and efficient representative" and declared from Cuthbert: "I am not prepared to believe that the colored people will cast him [Whiteley] aside simply because someone else wants to go to Congress." More corroboration arrived from Camilla. Referring to "Major Whiteley as our leader," Isaiah Arnold deplored efforts by Joiner and Wiseman to convince blacks that change was needed. He dismissively referred to the "few malcontents of Albany."[17]

Differences of opinion were evident when district Republicans settled on delegates to the Albany convention. At Newton, in Baker County, Republicans met on June 26. Henry and James Singleton, visiting from Dougherty County, acted in Putney's interest. Despite their efforts, Baker County Republicans endorsed Whiteley and named two delegates to the Albany convention. Strident disagreement occurred when Dougherty County Republicans met at the courthouse on the last Saturday in June. Arnold, Joiner, Putney, Wessolowski, and Wiseman worked against the incumbent. All but Joiner were white. Most blacks defied them. Ishmael Lownon and Sylvester Wilson (both black) angrily denounced Whiteley's foes. That did not prevent the convention from tapping an anti-Whiteley delegation. The hand and influence of Whiteley was long—even feared—but not omnipotent. At Morgan, in Calhoun County, black and white Republicans gathered on July 4. The question of whom to endorse made for extreme contention, extending the meeting until near midnight. At that late hour, according to a witness, "the adherents of Major Whiteley were driven to the wall." Putney claimed the allegiance of the delegates who were selected. In the weeks before the election, Frank Putney had some reason for hope.[18]

About this time, late in June, Congress recessed and Whiteley returned to Georgia. Once back home, he made gaining the nomination and mending party fences an immediate priority. "We are again at our post," Whiteley began a *Bainbridge Sun* editorial. The candidate alluded to the current "senseless bickerings" and "discord and dissension." If "internal warfare" continued, he predicted Republican failure.[19]

Whiteley wasted no time in shoring up his allegiances. He spoke for over three hours at Albany on July 4. Although opposition to his renomination centered there, Whiteley counted far more friends than opponents among the Dougherty County Republican faithful. Some whites and large numbers of blacks turned out at the courthouse that holiday Saturday to hear him cover a wide range of topics. The freedpeople were most interested in one declaration. A witness reported that Whiteley confirmed his vote for the Civil Rights Bill and that he "was proud of it."[20]

A week later, on July 11, Whiteley made the thirty-five-mile trip from Bainbridge to Thomasville. The loyalties of the Thomas County delegation to Albany were at stake. William Clark was also present at this gathering. Whiteley spoke first, ridiculing Clark and responding with sarcasm to the opposition of the man who, he believed, hid his overreaching ambition behind ostensible concern for Republican principles. Clark unsuccessfully attempted to make the case that Whiteley did not have the freedpeople's interests at heart. The delegates endorsed Whiteley, and one who was present decided that the lesson was "the homemade scalawag can head off the carpetbagger."[21]

The congressman appeared several days later at Camilla. A large number of blacks lived in or near the small Mitchell County seat of government, and freedmen composed the majority of those gathered to hear him. Whiteley was among friends and was sure of himself and his message. Warming to the receptive audience, he endorsed the Civil Rights Bill and predicted its passage. When Whiteley defiantly promised enforcement of the law in Camilla, he "brought the house down."[22]

He spoke at Bainbridge on Saturday, July 18. Arriving early from the country that morning, blacks and whites took positions under the trees that dotted the courthouse grounds with shade. Whiteley moved quickly to the attack, disparaging Democrats as compassionless and championing a Republican Party that looked to the future and not the past. He pointed out that the Democrat-controlled legislature had recently repealed a long-standing provision that allowed individuals to exempt $200 worth of private property from levy or sale. That exemption included agricultural tools, cooking utensils, and necessities of life. This safety net, which Whiteley reasoned provided "the poor man and his family at least a living," no longer existed. With the measured words of a man sure of his target, the congressman drew a picture of the constable who "invades the kitchen and pantry . . . the skillet and the milkpan are paraded before the Court House door for sale." He faulted Democrats who made demagogic racial appeals and dwelled on the imagined evils of the Civil Rights Bill. It was the same kind of irrational reasoning, he reminded listeners, that had led to secession and disaster in 1861. In over three hours of oratory, southwest Georgia's most controversial politician "fought Democracy to the bitter end."[23]

Within the week, on July 22, Second District Republicans met in convention at the Dougherty County courthouse. Whiteley did not fear Clark or Putney and was confident of renomination. Benjamin Brimberry, the state senator from Camilla, was present. Another ally, Louis Guild, had made the trip from Morgan. Whiteley was not the choice of Dougherty County residents Charles Arnold, Charles Wessolowski, and Isaac Wiseman. Nonetheless, the question was less Whiteley's renomination (assured) than establishing party unity (anything but assured). The candidacies of Putney and Clark had collapsed. Putney's name was withdrawn at Albany, and Clark received no consideration. Decatur County delegates placed the incumbent's name in nomination. William H. Noble, a black minister in Thomasville, offered token opposition. Whiteley was selected on the first ballot. In the time-honored practice, a committee of three escorted him to the podium. The scene, reassuring to some, seemed all too familiar to others. Whiteley accepted the nomination and in an hour-long speech pledged to push the cause forward.

Yielding to political reality, Charles Arnold commented in the *Albany Republican* that Whiteley's nomination "had not been unlooked for by us." He continued: "suffice it to say that the opposition met with a severe defeat." Arnold also announced the end of the *Albany Republican* and endorsed Whiteley in its final issue.[24] So concluded the internal challenge to the incumbent and the existence of one of the shortest lived Republican newspapers during Reconstruction.

Whiteley had much bigger worries, however. Several days after the Republican convention, a Democrat wrote: "we now know who we have to oppose. . . . Whiteley is again upon the track and it behooves us to put out our strongest man."[25] It was not certain exactly who that was. On August 20, a month after the Republican convention, Democrats would name Whiteley's opponent at Albany. Meeting in various counties, delegates were designated, and sometimes they committed to one of the men seeking the congressional nomination. Herbert Fielder, a Cuthbert attorney, was the favorite. The *Cuthbert Appeal* considered him the candidate "to defeat Whiteley and rescue the old 2d from Radical rule and oppression." On August 4, Randolph County Democrats deliberated, selected delegates, and pledged themselves to Fielder.[26] Powhaten B. Whittle was the preference at Valdosta when Lowndes County Democrats met. In Clay County's Fort Gaines, a citizen proposed Richard E. Kennon, who practiced law locally. As Kennon's promoter warned, "Whiteley is a strong man . . . and in selecting a man to beat him we must not permit ourselves to take up this man or that."[27]

On August 20, at noon, the Democrats met in convention at the Dougherty County courthouse. The weather was predictably hot. Much less predictable was who would gain the nomination. Various business was conducted, a recess followed, and the nominating did not begin until mid-afternoon. Seven men—Flourney Clark, Herbert Fielder, James T. Flewellen, Richard Kennon, Archibald McIntrye, Robert G. Mitchell, and Powhaten Whittle—were placed in nomination. Fielder commanded the largest following but, as the lengthy balloting continued inconclusively, could not gain the necessary two-thirds support necessary. The name of the Albany lawyer William E. Smith appeared on the sixteenth ballot; he assumed the lead, and finally, on the thirtieth ballot, received the nomination.

That evening the convention reassembled. An illness limited Smith to a brief speech; rallying the partisans was left to others. Richard Kennon, James Flewellen, and William Fleming proved able substitutes, and "Major Whiteley got it heavy from all sides and by all hands." The convention passed resolutions condemning the Civil Rights Bill and pledged that "the scalawag Whiteley will be driven into obscurity."[28]

William Smith, a former county ordinary and solicitor general, forty-four years old in 1874, had been a Whig before the war. His opposition to secession had not prevented him from serving the Confederacy with distinction. Smith had captained the Albany Guards and fought with the Army of Northern Virginia. Wounded at King's School House in Virginia in June 1862, he had lost his leg. The injury had forced his military retirement, but in 1863 he had been elected to the Confederate Congress. Smith practiced law in Albany, where he lived with his family.

Like Nelson Tift and Gilbert Wright before him, Smith enjoyed the support of the overwhelmingly Democratic press in the Second District. Noting Smith's honorable loss of limb, the *Thomasville Times* assured voters that Smith "can outrun Whiteley on one leg." The *Quitman Reporter, Valdosta Times,* and other journals fell into line. Governor James Smith wrote Smith and offered assistance.[29]

One Democrat advised Smith to make Whiteley "'tote' the civil rights skillet wherever he goes." Smith intended to do just that.[30] He soon penned a message to Second District residents that focused on the Civil Rights Bill. According to Smith, the legislation was an unwarranted transfer of power from the state to the federal government. More important, he feared the daily consequences. Not allowing a black man or woman to purchase a circus ticket was wrong and unlawful, Smith reasoned. Yet he considered requiring blacks to sit in a designated area a proprietor's reasonable prerogative. Acknowledging that accepted form separated the races and that whites wanted the races kept distinct, Smith reasoned that "unless the black man dislikes his own color, the arrangement ought to suit him." Nothing angered or frightened whites so much as the prospect of integrated public schools. Democrats argued that white

William E. Smith. Courtesy of Georgia State Department of Archives and History, Atlanta.

and black children, although instructed separately, gained the same education. The contemplated civil rights law represented for Smith a misguided effort to "give the black man a social status and the courtesies of polite life, without first preparing him for it."[31]

Whiteley also realized the power of the written word. In the widely circulating *Bainbridge Sun,* he addressed Second District residents in a long open letter. Writing "as your representative," Whiteley noted accomplishments that included bringing patronage positions to Georgia, gaining subsidization for river improvements, and increased postal facilities and service. The number of citizens shackled by political disabilities had fallen from three hundred to none, he related. Returning to a familiar theme he would continue to sound, Whiteley portrayed Democrats as lacking concern for the Georgian of modest or less means. State Democrats and their regressive tax policy penalized the "poor soldier" and drove "the widow and the orphan out upon the cold charities of the world."

Appealing to readers, Whiteley defended himself against Democrats "eager to find cause to condemn me." Georgia Democrats had contemptuously referred to the legislation he sponsored dealing with elections during the last session as "Whiteley's Election Bill." Eschewing political motivations, Whiteley explained that the bill "was offered to secure good order and prevent fraud," and "if the Democratic party desire that end, why they should be so sorely exercised in regard to it." As for the Civil Rights Bill, Whiteley downplayed its effect and maintained that the measure merely envisioned guaranteeing blacks "public rights." In their private lives, Whiteley explained, people controlled whom they did or did not associate with. A person's privacy, home, and associations, he argued, could never be threatened by a federal law. "Social equality can only exist by your own choice and consent," he rationalized. Couching a radical idea in more palatable terms, he reasoned that extending civil rights to blacks promoted a more content and industrious workforce. Cooperation between those who owned capital (whites) and others providing the labor (blacks), was essential. Whites could expect "peace and prosperity," he continued pragmatically, and blacks "will rejoice in rights that will gladden their hearts." He pleaded: "I ask you to carefully ponder over these inquiries and say if your Representative has betrayed either race in his support of the Civil Rights Bill."[32]

Beginning in the hot summer and continuing into the cooler autumn, Whiteley traveled throughout the rural district. He advertised his speeches at Quitman and Dawson on successive Saturdays, and he challenged his Democratic opponent: "I invite the Hon. Wm. E. Smith to attend each of these appointments, and discuss the issues of the day upon equal terms."[33]

Wherever Whiteley spoke—Cairo, Morgan, Thomasville—the incumbent listed what he had done for southwest Georgians in Washington. In a district where poverty was chronic, he made a proletarian pitch, championing the downtrodden. The Democratic Party emerged as the purveyor of "caste, prejudice, intolerance, [and] hate." Affirmation of the Civil Rights Bill, with some qualifications, was also standard. Answering those who played racially to the white man's fears, Whiteley warned: "passion not reason is what they invoke."[34]

Whiteley made one of his earliest appearances on September 12 at Quitman. A ride west over the Atlantic and Gulf Railroad took him to the Brooks County seat of some thirteen hundred people. None of the residents was more opposed to Republicanism than J. C. Gallaher, a one-armed former Confederate major, and the editor of *Gallaher's Independent.* He was one of about two hundred people assembling at the courthouse to hear Whiteley. The incumbent delivered what became his standard reelection speech. Anxious to convince whites, he pointed to his efforts to remove political disabilities. Whiteley documented the appropriations he had gained for improving Georgia rivers and also his successful efforts to increase the number of post offices in the district. Attempting to calm white fears, he explained that the Civil Rights Bill would not result in whites and blacks sitting on the same railroad car and attending school together. Gallaher described as "good advise" Whiteley's admonition to the freedpeople regarding the value of work and upright behavior. On balance, however, Gallaher objected to Whiteley's "self-glorifying" and how he seemed to base his appeal to blacks on what the Civil Rights Bill would do for them, as he played down the consequences to whites. The demonstratively anti-Republican editor mocked Whiteley with a wood-engraved political cartoon capturing his alleged falseness.[35]

William Smith belatedly began his campaign several weeks after Whiteley, and proved a ponderous and unexciting candidate, possessing none of his opponent's flair for politics and not as accomplished at repartee. The decision not to accept Whiteley's debate invitation was well advised.

At Nashville, in Berrien County, Smith made his first appearance on September 22. In a county where 90 percent of the population was white, Smith could be sure of a sympathetic audience. At Nashville, and elsewhere, he condemned, in a rote-like way, civil rights legislation as unnatural and unnecessary. His opponent, he reminded listeners, favored forcing on Georgians the dangerous vision of Radical Republicans. If Whiteley minimized the consequences of a civil rights law, Smith maximized them. It was much the same message elsewhere. The limp the one-legged candidate walked with testified to past sacrifices. A decade removed from the war, the Nashville crowd and other audiences concluded that the ex-Confederate was conducting an equally gallant campaign.

No effort was spared to bring about the downfall of the man state Democrats considered Georgia's most infamous congressman. Spokesmen entered the district to praise Smith and denounce his opponent. John B. Gordon and Benjamin H. Hill were the two most prominent visitors. Gordon had been the governor of Georgia in the 1850s and was heralded even more as a Civil War general. Hill was a former United States senator and Confederate congressman. They spoke together on several occasions. Both provided the oratory at Thomasville, the Thomas County seat, on September 30. Whites from Dougherty, Mitchell, Brooks, and Lowndes counties arrived on excursionist railroad cars and joined local Democrats assembled under a grove of oak trees on the Fletcher Institute campus. An estimated fifteen hundred people were there. Smith spoke briefly before deferring to Gordon. One listener noted "the mere presence of Georgia's greatest soldier" and the scathing indictment of Republicanism delivered by Gordon and Hill. On October 1, the next day, the exercise was repeated at Bainbridge in front of another huge crowd. Former Confederate soldiers strained to shake Gordon's hand, Whiteley was denounced in his own political backyard, and much Democratic barbecue was consumed. That Smith barely spoke was irrelevant.[36]

All of white society seemed to have a stake in the outcome. At Bainbridge, when the local Central Democratic Club met, an invitation was extended to women, who did not usually attend political events. Whiteley's opponents maintained that what he advocated threatened society and that as members of society, women had a place at the meeting. That the civil rights measure invited black ravishment of Caucasian women was assumed. The *Thomasville Times* decided that the white man who voted Republican "ought to have his wife and daughters confiscated by the government for the benefit of the negroes."[37] When a young widow and her daughter took some flowers to the cemetery in Albany, a black man accosted them and made some distasteful remarks. The *Albany News* cited the Civil Rights Bill as encouraging such impudence and declared: "Whiteley is the Head Devil in this part of the State—let him look to his personal safety."[38]

Opponents condemned Whiteley in unprecedented terms. The *Albany News* decried the "social equality propagandist," his "leveling dogma," and the "pandora's box of evil and infamy Mr. Whiteley voted to open upon the country."[39] The *Cuthbert Appeal* labeled Whiteley the "radical Civil-Rights-social equality white skinned negro candidate."[40]

The few whites supporting (or even suspected of supporting) him endured severe ostracism. Some Bainbridge residents turned on W. M. Cooper, a fellow citizen, because they believed him sympathetic to Republicanism. The embattled man felt compelled to publish a note in the *Bainbridge Democrat* announcing: "I am opposed to Radicalism, the Civil Rights bill, Whiteley, and the Devil." A heightened political awareness was unmistakable. At Democratic meetings crowds were large, more enthusiastic than usual, and obviously committed to defeating Richard Whiteley.[41]

The rumor that Whiteley had fathered an illegitimate child by an unknown woman in Washington had circulated previously in the Second District. Only now, though, during the campaign, were charges to that effect made public, by an anonymous Bainbridge resident, and happily printed by Benjamin Russell in the *Bainbridge Democrat.* The letter's author maintained that Whiteley had "licentiously and lustfully violated the most sacred of all obligations." The allegations, though they do not seem to have dogged Whiteley during the campaign, further called his character into question.[42]

This barrage forced Whiteley to the defensive. In the *Bainbridge Sun*'s columns and at speaking engagements, he continued to explain that the social relations of whites and blacks were not affected by the contemplated civil rights legislation. State laws gave proprietors latitude regarding arrangements on railroad cars, steamboats, and places of amusement. Neither did his reading of the bill force integrated schools. Acknowledging whites' concerns about schools, he promised: "I shall move to strike out this portion of the bill."[43] Some agonized about blacks buried in white cemeteries. Whiteley doubted "that the bones of a colored person would interfere with our rest in the grave," and neither "would we be the less prepared for the trial and judgment that must follow that sleep." Whiteley could only hope that his logic and pleading would have effect. In moments of honest introspection, though, he must have doubted that he could shake white fears.[44]

Politics competed for attention that fall with the usual affairs of daily life. Cotton-laden wagons were a familiar sight by September. At the Atlantic and Gulf depot in Thomasville, where much of the cotton was shipped, activity was steady. Thomasville residents noted the progress of the Mitchell's Hotel building; three stories had been raised, and an admirer predicted the hotel would be "one of the finest in the state."[45] At the small Clay County courthouse in Fort Gaines, the convening of Superior Court woke the sleepy village. Meanwhile, at Camilla, "great work" was accomplished at a revival. In Brooks County, a large crowd turned out for competition between the Social Baseball Club of Quitman and a visiting Florida team. The opposition was leading thirteen to three when heavy rain ended the game, saving the home nine from further embarrassment.[46]

The facade of normality masked a revived pattern of intimidation. Dramatically increased violence, so evident elsewhere in the South during the fall political season, was apparent in the Second District of Georgia. Edward C. Wade, United States commissioner for the Southern District of Georgia, was aware of extreme disorder. Writing from Quitman, Wade informed Henry Farrow that "the condition of affairs is worse than I have language to describe." Wade, a longtime Quitman resident, had been well respected before his conversion to Republicanism in 1872. He wrote of threats and concluded: "no fair election can be held here."[47] In September, the white Republican Louis Guild—the Calhoun County physician connected to the Internal Revenue Department—wrote to alert United States attorney general George Williams to the violent tactics being used to defeat Whiteley. Democrats mistreated black and white Republicans; "armed bodies of *ku klux* are frequently patroling."[48]

Solomon Wise Parker in Dawson, a lawyer and former solicitor general, gave Attorney General Williams more testimony from southwest Georgia. He predicted that intimidation and ballot box fraud would carry the day for the Democrats. Having lived in the area his entire life, Parker claimed some understanding of the population. He explained to Grant's attorney general that many of them were "hot headed unreasonable kind of people" who "think the Negro ought to be their Slave." He added: "it has been said upon the streets in this town that I ought to be hung for advocating the return of the Hon. R. H. Whiteley to Congress."[49] Benjamin Brimberry, the state senator from Camilla, described a menacing situation in Mitchell County. A group of whites had interrupted a Republican Club meeting recently. Hardships awaited any white man, Brimberry wrote to Commissioner Edward Wade, "who dares say he intends to vote or act with the Republican Party."[50] Wade understood the mentality and speculated: "God only knows what we are coming to."[51]

Whiteley shared that concern. He got a personal taste of the bitterness at Valdosta early in September. About a dozen men, clanging pots and ringing bells, shouted insults as Whiteley stepped from an Atlantic and Gulf railroad car. Over the cacophony, Whiteley heard profane references to the Civil Rights Bill, and as for him specifically, the threat that "no damned radical ought to be allowed to walk the streets." Joshua Griffin, a leading Republican, escorted Whiteley to his home. The crowd followed, keeping up a barrage of insults, and after Whiteley and Griffin entered the house, some fired shots into the air. The eventful visit,

Whiteley wrote the next week in the *Sun,* called into question whether "in a free country a candidate if not a Representative could visit the people."[52]

These were among the last words Whiteley ever communicated through the newspaper. Two weeks later, the office of the *Bainbridge Sun* burned to the ground. One of the worst fires in the town's history began shortly after eight o'clock on Sunday morning, September 20. Flames apparently spread from a stable just behind the Sanborn Block Building. Within minutes, various stores were up in flames, and the fire, crossing West Street, engulfed the Presbyterian Church, even as the bell in its belfry sounded the alarm. The entire block south of the courthouse was threatened before the Stonewall and Oak City fire companies, aided by freedmen, finally brought the blaze under control. That Sunday morning, or soon thereafter, Whiteley inspected the charred remains of the *Sun* press and his law office. He bitterly attributed the fire to political arsonists.

He was probably correct. Thomas Swearingen and John Higdon, both local Republicans, had been recently victimized by arson. The latest fire had started on a Sunday morning when no one had been present to sound an alarm. A consequence of the fire also suggests criminal activity: the silencing of the *Bainbridge Sun,* a party journal that reached a wide reading (and voting) public. Destroying a newspaper press was a well-established tradition in America. It is also possible that the fire was accidental. Two months earlier, a major fire had caused considerable destruction in Bainbridge. Whatever the truth, arson or not, Whiteley had lost the forum from which he addressed most voters. The *Sun* office in the Sanborn Block Building and the press was all but completely destroyed.[53]

As usual, the state elections preceded the federal elections by a month. On October 7, Governor James Smith carried every county but three and was easily reelected, and the Democrats routed Republicans in the legislative races. The tallies could only have discouraged Whiteley. The trend held in the Second District, where Smith won convincingly. Whiteley had proclaimed at the Bainbridge courthouse square that his reelection depended on gaining a large majority in Decatur County. The defeat of Republican legislative candidates John Hayes and Alexander Nicholson in the party stronghold of Decatur did not bode well.

William Smith continued to batter Whiteley with the Civil Rights Bill. In early October, he appeared before audiences on successive days at Dawson, Cuthbert, and Georgetown; after honoring the Sabbath on October 11, he followed with five days of speechmaking at Morgan, Fort Gaines, Blakely, Colquitt, and Newton. At the Early County courthouse at Blakely, on October 14, blacks and whites listened to Smith outline the mutually beneficial relationship between white landlords and black tenants. He warned freedpeople of their "pretended political friends." Treating freedpeople fairly and opposing the Civil Rights Bill, Smith insisted, was not incongruent. At every engagement, he condemned the legislation, hammering away at the theme with numbing but telling efficiency. His opponent had voted for the measure once and, if given the chance, Smith assured audiences, would surely do so again.[54]

Whiteley campaigned even harder, in far more modest settings, and summoning all his political skills. At Quitman, Whiteley worked at solidifying his base, warning blacks against believing Democratic promises. One observer wrote of him "prowl[ing] at night among the cabins and haunts of his colored constituents."[55] Whiteley described to whites a Democratic Party that offered them nothing and whose policies penalized those who had little. No place seemed too small. In Decatur County, the self-proclaimed "working man's candidate" or the "peoples candidate" appeared at rural precincts such as Higdon's Store, Whigham, and Limesink.[56] There and elsewhere, falling back on his considerable political savvy, Whiteley targeted "hot-headed Democrats" who, he charged, do nothing but "whittle on goods boxes and talk politics."[57]

In October, after the *Sun* fell silent, Whiteley issued a circular further qualifying his civil rights position. He explained: "the civil rights bill as passed the Senate and I voted on it in the House as your Representative does not require either mixed schools, or a mixture of the races in the same cars."[58] The *Thomasville Times* responded by recalling the story "of the thief who, to conceal his own villainy, joined loudest in the hue and cry of 'Stop Thief.'" Most considered Whiteley's efforts to minimize the contemplated legislation's effect labored at best and dishonest at worst. Because he championed the Civil Rights Bill before largely black audiences and took a different position in front of whites, Democrats chastised him as "Slippery Dick Whiteley."[59]

"As the election draws near," a Thomasville resident observed, "politics absorbs everything else." On Tuesday, November 3, William Smith decisively defeated Whiteley. He received 12,050 votes and Whiteley 9,731. The much-reviled scalawag's demise touched off enthusiastic celebrations. Framed by torches and, surely, warmed by spirits, citizens staged a nighttime parade at Camilla. A festive atmosphere prevailed at Blakely, where townspeople assembled at the courthouse square early on Saturday evening, November 7. Torchbearers, the Early County Guards, and the Blakely Cornet Band made up part of the procession that began there. Some participants waved signs with crude etchings. One pictured

Whiteley with two faces. One face, colored black, was shown as spreading the word of social equality to blacks; the white face denied to whites that civil rights would affect them.[60]

Whiteley was far more disappointed than surprised by this defeat. The causes, he realized, could be attributed to the fears and the level of political excitement that the issue of civil rights raised. Politically slumbering Democrats had been awakened by the warnings of the consequences of the Civil Rights Bill becoming law. Over three thousand more Democratic votes had been cast in 1874 than two years earlier when Whiteley had defeated Gilbert Wright. At Fort Gaines in Clay County, one observer noted: "the Democrats were aroused to the importance of the issue . . . and nearly every man turned out."[61] That was true elsewhere. "The support of the civil rights bill," another Democrat wrote from the county seat of Morgan, "has lost Mr. Whiteley many votes in Calhoun."[62] A white Bainbridge resident, who had previously voted for Whiteley, cast his ballot for Smith because "never, never, will we consent for them [blacks] to be forced upon us, upon terms of social equality at these places."[63] All Whiteley's instincts, persuasive abilities, oratorical powers, and shrewdness could not overcome this mindset. In his published address opening the campaign, Whiteley had warned whites: "you will be told by designing politicians that the object and effect of the Civil Rights bill will be to force social equality." His victorious opponent and others had done so, and the majority of listeners had believed them. For many voters, it had been more important to defeat Richard Whiteley than to elect William Smith. An inflammatory issue, more than a candidate, had defeated Whiteley.

In Bainbridge, contemplating the consequences of defeat and the seemingly bleak future of Republicanism in Georgia, Whiteley apparently considered moving his family to Washington and practicing law. More immediately, though, there was the final session of the Forty-third Congress to participate in, and he prepared for the trip to Washington. The railroad journey to the nation's capital would seem longer this time.[64]

10 *The Ablest and Strongest Radical in the District*

In December 1874, when the Forty-third Congress reconvened, Whiteley would join many lame-duck Republicans in Washington. In the midterm elections, Democrats gained control of the House of Representatives for the first time since the beginning of the Civil War and, incredibly, turned a Republican seat majority of 110 into a 60–seat Democratic one. In the Northeast, the Midwest, and the far West, concerns about race, the poor economy, and scandals connected to the Grant administration damaged the Republican cause. The civil rights question had utterly devastated southern Republicans; so had violence directed at their party. As Congress opened in December, Grant in his annual message called for a congressional committee to investigate the political lawlessness. Not a single Georgia Republican had won a seat to the Forty-fourth Congress; elsewhere, southern Republicans had fared little better.

Writ large, Richard Whiteley's loss offered a sign of the political times and was indicative of the Republican Party's future in the South. On a smaller and personal level, defeat caused Whiteley to make plans to return to Bainbridge and his law practice on a full-time basis. Early in December, after settling in at the National Hotel on Pennsylvania Avenue, Whiteley informed Ben Perley Poore, Congress's unofficial historian: "my residence for the session will be the National Hotel and . . . I shall be alone." Only ten weeks of the Forty-third Congress remained. Stepping from his hotel each morning, Whiteley dressed warmly, for the winter was brutal. On several occasions the temperature fell below zero, freezing the Potomac River from bank to bank by mid-January.[1]

"For about four years I have had the honor to represent you in Congress," Whiteley had reminded voters during the recent campaign. He continued: "however, some of you may differ with me as to the course I have thought best to pursue, I hope all will concede that my motives have been good." Whether they did or not, that period of representation was coming to an end. Whiteley attended to different concerns in his final weeks in Washington. They included acting in behalf of the African Methodist Episcopal Church at Marietta, Georgia. In 1864, William Sherman's Army of the Tennessee had taken pews, doors, and even the pulpit from that church, and Union soldiers had built rough coffins from the confiscated materials. Whiteley introduced a petition calling for compensation in the amount of $700 for the African Methodist Episcopal church. Increasing the navigability of Georgia rivers remained important. On January 11, 1875, he asked for more funds for improving the Flint and Chattahoochee rivers. His requests were partly complied with. A significant appropriation, $25,000 for the Chattahoochee and $5,000 for the Flint, was eventually provided. Yet the congregation at Marietta continued to wait for reimbursement.[2]

Earlier, during the recent campaign, in what he could not have known would be the last issue of the *Bainbridge Sun,* Whiteley had criticized Democrats' extremism in Georgia. He decried their demagogic misrepresentations and charged them with appealing to the "passion and prejudice of people," asking: "Is it to be wondered at, that we meet and see so much lawlessness?" A week later, the press had been consumed by flames. Now, in Washington, embittered by the campaign and the destruction of the *Sun,* Whiteley turned with strong purpose toward rectification. A week after the session began, Whiteley asked Congress to establish a commission for investigating political conditions in the South. A week later, just before the Christmas recess, he introduced a measure similar to the election bill he had sponsored the previous session. He proposed placing deputy marshals at the polls and keeping ballots, votes, and tally sheets. The resolute congressman began 1875 as he ended 1874. On January 18, he called for the establishment of an additional district judge, district attorney, and marshal for the state of Georgia. Whiteley's proposals reflected the concerns of a man fully cognizant of extreme and longstanding election irregularities. They also represented the actions of an angry man who had personally confronted defiant elements in Georgia's Second Congressional District. Although none of his initiatives concerning elections cleared committee, he became in the last weeks of the Congress a leading spokesman regarding the southern situation.[3]

The eternal patronage struggles continued. As the New Year opened, "Specks" reported, "it cannot be denied that Whiteley controls the patronage of the state."[4] Alexander Allen, a Bainbridge lawyer, begrudgingly admitted Whiteley's influence. Any personal friendship between him and Whiteley had vanished by 1875. Swallowing his pride, though, Allen did write Whiteley seeking an appointment for his brother. Expecting little, Allen informed his brother, "Whiteley is such a skunk of a Radical that I suppose that he will not serve me or you either."[5] A battle over the Macon postmastership drew Whiteley's attention. In 1873, he had helped Edwin Belcher, a black man, gain that position. Jefferson Long, the influential black Republican in Macon, charged Belcher with poor management and financial abuses at the post office. Whiteley defended Belcher in visits to both President Grant and postmaster general Marshall Jewell in January. Among the reasons to resist a change, Whiteley must have maintained, was the necessity of keeping blacks in office. As the controversy continued, "Specks" reported: "it remains to be seen whether Whiteley has the power to keep Belcher."[6]

It also remained to be determined whether he had the power to remove Charles Arnold from the position of postmaster at Albany. Whiteley's efforts to replace him with Frank Putney were probably partly attributable to Arnold's opposition in the last campaign (apparently Whiteley did not bear a grudge against Putney). Removing Arnold also had a direct bearing on Benjamin Brimberry's becoming the deputy collector of internal revenue in the region. Putney held that position, but if he gained the Albany postmastership, Brimberry could succeed him as the deputy collector. It is impossible to say whether helping his longtime friend Brimberry or punishing a foe such as Arnold was foremost for Whiteley. He could take satisfaction in either. It was the kind of Machiavellian maneuvering at which he excelled. Once again he called on Grant at the White House. According to the *Savannah Morning News*'s correspondent in Washington, Whiteley made "strenuous efforts" to force Arnold from the Albany postmastership.[7]

Whiteley also remained an implacable enemy of Sam Bard. He had bitterly fought Bard's appointment as the Atlanta postmaster the previous spring. Benjamin Conley, long desiring some position, wanted the postmastership and enlisted Whiteley's support. "Specks" soon wrote: "Whiteley is chaperoning the slaughtering party and pressing Sam Bard." Whiteley believed that removing Bard was in the interests of the state

Republican Party, and particularly if Conley replaced him. Appointing Conley would mean rewarding one loyal to Republicanism and punishing another who had not been. Whiteley had a special distaste for Bard. As with the postmaster situation at Macon and Albany, the question remained temporarily unresolved.

The fifty-six working days that closed out the Forty-third Congress were surprisingly eventful. Acting on the reality that Democrats controlled the next House, Republicans considered civil rights and enforcement legislation. A bill passed that resembled the controversial civil rights legislation that had been considered during the last session: the Civil Rights Act of 1875. It gave blacks equal access to railroad cars and hotels, as well as accommodations and places of amusement, but did not provide for integrating schools and mixing in cemeteries.

In the heat of the recent campaign against William Smith, Whiteley had backed up, prevaricated, and compromised his position on civil rights. Doing so represented the maneuvering of a politician desperately seeking reelection. His support of the Civil Rights Act of 1875 was the act of an exiting congressman free to vote his conscience.[8]

Whiteley was equally committed to protecting southern Republicans. Recent election crimes had revived the cry for action against political outlaws in the South. The violence that marred the recent election in the Second District fit into the context of trouble throughout the region during the political season. In Tennessee, a black candidate for the legislature was murdered. In Alabama's Black Belt, in two separate incidents, two men who had campaigned for the Republican Party were ambushed and killed. By means of a campaign of intimidation in Louisiana, Democrats had temporarily replaced Republican governor, William P. Kellogg. Attorney General Williams had sent troops during the election to keep order in Arkansas, Alabama, Georgia, Louisiana, South Carolina, and Tennessee. Adding immediacy to the situation since the election was the debacle in December at Vicksburg, Mississippi, where virtual race war resulted in the deaths of about three hundred blacks. Unless action was taken, Republican principles would be squandered, and the debilitated southern wing of the party would face impotency.

As Whiteley left the House of Representatives in 1875, much as when he had first entered Congress four years earlier, Democrats and Republicans disagreed about southern conditions. The congressman may have fatalistically reflected that little had changed. The situation in the ex-Confederacy was the subject when southern House Republicans caucused on the night of December 19. Several congressmen, including Whiteley, were appointed to a committee that was to meet with a similar committee drawn from the Senate. Alexander White (Alabama), Horace Maynard (Tennessee), James H. Platt (Virginia), and John Lynch (Mississippi) were his fellow House members; all but Lynch had been defeated the previous fall. Drafting a major piece of enforcement legislation was their purpose. House Republicans caucused frequently at night and considered corrective action in January and February. On the evening of February 12, Republicans continued their discussions past midnight. Whiteley spoke that night, and though what he said is not known, he must have provided a personal perspective from Georgia.

The Force Bill devolved out of these concerns. The proposed legislation increased the power of federal deputy marshals and election supervisors, provided guidelines for vote counting, and prohibited unreasonable poll taxes. Allowing the president to suspend the writ of habeas corpus was the most controversial provision. The battle split the House during the final days of Congress. Democrats replied to Republican demands for order by pointing to a partisan "outrage mill" that generated mythical crimes for political reasons. Dominating debate on February 27, with discussion carrying beyond midnight, the bill passed by a vote of 135 to 114. Whiteley cast his vote for the Force Bill during the early hours of February 28. The Forty-third Congress ended several days later without the Senate considering the measure.[9]

As he had before, Whiteley remained in Washington as the Senate made final patronage decisions in executive session. He lost the battle to keep Edwin Belcher on as postmaster at Macon. Blaming Postmaster General Jewell, Whiteley would soon write blisteringly of "the supreme folly of Jewell who has as much conceit and as little brains as you could hope to find in one man." Nor was he successful in having Frank Putney replace Charles Arnold as Albany postmaster. The outcome at the Atlanta post office did please him. Whiteley had played a significant role in engineering Bard's exit and Benjamin Conley's appointment. The assignment of Benjamin Brimberry as the deputy collector of internal revenue provided further satisfaction.

With a distinct melancholy and understanding that his career as a congressman was over, Whiteley packed his bags at the National Hotel in March. Leaving behind a place and a life was difficult. He told friends and colleagues goodbye, and departed the nation's capital on a southbound train on the evening of March 19. It is impossible to know whether his farewells included Catherine Carmody, or their daughter Cecilia, by now a little girl three years old.[10]

Richard Whiteley was forty-five years old when he returned to private life in Bainbridge. He could look to the future optimistically. He and Margaret and their four children lived in a fine home. Providing liberally for his family was easy for a man who practiced law profitably and owned hundreds of acres of land. His career as an editor had ended, however. Thoughts of reviving the *Bainbridge Sun* never advanced past the thinking stage.

The Bainbridge Whiteley returned to differed mostly only in detail from other small southern towns. Occasional events such as the arrival in 1875 of John Robinson's Great World Exposition punctuated periods of relentless tedium. If somewhat disappointed by the advertised (but largely absent) musicians, clowns, and wild animals, the crowd enjoyed the equestrian performances. Some residents watched and others played baseball; the *Bainbridge Democrat* announced the sport "is all the rage."[11] The arrival and placement of a 518-pound fire bell in a tower on the courthouse grounds caused local comment. Eliciting far less favorable notice was the deteriorating Female College building. Started before the war but abandoned when the conflict began, the building, battered by the elements and fifteen years of neglect, was a "colossal pile of bricks and mortar."[12]

If Bainbridge was typical in some ways, it was different from other southern municipalities in one respect: Republicans maintained political control of local government. Attempting to rouse Democrats before a local election in January 1875, the *Bainbridge Democrat* had remarked: "we hope our readers have not forgotten Whiteley . . . and the attendant deviltries of Radicalism." On January 6, with more blacks than whites voting, the Republicans triumphed. Two allies of Whiteley, William W. Harrell (sheriff) and Thomas Hampton (clerk of the Superior Court), among other Republicans, were elected. Randall Kinney, the well-known black man, became coroner.[13]

Whiteley's departure from Congress did not end his political involvement. He maintained contact with some state Republicans and probably some national party members as well. Within a week of returning to Bainbridge, he received a letter from Benjamin Conley. Their mutual interest in the state Republican Party caused the disillusioned Whiteley to reply: "I have seen so many evidences of the perversity of our friends and their jealousy that I fear to express my opinion in regard to matters beyond my immediate locality."[14] Later in 1875, when Henry Farrow successfully sought reappointment as United States attorney general in Georgia, Whiteley endorsed him as "a man of ability, nerve and character." No less important, in Whiteley's mind, he considered Farrow a "pronounced Republican."[15]

Whatever people thought of the ex-congressman, and some disapproved of him for any number of reasons, his family did not share that opprobrium. The Whiteleys remained well liked and active in the community. Charles was still attempting to recover his health. His wife, Josephine, gave birth to their second child the month Whiteley returned from Washington. In their midteens, Montie and Richard continued their educations at the local white school, where a new principal pledged: "it will be my object to give to the citizens of Bainbridge a first class school."[16] Both boys were also involved in local baseball. Hortense was six in 1875, and Zena celebrated her fourth birthday in July. Their lives, though surely more privileged, were also similar to those of other girls their age. Hortense did perform in a play put on by children on November 4 in the dining room of the Sharon Hotel. A member of the audience concluded that she looked "as etherial [*sic*] and angelic as the winged seraphim she represented."[17]

Just as her husband's victories had no bearing on Margaret's standing locally, neither did his defeat. On May 6, 1875, at a parade, dinner, and ball marking the seventh anniversary of the Oak City Fire Company, Margaret presented the firemen with a cake. She was also the unofficial patron of the Bainbridge Stars, a baseball team, which formed that spring. The Stars, outfitted in white uniforms trimmed in blue, competed against other clubs in the area. Montie played various positions (catcher, pitcher, and shortstop), gaining recognition for his abilities. Richard often acted as a "scorer." After a contest against the Occidental Club of Quincy, the *Bainbridge Democrat* thanked "our young friend R. H. Whiteley" for making game details available to the paper.[18] Charles played the organ when a spelling bee benefit was staged for the Stars at Hopson Hall on July 2, and one listener complimented him as "more than an ordinary performer."[19] Later that month, the Stars took the field against the visiting Wide Awakes from Valdosta. Montie handled the catching duties, and Richard scored the game. Charles umpired and magnanimously gave the "visiting club the benefit of all doubts." Margaret Whiteley was also evenhanded. She provided the Wide Awakes and the Stars with ice cream after the game.

The marriage of Richard and Margaret Whiteley seemed solid. On November 29, 1875, they celebrated their twenty-fifth anniversary. Custom may have dictated separate public observances. Friends of the ex-congressman came by the law office, champagne was opened, and toasts were offered to the marriage. Several blocks away on Evans Street, local women called on Margaret at home.

Although their Sanborn Block Building law offices had been destroyed by the fire the previous September, Whiteley and John Donalson entered their sixth year as partners in 1875. They established new offices in a recently constructed two-story brick building across from the courthouse on Broughton Street. Henry B. Ehrlich, who owned the building, sold groceries on the first floor. The Ehrlich Building was one of the most handsome in town, and it was fitting that it housed the firm of Whiteley and Donalson.[20]

Court and litigation, presumably, kept Whiteley busy. When Superior Court convened in May 1875, Whiteley became involved in a trial that gained wide local attention. Several months earlier, on the night of December 10, 1874, Ferdinand Miller had shot and killed Tommie R. Cloud at a Bainbridge bar. Richard Sims, a local lawyer, had been drinking with Cloud. As words and passions between Cloud and Miller escalated, Sims fired a pistol shot without effect. Authorities later charged him with intending to kill Miller. An active Democrat, Sims had strongly opposed Whiteley. That did not prevent him from asking the Republican to act with his defense team. Nor did past political differences preclude Whiteley from agreeing to do so. He helped gain Sims's acquittal.

Some progress among the local freedpeople heartened Whiteley. Blacks in Bainbridge continued to attend the Whittier School. Some freedpeople worshipped at the African Methodist Episcopal Church or at a local Baptist church attended exclusively by blacks. An August revival attracted many, and about twenty blacks were baptized in the Flint's waters down at the wharf. The freedman Hiram Wood, a model citizen, belonged to the police force. The *Bainbridge Democrat* praised him as "ever watchful, on the alert, and always at his post." Whites and blacks were saddened when Alexander Nicholson was thrown from a mule in September and killed. Nicholson had served in the legislature as a Republican but was widely liked by whites. As elsewhere in the South, the fire company that Bainbridge blacks organized was largely social in purpose. A black baseball team also took the field. Other realities, Whiteley realized, tempered these signs of racial accord. Freedpeople remained chronically poor.[21]

Whiteley must have noted an increasing sense of patriotism among fellow townspeople. Whites in Bainbridge observed the Fourth of July in 1875 for the first time since before the Civil War. A ceremony Margaret participated in on November 11 provided more encouragement: an audience gathered at Hopson Hall for the presentation of a silk American flag to the local militia company, the Bainbridge Independents. Presumably, Whiteley looked on as his wife handed the flag to William Fleming, a local lawyer. If Whiteley did not pen the words his wife read when she presented the flag, he certainly agreed with them. Margaret asked: "May

I not assume that we have returned out our first love and recognize this emblem as the common flag of our country, the standard of a common brotherhood?" Like much about her, the extent of Margaret's interest in politics cannot be known. Nonetheless, she was an intelligent woman, with considerable self-confidence, and it would have been natural for her to have such an interest.[22]

Almost a year of private life in Bainbridge had passed for Whiteley when Judge Gilbert Wright (his opponent in 1872) convened Superior Court early in February 1876. The *Bainbridge Democrat* had recently announced: "there are a good many prisoners in jail, and the Judge is endeavoring to clear it out." Blacks were a large majority of the prison population, and Whiteley provided legal counsel to some. Among his clients were Joe Daniels and Calvin Mills, both freedmen, charged with larceny. After pleading guilty on Whiteley's advice, they began a six-month stay in the county jail.[23]

Some inmates languished in the two dungeons at the two-story brick jail. Deprived of ventilation or any light, these prisons were "totally unfit for the occupancy of even the most hardened criminal," a critic declared.[24] Life outside the jail walls was not much better for many whites and blacks. Local farmers had suffered terribly in the last few years as the depression wore obdurately on. Some abandoned crops, forced sometimes to turn unfed horses out to grass. Landlords at times could not pay freedmen tenants. Over nine hundred farmers belonged to and placed some faith in the recently formed Patrons of Husbandry or Grange chapter. Julius Steininger, who owned the Flint River Stores, noted "alarming" insolvency that spring, and he urged the creation of a stock company to raise funds for the poor.[25]

Whiteley understood the unforgiving realities. He also attributed some problems to indolence. On Saturday, April 22, 1876, Decatur County Republicans transacted political business at a Bainbridge meeting. As he had since the war, Whiteley handed out advice to the freedpeople. He impressed upon them that "making bread and meat" should be their most important concern and urged them to obey the law and act responsibly. Even the normally hostile *Bainbridge Democrat* categorized the ex-congressman's remarks as "quite salutary."[26]

Whiteley empathized with the poor, although his family lived in a world far removed from want. Many of Bainbridge's gentility were present on the evening of March 8, 1876, for the town's first Grand Masquerade Ball. Dinner, dancing, and the unmasking of the participants highlighted what one participant termed "the most elegant and successful affair ever witnessed in our city." Judges determined that a "Blacksmith" and a

"Schoolgirl" wore the best costumes. Whiteley presented the prizes and made "a neat little speech."[27] In May, when the Oak City Fire Company commemorated its eighth anniversary, guests enjoyed food, dance, and the cake prepared by Margaret. In the meantime, the Bainbridge Stars prepared for the coming season. Noting Montie's selection as captain, the *Democrat* pronounced him "one of the very best players in Georgia."[28]

The centennial year of 1876 was one of political significance, since a presidential election would be held. The biennial rite in Georgia of contests for the governorship and the legislature was set for October. A month later, voters would make a presidential selection and send nine congressmen to Washington. In private moments, Whiteley was more than ever pessimistic about the future of Republicanism in the state. No Republicans represented Georgia in Congress. White attrition from the state Republican Party continued, there was almost no newspaper backing, and factionalism divided Georgia Republicans. His friend and ally, Benjamin Brimberry, was the only Republican sitting in the state senate. What Whiteley had once envisioned—a respectable and viable alternative to the Democratic Party in Georgia—seemed virtually impossible. Charles Nordhoff, a somewhat celebrated journalist, visited six southern states and published his observations in his book *The Cotton States in the Spring and Summer of 1875*. When he asked a prominent Georgia Republican about the condition of Republicanism in the state, Nordhoff was told: "I don't know that there is any Republican Party in the state."

Georgia Republicans held their state convention at Atlanta on May 3–4. Many of Whiteley's political friends attended. Among them were Amos Akerman, Edwin Belcher, Benjamin Conley, Henry Farrow, Andrew Sloan, and Edward Wade. Some enemies, or at least men Whiteley had been at odds with, were also present, including Charles Arnold and Jefferson Long. At Cincinnati, Republicans would nominate a national ticket in June, and settling on the Georgia delegation was the most important task for Republicans at Atlanta. James G. Blaine, Benjamin H. Bristow, Roscoe Conkling, and Oliver P. Morton were the leading candidates to succeed Grant. Differing opinions among national Republicans were reflected at the state convention, where each claimed support. Republicans agreed to a twenty-two-member delegation to the Cincinnati convention, and its members pledged allegiance to several of the candidates.

Whiteley apparently did not attend the convention. Although he was promoted as one of the four at-large delegates to Cincinnati, he was not selected. Whiteley supported Blaine for the presidency, and he helped assure that the two delegates from the Second District (Edward Wade and

Frank Putney) were pledged to the former speaker of the House. In his absence, Whiteley was appointed to the large (seventy members) State Central Committee that was formed at the convention.

The next month, in Cincinnati, Republicans nominated Rutherford B. Hayes for president and William A. Wheeler for vice-president. In St. Louis in June, Democrats settled on a ticket of Samuel J. Tilden and Thomas A. Hendricks.[29]

Whiteley remained the nominal party leader in the Second District. Acknowledging that he was busy practicing law, the *Bainbridge Democrat* conjectured: "so far as we know, [Whiteley] is out of politics." There was no reason to assume otherwise. Whiteley did not make public any political intentions during the spring or summer. Another campaign, though, and possibility of a return to Washington, appealed to him. One of the traits that made him an effective lawyer, a certain contentiousness, also pulled Whiteley to the political stage. He took satisfaction, even if success was not a corollary, in challenging a political opponent and party he held as reactionary and unresponsive to the people, black and white. The excitement and competition of a campaign attracted him, as well as the righteousness of his message. Second District Republicans would select someone on August 9 at Albany. Whiteley declined to seek the nomination, but he coyly admitted he would accept the nomination if the convention offered it to him. In Bainbridge, and elsewhere in the district, conventional wisdom held that Richard Whiteley was the candidate-in-waiting.[30]

A veteran candidate like Whiteley did not need to compose any formal acceptance remarks. If he did, though, he could have done so before traveling to Albany for the convention, for his nomination was not in any doubt. Blacks had always composed a sizeable percentage of the delegates at the Second District convention. An even larger than usual number of freedmen assembling at Albany on August 9 was an indication of the diminishing Republican support among district whites. The delegates nominated Whiteley by acclamation on the first ballot. He had recently expressed confidence to a Bainbridge resident that he could win, and he must have made that clear in his acceptance speech. Events at Albany did not surprise the *Southern Enterprise* in Thomasville; its editor considered the choice "cut and dry" and, given its inevitability, pronounced the convention a "perfect farce."[31]

Delegates at Albany who heard Whiteley pledge a strong campaign did not question his abilities. Democrats also warily respected the veteran Republican. "From our knowledge of his untiring efforts as a canvasser, and his unblushingness in political scheming," the *Early County News* warned, "we know that the contest in November will not be child's play."[32] The *Dawson Journal* echoed: "Whiteley is the ablest and strongest radical in the district." An objective Democrat might despise Whiteley but also conceded his political skills.[33]

Over a month later, in mid-September, Second District Democrats intended to nominate a candidate at Thomasville. William Smith had made known his intention to seek reelection. In the weeks before the convention, Democrats in Baker, Clay, Decatur, Dougherty, Early, Terrell, and Worth counties pledged their support. Yet Smith could not take the nomination for granted. In the southeastern part of the district, in Brooks and Lowndes counties, some Democrats doubted the congressman's ability to defeat Whiteley. Henry M. McIntosh, editor of the *Quitman Reporter,* considered Smith "too tame, too dry, too slow to make this race" and no match for the "adroit and slick-tongued Whiteley." McIntosh attributed Smith's victory in 1874 to the Civil Rights Bill, which had stirred the electorate. Without that galvanizing force, he doubted Smith could inspire voters. "The man for the hour is one who can defeat Richard Whiteley," McIntosh averred. He considered Henry G. Turner, a Quitman attorney, a better choice. Charles R. Pendleton, editor of the *Valdosta Times,* also praised Turner, and cautioned against a hasty coronation of Smith.[34]

Democrats met at Thomasville on September 13. Henry Turner was a candidate for the legislature, but another alternative, James L. Seward, a Thomasville lawyer, claimed some allegiance. William Fleming, the Bainbridge lawyer, moved that William Smith be nominated by acclamation. Opponents of the incumbent forced a ballot vote, which made it necessary for the nominee to gain two-thirds of the delegates' support. On the first ballot, Smith was renominated, receiving twenty-seven votes to Seward's eight. Yielding to party loyalty, the *Quitman Reader* soon endorsed Smith. So did Pendleton of the *Valdosta Times,* declaring: "we heartily go into the fight for him against Slippery Dick Whiteley."[35]

The rematch between Whiteley and Smith was waged on a different battleground from that of 1874. Race did not loom as large. "Negro suffrage and the Constitutional amendments are finalities," the *Bainbridge Democrat* had recently editorialized. Acknowledging further that since the Civil Rights Bill was a "dead letter," Benjamin Russell predicted "less race antagonism than ever before" in the coming congressional campaign. Gaining a measure of economic stability had partly replaced fears of racial mixing. Attracting capital to Georgia and establishing a better balanced economy were given much priority.[36]

Even so, the Republican Party remained the party of the black man, just as surely as the Democratic Party was the home of the white man. Charles Nordhoff, the visiting journalist, after talking with state Democrats and Republicans in Georgia, decided that both parties "unite in maintaining the color-line in politics." Yet, increasingly, even blacks were voting Democratic. Some were dissatisfied with specific Republican leaders or Republicanism. Others were influenced by whites they trusted and believed had their interests at heart. More unscrupulous whites bought off blacks with money, whiskey, and other bribes.[37]

Whiteley had lost to Smith by over twenty-three hundred votes two years earlier, but he had some reason for hope. More blacks than whites lived in the district, which had been the strongest Republican region in Georgia during Reconstruction. That the civil rights question would not galvanize Democrats provided a glimmer of optimism; a certain apathy among white voters had helped him in the past. Whiteley intended to focus on the economic plight of many in the district. As in the past, he would portray state Democrats as callous and unsympathetic to the struggling masses. Another line of attack involved portraying Governor James Smith's administration as financially wasteful and extravagant. By offering his own egalitarian ideas, and saddling his opponent with the Democratic yoke, Whiteley might return to Congress. His hope and, he knew, his only chance was that white men could put aside anti-Republican predispositions. The challenge was to establish that a man could have the South's interests at heart and belong to the Republican Party.

As the campaign began, Whiteley served notice of his intentions when he issued a printed address to Second District residents. "If elected to represent the Second District, that has in the past honored me with its confidence," the candidate pledged, "I can but say that my vote and my voice shall be given and raised in behalf of what I honestly believe to be the permanent interest and glory of Georgia and our whole country." The economic regeneration blueprint he outlined included attracting outside capital and promoting manufacturing interests. Extrapolating statistics from the state treasurer reports, Whiteley charged that the state's debt under Rufus Bullock had been less than that of Governor James Smith. Financial retrenchment was a theme nationwide, and though it was most earnestly first advanced by Democrats, Whiteley borrowed the cause of fiscal responsibility.[38]

At Thomasville, he enlarged on these concepts at an early campaign appearance on Saturday, August 26, speaking to a mixed crowd of whites and blacks. Pointing out that they had controlled the legislature since 1870, he blamed state Democrats for contributing to the economic despair. Responsibility for repealing the Homestead exemption and forcing an inequitable tax burden on the lowest classes lay with that party. In a region wedded to agriculture, the former textile mill operative advocated the encouragement of manufacturing and the mechanical arts. Foreign capital and labor, he maintained, must be enticed to Georgia. Whiteley carefully avoided the subject of civil rights. The year was 1876, not 1868, and ever the felicitous politician, he adjusted with the times. Half the audience in Thomasville was white, and one noticed that Whiteley "addressed himself almost entirely to them."[39]

Charles P. Hansell, editor of the *Southern Enterprise* in Thomasville, commended Whiteley for avoiding "strictly a political speech" and pronounced him "a man of clear head, good foresight, and telling delivery."[40] Less convinced, another Democrat observed that Whiteley appealed "to the prejudices of the poorer classes by attempting to show that Democratic legislation was all in the interest of the rich against the poor." At Thomasville, Whiteley was at his best—or, some would argue, his demagogic worst.[41]

Despite the candidate's efforts, the race question trumped all else. Whiteley fought that mindset when he appealed to the farmer in Camilla or the merchant in Quitman. It did not matter that the crop lien system wore the farmer down or that the merchant faced bankruptcy. Within days of Whiteley's nomination, a Calhoun County resident referred to "the arch traitor to his race Richard H. Whiteley." What white man, the same outraged Democrat asked, could support a candidate "who would make the degraded negro the fireside companion of his wife and daughters?" In Reconstruction Georgia, no matter how exaggerated, these statements drew political blood.[42]

Achieving rapport with the freedpeople came much easier to Whiteley. He often spoke in expansive terms of freedom, citizenship, and the Republican Party. That was the timeworn but effective message at a black church or any place where freedpeople congregated. In Lowndes County, where three political clubs of blacks of about 250 each had been formed, Whiteley commanded significant loyalty. Meeting at the black Methodist church in Dawson, freedpeople were of the same mind. Even black women were joining clubs and "working faithfully and diligently for their brother Richard."[43] There was a reason for that. At Blakely, the candidate proclaimed he had never "been untrue to the interest of the colored population."[44] In the southern part of the district, where black Republican clubs organized in Lowndes County, freedpeople were urged to pay their poll tax. William J. Harrell, a Bainbridge doctor who had performed heroically during the yellow fever epidemic, campaigned for Whiteley among Early County freedpeople. Word arrived from Calhoun County that blacks were intent on providing him with "a telling expression of their friendship."[45] Miller County freedmen in their clubs supposedly swore on the Bible to vote for him. Whiteley's audience at Fort Gaines on October 21 consisted mostly of what a political foe called "his colored brethren."[46] In the familiar confines of Decatur County, Sampson McFarland, a freedman, labored politically for him. A Democrat confirmed the obvious when he conceded that the Republican "has considerable power over the colored men."[47]

William Smith spoke widely and frequently, describing a Republican Party riddled with corruption from the White House to the lowest patronage offices. Only months earlier, a resolution of impeachment against secretary of war William W. Belknap for receiving bribes had passed the House, adding to the list of scandals associated with the Grant administration. Whiteley suffered by association. Smith preached financial responsibility, honest government, and a departure from a recent past that he described as sordid and fraudulent. The Democrat also reminded crowds of his opponent's voting record and emphasized Whiteley's support of the Civil Rights Bill. Any blacks in the audience heard the incumbent talk of Republican deception and unfulfilled promises to their race.[48]

Smith campaigned almost daily in October. Democrats cheered him at Dawson on October 9, and from there he traveled on successive days to Cuthbert, Georgetown, Fort Gaines, Blakely, and Colquitt. Brass bands, partisan crowds, and often some blacks received him warmly on his trek through the western part of the district. After a break on Sunday, October 15, Smith moved on to Bainbridge, Thomasville, Quitman, Valdosta, Mill Pond, and Nashville before looping back east to Isabella, Moultrie, Camilla, and Newton. Richard Kennon, the Fort Gaines lawyer and the Tilden/Hendricks elector for the Second District, traveled with him. Kennon promised "to make it lively for Whiteley . . . and make him think he has outlived his day."

On Tuesday, October 10, Smith spoke at Cuthbert. The crowd at Powell's Hall heard him recount Whisky Ring activities and berate Republicans for plundering the government. He connected Ulysses Grant to the wholesale corruption. The *Cuthbert Appeal* decided that Smith, "while no orator, is a clear, forcible, logical reasoner."[49] Three days later, on October 13, Smith provided basically the same message at Blakely. He contended that the House of Representatives, controlled by Democrats, had at least thwarted some Republican excesses. Smith referred the audience to Whiteley's voting record, which conformed to the Radical line. About twenty blacks listened to Smith point out the disparity between Republican promises and reality for the freedpeople. On October 17, a Tuesday, the Democrat found himself before a large crowd in the courtroom at the Thomas County courthouse. He enlarged on Republican skullduggery. Richard Kennon followed, and "held 'Slippery Dick' up in a most unenviable light."[50]

Some 144,000 Georgians participated in the gubernatorial contest on October 4. Alfred Colquitt, the Democratic candidate, received over 111,000 votes, devastating his Republican opponent, Jonathan Norcross, who received approximately 33,000 ballots. Only six years earlier, over 83,500 Republican votes had been cast for Rufus Bullock. Such was the standing and descent of the state Republican Party. As elsewhere in Georgia, Democrats clearly held the upper hand in the Second District. Some 12,425 Democratic ballots, compared to 7,688 Republican ones, were cast in Whiteley's district. It was the informed opinion of the *Southern Enterprise* in Thomasville that the Democratic majority represented a margin "we believe Whiteley cannot overcome."[51]

He was undeterred. As Whiteley journeyed over the familiar trek around the district, he usually made favorable reference to Rutherford B. Hayes, economic development, and fiscal prudence. Corroborating his accusations of Democratic financial mismanagement involved presenting statistics from official state documents. He routinely (if selectively) referred to financial expenditures that reflected poorly on Governor Smith's administration. Less clinically, and presumably more effectively, Whiteley described a human toll of misery, flaying the opposition for ignoring the poor.

On October 16, at the Early County courthouse, whites listened skeptically as the candidate labored to minimize differences between himself and them. Conveying a shared interest in reviving prosperity in Georgia was the intent. According to one witness present that day at Blakely, Whiteley seemed "anxious to make the impression upon his white hearers that it was only an honest difference of opinion that caused him to be a Republican and them to be Democrats." Exactly what words he reserved for William Smith are not known. (Democratic papers continued to denounce but rarely quote Whiteley.) At Cuthbert, on October 19, and then at Fort Gaines two days later, the candidate called for retrenchment and reform.[52]

He made few converts. Republican affiliation, no matter his public reasoning, remained to most whites disreputable, morally unacceptable, and seemingly heretical. As Whiteley went forward, he received predictable denunciation. "Shall we suffer the resurrection," one asked, "of the office-seeking negro-loving renegade, Richard H. Whiteley?"[53] He was condemned in Randolph County as one who "will mix and mingle with bad negroes in their midnight league."[54] Another, associating Whiteley and his misdeeds with the bewitching hour, accused him of walking "over his mother's grave at midnight to consort with negroes and concoct schemes of self-advancement."[55] Assuming that Whiteley's departure from his wedding vows was common knowledge, the *Early County News* maintained that his "debaucheries in Washington were a disgrace."[56]

The Republican scoffed at epithets, was unfazed by insult, and usually more than held his own when challenged by white listeners. But Whiteley knew he could not win. In a quiet acknowledgement of that reality, he told a Blakely audience that, if defeated, he "would not cry." A sense of conviction, duty and instinct for political combat sustained him, but not the prospect of victory. On Saturday, November 4, he spoke at Thomasville. An unusually large number of women were present, and Whiteley urged them to make sure their husbands voted on the following Tuesday.

Election Day, November 7, merely established the margin of his defeat. Smith received 13,600 votes and Whiteley 8,015. Of the seventeen counties in the district, Whiteley carried only Decatur, and that by just 51 votes. Smith received about a thousand more votes than in 1874, and Whiteley fell to seventeen hundred votes shy of his total in that election. Samuel Tilden swamped Hayes in Georgia. Both a man and a philosophy had been thoroughly repudiated. Many felt a personal and political loathing for Whiteley and reacted jubilantly to his defeat. Death was the macabre motif. Albany residents paraded with his coffin. A mock corpse representing him was buried in front of Benjamin Brimberry's residence in Camilla, and a black Democrat preached his funeral. Celebrating Democrats hanged Whiteley in effigy from a line supporting the Tilden and Hendricks flag on the Cuthbert town square. For several days after the contest, passing townspeople ridiculed the likeness of the defeated Republican.[57]

The causes of defeat were specific and general. Democrats controlled the press, resources in each county, and, increasingly, many freedpeople. The poll tax disfranchised whites and freedpeople but more often black Republicans. Whites continued to identify Richard Whiteley with civil rights and black equality, and his message to the lower classes attracted few. "Because men are poor," the *Thomasville Times-Enterprise* reasoned, "they are not necessarily mean enough to be voting for a man who thought they were not as good as a negro."[58] After hearing Whiteley speak, a listener with no intention of voting for him admitted that the Republican's argument was "ingenious." That Whiteley had run a hard and fine campaign was beside the point.[59]

Whiteley struggled against more than William Smith and the Democratic Party. Declining Republican fortunes in the South, first a trend, had become a historical fact by the mid-1870s. No Republican governor sat in a single southern capital. Democrats had routed Republicans from state governments in all but Florida, Louisiana, and South Carolina, and the remaining anachronistic elements had short political futures. Although insufficient time had passed to provide perspective, an era had ended. Redemption had arrived. Nothing heralded its coming in the Second District of Georgia as clearly as the thorough repudiation of Richard Henry Whiteley. The day of the Republican was over and that of the Bourbon Democrat was just beginning. Whiteley was swept away by the tide of history.

Whiteley received letters of consolation and praise. In an election postmortem, Amos Akerman, Grant's former attorney general, wrote to Whiteley from his Cartersville home. Regretting that "things have for some time pointed that way," Akerman promised not to give up on Republicanism in Georgia.[60] Jonathan Bryant had been defeated for the congressional seat from the First District. The maverick Augusta Republican, now chairman of the State Central Committee, had alienated many state Republicans in the past, and had not been on friendly political terms with Whiteley. Now Bryant attempted a rapprochement with him in December. Admitting that "we have seemed to work at cross purposes since the first days of reconstruction," Bryant proposed to put differences aside in the interests of the state party. "Many of your personal friends," he wrote, "are also my personal friends."[61] At around the same time, Whiteley heard from William A. Pledger, a young black man with a future in the state Republican Party and editor of the *Athens Blade.* He and Whiteley had a passing acquaintanceship. Pledger acknowledged in a letter of December 2 that "you, sir, have been a friend of my race." As for past service to the freedpeople, Pledger thanked Whiteley for "standing by them in every measure."[62]

Defeat for Richard Whiteley made for disappointment. It also was a major contributing factor in his decision to leave Georgia. He seems to have considered moving to Washington and practicing law after the 1874 defeat. In 1876, following the election, he immediately took definitive steps. Not the nation's capital but Colorado was his intended destination.

Congress had designated Colorado a territory the year the Civil War began. Like that of much of the West, the territory's settlement had been linked to the discovery of gold and silver. The Rocky Mountains, extending through the future state's central part, yielded vast stores of gold and silver ore and other precious metals. This was the West, and for many easterners, the area had a galvanizing pull. Dreams of El Dorado brought thousands to the region. Almost ninety thousand people lived in the territory by 1870, and in the centennial year of 1876, when Colorado became a state, Denver was designated the capital. In a fitting historical coincidence, Whiteley had voted during his last term in Congress for Colorado statehood.

What Whiteley knew of Colorado impressed and intrigued him. Whiteley's law partner John Donalson had traveled to the territory in 1873 and had written back and praised the area in the *Bainbridge Democrat.* He must have spoken in greater detail to Whiteley. That he could do well as a lawyer Whiteley was confident. The lure of investing in gold and silver mines also interested him, always a man of enterprise. It can be assumed that Colorado's aesthetic appeal was a consideration. As with thousands of others, Colorado also conceivably offered Whiteley a new start and place. Searching for better opportunities had led Whiteley as a young man from Augusta to Greensborough, then to Athens, and finally to Bainbridge. A final move, to the Union's newest state, seemed to offer a promising prospect.

What Colorado was mattered. So did what it was not: the South, controlled by Democrats, and a place with little chance for change. Whiteley wanted to escape a mentality. For him, a repudiated Republican, the West provided a beacon of tolerance. For the maligned scalawag, a new social setting was quite possibly welcome. Other Republicans, sometimes politically disillusioned, left the South for the West in the 1870s. A number of Mississippi Republicans established themselves in Denver. Several years earlier, addressing Second District citizens, Whiteley had ventured that the harsh feelings of the war were "fast giving way to the realities of a life of peace and of union."[63] That optimistic assessment needed serious qualification. As the disenchanted Southerner explained later to a Coloradan, he "believed there was no hope of a change in the feelings or policy of the South." For whatever reason, or combination of reasons, Whiteley gave considerable thought to moving there. He made plans early in 1877 to visit Colorado and see the place for himself.[64]

11 *Major Whiteley Will Make His Mark*

On March 14, 1877, John Hayes, formerly associated with the *Bainbridge Sun,* wrote from Bainbridge: "Maj. W. has left for Colorado." In all probability, Whiteley traveled by train to Kansas City, Missouri, which was the most frequent point of westward departure. From Kansas City, taking the Kansas Pacific Railroad, he set out for Denver. A day and a half later, on March 27, having traveled some 640 miles across the Great Plains, he checked into the Alvord House in Denver.[1]

Although Denver was the largest city in Colorado, Whiteley was interested in another growing town: Boulder, about fifty miles north of Denver and in the north central part of the state. Exactly what led him to Boulder is not known. Maybe he had made connections with Orris Blake, who would become his law partner. Whatever the circumstances, Boulder was his destination.

First known as Boulder City, the settlement lay in a valley at the base of the Rocky Mountain foothills. Mountains and rocky peaks immediately to the west provided a dramatic backdrop to the small village; rolling plains buffeted it to the north and east. Boulder Creek, leading swiftly from the mountains, flowed through the town. One observer decided that "nature could have formed no prettier place for a town." Although picturesquely located, Boulder remained unremarkable for some time. Its economic situation began to change with the completion in 1873 of the Boulder Valley Railroad, which connected the town to Denver. The Colorado Central, linking Cheyenne and Denver in a north-south direction, soon provided better connections for the county seat of Boulder County. Gold and silver had been mined in the area previously, and the discovery of tellurium ore, a rare metal, contributed to growth in the mid-1870s. Mining camps and towns such as Caribou, Magnolia, Sunshine, and the appropriately named Gold Hill pockmarked the mountains just above Boulder. Unlike such mining camps with few pretensions as towns, Boulder assumed a more settled maturity during the decade.[2]

A tourist guide author wrote in 1878 that by moving to Colorado "one does not necessarily bid farewell to civilization or to the comforts of ordinary life."[3] That was an accurate observation with regard to Boulder. Aside from its stunning setting, Boulder was similar to towns of the same size in other parts of the country. Pearl Street, the major thoroughfare, ran from east to west and bisected the town. Merchants, lawyers, doctors, artisans, and others were located along it and other streets. At the newly constructed dry goods store of A. L. Welch, customers found laces, embroideries, cashmeres, velvet purses, and "an endless variety of things to please the ladies."[4] Some sense of the community's diversity was provided by Boston's Clothing Store, where available attire ranged from "miners' overalls to dress suits."[5] The hopeful sought appraisals of various ores at an assayer's offices. Patrons visited Chamberlin's Music Store and purchased sheet music, and for those so inclined, "instruments are furnished free." Brick buildings were replacing wooden structures. In 1878, residents followed with special interest the construction of Charles Boettcher's hardware store at the corner of Pearl and Twelfth Street. The second floor of the brick building, constituting a public hall, became known as Boettcher's Hall. On another corner, that of Front and Thirteenth Streets, the American House boldly stood for Boulder's unqualified and respectable permanence.[6]

Townspeople established the institutions they had known in the East; they attended any one of several churches on Sunday, and they recognized the value of education. Over five hundred students received instruction at the Boulder Public School on Front Street. The territorial legislature had created the University of Colorado in 1874, and in a community deemed "almost fanatically devoted to the cause of education," citizens pooled their financial resources and attracted the university to Boulder. A mile outside of town, on the south side of Boulder Creek, the University of Colorado opened in 1877. Political differences were evident and strident as Democrats, Republicans, and Greenbackers disagreed. Factions vied for control of town government. For local and national news, residents depended on the *Boulder County News* or the *Colorado Banner.*

Boys and young men played baseball, a wide cross-section enjoyed sleighing, and carriage rides offered spectacular vistas. Costumed revelers marked George Washington's birthday annually with a masquerade ball at Boettcher's Hall. In the year the Whiteleys moved west, Susan B. Anthony lectured at Boulder, and P. T. Barnum's troupe (including General Tom Thumb) performed. Men enjoyed billiards, and the saloons, another male domain, were rarely empty. Parallels with the East were unmistakable.[7]

The objective observer also admitted what Boulder lacked. Any list started with a courthouse. As it was, Boulder County records were kept at one location, those seeking the sheriff's services went elsewhere, and District Court convened at yet another place. Nor was the jail on Pearl Street a model of penological science. Ridiculed as the "crate," the jail was surrounded by a stone wall, but fleeing prisoners were undaunted, since the wall had "one hole sufficient to receive a man's body."[8] Boulder had some rough edges. Rain quickly turned dirt streets to mud. Cows sometimes roamed about, and one civic-minded individual pled for a law "denying the cows the freedom of the city."[9] Yet, on balance, the future was promising, and with booster-driven exuberance, the *News* proclaimed Boulder "the coming city of Colorado." About three thousand people lived there when Richard Whiteley arrived.[10]

In all likelihood, Whiteley first saw Boulder on the last day of March 1877, the day he registered at the Boulder House. Although the exact circumstances are unclear, he soon made the acquaintance of Orris Blake, with whom he would practice law. Blake must have informed the visiting Georgian of the favorable outlook for attorneys. It is also reasonable to assume that Blake, who had invested in the mines, apprised Whiteley of opportunities offered by the area's mineral deposits. Not a man to discount financial opportunities, Whiteley listened with keen interest. Whiteley would have met a number of Boulder residents; many impressed him as educated and sophisticated, and the genteel Southerner noted the social promise of this western town. Any number of considerations drew him to Boulder. He envisioned Montford and Richard attending the University of Colorado. A very acceptable school system would accommodate Hortense and Zena. The local Episcopalian congregation could meet spiritual needs. Whiteley had always taken advantage of opportunities, and that was what Boulder offered.

He returned to Georgia after several weeks in Colorado. Margaret, however enthusiastically or unenthusiastically, prepared to move. So did Montie, Richard, Hortense, and Zena. Charles and Josephine, with their two children, returned to Washington, where Charles began working as a civil servant in the surgeon general's office. The rest of the family made plans for a fall departure.

There was much to do in the summer of 1877. That did not, however, include selling the family home or land, which Whiteley kept. Packing and making arrangements for transporting the furniture that filled their Evans Street home was necessary. Whiteley attempted to collect some outstanding clients' debts and conclude any final litigating business. He would miss friends, some he had known for over twenty years. John Hayes was one of them. Although Whiteley had inspired extreme bitterness as a politician, he also claimed the personal friendship of many of those same people. The family's close relationship with John Donalson, a strong Democrat, would continue well after their departure from Georgia. As for the freedpeople, many of whom he counted as friends, there were also regrets. Whiteley would tell many residents of both races goodbye, and they reciprocated warmly. Others were glad to see the last of the infamous scalawag. Benjamin Russell of the *Bainbridge Democrat* certainly was. No copies of the *Democrat* exist for this time period, but, like other editors in the Second Congressional District who marked the ex-congressman's exit opportunity with a parting shot, Russell must have gleefully done so. (At the time of Russell's death in 1909, the local Bainbridge newspaper recalled the times when Whiteley had "ruled the district" and the Democratic editor's role in "driving him from power.")[11]

At some point, together or separately, the family made a last visit to the family cemetery plot. Tomasina, George, William, and possibly another of the Whiteley children who had died during the 1850s and 1860s were buried there, as well as Mary Devine, Margaret's mother. By September, all was in order, and the family bade their final goodbyes. A certain melancholy was tempered by excitement. In the years ahead, Bainbridge came to be known in the family as the "old home."[12]

The new home beckoned. In late September, after the long railroad trip over the plains, the Whiteleys reached Boulder. The "handsome family," welcomed by the *Colorado Banner,* moved into one of the finest homes in Boulder.[13] The house, recently built, was located a couple of miles northeast of town on a bluff or hill. The home had been designed by local architect George E. King and commanded a magnificent view of Boulder Valley and the mountains to the west. A large two-story Dutch colonial–style house, described as "sightly and beautiful," it had big bedrooms and parlors and suited the Whiteley family. Removed but not isolated, the residence was about a ten-minute carriage ride from town.

Whiteley had apparently arranged the purchase on his previous trip, and soon after their arrival, on September 26, he bought the home for $3,000 from James B. and Sarah Allen. About the same time, expanding the acreage, he purchased two adjoining lots. Aesthetics, comfort, and privacy were served by the house. It was here, at what would be called Whiteley Hill, that the family observed Thanksgiving in November 1877.[14]

The distance from Bainbridge to Boulder could be measured in more than miles. The western city's elevation was about fifty-four hundred feet, and the Whiteleys accepted colder winter months in exchange for relief from Georgia's summer. Miles of cotton fields characterized Georgia, but not a single acre of cotton was cultivated in Colorado. Whiteley's Decatur County was lush and green, a flat land of pines, hardwoods, and the statuesque live oak. Although Georgia farmers sometimes suffered through periods of little rain, the region generally enjoyed steady precipitation. Far fewer trees met the eye in mountainous Boulder, and rain was fairly uncommon in its arid environment.

The people also were different. While every other person in Bainbridge was black, less than 1 percent of Boulder's population were of African

Whiteley Hill. Courtesy of Carnegie Branch Library for Local History, Boulder Historical Society Collection.

descent. Most Bainbridge residents were Southerners, and if they had not fought in Rebel armies, they had supported the Confederacy. Much of Boulder's citizenry, having crossed the Great Plains from Pennsylvania, Illinois, New York, and other northern locations, had held different loyalties. Orris Blake, Whiteley's law partner, had been a major in an Indiana cavalry regiment. Mary Thomas, the principal at Boulder Public School, had lost two brothers fighting for the Union.

In a town not far removed from frontier status, where a person's worth was often evaluated at face value, Whiteley made a favorable impression. Boulder residents soon became acquainted with the slight ex-congressman from the South. Whiteley's affability stood him well; he greeted townspeople easily and comfortably, acquaintances became more than that, and he became well known. Even here, hundreds of miles from the nearest Civil War battlefield and a dozen years removed from the conflict, the southern expatriate would be known as "Major Whiteley" or the "major."[15]

About fifteen lawyers composed the local bar that Whiteley joined. Blake and Whiteley first received clients in a wooden building office on Pearl Street. As in Georgia, Whiteley handled divorces, drew up wills, and attended to other routine but cumulatively remunerative duties. On various levels, Whiteley represented clients, defending and prosecuting. Yet he made his name as a trial lawyer in district or superior court. In over ten years of legal practice in Georgia, as a solicitor general and a lawyer, Whiteley had earned a solid reputation. His skills would quickly become apparent in Colorado.

Practicing law in the new venue required adjustments. Conversance with often convoluted mining laws was required. That was especially crucial because the firm of Blake and Whiteley advertised "mining litigation a speciality."[16] Whiteley moved books he had brought with him from Georgia into his office and soon added others to his law library. Henry N. Copp's *Hand-book of Mining Law* and Robert Stewart Morrison's *Mining Rights in Colorado* were necessary additions. Whiteley began familiarizing himself with mining terminology, lode-claims, linear feet, tunnel rights, placer-claims, and more. He obtained *General Laws of the State of Colorado* (1877) and, for further illumination, Thomas A. Green's *Colorado Pleading and Practice.* He had barely settled in when the firm relocated. That first spring, in 1878, Blake and Whiteley moved down the street to rooms over Boettcher's brick hardware store at the corner of Twelfth and Pearl streets. Whiteley quickly gained the respect of fellow lawyers and the public. The *Boulder County News* noted that he and Blake were "old and experienced attorneys" and declared: "the new firm is a strong one."[17]

Margaret Whiteley rapidly became part of the community. As in Bainbridge, she became known for her graciousness, generosity, and skill with flowers. Church remained an important part of her world. Unlike in Bainbridge, Episcopalians had their own church, and they worshiped at a small chapel on Front Street. Margaret joined the Parish Aid Society there; by May 1878, the society was meeting at the Whiteley home, and she became its first president. There were various possibilities for working with flowers, and Margaret turned enthusiastically to that passion. Roses flourished under her care. Townspeople soon began receiving bouquets from this well-thought-of southern woman.

Hortense and Zena, now of school age, made the short carriage trip each morning to the Boulder Public School on Front Street. In her second-grade class, Hortense quickly made the honor roll, and soon exhibited precocious musical skills. Zena matched her high marks in school.

Montie was eighteen and Richard was sixteen when the family left Bainbridge. Both joined the first freshman class at the University of Colorado. A four-story brick building crowned by a tower and observatory, standing alone a mile south of Boulder Creek, served all functions for the university. For the Whiteley brothers, part of a class of fewer than fifteen students, there was instruction in a heavy classical curriculum. Putting aside their Greek, Latin, and mathematics, the boys also made time for pleasure. In February 1878, Richard, dressed as a sailor, attended the annual masquerade ball sponsored by the Boulder Hose Company No. 1. The next month, on March 22, Montie played the part of a slave-hunter in the local production of *Jackwood*; that a Southerner assumed that role may or may not have been coincidental.

Montford's baseball skills exceeded any thespian talents. As the weather warmed that year, the baseball-playing and -viewing population readied for the season. The former Bainbridge Star pitched, played outfield, and soon captained the Boulders. On June 27, 1878, Richard and Margaret Whiteley joined others on a railroad excursion to nearby Greeley to watch their son and his teammates play against the Greeleys. The Whiteleys enjoyed a tour of the recently established town, as well as the game, which the Boulders handily won. As she had in Bainbridge at similar events, Margaret contributed; the team thanked Montie's mother for the "splendid lunch" she prepared and "did ample justice to it."[18]

Whatever their talents, interests, or failings, all the Whiteleys attended the Episcopal chapel, where Rector Thomas V. Wilson presided. Local Episcopalians wanted to move from the confining chapel to a church, and the Parish Aid Society, directed by Margaret, raised money for constructing one. The Whiteleys gave generously to the church lot and building fund. In 1879, on the corner of Pine and Fourteenth streets, a Gothic-style church rose. A crowd turned out on December 3 when it was consecrated as St. John's Church. The Whiteley family was surely represented on that occasion. By the next year, 1880, Richard Whiteley was a vestryman.

Whiteley made many friends, and one of the best was Alpheus Wright, who had moved to Colorado from the East on the eve of the Civil War. Both men, who were about the same age, had overcome trying childhoods. Whiteley and Wright also shared an interest in mining. A strong Republican allegiance and taste for local politics further bound them. Wright's partisan credentials dated to the 1856 presidential election, when he had campaigned for John C. Fremont. Wright and Whiteley would become a powerful political team locally, and in some dark times to come, Wright would stand by his southern friend.

Always the partisan, Whiteley almost immediately became involved in civic affairs, and he quickly gained a high profile. A mayor and four aldermen ran town government and were chosen in annual elections. Local coalitions and parties, sometimes forming on Democratic, Greenback, or Republican lines, nominated tickets. At the National Party convention on March 16, 1878, Whiteley was nominated to become an alderman. Delegates to the Peoples' Party Convention also tapped him. No other candidate received the nomination of both parties. A little over five hundred residents went to the polls on April 2. As the nominee of both parties, Whiteley received 492 votes, easily more than any other candidate. In May, when the fire companies conducted their annual parade, bands and citizens joined the procession. At the conclusion, Whiteley shared the speaking billing with Mayor James P. Maxwell. He had been in Boulder only seven months.[19]

Trials that attracted much attention further placed Whiteley in the public eye. Boulder citizens were not appreciably more or less law-abiding than others back East. Yet in the mining camps—Gold Hill, Magnolia, Salina, and other rough places—violence was more common. As a lawyer, Whiteley assumed capital cases that often had their origins in the mountains but were adjudicated when District Court met at the county seat of Boulder. In the years ahead, Whiteley participated in trials that gained local and regional attention.

When Julius Baron murdered Daniel Webb at Salina in 1877, the crime allowed Whiteley the forum to start building his legal reputation. He and Blake represented Baron. Salina, several miles west of Boulder, was described as "a live mining town" and attracted its share of rowdy characters.[20] In Baron's saloon, on the night of November 11, 1877, Julius

Baron had shot and killed Daniel Webb in a dispute growing out of a card game. When District Court convened in February 1878, curious townspeople turned out. Blake and Whiteley sat with a repentant Baron. The district attorney and county attorney established that Baron, heavily inebriated, had fatally wounded Webb. The defense's expectations were limited, since Baron could only hope for the jury's mercy. He allowed: "I would rather have been killed myself than to have killed another."[21] Neither his nor his counsels' words saved Baron from a life sentence. Even so, the *Boulder County News* declared that Whiteley and Blake had conducted "an able defense."[22]

Whiteley also quickly assumed an active role in politics. He strongly supported the emerging demands of women for the suffrage. In the western states, where women first gained political rights, the question raised strong passions. A statewide referendum in October 1877 had resulted in the failure of a proposal granting women the right to vote in state elections. Several months later, on March 25, 1878, forty one men and women founded an Equal Rights League in Boulder. Whiteley was present that night at the Methodist Episcopal Church. He listened in agreement when Mary Hindman, a local resident, argued for the suffrage. The former congressman also joined the executive committee of the Equal Rights League in Boulder County.

In November 1876, when Richard Whiteley had lost the congressional election to William Smith, his career as a candidate (excluding local office) had ended. Nonetheless, he remained an enthusiastic Republican spokesman. Colorado residents would elect a governor, legislature, and congressmen in the midterm elections of 1878. Whiteley played a significant part. Questions concerning the amount and type of money in circulation were most crucial. Members of the recently formed Greenback Party advocated government-issued greenbacks, or paper money, a practice first created by the exigencies of the Civil War. More fiscally conservative interests in the Republican and Democratic parties opposed this inflationary plan and supported greenback limitations and the resumption of specie payments. Opinion varied widely in Boulder County, where Republicans composed the majority, but Democrats threatened their dominance, and Greenbackers, though widely outnumbered, worked with diligence and sometimes achieved results. When all three parties made their case in the fall of 1878, Whiteley proved a strong Republican asset.[23]

Just as Whiteley had to make adjustments in his legal profession, he also faced orientation to a different political world. Previously he had spoken frequently to black audiences and often about Reconstruction questions. In the West, Reconstruction was less important, and there were far fewer freedpeople. Rather than farmers, his listeners were often miners. Reaching them required making carriage trips through the pine- and cedar-timbered mountains to speak at outposts like Salina and Sunshine and other mountain settlements. Gold Hill, at an elevation of eight thousand feet and twelve twisting miles from Boulder, was especially remote. Even so, granting differences in the time, place, and issues, something else became clear. The nimble politician understood the dynamics of a political audience on both sides of the Mississippi River.

Whiteley, Charles M. Campbell, and Henry Neikert made the winding trip up through Boulder Canyon to Salina for an engagement on August 22, 1878. Campbell was a local businessman who chaired the Republican County Committee; Neikert was seeking a senate seat. According to a listener, Whiteley examined the finance question from "the standpoint of historical experience, common honesty and common sense." Greenbacks were not redeemable in coin and were not, therefore, real money, and to assume otherwise, he claimed, amounted to "fiat folly, hocus pocus nonsense."[24] Mentioning his credentials as a former congressman and an "old campaigner," the *Boulder County News* pronounced Whiteley a "powerful speaker."[25] The *Boulder County Courier* concurred: "Major Whiteley's speech was a masterpiece of argument and eloquence."[26]

About a week later, early in September, the same threesome made their way to Magnolia, a mining camp within ten miles of Boulder. "The major" provided a two-hour discussion of the financial questions, speaking in his "happy, effective style."[27] On September 7, at Nederland, a pastoral mining town sixteen miles west of Boulder, the Republican team was warmly received. As he often had in Georgia, Whiteley pitched his argument toward the "laboring man." It was not a lack of circulating medium that caused problems but rather the reluctance of wealthy men to invest in enterprises. After listening, one person in the audience became convinced that "Major Whiteley will make his mark wherever he goes in this campaign."[28] At Longmont, in the northern part of the county, Whiteley spoke alone on September 21 and succeeded in "getting out one of the best audiences that town has accorded to any speaker." In the week before the October 1 election, Whiteley appeared almost nightly, beginning his comments at 7:30 P.M. Audiences at Salina, Upper St. Vrain, Louisville, and Valmont listened, and many were persuaded.[29]

Election Day results pleased Whiteley. Republicans claimed a four-hundred-vote plurality in Boulder County and swept the state. An election postmortem, noting the former Georgian's "cool and argumentative" speeches, asserted: "no one is more deserving of praise than Mr. R. H.

Whiteley, who did splendid service in the cause of honest money." The former scalawag obviously retained a taste and facility for campaigning.[30]

Soon after the war, in Bainbridge, Whiteley had taken an avid interest in bringing a railroad to town. In Boulder, as an apostle of progress, he outlined a vision for a better town. On April 1, 1879, after residents reelected the comparative newcomer an alderman, the *Boulder News and Courier* explained there were "no party issue nor special axes to grind" so his victory could be construed as a personal vote of confidence. That was not the only contest Whiteley won that spring. In May, residents elected him president of the School Board. The incumbent was stepping down, little campaigning seems to have been involved, and Whiteley triumphed easily.[31]

Whiteley's law partnership with Orris Blake ended that summer. Health problems, limiting Blake's professional activities, may have caused the dissolution. Even so, the daily law office routine for Whiteley remained much the same. In the absence of a courthouse, he and other lawyers continued to endure inconveniences. Judges, bailiffs, jurors, other lawyers, and prisoners carried on in varying degrees of discomfort. When Judge William E. Beck gaveled the October District Court into session in 1879, in a courtroom located in the Van Fleet Building on Pearl Street, Whiteley appreciated some improvements at the new location. Accommodations were more spacious, and the setting was "free from the noise and dust of the street which was a terrible annoyance to spectators when anything of interest was transpiring before the Court." The need for a courthouse remained acute.[32]

The family maintained a close connection with the University of Colorado. Montie and Richard, sophomores during 1878–79, were often there. Richard, the more academically inclined, belonged to the University Literary Society, and law also interested him. On February 12, 1879, at a meeting of the Literary Society, Richard argued affirmatively the question "Is an advocate justified in defending a man whom he knows to be guilty?" The influence of his father was obvious.[33] As the academic year closed that summer, the Whiteleys hosted a party for faculty and students on June 20. Guests enjoyed music and games, and Margaret's touch was evident at a "table filled with flowers and all the delicacies of the season." Her husband thanked all for coming and, noting the young women, declared they made possible "the highest type of social enjoyment."[34]

Whiteley Hill became a place of gatherings for all ages and sexes. With taste, and considerable money, the Whiteleys made improvements to the home and grounds. A fence soon enclosed the property. Thirty-

Richard H. Whiteley Jr., 1882. Photograph in Mary Rippon Collection, Archives, University of Colorado at Boulder Libraries.

eight trees had been set out almost immediately, and flowers and shrubbery were added. Honoring Margaret's wishes, Whiteley had a conservatory built for her flowers. A large bay window was added to a room facing the mountains and admitting favorable light. An amazed visitor noted: "to give the names of all the flowers would be a difficult task."[35]

Whiteley engaged a contractor to build a brick barn that blended with the home's architectural style. The *Boulder County News* decided the barn was more elaborate than the homes of most people and that "the Major must keep some high-priced stock to require such quarters."[36] On July 25, 1879, when Zena turned eight years old, a number of her friends came to her birthday party. "Associates of both sexes," the *Colorado Banner* explained, "went home full of jam, cake, pies, tarts, and other good things."[37]

On January 1, 1880, the Whiteleys greeted numerous guests who rode out to their home. Holding Open House on New Year's Day was traditional in Boulder. Disaster was narrowly averted a week later on January 8. Late that Thursday morning, untended hot ashes in the barn apparently ignited a large fire. Richard and Montie were home and acted quickly as the flames spread, removing a carriage and the horses from danger. In the meantime, fire companies rushed to the scene and, with the help of a strong wind, prevented the fire from reaching the house. In the *Boulder News and Courier*, Whiteley thanked the firemen and other citizens who had helped contain the fire. "Major Whiteley's barn looks all right again," one observer noted, "but he does not want any more fires."[38]

Family name and pedigree meant less in the newly opening West than other areas of the country. Even so, lines of demarcation existed. The Whiteleys circulated in the most prestigious circles. On February 6, 1880, they dressed in masquerade attire to attend a Leap Year Party at Boettcher's Hall, described as the "greatest social event of the season." Whiteley's attire, highlighted by a Napoleon blue grosgrain haversack and alligator boots from Georgia, caused one fellow reveler to note: "Major Whiteley was elegantly dressed."[39] Whiteley mixed easily, unencumbered by any political resentments that might have complicated a similar situation in Georgia, and obviously enjoyed himself. He and Margaret entertained often on Whiteley Hill. On one occasion, a guest recalled delectable party fare, games of whist, and conversation in "large and airy parlors brilliantly lighted."[40] A guest at another party there commented on "the graceful and easy manner in which the major and his estimable lady seek to please their guests." The couple apparently complemented each other well.[41]

Easter Sunday, March 28, 1880, was a special day for Boulder Episcopalians; the congregation observed the occasion at their recently completed St. John's Church. Margaret Whiteley provided the calla lily that formed the centerpiece of a flower cross that Easter. Independence Day, 1880, was commemorated in another way; hundreds turned out for baseball, a horse race, and oratory. Befitting his standing, Whiteley reminded the audience that the republic's safety was dependent on an educated citizenry and honest public officials.

The most celebrated event of 1880 in Boulder was not Independence Day but the visit of Ulysses Grant later that summer. The possibility of investing in some mines brought him to Colorado. Elaborate preparations were made to welcome the former president on August 21. Margaret belonged to the Committee on Decorations, and her husband headed a reception committee that included the university president and several other prominent men. On the evening before Grant's arrival, the receiving party of eight met him at the Glenarm Hotel in Denver. Grant at once recalled the former congressman from their Washington years. Acting as spokesman, Whiteley explained their purpose and introduced the group to the ex-president. The next morning the party took the Colorado Central Railroad to Boulder. Arriving on Saturday morning, Grant stepped from the train to loud cheers, and, mounting a horse, he joined the procession that moved up Pearl Street, which was draped with flags and bunting. Hundreds shook his hand at a Boettcher Hall reception that afternoon. An exclusive few dined with Grant that evening at the Brainard Hotel. Richard and Margaret Whiteley were among those sitting at the presidential front table.

With much less fanfare, Charles Whiteley had visited Boulder the previous month. Health problems still plagued him. An extended stay in a very remote part of Florida where he seems to have pursued agricultural interests, financed by his father, who hoped the climate would have a beneficial effect, had not provided the hoped-for results. "If he had to die," Charles explained on his return to Washington, he wanted to "be among civilized people." He supported his wife and two children by working in the surgeon general's office. His visit was, it may be assumed, a pleasant one.[42]

Since 1868, every four years, Whiteley had campaigned for a Republican presidential candidate. The move to Colorado changed nothing. In 1880, Whiteley spoke widely for the Republican nominee James Garfield, who had sat next to him in Congress. Chester A. Arthur was the vice-presidential candidate. On July 21, when the local Garfield and Arthur Club met, Whiteley was a featured speaker. The administration of Rutherford B. Hayes was ending, and by Whiteley's interpretation, times were prosperous. Given those facts, he maintained that the electorate should keep the Republicans in power. Would a family dismiss the physician who had served them well? How wise would it be, he continued rhetorically, to discharge a lawyer who had provided appropriate legal advice? On a lighter note, he praised the women's decorating efforts and speculated that if Republicans applied themselves with equal diligence, the election would be "a simple walk over." Early in August, at another Garfield and Arthur Club meeting, Whiteley had indicted the opposition on various counts. The *Boulder County Herald,* supportive of Grover Cleveland, noted the comprehensive attack, and facetiously remarked that Whiteley forgot to blame the Democrats for drought conditions in Colorado.[43]

At Longmont, fourteen miles north of Boulder, Whiteley addressed citizens in behalf of Republicanism. Charles Campbell, a fellow Boulder Republican, traveling with him, labeled Whiteley's effort "one of the finest political speeches he ever heard." A week later, Whiteley and Campbell made the steep ascent through Boulder Canyon to Gold Hill, where Whiteley "fairly excelled himself handling the political questions and the Democratic party without gloves." On November 2, joining others across the state, residents of Boulder County cast their first presidential ballots as Coloradans. Much to Whiteley's satisfaction, Garfield carried Boulder, Colorado, and a majority of the states and was elected.[44]

Less than a year later, Garfield was dead. Shot by an assassin on July 2, 1881, at a Washington railroad station, Garfield lingered two and a half months before dying. On September 25, the day of Garfield's funeral, Whiteley, university president Joseph A. Sewall, mayor John A. Ellet, and several minister, eulogized the president from under a tent on a vacant Pearl Street lot. Noting that he was speaking from "head and heart," Whiteley recalled their days as fellow congressmen. He described Garfield in platitudes as an upstanding lawyer and statesman who had served his country well in peace and war.[45]

Never without an opinion, or the compunction to express it, Whiteley played a prominent part in a courthouse-building campaign that year. Most citizens considered the erection of a courthouse long overdue. How to finance its construction and where to locate it was a more involved question. Whiteley and others favored building the courthouse on the public square, heretofore a barren area, centrally located between Pearl and Spruce Streets. Exactly what would be done with the square, set aside in 1860 for the "public use," was a critical public issue by the spring of 1881.[46]

"Erect a courthouse," Whiteley admonished the people, and provide a center of government. Asked about refurbishing the square as a park, he replied that doing so represented "so much [money] thrown away."[47] Several hundred residents filed into Union Hall on the evening of March 23, filling the room, forcing some of the overflow audience to stand. Whiteley presented a report from a committee of consulted lawyers. In remarks that drew laughter, he reminded his listeners that an opinion delivered gratis by a lawyer was of little importance. Rising later, after various opinions had been stridently advanced, he called for "harmony" and pled: "let us drop this bickering." He envisioned Boulder residents uniting, and providing for new buildings and attracting railroads, and that was not possible in their divided state. One witness concluded that "the major's speech was frequently very eloquent." Whiteley contributed to what a participant described as "the most spirited town meeting Boulder ever had."[48]

Eventually, building the courthouse on the centrally located site was agreed on. The task of raising funds ($42,000) for its construction remained. In October and November 1881, Whiteley stumped throughout the county for the bonds. Support for the courthouse transcended party lines and made for unlikely alliances. Whiteley, Judge Granville Berkley, and Joseph Wolff traveled and spoke together. Theirs was a formidable if strange triumvirate. Berkley was a leading local Democrat and Wolff an outspoken Greenbacker. The threesome passed through Boulder Canyon to Nederland on October 28. At the mountain town, Whiteley remarked on the ironic circumstances of their collaboration. He colorfully described Berkeley as a "Democratic lion," mentioned the "gory Greenback Wolff," and, identifying himself as "the Republican lamb," asked, "imagine us all lying down together." More seriously, he vividly described bailiffs escorting jurors to a deliberating room over a music hall. The picture Whiteley drew of grand juries conferring in the county jail was (if somewhat amusing) equally appalling. Jail conditions were abysmal and degrading. Most arrested parties were not guilty, Whiteley informed the naive, but in Boulder they suffered indefinitely in what he described as "a cage not fit for beasts."

He made the same pitch at Caribou, Salina, Goss School House, Gold Hill, and elsewhere. Getting to the mining camp of Gold Hill required a steady ascension from Boulder of some two thousand feet. At Salina, a week before the November 8 vote, Whiteley pronounced the county clerk and recorder's office "not fit for a one-horse lawyer's office." On November 8, by an overwhelming vote of 984 to 340, Boulder County residents approved the bond issue. Whiteley had played no small role. The uninformed observer, having followed Whiteley's efforts, would have concluded that he was one of the county's most longstanding citizens.[49]

The prominent Republican made no money from politics, but that was immaterial since he had a lucrative law practice. In the same year he campaigned for the courthouse, Whiteley represented the Greeley,

Salt Lake and Pacific Railroad in county court. His retaining fee would not have been small. At times, he traveled to Denver to practice in the United States District Court. Profits also accrued from mining investments. Orris Blake, his former law partner, was often a joint investor. In 1877, even before the family followed him to Boulder, Whiteley had acquired an interest in the Silver Bell Lode. In 1878, he diverted more of his earnings to the Ogallalah Lode; and in 1880 he claimed a financial interest in the Gold Cliff Lode; and the Prince Albert Lode soon attracted his attention. Around that time, the *Boulder County Herald* noted renewed mining activity and predicted: "more work will be done and greater results accomplished than any time since the telluride excitement of seven years ago." Whiteley hoped to capitalize.[50]

By Thanksgiving 1881, the Whiteley family had lived in Boulder for four years, and had become a valued part of the community. Zena had her friends and interests. For Hortense, there was music, and a local listener had even observed: "her voice is gradually but surely being ruined, by being overtaxed." Richard, handsome and dark-haired, was a familiar figure on the small University of Colorado campus. As the president of the Phi Alpha Upsilon Society, he delivered a paper on May 20, 1881, denouncing nihilism. Montie left the university at the end of his junior year in 1880. In July 1881, his announcement of marriage to Mina A. Andrews, the well-bred daughter of a local family, surprised people. Why they married secretly is not known. Montford accepted a clerk's position at the hardware and grocery store of Hansborough Brothers; in his free time, as a member of Boulder Hose Company No. 1, he participated enthusiastically in the competitive contests waged between fire companies in Colorado.[51]

Margaret Whiteley was a mother, wife, and leading lady in Boulder. When her son was hired at Hansborough Brothers, she sent the proprietors a bouquet. Maybe Margaret's pride were the large calla lilies with which she sometimes crowned her fragrant brilliant bouquets. On Friday evening, February 10, 1881, guests had gathered at Whiteley Hill for card games, fruit, cake, and coffee. After admiring her sweet-smelling flowers, one incredulous observer decided it was easy to "forget that he is in mid winter, surrounded by fields of snow."[52] That spring, the strong Episcopalian was the "moving spirit" in organizing an amateur opera to benefit St. John's Church.[53]

Richard Whiteley was a successful lawyer, a popular man, and an admired civic leader. It is easy to imagine him as the generous host conversing with guests at his home, or exchanging greetings with one of his many acquaintances on Pearl Street. The public weal was his passion.

*Montford Whiteley (*first fireman, left of photo*). Courtesy of Carnegie Branch Library for Local History, Boulder Historical Society Collection.*

In the last month of 1881 he spoke of "Boulder's progress."[54] Building a courthouse to serve county citizens fit his definition of advancement. So did dealing with the "suppression of evils resulting from the visits of tramps to the town," as a motion he put before the city council said. He directed other improvements as superintendent of education.[55] He regaled his new (and undoubtedly amazed) Boulder friends with stories of campaigning in Reconstruction Georgia. In Colorado, controlled by Republicans between the late 1870s and early 1890s, Whiteley was much more comfortable. The setting, time, and issues had changed, and he easily adapted. During the 1878 midterm elections, in one mountain mining camp, an impressed listener concluded that Whiteley "had hard work to condense into a two hours' speech all that he would like to say on the finance question." His interests—public interests—were many, and he had quickly become identified with the present and future of Boulder. The unconventional move from the South to the town on the edge of the Great Plains had been undertaken with no assurances of success. He could now look toward the mountains from his family home and reflect on the move with satisfaction.[56]

12 *Peace to His Ashes*

Richard Whiteley was fifty-two years old in 1881 and a busy man. A fellow citizen described him as "one of Boulder's highly honored and esteemed citizens" and cited his efforts as an "enthusiastic worker in the support of all her institutions."[1] That included the cause of education. Late in 1881, speaking publicly as president of the School Board, Whiteley had urged construction of a new school. Classes were crowded in the eight-room Boulder Public School on Front Street. Children caught colds and worse in the poorly ventilated building. The parents of Lora Colton blamed her sickness and resulting near death on the situation. Under the circumstances, the stewardship provided by the president of the School Board was crucial. On May 1, 1882, Whiteley stood for reelection, and the *Boulder County Herald* decided that on that referendum "hangs the question of the welfare of 500 children." As the *Herald* concluded, "at this time more than any other, such a man as Major Whiteley is needed on the board."[2] Women in Colorado could vote in elections concerning school or educational questions. Some not only cast their ballot for Whiteley but also actively campaigned for the incumbent. The standing of the man who received 238 of the 243 votes cast was obvious. Work soon began on a two-story Italianate brick school on Pine Street.[3]

Another dilemma Whiteley took a close interest in was not solved so easily. Boulder residents chronically suffered with too little water—a common problem in the arid West. Water was obtained from a reservoir above Boulder and conducted to town by iron water mains and supply pipes, but water pressure was often weak. In the summer, when it rained less and watering lawns was necessary, shortages were especially acute. The situation was much more than inconvenient; a fire was potentially disastrous.

Whiteley appealed for a solution when the firehouse of the Boulder Hose Company No. 1 was dedicated at its Pearl Street location on July 1, 1882. He did not expect to speak, but, never at a loss for words, he responded when called on "in his usual happy vein." He commended the brotherhood of the firemen. The timing was perfect for another pitch. "Water is the one and necessary thing which we must have," Whiteley asserted, and urged firemen to "raise the cry of 'more water.'" He remained the undoubted and committed public advocate.[4]

That summer Richard Whiteley Jr. and five classmates became the first graduates of the University of Colorado. On the eve of commencement, June 7, 1882, the farewell class dinner was held at the Whiteley home. Toasts were offered, and guests enjoyed food "Mrs. Whiteley alone can spread."[5] The next day, at the university, Richard Jr. emotionally delivered the farewell address. "To you who are destined to graduate in future years," the exiting senior stated, "we commend our University." His father and mother listened with understandable pride. An addition to the Whiteley family three weeks later made the summer more eventful. Montie's wife, Mina, gave birth to a baby boy.[6]

The fall of 1882 was a time of leave-takings for the family. Richard traveled across the country to begin studying law at Harvard. Hortense departed around the same time, heading north for training in music at Hellmuth Ladies College in London, Ontario. Several months later, on November 14, Margaret left with Zena by train for Georgia, where they spent several weeks in Bainbridge seeing old friends. Many former acquaintances inquired about Margaret's husband and the *Bainbridge Democrat* learned and reported that he was "doing a very lucrative business in Law and Mining."[7]

On a typical day, Whiteley might consult with clients and handle any work that went with representation. If they could not afford it, he sometimes asked for no compensation. Most of the time, at his Pearl Street office, Whiteley went about his living rather inconspicuously. On other occasions, circumstances thrust him on the public stage. In 1882 he gained considerable attention as a defense lawyer in two murder cases.

Few people in Boulder County did not recognize the names Nettie Still and Alpha Ray when District Court opened in May 1882. A year earlier, on the night of May 16, 1881, Still had murdered Ray. Suspecting the thirteen-year-old girl of being romantically involved with her husband, Still had shot her at Still's Nederland home. A grand jury had indicted Still for murder, but her pregnancy had delayed the trial for a year. Whiteley headed the defense team, which included James North and A. P. Rittenhouse. District attorney J. McD. Livesay prosecuted.

If jurors and the curious public had any preconceived image of a murderess, Nettie Still did not fit that stereotype. On May 8, the trial's first day, she was tastefully attired as she took a seat in front of Judge Chester C. Carpenter. Her husband, Charles Still, sat nearby and held their three-month-old baby. A year had passed since the crime, but the facts remained. On her deathbed, Alpha Ray had revealed that Nettie Still had cursed, kicked, and then shot her. Who committed the crime was beyond dispute. A more pertinent consideration, Whiteley contended, was the defendant's state of mind when she did so. The defense entered a plea of not guilty based on a state of temporary insanity. Twelve jurymen heard testimony for over a week, and crowds filled the courtroom. Considering the subjective nature of insanity, the *Boulder County Herald* believed the case provided "perhaps the most important murder trial that was ever tried in Boulder County."[8]

Demonstrating that Still was not responsible for her actions, Whiteley documented for the jury a pattern of abnormal behavior in recent years. Once the defendant had hidden in a treetop. She had delusions that someone wanted to kill her. Dr. Frederick J. Bancroft, a Denver physician with some expertise in the field of insanity, had examined Still. Whiteley posed various questions to Bancroft. Extemporaneously outlining Still's bizarre behavior in a "remarkable summary," Whiteley concluded with a crucial question, asking Bancroft: "What would you say as to her condition and actions previous to, at the time of, and after the homicide?" The doctor answered, "it was the action of an insane individual."[9] Many citizens in Boulder were far less certain. On the morning of May 17, the curious crowded the courtroom in the Van Fleet Building for the closing arguments. One witness noted "the major's eloquent plea in behalf of the unfortunate woman." Whiteley portrayed Still as a mentally unbalanced and ultimately pitiful woman, in a presentation that lasted over three hours. Most of the jury members agreed and, rejecting District Attorney Livesay's admonition to ignore the "insanity dodge," acquitted the defendant. Some residents believed justice had miscarried, and others placed greater faith in the judicial system. That Whiteley had won a major legal victory was undeniable.[10]

Another murder trial involving Whiteley, later that year, was almost as compelling locally. On July 9, 1882, James R. Pollock had killed Robert

Sanderson in the nearby mining community of Ward. Both men worked in the Celestial Mine. Following a disagreement, Sanderson had jumped at Pollock in the shaft house, and Pollock had fired the fatal shots. He fled but was captured two weeks later and jailed in Boulder. The crime, flight, and apprehension of the locally well-known man attracted wide attention. When a *Boulder County Herald* reporter attempted to interview the jailed prisoner, Pollock insisted first on consulting his lawyer—Richard Whiteley. A week later, speaking with the *Herald,* Whiteley maintained that Pollock was an "innocent man." The *Herald* responded: "if any one else had told us this we should have believed it was intended as a joke." A grand jury indicted Pollock for manslaughter and murder.[11]

District Court opened that fall, and many in Boulder followed the trial over the first three days of November. Whiteley and Alpheus Wright based their client's innocent plea on the grounds of self-defense. Among the witnesses called was Dr. William R. Earhart. While attending to Sanderson before he died, Earhart had found a knife in his pocket. In cross-examination, Whiteley led the doctor by asking "Was it a deadly weapon?" He failed, though, to get Eliel L. Sharpneck, who had witnessed the crime, to state that Sanderson had drawn the knife on Pollock. Both sides made long concluding arguments on Friday, November 3. Appealing to the jury, Whiteley claimed that the man before them had no motive for killing Robert Sanderson and had responded to a personal threat rather than acting with premeditation. He also pointed out that Pollock was almost fifty, married, and the father of three young children. In what was described as a "very eloquent" three-hour closing argument, Whiteley pleaded with the jurors not to deprive the family of their provider. They deliberated through Friday night and the next morning returned a verdict of manslaughter. That Saturday morning, before the sentencing, Whiteley asked for a humane punishment, again drawing an affecting picture of Pollock's dependents. Judge Carpenter sentenced him to nine years of hard labor at the state penitentiary. Pollock thanked God and Carpenter for the extended mercy. No doubt he privately expressed his appreciation to Whiteley.[12]

Whiteley's impassioned appeal to the Pollock jury was one of the last he delivered in the courtroom on Pearl Street. For several months, residents had been following the progress of the rising courthouse, and in March 1883, the building was dedicated. The imposing granite structure, crowned by a clock tower, had few architectural critics. Whiteley, who undoubtedly considered the building handsome, appreciated its functional comforts. He would be there often.

In the courtroom, in trials of small and large significance, Whiteley acted with and against fellow lawyers. Alpheus Wright had helped defend James Pollock; nonetheless, Wright had aided with the prosecution of Alpha Ray, whom Whiteley had defended. Charles Dabney, James North, and other lawyers proved worthy allies and adversaries. Since Whiteley almost invariably represented the defense in capital cases, District Attorney Livesay was often the opponent. In the courtroom there was anger, contention, and guile. Yet camaraderie also existed among the lawyers. In June 1883, Whiteley joined other attorneys who squared off in a friendly baseball game against Boulder merchants.

Richard Whiteley Jr. hoped eventually to join the local bar. After finishing his first year at Harvard Law School, he returned to Boulder. On July 13, 1883, the day before he turned twenty-two, a lavish birthday party was given in his honor at Whiteley Hill. Nobody walked there, and that evening "carriages were in a great demand."[13] Guests danced to waltzes by the light of Chinese lanterns, and Hortense, who had recently arrived home from the Hellmuth Ladies College, played the piano. Some ladies wore "elegant costumes," guests enjoyed refreshments in Margaret Whiteley's "beautiful conservatory," and "the occasion was a complete success."[14]

Whiteley could be a pleasing host, but in the courtroom or the political arena, he was a hard adversary. He remained an outspoken advocate of making more water available locally. The continuing water dilemma caused him and others consternation, aggravation, and discomfort during the summer of 1883. The elevated and removed location of Whiteley Hill exacerbated the situation for the family. As June ended, Whiteley complained that there had been no water at his home in two days. He facetiously suggested: "if you want to see what a beautiful water system you have, go look at the water gauge." He guessed there was less than ten pounds of pressure on the pipes; a check revealed he was right. Citing the danger of fire, the *Boulder County Herald* concluded: "it is high time this matter were attended to." The water problems continued.[15]

Whiteley resumed the battle against local Democrats and Greenbackers that fall. County elections were held in November, and local Republicans met to select a ticket in Boulder on October 10, 1883. "In fitting complimentary terms," Whiteley nominated Judge Sylvester S. Downer for county judge. The resolution he offered—to apportion officers among the county's Boulder, Valley, and Mountain districts—appeased disagreeing delegates, and he was credited with an "edict of justice."[16] At Berlin's Hall, Whiteley spoke at a Republican rally on election eve. On November 6, the next day, voters gave majorities to almost the entire Republican ticket.[17]

Several months later, when District Court opened in February 1884, Whiteley again stepped up onto the public pedestal. A cause, not a party issue, attracted his attention. In many towns, for revenue purposes and also to limit the number of liquor establishments locally, saloon proprietors were required to pay a substantial licensing fee. The Boulder City Council had recently raised the fee from $250 to $400. As a consequence, fifteen saloon keepers petitioned the City Council and cited their inability to pay the fees and support their families. As were most western saloon operators, they existed on only marginal economic means. Some resorted to serving customers on Sunday, a violation of Colorado law, and when District Court convened in February 1884, an unprecedented number of indictments (forty-one) were handed down for selling liquor on the Sabbath. As battle lines formed, saloon keepers created an association of mutual protection, and approached Whiteley and Alpheus Wright about legal representation. The opportunity to land a blow for the struggling saloon keeper was one Whiteley accepted with some relish. Striking against the prohibitionist forces, whom he considered pietistic and heartless, also offered satisfaction. He understood that a juror was much like a voter, quite possibly holding preconceived notions, even convictions, but persuadable if appealed to effectively. Whiteley would make a critical difference.

The case of Albert T. Henry, who pleased his customers with bourbon and more at his Pearl Street Saloon, was heard first. The defense strategy involved juxtaposing the precariously fixed saloon keeper and the powerful interests that would callously close him down. Whiteley's purpose became clear when he cross-examined Dr. Elmore Palmer. A noted liquor foe, Palmer was associated with raising money to prosecute those accused of violating the Sunday law. Whiteley began his examination by prodding "You have met and organized and aided in the raising of a fund to prosecute and convict in these cases, have you not?" When Palmer equivocated, Whiteley queried closer, "then state what you have done." Palmer admitted a fund had been started. Asked if he had contributed, Palmer compromised the truth. After Whiteley pressed: "Would you say on oath that [you] did not?" Palmer unconvincingly replied, "I would not say. I have forgotten." Whiteley had made the telling point that the poor saloon man stood at the mercy of conspiring, stronger, and untruthful elements.[18]

When the jury acquitted Albert Henry, the county attorney dropped the prosecution and all the cases involving Sunday restrictions. Having no legal case, for Henry had blatantly broken the law, Whiteley had played to the jurors' compassion and prejudices. Appreciative saloon keepers throughout the county praised (and surely toasted) Whiteley and Wright. Several days later, after being told that that further advice was needed, the two men walked into a surprise party where appreciative saloon keepers had gathered from "every camp and town in the county." Albert Henry, quite possibly an unwitting hero, thanked them in a short speech, and on behalf of the saloon keepers presented to each lawyer an inscribed, gold-headed ebony cane. Whiteley and Wright, basking in the continuing victory celebrations, showed their canes around Boulder, and by that afternoon "one half of the male portion of the city had seen those canes."[19]

The larger question of alcohol and its availability carried over into town politics that spring. Local temperance proponents had recently formed the Prohibitionist Party. Some of its members favored drastically raising the liquor license fee. Others supported blanket prohibition of the sale of alcohol. Meeting on March 22, 1884, at City Hall, the Prohibitionists drew up a platform and nominated mayoral and aldermen candidates. It was their conclusion that the sale and consumption of alcohol constituted "the greatest evil of the country."[20]

Less than a week later, on March 28, Whiteley was present when the Citizens Party (Republicans) met at City Hall and named its mayoral candidate and slate of aldermen. James P. Maxwell, who claimed the distinction of having served in the territorial and state legislature, warned, "we are to face a new enemy." He noted that Prohibitionist Party members "have seen fit to call us the whiskey party." Maxwell resented the imputation. So did Whiteley, who rose and stated that the Republicans did not kowtow to any interests. Alpheus Wright had recently become acting mayor. Whiteley emphasized his friend's stewardship, and on Whiteley's motion, Wright was unanimously nominated to fill the post full-time. The verdict of the brief but "hotly contested" election elated Whiteley. On April 1, 353 Boulder residents voted for Wright, and 272 recorded their support for another candidate. Whiteley's influence was not insignificant.[21]

In the summer of 1884 nothing seemed to hint at imminent change in Richard and Margaret Whiteley's life. In fact, the public record reflects much continuity. Margaret Whiteley complained that hours passed sometimes without a drop of water on Whiteley Hill. That caused extreme despair to a woman devoted to roses. "My prettiest ones," she lamented, "are almost all ruined for lack of water," and the "grass is parched and brown, and all because we can not get the water for which we pay."[22] Different concerns occupied her husband. At Berlin's Hall, on June 7, Republicans endorsed the recently nominated ticket of James G. Blaine and John A. Logan. Amid martial music and fireworks, there was oratory, some supplied by Whiteley, as the campaign was kicked off. Judge Granville Berkley died around the same time; Whiteley presided over a committee of fellow lawyers that considered how to mark Berkley's passing. He took advantage of one opportunity that must have caused him to feel nostalgic about his Reconstruction days in Georgia. Few blacks lived in Boulder, but some of those who did gathered outside of town at Turner's Grove on August 1 for an Emancipation Day celebration. Prayer and singing formed part of the commemoration, and attending were "a fair sprinkling of white people who sympathize with the freedmen in their jollification." Richard Whiteley spoke. He remained a public-spirited man whom almost everyone in Boulder knew, and most liked. His standing was about to take a precipitous fall.[23]

A series of events that would stun Boulder began on July 15, 1884. With cause, Margaret suspected (or knew) that her husband was involved in a relationship with Mollie Strickland, a local woman. On the evening of July 15, finding the two walking together, Margaret approached them. Whiteley knocked her down, and when she got up, struck her to the ground again. Some witnessed the altercation, and the incident became the object of considerable gossip.

Mary G. Strickland (known as Mollie) was the oldest daughter of Wade H. and Elizabeth Strickland. He was a well-liked miner, and the family lived in Magnolia, a mining community above Boulder. Mollie, twenty-one years old, was thirty-three years younger than Whiteley. Some evidence indicates she was a prostitute. Margaret did not know Mollie well, possibly not at all. They were of different generations, social classes, and moral outlooks. Whatever their familiarity, it was her husband's relationship with Mollie—a liaison apparently of some duration—that jeopardized and then ended the marriage.

Continuing to accept infidelity and physical abuse would have been difficult for any woman. It was exceedingly so for Margaret Whiteley, who was deeply devout and the embodiment of Victorian rectitude. She was a woman of means, fortitude, conviction, and as circumstances, proved, certain recourse. As one Boulder resident stated later, Margaret was "tolerant of the weaknesses though not the vices of others." Richard Whiteley was a man with vices.[24]

How untenable their marriage was became clear a month after the public confrontation. On August 12, Margaret filed for a divorce. She based the action on a pattern of domestic abuse, and though Margaret specifically cited the July 15 incident, she charged there had been past physical mistreatment. Whiteley appeared that afternoon in county court before Judge Sylvester Downer. He did not contest the divorce. About 2 P.M. on Tuesday, August 12, their thirty-three-year marriage abruptly ended.

That same afternoon the situation took another extraordinary turn: Whiteley married Mollie Strickland within two hours of the divorce. Justice of the peace Hyram E. Rowland married them because outraged local clergymen refused to do so. As it was, fearing violence against Whiteley, the sheriff and several policemen were summoned to provide protection. Alpheus Wright, Whiteley's longtime friend, witnessed the wedding ceremony.

Public reaction was immediate, definitive, and passionate. As the *Boulder News and Banner* reported, the developments were "the matter on every tongue." Angry and shocked townspeople categorically condemned Whiteley. Margaret Whiteley, well liked and respected, emerged the innocent and pitiable victim. The physical brutality she had suffered gravely affronted the community. Then her ex-husband's immediate marriage to another woman, a heartless and humiliating act, compounded feelings. The shocking news spread to the remote mountain cavities of Gold Hill, Nederland, and Salina and other Boulder County locations. People knew Richard Whiteley as a lawyer, politician, and civic leader. It was hard to conclude whether the presumably upright lawyer's abuse of his wife or his immediate remarriage was more astonishing. The situation drew notice in at least one Denver newspaper. According to the *Boulder News and Banner,* what transpired "shocked the public sensibilities as hardly any other occurrence in this city has ever before."

The divorce settlement clearly indicated where blame lay. Margaret kept Whiteley Hill and everything in the residence. Whiteley also conveyed to her all their Georgia property (with an estimated worth of $25,000), which included their former Bainbridge residence. Georgia bonds valued at $4,000 became Margaret's as well. Whiteley retained his law library, trunk, and clothing. With those possessions, he moved out of the family home in a cloud of disgrace.[25]

At least publicly, Whiteley remained silent about their parting. He explained that he could not live happily with Margaret, and was willing to give her the family property. Those simple facts should, he stated, satisfy Margaret and the public. He did not enlarge any further. Few accepted that rationalization, and the vast majority of Boulder agreed with the *Boulder County Herald,* which declared, "we have no excuse whatever to offer for the major."

It is not known how much or little the Whiteley children knew of their parents' differences and their father's relationship with Mollie. The

Boulder County Herald commiserated: "The family deserve and receive the sympathy of the people of Boulder." All but Charles were in Boulder during this wrenching time. Richard had returned from Harvard in July for the summer, and Hortense had recently arrived from school in Canada. For Hortense and Zena, fifteen and thirteen years old, the circumstances must have been devastating. All of the children supported their mother.[26]

The events of the summer of 1884 raise far more questions than can be answered. What were the problems that separated a man and woman who had been married for over three decades and had ten children together? How did Whiteley meet Mollie, and how long had they conducted an improper relationship? What was their attraction to each other? Why did Whiteley not at least allow a respectable period of time to pass before marrying Mollie? When considered along with his fathering of an illegitimate child by Catherine Carmody in Washington, does Whiteley's conduct point to a pattern of frequent immorality? Did he hit Margaret when under the influence of alcohol? Does Whiteley's physical abuse indicate that the private man was far different from the appealing public figure? The answers, simple or complex, are not known. It is certain that what occurred irrevocably stained the remaining life of Richard Whiteley.

Whiteley was fifty-four years old when the marriage ended. Several years earlier, a fellow resident had described him as "a man of sterling worth in society." That reputation was severely tarnished and sullied. In the small town of Boulder, there was no escaping the public opprobrium. He faced certain ostracism. Some friends remained steadfast, but others deserted him. Episcopal Church rules prevented him from taking Communion, and the former vestryman stopped attending St. John's Church. A public man had been brought down publicly. It was a degrading and long fall for the former master of Whiteley Hill.[27]

The short and unsatisfying statement that he could not live contentedly with Margaret is Whiteley's only known public explanation for their divorce. Leading a more contented existence, he apparently assumed, was possible with Mollie, and he began a new life with her. Despite the financially disastrous divorce, he remained a man of some means. In October 1885, he paid Henry C. Woodworth $4,000 for a home on the western edge of Pearl Street. Located on the corner of Seventh and Pearl streets, this house was within easy walking distance of his office. Whiteley appreciated the home for more than its convenience. The harmonious and distinguishing lines of the Gothic Revival cottage reflected the inspiration of George King, who had also been the architect of Whiteley

Hill. King had designed the home for William Arnett, a businessman, who had spared few expenses in its construction, completed in 1877. Two stories tall, built of red brick, crowned by a shingled mansard roof and framed by a wrought-iron fence, the house was described as "the gem of the city." The unconventional couple, accepted by some, a curiosity to others, and shunned by probably more, moved in. Major Whiteley had entered a period of social retreat.[28]

Whiteley's address, financial holdings, and local standing were diminished and changed by the divorce, but it did not have a devastating effect on his professional life. Three months after his divorce, in October 1884 in District Court, Whiteley defended John Paul, who had fatally wounded a man outside a saloon in Gold Hill. On Saturday evening, September 20, 1884, John L. Herzinger had viciously struck Paul in the face with a piece of ore; angered, Paul had retrieved a pistol and fired at Herzinger as he fled the saloon. The shots miscarried and struck Mike Joy, who was outside. Whiteley attempted to mitigate his client's crime by charging that Herzinger had precipitated the tragic chain of events. He rigorously cross-examined Herzinger. Accusatory questions posed by Whiteley caused Herzinger to protest "that is a lie," and declare from the stand: "I tell you it is pretty hard to testify." Whiteley continued relentlessly. As for his past relationship with Paul, Herzinger claimed to have "liked him very much." Whiteley immediately challenged: "Did you like him on the night in question?" A jury sympathetic to Paul found the defendant guilty of voluntary manslaughter, and Judge Charles Carpenter issued a lenient four-year sentence.[29]

When Whiteley represented William W. Likens in the spring of 1885, he defended a man held in low repute locally, who had been indicted for forgery. He realized the obstacles, given Likens's well-earned reputation for dishonesty and the state of opinion in Boulder. On May 21, amid much public attention, the jury found Likens guilty. Whiteley immediately demanded that the twelve men be polled. His challenge changed nothing, and Judge Charles Carpenter also denied Whiteley's request for a new trial. When Whiteley asked that Likens be allowed to return home before the sentencing, the magistrate refused. On May 25, at the sentencing, the psychologically and physically broken Likens took his seat between his wife and Whiteley. On behalf of Likens, Whiteley rose and reasoned that a hostile public inevitably influenced the jury, and he asked the judge "to be as merciful and as lenient as the law allows." Carpenter sentenced the haggard Likens to four years at the state penitentiary in Canon City. Even his many detractors were moved by the pathetic scene that played out the next afternoon at the courthouse when the handcuffed prisoner told his family goodbye and, escorted by Whiteley and a guard, traveled by carriage to the depot. Such was Likens's notoriety that a crowd had gathered there also. For his own reasons, and not uncommendable ones, Whiteley made the railroad trip to Canon City with Likens.

Whiteley remained involved in local political affairs. In the spring of 1885, a mayor and aldermen would be selected. As with the previous year's contest, the liquor question dominated. Temperance elements favored raising the saloon license fee to $1,000. That represented a dramatic increase from the existing fee of $400. Dr. Charles C. Brace headed what was called the "high license" ticket. Whiteley objected that although some proprietors could afford the increase, others would have to close. If their livelihood was jeopardized, Whiteley continued, the public also stood to suffer. Those saloon proprietors who remained in business would have a monopoly, and customers could expect to pay more in their establishments. Whiteley and others rallied around the theme of "anti-monopoly."[30]

On April 2, 1885, when the Citizens (or Republican) Party met, Whiteley read resolutions opposing raising license rates. James W. Develine, owner of the Boulder Iron Foundry, was mentioned as a candidate for mayor. When Develine professed an unfamiliarity with city business, Whiteley asked the Irishman if he had time for the office's duties. Develine replied affirmatively, and Whiteley assured him: "Well, then you are the man we want."[31] The party emphasized "anti-monopoly," and the *Boulder County Herald* stated its willingness "to bet Major Whiteley wrote that platform." Given his convictions and influence, it was a reasonable assumption. Develine may have been the mayoral candidate, but real power lay in the hands of Richard Whiteley.[32]

Arguably Boulder's most controversial citizen, Whiteley spoke at least once during the brief campaign. The front of John and Sarah Williams's saloon provided the appropriate venue. On Monday, March 23, a noon crowd gathered to hear Whiteley sound the "anti-monopoly" battle cry. "Go before the people and ask them," he urged, "if in addition to the other monopolies they are willing to have a whiskey monopoly?" Was it ethical, Whiteley asked, to "give the right to sell liquors in this town to a few?" Some may have questioned the major's personal sense of ethics. On Election Day, early in April, voters in the four wards gave a seventy-vote majority to the high-license ticket and Charles Brace.[33]

In the fall of 1886, when local Republicans settled on a county ticket, Whiteley played a heavy-handed role. The *Boulder Sentinel,* reacting to the expressed dissatisfaction of some Republicans, asked: "Does Major Whiteley carry the Republican party in and about his wearing apparel?" In a reference that needed no clarification, the paper wondered if county

Republicans bowed before "the gentleman from Georgia with the savory reputation?"[34]

Although Whiteley did not live with his family, he continued to have contact with them. He wanted that, and it was inevitable in a small town like Boulder. Whiteley surely continued to attend some of Montie's baseball games, and he took pride in his son's contributions to the Boulder Hose Company No. 1. Fire companies in Colorado competed annually at Georgetown in "wet" and "dry" contests. In August 1886, Montie captained an eighteen-member team that pulled their hose cart a designated distance and "procured water" in thirty-six and a half seconds, earning a $100 first prize and wide acclaim in Boulder. No doubt, on the streets of Boulder, his father accepted congratulations.[35]

He also approved of Richard. In June 1885, almost a year after his parents' divorce, Richard graduated from Harvard Law School. He returned to Boulder, moved in with his mother, Hortense, and Zena at Whiteley Hill, and began to practice law, inevitably opposing his father in court—doing so for the first time in 1886. Although he was not a man as given to dispute as his father could be, Richard followed him into politics. He became a well-known local Republican and ran for the state senate in 1888. To his father's delight, Richard unseated the incumbent. The elder Whiteley also endorsed his son's much-publicized (but ultimately futile) attempt to have a statute passed regulating railroad rates.

Whiteley followed his daughters' lives with love and interest. Hortense's instruction at the Hellmuth Ladies College had concluded, and following study at the preparatory department at the University of Colorado, she entered the university in 1887. She also performed often at local university functions. On the last day of May 1886, when the Philomathean Society met, Hortense "exhibited rare skill in rendering on the piano a selection from Mendelssohn."[36] Zena was in her last year of high school that year. On February 12, at a school program honoring Abraham Lincoln, she read an essay commemorating his death. At her graduation in May, she provided the "class prophecy," exhibiting "great inventive genius in being able to dispose of so many young people." She soon joined Hortense at the university.[37]

Margaret, almost fifty at the time of the divorce, continued to live at Whiteley Hill. She never remarried. Her life centered around her family and many friends. In the spring of 1886, water was especially scarce, but the resourceful woman took advantage of an exception that allowed water to be drawn from a central well after 11 P.M. She simply stayed up late and obtained water for her flowers. In a town of Boulder's size, and sharing a family, she had to have some contact with her former husband.

Some evidence indicates that their relationship was not overtly acrimonious.

Whatever the exact relationship between Whiteley and his family, all were saddened by the death of Charles Whiteley on December 17, 1886, in Washington, from the kidney problems he had long suffered from. Charles was thirty-seven years old. Josephine and their three children survived him. At least Richard and Margaret could share grief.

The death of Charles dampened the mood at the wedding, two weeks later, of Richard Whiteley to Ella Tyler. A member of a prominent local family, Ella became in 1886 the first female graduate of the University of Colorado. On January 1, 1887, Rector Thomas Wilson and Bishop John F. Spaulding married the couple. The ceremony took place on Saturday night at the fine home of Clinton and Sarah Tyler north of Boulder. The marriage grafted together two of the most respected families in the county. Following a honeymoon in nearby Estes Park, Richard and Ella made a temporary home at Whiteley Hill.[38]

In the late 1880s, Margaret Whiteley continued to do what her former husband could not: lead a life free of burdening guilt. In February

*Margaret Whiteley (*sixth from right*). Courtesy of Carnegie Branch Library for Local History, Boulder Historical Society Collection.*

1888, she hosted teas on successive days at Whiteley Hill. "Mrs. Whiteley employed her usual tact," a guest wrote, "in trying to invite all her friends so that none should feel any slight." The scene—crowded parlors, much conversation, and fine food—was reminiscent of past times at Whiteley Hill.[39] Margaret grew, picked, and arranged a bouquet of "rare flowers" that drew praise locally in 1889. Five years had passed since the divorce.[40] John Donalson, Whiteley's former law partner in Bainbridge, handled her Georgia property and any business relating to Margaret's holdings. All did not go well. Ann Desverges had bought their Bainbridge home in 1886 but had not paid Margaret the balance. As the situation strung out, she wrote Donalson: "I think Mrs. Desverges has acted very shabby in the matter and don't care if the place is sold away from her."[41] She held Mollie Strickland Whiteley in even less favor and referred to her contemptuously as "that woman."[42]

Her former husband struggled with a deep sense of remorse in the last years of his life. The self-inflicted damage done to his name and the grief and embarrassment caused his family burdened Whiteley heavily. One who knew the lawyer speculated that "for his weakness, he paid a dear penalty."[43] In the meantime, his marriage to Mollie fell apart. They were of different worlds. Age was only one chasm that separated them. Mollie lacked all social standing or sense of etiquette and was barely literate. Simply adopting the surname Whiteley did not endow her with the qualities of the genteel. Bridging their differences proved impossible. The circumstances of his divorce tormented him, and possibly Whiteley blamed Mollie for breaking up his marriage to Margaret, further weakening their relationship. For Mollie's part, she resented her husband's relations with his family. On one occasion, she destroyed the pictures of Hortense and Zena that Whiteley kept in his law office. As the marriage deteriorated, they slept in separate rooms. He took meals at a local hotel and feared Mollie might poison him. Efforts to divorce Mollie, apparently pursued by Whiteley, all failed. In 1890, Margaret would write of her ex-husband: "he has been very unhappy for years."[44]

Despite his private despair, the major seems to have regained some of his local standing by the late 1880s. Sentiment against him, as time passed, somewhat dissipated. When citizens confused him with his son Richard, who was handling some accounting work, the *Boulder County Herald* observed: "Major Whiteley has been bothered no little by persons coming to him to settle."[45] Early in 1888, Whiteley made improvements on his and Mollie's Pearl Street house. Later in the year, he somehow dislocated his shoulder, but by the fall was reported to be out on the streets, with the qualification that he would "attempt no more acrobatic feats for the present." When he contracted yellow fever in the fall of 1888, he insisted that the disease was preferable to the shoulder injury. Making money in mining ventures continued to be important; on October 1, 1887, he bought an interest in the Grand View Lode. At other times, acting as the grantor, he sold property.

Whiteley gradually gave up his campaigning in the midterm and national elections. Since 1872 he had obtained, every other year, a copy of Edward McPherson's Washington-based biannual *Hand-book of Politics,* whose contents could only have interested the closest Washington observer. Whiteley stopped getting the handbook after 1882. Still, he did not ever abandon local politics. In the county elections of 1889, the *Boulder County Herald* defended Whiteley when it was rumored that he had participated in a devious Republican intrigue.

Sometime after the publication of Ulysses Grant's well-received memoirs in 1885, Whiteley obtained that two-volume work. He could read it with a unique perspective—he had fought against the general but acted politically with the president. He also acquired John A. Logan's book *The Great Conspiracy,* dealing with the Civil War era, and the *Personal Memoirs of P. H. Sheridan* became part of his library of approximately three hundred volumes. He continued to consult and read legal works. When he defended Nettie Still, Whiteley had to reach no further than his office shelves to consult William A. Hammond's *Treatise on Insanity* and *A Treatise on the Medical Jurisprudence of Insanity,* written by Isaac Ray. It was a man who took pride in his profession and performance who around this time added to his library Richard Harris's work *Before and at Trial: What Should Be Done by Council, Solicitor and Client.*[46]

Whiteley clearly remained a force in the courtroom. In April 1888, he represented Louis Garbinio before the City Council, which had revoked Garbinio's liquor license as punishment for his selling liquor on Sunday. The words of an observer who colorfully described the council meeting give a sense of Whiteley's power of persuasion: Whiteley "anointed the heads of the refractory [City Council] members" and "struck them dumb with his oratory." When Garbinio regained his license, the "penitent client" thanked "the Major." Gabrinio had brashly offered $500 to anyone who could prove he sold liquor on Sunday. Some of the money, better spent, was presumably used to pay Whiteley.[47]

In February 1889, when Judge Sylvester Downer convened District Court, the most anticipated case was that of the indicted murderer Alma Green, whom Whiteley defended. Green, who was twenty-eight years old, was a servant on A. C. Goodhue's local farm, where Sam Dudley, nineteen years old, worked as a farm hand. The boy had often insulted Green and made crude references to her virtue. On January 4, 1889, angered by the latest insult, she took a pistol from a closet at the Goodhue home, aimed the gun at Dudley, and demanded he take his words back. He refused, the pistol went off, and he was killed almost instantly.

Six weeks later, when District Court opened, local attention rivaled that for the Nettie Still trial seven years earlier, which had also been the last time a woman had been tried for murder in Boulder County. Unusually large numbers of women, undoubtedly sympathetic to Green, were present when Whiteley delivered a "spirited" opening argument on February 11, 1889.[48] He maintained that the shooting was accidental. And even if the jury decided that Green meant to shoot, her counselor argued, the action was justified. Whiteley, a consummate judge of human nature, shrewdly put her on the stand, where her behavior elicited sympathy. As he directed the examination, the shaken and nervous woman recalled the victim's transgressions. Speaking emotionally, haltingly, "as if in a dream," she confided that she had not meant to shoot the gun and had "never before nor after fired a pistol."[49]

On February 13, when Whiteley and District Attorney C. E. Garrigues delivered closing arguments, every seat in the courtroom was taken. Whiteley portrayed for the jury a helpless and intimidated woman. He described Alma Green as naive, and he "appealed eloquently to the sympathy and manhood of the jury." Garrigues presented her in very contrasting terms. An observer judged Whiteley's effort the superior one, and it became "evident from the start that he had the sympathy of the jury and audience." The jury deliberated only minutes before pronouncing the defendant not guilty. Green collapsed, and the audience broke out in spontaneous applause. Whiteley took satisfaction from prevailing in a case of which one observer said "no trial that ever occurred in the county perhaps excited more general interest."

The scars of the divorce remained, but Whiteley's rehabilitation with his family continued. With the passage of time, a certain sadness and resignation, more than bristling hostility, characterized Richard and Margaret Whiteley's relationship. Mindful of her former husband's failings, Margaret also respected his strengths. Those included solicitude for his family. Hortense and Zena were delighted in 1890 to receive a grand piano from their father. He talked regularly with Montie and Richard. When District Court convened in February 1890, Whiteley and his son defended Albert Kruger, a father of five children, none older than six, who had stolen some horses. Acting on his own, Whiteley defended four Swedish immigrants who were charged with arson in Coal Creek Canyon. It would be one of his last cases.[50]

If Whiteley thought much about death, and how he would be remembered, it is impossible to know. At any rate, in 1890 he seems to have showed no signs of slowing down. He was professionally active and had regained a measure of social respectability. Life for him was vibrant and well worth living, and despite times of intense personal self-recrimination, Whiteley felt he had much more to do. But on Friday, September 26, he suddenly and unexpectedly died. On the previous day, Thursday, as was his practice, he had been about town and had talked with various people. That night, as he often did, he spoke with Montford. Neither Montie nor anybody else noticed anything unusual about him. Yet Whiteley complained to Mollie of head pains early Friday morning, and he soon became unconscious. She summoned a doctor, who was there by 7:30, and Montie and Richard arrived a couple of hours later. They called for two more doctors, but Whiteley never regained consciousness. He died around noon. Blood vessels had burst in his brain, causing apoplexy, and death. He was sixty.

The death of this notable man saddened and shocked townspeople. On the next day, Saturday, many attended the funeral at the Pearl Street residence. Minister Marion W. Hissey of the Methodist Episcopal Church officiated. Local lawyers acted as pallbearers. Margaret, Montford, Richard, Hortense, and Zena were surely present. Mollie Strickland, still not thirty years old, seemed an unlikely widow. Later that afternoon, at the cemetery on the southern edge of town, Richard Whiteley's remains were laid to rest.[51]

Whiteley had made a lasting, if ultimately marred, impression in thirteen years in Colorado. Local lawyers met two days after his funeral and drafted several resolutions. Those who had acted with and against him in court spoke "feelingly" of the man they described as kind, generous, and the ablest member of the bar.[52] Boulder citizens remembered a generous man, an advocate of public education, and a strong civic promoter. The *Boulder County News* outlined an eventful life. "He had many noble and generous qualities," the newspaper affirmed, and volunteered "there was something about his character, and genial disposition that drew men irresistibly to him and held them." Whiteley's passing also resurrected memories of personal scandal. The *News* alluded to "the grave mistakes which doubtless darkened and embittered the last years of his life."[53] The *Boulder County Herald* also noted his public contributions, loyal friends, and again, unusual kindness, adding that "the one great fault of his life weighed heavily upon him." Boulder knew what that was. The *Herald* concluded: "peace to his ashes." Richard Whiteley had not known much of that in his final years.[54]

Conclusion

Richard Henry Whiteley was an indefatigable advocate of causes. Though he never used the term "social justice," that was his unremitting goal. Whatever the aim—helping attract a railroad to Bainbridge or proselytizing for building a courthouse in Boulder—Whiteley was a man of vision. There was always a battle to be waged for this most public of men. The status of the ex-slaves was Whiteley's most important cause and accounts for this biography. For a dozen years after the Civil War, his compulsion to participate intersected with the unresolved issues of race and Reconstruction. Driven by an elemental need to speak, be heard, and make a difference, he understood and attempted to implement change. For Whiteley, and indeed any white man who did likewise in the Reconstruction South, certain notoriety awaited him.

Henry Caleb understood that. On October 1, 1871, testifying in Washington before the Select Committee to Inquire into the Condition of Affairs in the Late Insurrectionary States, Caleb responded to a question about the status of white Republicans in Georgia: "They called me by the worst name you can give a man down there, that is, a radical."[1] In Alabama, Samuel F. Rice also appeared before another congressional committee that investigated political disorder. He stated: "Whigs and Democrats used to abuse each other very fiercely in speeches and newspapers but such things scarcely ever affected our social relations." The situation had changed after the war. Rice continued: "I notice what I never noticed before, that the estimate of a man is more controlled by his politics than by anything else."[2]

Whiteley could have empathized with both men. What defined him as a politician, infusing his career with enduring importance, alienated him from the vast majority of Georgia whites. He endorsed full citizenship for the ex-slaves. The Reconstruction Acts and Fourteenth and Fifteenth Amendments gave him a political philosophy to act, speak, and vote by. By describing a better future, the Republican inspired blacks in Camilla, Thomasville, and other southwestern Georgia outposts. He showed the freedpeople the connection between politics, power, and their personal lives. They turned out to hear him and, time and again, to vote for him. (Regrettably, the lack of any surviving records left by members of Whiteley's black constituency prevents a more precise understanding of their view of him). A man of unswerving conviction, he spoke of "the rights of an emancipated race"[3] and "the legal and political equality of both races." A central point should not be lost in the story of Whiteley's biannual struggle for political survival between 1868 and 1876. He fought against Nelson Tift, Gilbert Wright, and James Smith, white Democrats all; but, more important, Whiteley fought for black Southerners.[4]

An inimitable sense of jurists' loyalties, passions, fears, weaknesses, and collective psyche made him a fine lawyer, and the same instincts contributed to his effectiveness as a political candidate. In the outback of southwest Georgia, Richard Whiteley addressed voters at on courthouse squares, from rural black pulpits, at isolated crossroads, and anywhere else an audience could be raised. He spoke well and convincingly and exhibited an instinctive gift for politics. These abilities were critical, given the unforgiving nature of grassroots Reconstruction politics. Some enemies considered him politically duplicitous, malleable, and insincere, depending on the time, place, and audience. Certainly he was shrewd and sly, but he acted on a basic truth. In its most unvarnished guise, political survival for a southern Republican politician depended on getting blacks to the polls, winning over or appeasing some whites, and minimizing the certain obstruction of Democrats. Whiteley understood that pragmatic considerations sometimes trumped principle, and that principle could never be served out of office. This was the man who, after he arrived out West, attempted to organize a migratory movement of blacks from southwest Georgia to Colorado. Whiteley understood that the promise Reconstruction heralded, by the mid-1870s, was an illusion in Georgia and the South. Though very few or none actually left Georgia, Whiteley's efforts at attracting blacks to Colorado to improve their lives clearly offers an antidote to charges that the vote-grabbing scalawag was not genuinely interested in the freedpeople. His thinking also anticipated the later exit of the Exodusters to Kansas.

Despite the charges and epithets of Democrats, Whiteley did not scorn the South. He possessed a deep affection for his adopted home. That sentiment accounted for his opposition to secession. Fearful of the consequences of war, and mindful of the Union, Whiteley had resisted the South's course. Yet, following secession, he loyally served the Confederacy for the conflict's duration. Rather than contempt, it was his regard for the South that guided his political conduct after the war. When Democrats resisted the proposed Fourteenth Amendment, they jeopardized Georgia's readmission to the Union. Whiteley argued that the South's resurrection (economic and psychological) could begin only after the region had resumed its place there. Always a proponent of economic development, he called for putting racial prejudices aside. Racial cooperation was necessary, since "we must meet a living present as practical men who have a country to develop." In Washington, Congressman Whiteley represented Georgians of both races and parties. Those who disparaged him as an ingrate, the caricature of the heinous scalawag, misjudged both southern Republicans and Richard Whiteley. Terry Seip has convincingly written that southern Republicans, contrary to previous supposition, represented the region's economic interests. Although how Whiteley voted on such questions has not been my focus, the congressman's record is clear. It was, Whiteley stated, "the best interests of the district" that caused him to work for improving Georgia rivers. The integral part he played in removing Georgians' political disabilities Whiteley considered part "of my good fortune." If some saw an inherent contradiction between his Confederate past and Republican present, their reasoning was lost on Whiteley.[5]

One can reasonably measure the politician by examining his speeches, correspondence, and voting record. Assessing the private man is more difficult, but some assumptions suggest themselves strongly. Always ambitious, he set out early in life to become a man of influence. His nature would not tolerate anything less. His ability, work ethic, and drive were apparent from the outset. These traits served him well in overcoming the absence of a father, humble Irish roots, and almost no formal education. The trajectory was always up—factory boy, textile mill owner, army officer, lawyer, solicitor general, congressman. This is not the path of the unambitious. Gregarious and unpretentious, and a man of considerable charm, Whiteley gained friends and admirers. He valued fine possessions and money, and he acquired both. Possibly his memories of a hardscrabble childhood accounted for his compassion for those who had hard lives, both blacks and poor whites. Whatever the case, his empathy was certain. At the Georgia state constitutional convention, delegate Whiteley worked for the homestead and relief clauses. In Colorado, he battled for the marginally fixed saloon keeper. A consistent and unmistakable pattern emerges. Whiteley provided legal services to the poor for a nominal fee or free. What best exemplifies his compassion were his efforts on behalf of the freedpeople, a downtrodden population with a collective past of exploitation and apparently a little brighter future.

There was also a complex and dark side to this enigmatic figure. Whiteley was an inscrutable man of contradictions. Although he made public references to the Almighty, this churchgoing man fathered an illegitimate child, and more than once his sexual desires overcame his will to pursue a morally higher course. He supported the rights of women but physically abused his wife. A man of society and the gentry, he violated its conventions by ruining his marriage to a good woman and immediately marrying a younger woman of dubious qualities. Any evaluation of Whiteley's character involves his divorce and remarriage. With so little available evidence, understanding what divided him and Margaret Whiteley is not possible. His actions in the summer of 1884 remain perplexing and intriguing, and present a large and unresolved question. Who can understand the dark recesses of a man's mind that can sometimes govern his actions, catapulting him into danger and infamy?

Regardless of his personal life, Whiteley's significance lies in the part he played in politics after the Civil War. In the end, Reconstruction failed. Privileges and rights granted to blacks after the war were gradually withdrawn. What Whiteley called a "new era of freedom," first compromised during Reconstruction, ended as the South developed into a Jim Crow society as the nineteenth century ended. Although the South lost the war, the southern white man's judgment of the black man's place became the reality. With little northern interference, southern whites soon relegated the freedpeople to a secondary citizenship. Blacks lost the right to vote. Opportunities for them to become educated, begun boldly during Reconstruction, similarly dissipated. The vast majority of blacks remained poor, unable to advance economically, often mired in the cruelties of crop-lien peonage. The descent began during Reconstruction. Klansmen, White Leaguers, and politically violent whites compromised the freedpeople's status. Other impediments to true citizenship, more deftly delivered than the vigilante's bludgeon, had equally devastating consequences for blacks. The poll tax in Georgia was a classic example. The flush times of the Republican Party in the South—the late 1860s—became part of a distant past. The party in Georgia and the South became little more than a clearinghouse for dispensing federal patronage. As the southern wing of the Republican Party slid toward political oblivion, its commitment to the principles of the party of Lincoln became obscure. By the late nineteenth century, the egalitarian words that were perfunctorily written into the Republican Party platform every four years had become meaningless.[6]

Earlier, at the racial crossroads of Reconstruction, a comparatively few white men had taken a stand for justice and the Constitution. Some of the most heroic of them were Southerners. Thomas Settle of North Carolina was one; another was Congressman Horace Maynard of Tennessee, who argued that blacks deserved the right to vote, testify in court, and participate fully. A colleague of his in the House of Representatives, George Whitemore of Texas, forthrightly agreed. Charles Hays, congressman from Alabama, who had owned much property before the war, including human chattel, became an outspoken Republican and advocated on the House floor what became the Civil Rights Act of 1875. In Mississippi, Robert Flourney, a prominent Republican though never elected to office, advocated a racially integrated society far ahead of his time.[7]

Richard Whiteley of Georgia belonged among that group. His was a path of tolerance and patience, with an informed view to the future and the black race's achievable place there. Here was a man who stood on makeshift platforms with blacks, calling for justice and respect for the Constitution. Whiteley's was a persistent but increasingly isolated voice. At one point, he asked: "Are we not one people?" The answer, for the time being, was a resounding no. He confronted a cultural milieu that overmatched his abilities, however persuasive, and his ideas, albeit enlightened. Whiteley became the incarnation of Radicalism and the most loathed Republican in southwest Georgia. By the time he left for Colorado, Georgia Republicanism lay in shambles, and blacks were well on their way to the inferior station they would occupy indefinitely. As for the freedpeople, Whiteley philosophized that "a civilized world, which sympathizes with the weak, the ignorant, the despised, of every land, will not remain silent in the presence of injustice." But that is precisely what happened. Whiteley faced political repudiation. He was resoundingly defeated in the 1874 and 1876 elections. Nonetheless, measured against a longer yardstick that stretches into the twentieth century, the convictions of Richard Whiteley were vindicated.[8]

Afterword

The Whiteley family continued to be prominent in Boulder in the years following Richard Whiteley's death. In 1892, two years after his father's death, Richard and his wife and their small son moved into a new home on the corner of Seventeenth and Pine streets. The "Poplars," as the striking two-story stone structure would be known, became a Boulder landmark. Leaving the family home on Whiteley Hill, Margaret, Hortense, and Zena soon resided there. Richard concentrated on an extremely successful corporate law practice and remained one of Boulder's most well-respected citizens. Montford, also held in high regard, served as mayor from 1899 to 1905, before moving with his family in 1912 to Fort Morgan, Wyoming. Early in the 1890s, both Hortense and Zena graduated from the University of Colorado. Hortense taught Greek and Latin at the State Preparatory School (connected to the university) and married Fred Hellems, the dean of the University of Colorado.

The family also faced bizarre tragedy. Few people knew (as was his wish) of Richard's countless private acts of charity. His struggle with epilepsy, however, was well known because the unpredictable seizures sometimes occurred publicly. A severe attack, causing the lawyer to fall and strike his head in front of his office, resulted in Richard Whiteley's death in 1912. He was fifty-one years old. A decade later, in 1922, a car accident in Boulder took the life of Hortense Whiteley, eulogized in the local newspaper as one of the town's "most loved and highly respected women."

Margaret Whiteley lived at the "Poplars" from the early 1890s until 1913. Soon after Richard's death, she wrote John Donalson in Bainbridge, "It is so hard not to see my dear boy." In 1913, an incredible life begun some eighty years earlier in Ireland, which included the distinctively American experiences of the Civil War, Reconstruction, and western settlement, ended when she died at the "Poplars." Zena Whiteley, civically active and prominent in the Episcopalian Church, married her brother-in-law, Fred Hellems, in 1926. Returning often to Boulder to attend football games, Montford remained well known locally. He died in 1933 at Fort Morgan. The last of the children, Zena, passed away at Boulder in 1958.

Mollie Whiteley never remarried. She moved from the Pearl Street home that she and Richard Whiteley had shared, but she remained in Boulder until shortly before her death in 1936. Those attending the service at Columbia or Pioneer Cemetery knew little or nothing of the man next to whom she was laid to rest. Richard Whiteley had died almost a half century earlier.

NOTES

Introduction

1. *Macon American Union,* March 11, 1870.
2. *Bainbridge Weekly Sun,* July 30, 1874.
3. Olsen, *Reconstruction and Redemption in the South,* 1; Tunnell, *Edge of the Sword;* Campbell, *Grass-Roots Reconstruction in Texas 1865–1880.*
4. Trelease, "Who Were the Scalawags?" 445; Tunnell, *Edge of the Sword,* 2–4; Dunning, *Reconstruction, Political and Economic 1865–1877;* also representative of this school are Fleming, *Civil War and Reconstruction in Alabama,* and Garner, *Reconstruction in Mississippi.*
5. Baggett, *The Scalawags;* 1–6; Donald, "The Scalawag in Mississippi Reconstruction"; Trelease, "Who Were the Scalawags?"; on a state level, see revisionist works such as Harris, *The Day of the Carpetbagger;* Shofner, *Nor Is It Over Yet;* Wiggins, *The Scalawag in Alabama Politics, 1865–1881;* Tunnell, *Crucible of Reconstruction;* on a broader level, see Foner, *Reconstruction;* Current, *Those Terrible Carpetbaggers;* Abbott, *The Republican Party and the South;* and Degler, *The Other South.*

Chapter 1: An Irishman in America

1. Registers of First Garvagh Presbyterian Church, First Garvagh Presbyterian Church, Garvagh, Ireland, Co. Londonderry; Georgia State Census 1840, Richmond County, reel 49, 274; Bixby et al., *History of Clear Creek and Boulder Valleys, Colorado,* 696; *Portrait and Biographical Record of Denver and Vicinity,* 331; Barnes, *The History of the Congress of the United States,* n.p.
2. Buckingham, *The Slave States of America,* 166–69; Bixby et al., *History of Clear Creek and Boulder Valleys,* 696–97; White, *Statistics of Georgia,* 506; a standard history of Augusta is Cashin, *The Story of Augusta.*
3. *Macon American Union,* March 11, 1890. Woodward, *The Augusta Directory and City Advertiser for 1841,* 79; Georgia State Census 1840, Richmond County, reel 49, 274; Roll and Record Book of Session of First Presbyterian Church, Augusta, Ga., from November 1838 to April 1856, reel 2, 43, Augusta Genealogical Society Library, Augusta, Georgia; Cashin, *Story of Augusta,* 39, 79, 94, 106.
4. Thomson, *A Tradesman's Travels,* 17–18, 114–16; *Augusta Daily Constitutionalist,* May 28, 1847; *Atlanta Daily New Era,* February 27, 1868; Buckingham, *The Slave States of America,* 169; Jones and Dutcher, *Memorial History*

of Augusta, Georgia, 242–43, 396–97; for textiles in Georgia, see Griffin, "The Origins of the Industrial Revolution in Georgia," 354–75.

5. *Augusta Daily Constitutionalist,* May 28, 1847; Richmond County Marriage License Book 1839–55, book B, 132, Office of the Probate Judge, Augusta, Georgia; *Boulder County Herald,* September 28, 1881.

6. *Augusta Daily Chronicle and Sentinel,* May 28, 1847; Georgia State Census 1850, Richmond County, reel 81, 498, 659; Thompson, *A Tradesman's Travels,* 17–18, 114–16.

7. Georgia State Census 1850, Greene County, reel 71, 109; Greene County Georgia Marriage Licenses, 1849–52, n.p., microfilm, Georgia Department of Archives and History (hereafter GDAH), Atlanta; Griffin, "The Textile Industry in Greene County, Georgia before 1860," 82; Bixby et al., *History of Clear Creek and Boulder Valleys,* 696–97; Charlene Fullerton Whiteley Gellatly to Secretary of the University (Princeton), March 22, 1954, Alumni File of Princeton University, Seeley G. Mudd Manuscript Library, Princeton, New Jersey; *Portrait and Biographical Record of Denver and Vicinity,* 331.

8. Bixby et al., *History of Clear Creek and Boulder Valleys,* 696; Tax Digests, 1852, 1853, 1854, Clarke County, Office of the Probate Judge Office, Athens, Georgia; Georgia State Census 1860, Decatur County, reel 119, 123; Decatur County, Georgia, Court of the Ordinary, 1860, 2, microfilm, GDAH; Thomas, *A Portrait of Historic Athens and Clarke County,* 47; *Portrait and Biographical Record of Denver and Vicinity,* 331.

9. Clarke County, Georgia Superior Court Minutes, 1853–56, book 19, microfilm, GDAH.

10. U.S. Bureau of the Census, *Eighth Census, 1860, Population,* 72–73; Johnston, *City of Bainbridge and County of Decatur Georgia,* 5, 7–8, 12; *American Missionary Magazine* (June 1868), 126–27; *Bainbridge Southern Sun,* quoted in *Macon American Union,* March 11, 1870; for Sanborn, see Jones, *History of Decatur County,* 215.

11. Tax Digests, 1856, 1857, 1860, Decatur County, microfilm, GDAH; *Bainbridge Southern Georgian,* July 22, 1859; Georgia State Census 1860, Slave Schedules, Decatur County, reel 144, 248.

12. *Bainbridge Southern Guardian,* July 22, 1859; Deed Book of Decatur County, Office of the Probate Judge, Bainbridge, Georgia, L, 141–42; Johnston, *City of Bainbridge and County of Decatur Georgia,* 19.

13. *Bainbridge Southern Guardian,* May 21, 1858, November 19, 1858.

14. Ibid., February 11, 1859.

15. Ibid., July 22, February 11, 1859.

16. *Bainbridge Argus,* June 10, September 16, December 2, 1856, July 15, 1857, January 20, 1858; *Bainbridge Southern Guardian,* May 20, 1859, February 7, 1860; U.S. Bureau of the Census, *Eighth Census, 1860, Population,* 72–74; *American Missionary Magazine* (June 1868), 126–27; Johnston, *City of Bainbridge and County of Decatur,* 9; Decatur County Historical Society, *Decatur County, Georgia, Past and Present 1823–1991,* 7.

17. *Bainbridge Southern Sun* quoted in *Macon American Union,* March 11, 1870; Bixby et al., *History of Clear Creek and Boulder Valleys,* 697; Georgia State Census 1860, Slave Schedules, Decatur County, reel 144, 248; Masons Book, Orion Lodge No. 8, Free and Accepted Masons from May 26, 1855, to December 26, 1857, in possession of Benny Brooksip, Bainbridge, Georgia.

18. *Atlanta Daily New Era,* February 27, 1867.

19. *Bainbridge Southern Sun,* quoted in *Macon American Union,* March 11, 1870; *Atlanta Daily New Era,* February 27, 1868.

20. "Petition of Hugh M. King," Decatur County Superior Court, Superior Court Pleadings 1850–69, Office of the Probate Judge, Bainbridge, Georgia; Bixby et al., *History of Clear Creek and Boulder Valleys,* 697; *Boulder (Colo.) County Herald,* April 9, 1913; Grice, *The Georgia Bench and Bar,* 261–63, 350–53; Bryant, *How Curious a Land,* 50–51; for the wiles of a trial lawyer in Georgia, see Smith, "Some Recollections of Law and Lawyers of Other Days," 71–72; Jones, *History of Decatur County,* 418.

21. For sectional controversy during the 1850s, see McPherson, *The Battle Cry of Freedom.*

22. *Bainbridge Southern Georgian* quoted in *Bainbridge Argus,* January 20, 1858; Johnson, *Under the Southern Cross,* 8; for sectional debate in Georgia, see Carey, *Practice, Slavery, and the Union in Antebellum Georgia.*

23. *Bainbridge Southern Guardian,* March 25, 1859, October 22, 1858, May 3, 1860.

24. *Bainbridge Southern Guardian,* December 9, 1859; *Bainbridge Southern Sun,* May 6, 1870; Bixby et al., *History of Clear Creek and Boulder Valleys,*

25. *Bainbridge Southern Guardian,* May 31, 1860.

26. *Macon Daily Telegraph,* May 14, 1861; Henderson, *Confederate Soldiers of Georgia,* 1:704; Johnson, *Under the Southern Cross,* 8; Jones, *History of Decatur County,* 368; Georgia State Census 1860, Slave Schedules, Decatur County, reel 144, 248.

27. *Macon Daily Telegraph,* May 14, 1861; Service Record of Richard H. Whiteley, Compiled Service Records of Confederate Soldiers Who Served in Organizations from the State of Georgia (St–Z), reel 199, GDAH; *Portrait and Biographical Record of Denver and Vicinity,* 331–32; McWhinney, *Braxton Bragg and Confederate Defeat,* 1:154–97; Henderson, *Confederate Soldiers of Georgia,* 704; Boatner, *The Civil War Dictionary,* 430; Mortality Schedule for Decatur County, 1860, GDAH.

28. Richard Whiteley to Samuel Cooper, March 12, 1862, in Compiled Service Records (St–Z); Service Record of Richard Whiteley, in Compiled Service Records, Second Battalion Sharp Shooters (K–Z), reel 164; Service Record of Richard Whiteley, in Compiled Service Records (A–J), reel 163, (K–Z), reel 164, GDAH; J. J. Cox to Captain Joseph B. Cumming, January 10, 1863, in U.S. Congress, *War of the Rebellion: A Compilation of the Office Records of the Union and Confederate Armies* (hereafter cited as OR), ser. 1, vol. 20, pt. 1, 841–42; John Jackson to John Ingram, October 3, 1863, *OR,* ser. 1, vol. 30, pt. 3, 82–85; *Macon American Union,* May 6, 1870; the standard history of the Army of Tennessee is Connelly, *Army of the Heartland,* and *Autumn of Glory;* Robinson, *Justice in Grey,* 362–63.

29. Richard Whiteley to Captain S. A. Moreno, October 4, 1863, *OR,* ser. 1, vol. 38, pt. 3, 89; John Jackson to S. Cooper, June 1, 1863, Compiled Service Records (St–Z); Henderson, *Roster of the Confederate Soldiers of Georgia,* 704.

30. Whiteley to Moreno, October 4, 1863, *OR,* ser. 1, vol. 38, pt. 3, 89–91, 655, 718–19; *Macon American Union,* May 6, 1870; Bixby et al., *History of Clear Creek and Boulder Valleys, Colorado,* 697.

31. *Bainbridge Weekly Sun,* July 30, 1874; Compiled Service Records (K–Z); for

experiences of soldiers in the Army of Tennessee, see Daniel, *Soldiering in the Army of Tennessee.*

32. *Boulder News,* October 2, 1890; *Macon American Union,* May 6, 1870; Johnston, *City of Bainbridge and County of Decatur,* 17.

Chapter 2: An Avowed Republican

1. Johnston, *City of Bainbridge and County of Decatur,* 13, 17; Minutes of [Bainbridge] City Council (1865–1868), City Hall, Bainbridge, Georgia, 2; William Clark to E. A. Ware, February 7, 1868, reel 10, Records of the Superintendent of Education for the State of Georgia, Bureau of Refugees, Freedmen, and Abandoned Lands, 1865–70, RG 105, National Archives Branch, Eastpoint, Georgia (hereafter cited as Records of the Superintendent of Education, Georgia); McQueen McIntosh to Brigadier General Davis Tillson, December 6, 1865, reel 24, Records of the Assistant Commissioner for the State of Georgia, Bureau of Refugees, Freedmen and Abandoned Lands, 1865–69, RG 105, National Archives Branch, Eastpoint, Georgia (hereafter cited as Records of the Assistant Commissioner, Georgia); for the South after the war, see Foner, *Reconstruction,* 124–29; Roark, *Masters without Slaves,* 120, 183–88.

2. *Bainbridge Weekly Democrat,* September 3, 1874; Georgia State Census 1860, Decatur County, reel 119, 123; Georgia State Census 1870, Decatur County, reel 146, 32; Deed Book of Decatur County, Office of the Probate Judge, Bainbridge, Georgia, N, 490; Mortality Schedule for Decatur County, 1860, GDAH; *Boulder News and Courier,* June 22, 1883.

3. *Bainbridge Argus* (November 8, 1865) quoted in *Macon American Union,* March 25, 1870; *Bainbridge Southern Georgian,* October 10, 1866, January 13, 1869; Grice, *Georgia Bench and Bar,* 255–58, 301–4; Jonathan Bryant, *How Curious a Land,* 51–52.

4. Foner, *Reconstruction,* 183; Stampp, *The Era of Reconstruction 1865–1877,* 62–64; Conway, *The Reconstruction of Georgia,* 51–52.

5. *Bainbridge Argus* (November 8, 1865) quoted in *Macon American Union,* March 25, 1870; *Bainbridge Weekly Democrat,* October 9, 1873; Johnston, *City of Bainbridge and County of Decatur,* 17.

6. *Bainbridge Southern Sun,* February 24, 1870.

7. *Bainbridge Argus* (November 8, 1865) quoted in *Macon American Union,* March 25, 1870; *Bainbridge Southern Sun,* February 24, 1870.

8. Foner, *Reconstruction,* 68–69, 180, 184, 189, 196–202, 227–32, 239; Stampp, *Era of Reconstruction,* 67–68, 79–82, 99–102, 110; a general history of the Freedmen's Bureau is Bentley, *A History of the Freedmen's Bureau.* In Georgia, see Cimbala, *Under the Guardianship of the Nation.*

9. U.S. Congress, "Condition of Affairs in Georgia," 118–19; Cimbala, *Under the Guardianship of the Nation,* 46–47, 107, 131, 164.

10. Robert R. Terrell to W. F. White, February 19, 1867, box 11, in Sub Assistant Commissioner Letters Received (Bainbridge 1867–68), Records of the Assistant Commissioner for the State of Georgia, Bureau of Refugees, Freedmen and Abandoned Lands, 1865–69, RG 105, National Archives (hereafter NA), Washington, D.C.

11. Minutes of [Bainbridge] City Council, 1865–1868, 22, 24, 82; "St. John's

Church Records, Bainbridge, Ga.," 2; *Bainbridge Southern Georgian,* October 10, 1866; *Savannah Daily Republican,* January 27, 1868.

12. Newspaper clipping, in Minutes of [Bainbridge] City Council, 1866–1868, 79, 94–95; *Bainbridge Argus,* February 3, 1858; *Thomasville Semi-Weekly Southern Enterprise,* January 8, 1867.

13. William Subers v. Isaac Grass, Decatur County Superior Court, April Term 1865, Superior Court Old Interrogatories 1854–74 file; Minutes of the Superior Court, Decatur County (1863–68), Office of the Probate Judge, Bainbridge, Georgia, book G; for sentiment toward Union troops, see Sefton, *The United States Army and Reconstruction,* 53–54; for animosity directed at soldiers in southwest Georgia, see Andrews, *The South since the War,* 295, 320.

14. *Index to the Congressional Record* (43rd Congress, 2nd session), x; Deed Book of Decatur County, Office of the Probate Judge, Bainbridge, Georgia, book o, 219, 374, 402; book Q, 65–67, 278, 413.

15. *Albany Tri-Weekly News,* June 6, 1867; *Thomasville Semi-Weekly Southern Enterprise,* June 11, December 20, 1867.

16. Charles Robbins to Gilbert Eberhart, May 24, May 16, July 2, 1867, reel 8; Charles Robbins to E. A. Ware, September 29, 1867, reel 9, Records of the Superintendent of Education, Georgia; William Clark to Rev. Edward Smith, November 30, 1868, reel 4, American Missionary Association Papers (hereafter AMA Papers), microfilm, Robert Strozier Library, Florida State University, Tallahassee; *Albany Tri-Weekly News,* June 6, 1867; Litwack, *Been in the Storm So Long,* 486; Jones, *Soldiers of Light and Love,* 50, 77–83, Cimbala, *Under the Guardianship of the Nation,* 113, 119.

17. Charles Robbins to Edmund Ware, September 29, 1867, reel 9, Records of the Superintendent of Education, Georgia; for resentment directed toward teachers, see Jones, *Soldiers of Light and Love,* 182–83.

18. *American Missionary Magazine* (June 1868), 126–27, (May 1869), 101; William Clark to Rev. Edward Smith, November 19, 1867, February 10, 1868, reel 3, AMA Papers; for the American Missionary Association, see Richardson, *Christian Reconstruction.*

19. William Clark to Edward Smith, October 26, 1868, reel 4; Clark to Edward Smith, February 10, 1868, reel 3, AMA Papers.

20. Foner, *Reconstruction,* 251–61, 291–307; Stampp, *Era of Reconstruction,* 142–44, 294–99; Abbott, *The Republican Party and the South,* 90–91, 108, 112, 176–77; for the Union League in the Deep South, see Fitzgerald, *The Union League Movement in the Deep South;* Drago, *Black Politicians and Reconstruction in Georgia,* 76–79; for accounts of League activities in Georgia, see U.S. Congress, *Condition of Affairs in the Late Insurrectionary States, Georgia,* 6:48–49.

21. For the Republican Party in Georgia, see Shadgett, *The Republican Party in Georgia,* 2–5; Nathans, *Losing the Peace,* 17–42; Smith, "The Republican Party in Georgia 1867–1871," 66–67; Abbott, *Republican Party in the South,* 74–75, 176; "Circular Grand Council Chamber, Union League Association in Georgia, February 5, 1868," Broadside Collection, Special Collections, Hargrett Rare Book and Manuscript Library, University of Georgia Libraries, Athens; Fitzgerald, *The Union League Movement in the Deep South,* 2.

22. *New York Times,* March 13, December 11, 1867; U.S. Congress, "Affairs in Georgia," 26; U.S. Congress, "Report on Joint Committee on Reconstruction," 162–63; Foner, *Reconstruction,* 268–69, Rable, *But There Was No Peace,* 61–64;

Bartley, *The Creation of Modern Georgia,* 48; Abbott, *Republican Party and the South,* 81–82, 96–97.

23. "Returns of Qualified Voters under the Reconstruction Act," vol. 25, Decatur County, roll 4–351, microfilm, GDAH; Duncan, *Entrepreneur for Equality,* 26; Nathans, *Losing the Peace,* 32–34, 49–50, 54; Smith, "The Republican Party in Georgia 1867–1871," 61–62.

24. Bixby et al., *History of Clear Creek and Boulder Valleys,* 697; *Congressional Globe* (42nd Congress, 3rd session), 2:1550–51; *Bainbridge Southern Sun,* February 24, 1870; *The Sun and Columbus Enquirer Weekly,* May 19, 1874.

25. *Bainbridge Southern Sun,* July 30, 1874; for discussion of other white Southerners and motivations for joining the Republican Party, see Baggett, *The Scalawags,* 206, 260–71; Foner, *Reconstruction,* 297–99.

26. *Macon American Union,* March 11, 1870.

27. C. W. Robbins to John R. Lewis, December 28, 1867, reel 19, Records of the Assistant Commissioner, Georgia; William C. Carson to William White, November 13, 1867, box 34, in Sub Assistant Commissioner Letters Received (Thomasville 1865–68), RG 105, Bureau of Refugees, Freedmen, and Abandoned Lands, NA; "Returns of Qualified Voters under the Reconstruction Act," Vol. 25, Decatur County, 14; "Reconstruction Registration Oath Books," 42:477; microfilm, GDAH. Finding suitable living accommodations was often difficult for northern teachers; see Richardson, *Christian Reconstruction,* 173.

28. *Bainbridge Southern Sun,* February 17, 1870.

29. Testimony of Judge Glenn and Robert Malloy, folder 1, box 2388, "Proceedings of the Military Commission which convened at Bainbridge, Georgia," Records of the Office of the Judge Advocate General, Army Court Martial Case Files, 1869–94, RG 109, NA; William Clark to Caleb Sibley, June 16, 1868, box 11, "Georgia District, Bainbridge Letters Received (January–December, 1868)," Records of the Bureau of Refugees, Freedmen, and Abandoned Lands, RG 105, NA; Lizzie Parsons to Rev. E. M. Cravath, December 11, 1870, reel 7, AMA Papers; for Adam Bruton, Benjamin Bruton, John Higdon, Randall Kinney, Alexander Nicholson, and Benjamin Powell, see Georgia State Census 1870, Decatur County, reel 146, 2, 9, 17, 49, 76; *Bainbridge Semi-Weekly Democrat,* February 29, 1872; *Bainbridge Southern Sun,* February 11, 1869, July 14, 1870.

30. *Bainbridge Southern Sun,* November 17, 1870.

31. Perman, *The Road to Redemption,* 43–46; Bixby et al., *History of Clear Creek and Boulder Valleys,* 697; *Bainbridge Southern Sun,* November 17, 1870; *Thomasville Semi-Weekly Southern Enterprise,* November 19, 1867; Nathans, *Losing the Peace,* 54–55.

Chapter 3: The Only Freedman's Lawyer in the Place

1. *Atlanta Daily New Era,* January 10, 9, 12, 1868; Hume, "The 'Black and Tan' Constitutional Conventions," 209–11; for Atlanta at the end of the war, see Smith, *Atlanta 1847–1890,* 113–18.

2. *New York Herald,* December 13, 1867; *Journal of the Proceedings of the Constitutional Convention,* 10–14; Hume, "The 'Black and Tan Constitutional Conventions," 211; for Blodgett, see Duncan, *Entrepreneur for Equality,* 21.

3. *Atlanta Daily New Era*, February 27, 1867; *Savannah Daily Republican*, January 16, 1868.

4. *Savannah Daily Republican*, February 24, 1868; *New York Times*, April 12, 1868.

5. *Journal of the Proceedings of the Constitutional Convention*, 117–18; Seip, *The South Returns to Congress*, 199–203.

6. *Journal of the Proceedings of the Constitutional Convention*, 117–18, 170–75; U.S. Congress, *Condition of Affairs in the Late Insurrectionary States, Georgia*, 6:384; *Savannah Daily Republican*, January 13, 168; *Augusta National Republican*, January 23, 1868; Abbot, *The Republican Party and the South*, 52, 151–52.

7. *Atlanta Daily New Era*, January 17, 1868; *Milledgeville Federal Union*, December 24, 1867; Hume, "The 'Black and Tan' Constitutional Conventions," 214–20; Duncan, *Entrepreneur for Equality*, 31–33; Henri H. Freeman, "Some Aspects of Debtor Relief in Georgia during Reconstruction," 1–2, 25, 28–30.

8. *Atlanta Daily New Era*, January 17, 1868; *Savannah Daily Republican*, January 20, 1868; undated *New York Tribune* clipping, Records Relating to the Appointments of Federal Judges, Marshals, and Attornies, 1853–1901, Georgia, RG 60, NA.

9. *Savannah Daily Republican*, March 9, 1868; Foner, *Reconstruction*, 366–68; Thompson, *Reconstruction in Georgia*, 180.

10. *Atlanta Daily New Era*, January 17, March 8, 1868; *Athens Southern Watchman*, March 18, 1868; *Georgia Weekly Telegraph* (Macon), March 13, 1868; *New York Times*, March 13–14, 1868; Hume, "The 'Black and Tan' Constitutional Conventions," 224–25; Baggett, *The Scalawags*, 51–52; Harris, *The Day of the Carpetbagger*, 139–48; Taylor, *Louisiana Reconstructed 1863–1877*, 151–52; Abbot, *The Republican Party and the South*, 148; Hill, *The Georgia State Constitution*, 7–9; Duncan, *Entrepreneur for Equality*, 37–38; Shadgett, *The Republican Party in Georgia*, 7–8; for text of constitution, see *Journal of the Proceedings of the Constitutional Convention*, 540–62.

11. *Atlanta Daily New Era*, March 12, 1868.

12. *Dawson Weekly Journal*, April 9, 1868; *Bainbridge Southern Georgian*, December 31, 1858; Fair, "Nelson Tift," 338–74; Works Progress Administration, *Historical Background of Dougherty County*, 1, 5, 12–15; Thronateeska Chapter, Daughters of the American Revolution, *History and Reminiscences of Dougherty County*, 186–88; O'Donovan, "The Journal of Nelson Tift 1835–36," 66; *Georgia Weekly Telegraph* (Macon), April 3, 1868; Georgia State Census 1860, Slave Schedules, Dougherty County, reel 145, 313; Conway, *The Reconstruction of Georgia*, 157; Nathans, *Losing the Peace*, 80–88.

13. Trelease, *White Terror*; for violence, see also Gillette, *Retreat from Reconstruction*; Rable, *But There Was No Peace*; Swinney, "Suppressing the Ku Klux Klan"; for Asburn, see Trelease, *White Terror*, 76–79.

14. U.S. Bureau of the Census, *Ninth Census, 1870, Population*, 20–22; Lee W. Formwalt, "A Garden of Irony and Diversity" (essay on southwest Georgia), in *The New Georgia Guide* (Athens: University of Georgia Press, 1996), 504–6; Works Progress Administration, *Historical Background of Dougherty County*, 45–46.

15. Andrew Clark to William White, August 22, 1867, reel 17, William Clark to Caleb Sibley, June 24, 1868, reel 21, C. W. Robbins to William White, August

20, 1867, reel 12, Records of the Assistant Commissioner, Georgia; Andrew B. Clark to O. H. Howard, October 31, 1868, box 1; W. C. Morrill to O. H. Howard, September 30, 1868, box 2, Sub Assistant Commissioner Letters Received (Albany, 1866–68), Bureau of Refugees, Freedmen, and Abandoned Lands, RG 105, NA; *Dawson Weekly Journal,* December 15, 1870; Bloom, "The Georgia Election of April, 1868," 45–46.

16. C. C. Hicks to Major J. R. Lewis, October 9, 1867, box 1, Letters Received, Third Military District, 1867–68, Records of the United States Army Continental Commands, RG 393, NA.

17. *Augusta National Republican,* April 17, 1868.

18. *Bainbridge Southern Sun,* February 17, 1870; *Cuthbert Weekly Appeal,* April 16, 1868; *Atlanta Daily New Era,* April 10, 1868; unknown Freedmen's Bureau agent to O. H. Howard, November 10, 1868, box 2, Letters Received (Albany, 1866–68); Wight and Thomas to William White, April 6, 1867, box 24, in Sub Assistant Commissioner Letters Received (Newton), RG 105, NA. Blacks across the South demonstrated a desire to own land. For examples in Georgia, see U.S. Congress, "Report on Joint Committee on Reconstruction," 41, 101, 175.

19. *Cuthbert Weekly Appeal,* April 16, 1868; Perman, *The Road to Redemption,* 24–25, 30, 42–48; Tunnell, *Edge of the Sword,* 142–44.

20. *Cuthbert Weekly Appeal,* April 16, 1868; *Dawson Weekly Journal,* April 9, 1868.

21. *Dawson Weekly Journal,* April 9, 1868.

22. *Cuthbert Weekly Appeal,* April 16, 1868; U.S. Congress, *Condition of Affairs in the Late Insurrectionary States, Georgia,* 6:48; *Albany Tri-Weekly News,* October 19, 1867; Fair, "Nelson Tift," 340–41, 46, 49, 352–53; O'Donovan, "Philip Joiner," 56–71.

23. Bloom, "The Georgia Election of April, 1868," 42–49; for a contemporary's description of voting in Georgia, see U.S. Congress, "Condition of Affairs in Georgia," 14; for voting in the Second District, see Williford, *Americus through the Years,* 136–37; for activities of troops, see Swinney, "Suppressing the Ku Klux Klan," 192–94; Sefton, *The United States Army and Reconstruction,* 229–35; Rable, *But There Was No Peace,* 108–9; Drago, *Black Politicians and Reconstruction,* 93–94.

24. William Clark to Major J. R. Lewis, April 3, 1868, reel 10, Records of the Superintendent of Education, Georgia; F. O. Welch, W. C. Morrill, et al. to Lieutenant O. H. Howard, April 7, 1868, Letters Received (Albany, 1866–68); William Clark to William White, April 8, 1868, in Sub Assistant Commissioner Letters Received (Bainbridge, 1867–68), RG 105, NA.

25. William B. Dixson to James A. Jackson, April 26, 1868, General Reconstruction File, box 89, GDAH; *Atlanta Daily New Era,* May 7, 1868.

26. John Cain to General George Meade, April 24, 1868, box 4, Letters Received in Third Military District, 1867–68, RG 393, NA; J. H. Caldwell to William Chandler, book 6, 1116–21, William E. Chandler Papers, Library of Congress, Washington, D.C.; *Atlanta Daily New Era,* May 7, 1868.

27. Testimony of Jabez Donalson, 16–17, Robert Malloy, 28–30, folder 1, box 2388, "Proceedings of the Military Commission Which Convened at Bainbridge, Georgia," Records of the Office of the Judge Advocate General, Army Court Martial Case Files, 1869–94, RG 69, NA.

28. Whiteley to Clarke Swayze, January 19, 1871, in J. Cameron Swayze Papers, Kansas State Historical Society, Topeka, Kansas; Bixby et al., *History of Clear*

Creek and Boulder Valleys, 697; Duncan, *Entrepreneur for Equality,* 48–52, 70–77; Shadgett, *Republican Party in Georgia,* 11; Nathans, *Losing the Peace,* 100–101.

29. Frank Gallagher to O. H. Howard, November 10, 1868, box 2, Sub Assistant Commissioner Letters Received (Albany, 1866–68), RG 105, NA; U.S. Congress, "Condition of Affairs in Georgia," 118–23; U.S. Congress, *Condition of Affairs in the Late Insurrectionary States, Georgia,* 6:37; Litwack, *Been in the Storm So Long,* 282–88; Drago, *Black Politicians in Georgia,* 95–96; Rable, *But There Was No Peace,* 87.

30. William Clark to Sibley, February 24, 1868, reel 20, in Records of the Assistant Commissioner, Georgia; William Clark to William White, March 12, 1868, box 34, Sub Assistant Commissioner Letters Received (Thomasville, 1865–68), RG 105, NA.

31. William Clark to Mr. Smith, February 10, 1868, reel 3, AMA Papers; *American Missionary Magazine* 12 (June 1868), 126–27; for sentiment toward AMA representatives, see Jones, *Soldiers of Light and Love,* 81–82, 182–83; Richardson, *Christian Reconstruction,* 213–33.

32. William Clark to Caleb Sibley, June 24, 1868, William White to Frank Gallagher, May 25, 1868, reel 21, in Records of the Assistant Commissioner, Georgia; William Clark to William White, March 20, 1868, Georgia District, Bainbridge, Letters Received by Agent, January–December 1868, box 11, RG 105, NA.

33. William Clark to Sibley, December 24, 1867, reel 17; "Report of Murders and Cases of Assault with Intent to Kill in the Counties of Decatur and Miller to Date during the Year 1868," reel 32, Records of the Assistant Commissioner, Georgia; "Henry Clay vs. J. H. Thomas" and Robert Wright vs. Rares Dickinson, Register of Complaints, August 1, 1868–December 31, vol. 2, 1868, RG 105, NA.

34. Testimony of Jabez Donalson, Judge Glenn, Samuel W. Patterson, and Benjamin F. Barfield, folder 1, "Petition of Citizens of Bainbridge, Ga.," folder 2, box 2388, "Proceedings of the Military Commission Which Convened at Bainbridge, Georgia," Records of the Office of the Judge Advocate General, Army Court Martial Case Files, 1869–94, RG 109, NA; William White to Frank Gallagher, May 25, 1868, reel 21, Records of the Assistant Commissioner, Georgia; for military commission courts, see Sefton, *The United States Army and Reconstruction,* 30–31.

35. William Clark to Sibley, June 24, 1868, reel 21, Records of the Assistant Commissioner, Georgia; *Cuthbert Weekly Appeal,* November 26, 1868.

36. *Bainbridge Southern Sun,* February 17, 1870; March 23, 1871; *Bainbridge Democrat,* April 4, 1872; *Albany News,* April 4, 1872; Jones, *Soldiers of Light and Love,* 140–41; for another Republican in the South who sought respectability and support among whites, see Tunnell's biography of Marshall Twitchell, *Edge of the Sword,* 142–43.

Chapter 4: A Representative Man of New Georgia

1. *Bainbridge Southern Sun,* August 11, 1870.
2. *Bainbridge Weekly Sun,* July 30, 1874.
3. Georgia, Decatur County, Superior Court, 1868, filed complaint of Heil

Waugh, in Superior Court Pleadings, 1851–71, Office of the Probate Judge, Bainbridge, Georgia; "Court of Ordinary Minutes," Decatur County, Georgia, 1866–76, book C, 185–89, microfilm, GDAH; William Clark to J. R. Lewis, October 21, 1868, reel 23, Records of the Assistant Commissioner, Georgia; Tunnell, *Edge of the Sword,* 128–30.

4. Alexander Allen to brother, March 21, 1870, George Washington Allen Papers, Southern Historical Collection, University of North Carolina, Chapel Hill; R. H. Clark, T. R. R. Cobb, and D. Irwin, *The Code of the State of Georgia,* 78–79; *Atlanta Daily New Era,* July 25, 1868; *Bainbridge Sun,* February 24, 1870; Jones, *History of Decatur County,* 418.

5. "Presentments of the Grand Jury," Decatur County Superior Court Minutes Book (1859–63), F, 163, Office of the Probate Judge, Bainbridge, Georgia.

6. Richard Whiteley to Rufus Bullock, February 6, 1871, file 2, Names, GDAH; Clark, *Code of Georgia,* 78–79; *Albany News,* June 29, 1869; June 10, 1870.

7. *Macon American Union,* July 31, 1868; *Atlanta Daily New Era,* March 12, June 2, 1868; for Jefferson Long, see Matthews, "Jefferson Franklin Long," 145–50; and *Biographical Directory of the American Congress, 1774–1971,* 1305.

8. *Dawson Weekly Journal,* March 26, 1868; *Atlanta Constitution,* August 26, September 13, 1868; *Atlanta Daily New Era,* August 21, 1868; *Bainbridge Weekly Democrat,* October 29, 1874; *New York Tribune,* September 26, 1868; *New York Tribune,* clipping, n.d., box 223, Records Relating to the Appointment of Federal Judges, Marshals and Attornies, 1853–1901, Georgia, Department of Justice, RG 60, NA.

9. Trelease, *White Terror,* 113–59, 185; for Georgia, see 117–19; Bartley, *Creation of Modern Georgia,* 62–64; Rable, *But There Was No Peace,* 70–78; Foner, *Reconstruction,* 340–43.

10. Philip Joiner to John E. Bryant, September 30, 1868, in John E. Bryant Papers, Special Collections, William R. Perkins Library, Duke University; *New York Tribune,* September 26, October 23, 1868; Formwalt, "The Camilla Massacre of 1868," 399–426; Lewis Nicholas Wynne and Milly St. Julien, "The Camilla Race Riot and the Failure of Reconstruction in Georgia," *Journal of Southwest Georgia History* 5 (fall 1987), 15–37.

11. George R. Bullow to O. H. Howard, November 2, 1868, box 57, Incoming Correspondence of Rufus Bullock, Rufus Bullock Papers, GDAH.

12. William Clark to Sibley, June 24, 1868, reel 21, Records of the Assistant Commissioner, Georgia.

13. Shadgett, *History of the Republican Party in Georgia,* 14–15; Duncan, *Entrepreneur for Equality,* 75–76.

14. "Meeting of the State Central Committee of Union Republican Party of Georgia held at Atlanta, Wednesday, November 24, 1869," Duke Pamphlet Collection, Perkins Library, Duke University; *Macon American Union,* February 26, 1869; Duncan, *Entrepreneur for Equality,* 63–65, 79, 82–83; Drago, *Black Politicians and Reconstruction in Georgia,* 48–49.

15. Richard Whiteley to Joe Christie, February 1, 1870; Joe Christie to Richard Whiteley, January 24, 1870, file 2, Names, GDAH.

16. *Albany News,* July 2, 1869; *Bainbridge Southern Sun,* May 20, 1869.

17. William Clark to John R. Lewis, April 18, 1869, reel 12, in Records of the Superintendent of Education, Georgia.

18. *Bainbridge Argus,* April 17, May 15, 1869, August 6, 1870; *Bainbridge Post*

Search-Light, December 9, 1920; Richard Whiteley and John Donalson to William H. Stark, April 30, 1870, folder 1, Benjamin Conley Papers, Atlanta History Center, Atlanta.

19. *Bainbridge Southern Sun,* June 17, 1869; *Bainbridge Argus,* February 13, 1869; "St. John's Church Records, Bainbridge, Ga.," 5.

20. *Bainbridge Southern Sun,* June 30, 1870; copy of *The Poetical Works of Henry Wadsworth Longfellow* in Estate of Montford S. Whiteley, Boulder, Colorado; interview with Montford Whiteley, December 15, 1997, Boulder, Colorado.

21. *Bainbridge Southern Sun,* September 1, 1870; *Boulder County Herald,* November 13, 1889; "St. John's Church Records, Bainbridge, Ga.," 5; Gellatly to Secretary of the University, March 22, 1954, Alumni File, Princeton University; Georgia State Census 1870, Decatur County, reel 146, 32; n.a., *Portrait and Biographical Record of Denver and Vicinity,* 332, 741.

22. *Bainbridge Southern Sun,* January 27, 1869.

23. Ibid., November 25, 1869; *Bainbridge Argus,* September 11, 1869.

24. *Bainbridge Southern Sun,* November 25, May 27, 1869, March 9, 1871.

25. Ibid., July 8, 1869.

26. Ibid., February 18, 1869; *Bainbridge Weekly Sun,* June 1, 1872; William Clark to Edward Smith, February 15, 1869, reel 4; Clark to Smith, March 8, March 29, 1869, reel 5; Lizzie Parsons to Erastus Craveth, May 1, 1871, reel 7, AMA Papers; collaboration between the Freedmen's Bureau and benevolent associations was common; see Bentley, *A History of the Freedmen's Bureau,* 171–73.

27. Duncan, *Entrepreneur for Equality,* 93–97, 122–23; Nathans, *Losing the Peace,* 178; for Hill and Miller, see *Biographical Directory of the American Congress,* 1118–19, 1409, and Roberts, "The Political Career of Joshua Hill," 50–72.

28. *Atlanta Constitution,* January 8, 1870; *Atlanta Daily New Era,* February 11, March 18, 1870.

29. *Atlanta Daily New Era,* February 16, 10, 1870; *Journal of the Senate of the State of Georgia at the Annual Session of the General Assembly* (1870) (Atlanta: Public Printer, 1870), 86–99.

30. *Atlanta Daily New Era,* February 15, 1870.

31. *Macon American Union,* February 25, 18, 1870; *Atlanta Constitution,* February 22, 1870; *Washington Evening Star,* February 25, 1870; *Atlanta Daily New Era,* February 25, 1870; *Congressional Globe* (41st Congress, 2nd session), 2:1476; Duncan, *Entrepreneur for Equality,* 123–24.

32. *Bainbridge Southern Sun,* February 17, 1870, March 23, 1871.

33. *Bainbridge Argus* quoted in *Macon American Union,* March 25, 1870.

34. *Bainbridge Southern Sun,* May 12, 1870; *Bainbridge Argus,* June 4, 1870.

35. *Albany News,* June 10, June 24, 1870.

36. Benjamin Bruton to Governor James Smith, January 12, 1872, file 2, Names, GDAH.

37. *Bainbridge Southern Sun,* August 11, 1870; *Atlanta Constitution,* July 21, 1870; *Congressional Globe* (41st Congress, 2nd session) 6:5634; Shadgett, *History of the Republican Party in Georgia,* 21–23; Duncan, *Entrepreneur for Equality,* 129–31; Nathans, *Losing the Peace,* 190–94.

38. Richard Whiteley to Henry Farrow, August 15, 1870, Henry Farrow Papers, Hargrett Rare Book and Manuscript Library, University of Georgia Libraries, Athens.

39. Ibid.; *Atlanta Daily New Era,* September 28, 1870.

Chapter 5: Whiteley versus Tift: A Sequel

1. Richard Whiteley to Henry Farrow, September 16, 1870, Farrow Papers.
2. *Macon American Union,* September 15, 1870.
3. *Weekly Sumter Republican* (Americus), August 26, 1870; Duncan, *Entrepreneur for Equality,* 83–84.
4. "Address of Hon. Nelson Tift to the Press and People of Georgia," Nelson Tift Papers, Special Collections, Hargrett Rare Book and Manuscript Library, University of Georgia Libraries, Athens; *Albany Tri-Weekly Republican,* September 9, 30, 1870; *Dawson Weekly Journal,* September 15, 1870; for description of Albany, see *Albany News,* May 24, 1870.
5. Richard Whiteley to Henry Farrow, September 16, 1870, Farrow Papers; *Atlanta Daily New Era,* October 8, 1870.
6. *Albany News,* October 8, 1870.
7. *Atlanta Daily New Era,* October 8, 1870; for election, see Rogers, "Not Reconstructed by a Long Ways Yet," 257–82.
8. *Albany News,* November 15, 1870; *Atlanta Daily New Era,* October 8, 1870.
9. *Cuthbert Weekly Appeal,* November 18, 1870.
10. *Bainbridge Argus,* November 26, 1870; *Bainbridge Southern Sun,* November 24, 1870.
11. *Albany News,* October 7, 1870; *Dawson Weekly Journal,* December 8, 1870, August 27, 1874; *Bainbridge Weekly Democrat,* April 4, 1872; Dorris, *Pardon and Amnesty under Lincoln and Johnson,* 369–70; Abbott, *History of the Republican Party and the South,* 166–68; Drago, *Black Politicians and Reconstruction in Georgia,* 23–26; Perman, *The Road to Redemption,* 24–26.
12. *Bainbridge Southern Sun,* November 17, 1870.
13. *Weekly Sumter Republican* (Americus), November 18, 1870; Lewis Guild to Robert Clarke, November 30, 1870, Incoming Correspondence Files, Rufus Bullock Papers, GDAH.
14. *Albany News,* November 18, 1870; *Cuthbert Weekly Appeal,* November 8, 870.
15. *Albany News,* December 6, 1870; *Cuthbert Weekly Appeal,* November 18, 1870; Nathan, *Losing the Peace,* 87.
16. Lewis Guild to Robert Clarke, November 30, 1870, Incoming Correspondence Files, Bullock Papers, GDAH; Georgia State Census 1870, Calhoun County, reel 138, 604.
17. Minnie Hanson to Erastus Craveth, December 24, 1870, reel 7, AMA Papers.
18. *Albany News,* December 6, November 18, 1870; *Dawson Weekly Journal,* December 8, 1870; Dorris, *Pardon and Amnesty under Lincoln and Johnson,* 368–69.
19. *Bainbridge Argus,* December 24, 1870; *Tri-Weekly Republican* (Americus), December 23, 1870; *Cuthbert Weekly Appeal,* December 16, 23, 1870; Duncan, *Entrepreneur for Equality,* 13.
20. Minnie Hanson to Erastus Craveth, December 24, 1870, reel 7, AMA Papers.

21. U.S. Congress, "Report of Secretary of State David G. Cotting," and Affidavits of Dennis Barwald, Dennis J. Shepard, and William McCoy," in "Documents in Connection with the Contested Election Case of Tift vs. Whiteley," 10–15; Diary of Nelson Tift (1868–1871), February 13, 1871, in possession of Mr. C. S. Pritchett, Albany, Georgia (hereafter Tift Diary).

22. Richard Whiteley to Clarke Swayze, January 19, 1871, Swayze Papers; Tift Diary, February 18, 1871.

23. "Report of Secretary of State David Cotting," in "Documents in Connection with the Contested Election Case of Tift vs. Whiteley," 13–15; Duncan, *Entrepreneur for Equality,* 131.

24. Affidavits of David Barwald and Dennis Shepard, in "Documents in Connection with the Contested Election Case of Tift vs. Whiteley," 15–19.

25. Tift Diary, January 13, 1871; Rufus Bullock to Henry Farrow, January 24, 1871, in "Documents in Connection with the Contested Election Case of Tift vs. Whiteley," 2–3.

26. Tift Diary, January 17–18, January 20–25, January 27, 1871; Rufus Bullock to Henry Farrow, in "Documents in Connection with the Contested Election Case of Tift vs. Whiteley," 2–3.

27. U.S. Congress, "The Committee on the Judiciary, to Whom Were Referred the Credentials of Joshua Hill, H. V. M. Miller, Henry P. Farrow, and Richard H. Whiteley," 40; and for full report, see 1–65; *Congressional Globe* (41st Congress, 3rd session), 822–23, 871, 1632; *Macon American Union,* January 26, 1871; Tift Diary, January 28, 1871.

28. Richard Whiteley to Clark Swayze, January 19, 1871, Swayze Papers; Tift Diary, January 28, 1871; *Weekly Sumter Republican* (Americus), January 27, 1871; *Biographical Directory of the American Congress,* 1409; for Swayze, see Abbott, "Jason Clarke Swayze."

29. Tift Diary, January 31, 28, 1871; Henry Farrow to Nelson Tift, February 15, 1871, Farrow Papers.

30. Tift Diary, January 30, 1871.

31. Ibid., February 1, 1871.

32. Henry Farrow to Rufus Bullock, February 2, 1871, in "Documents in Connection with the Contested Election Case of Tift vs. Whiteley," 3–7; *Savannah Daily Republican,* February 11, 1871.

33. Tift Diary, February 3, 1871; *Congressional Globe* (41st Congress, 3rd session), 2:969.

34. Richard Whiteley to Rufus Bullock, February 6, 1871, file 2, Names, GDAH.

35. *Congressional Globe* (41st Congress, 3rd session), 2:1086.

36. *Bainbridge Argus,* April 1, 1871; Tift Diary, February 10, February 13, February 24, March 27; *Congressional Globe* (41st Congress, 3rd session), 3:1930.

37. *Appendix to the Congressional Globe* (41st Congress, 3rd session), 3:102; Affidavits of Solomon Council and Andrew Williams, in "Documents in Connection with the Contested Election Case of Tift vs. Whiteley," 21–22, 25–27.

38. Tift Diary, February 24, 1871.

39. Richard Whiteley to Clark Swazye, January 19, 1871, Swayze Papers.

40. Richard Whiteley to Joe Christie, Februrary 1, 1870, File 2, Names, GDAH.

Chapter 6: Congressman Whiteley

1. *The Sun and Columbus Enquirer Weekly,* May 19, 1874; *Bainbridge Argus* (November 8, 1865) quoted in *Macon American Union,* March 25, 1870; *Boulder County Herald,* July 25, 1883.

2. Martin, *Behind the Scenes in Washington,* 65, 50–52; Ellis, *The Sights and Secrets of the National Capital,* 442–43; Green, *Washington Village and Capital,* 198, 295.

3. *Sun and Columbus Enquirer Weekly,* May 26, 1874; Ellis, *The Sights and Secrets of the National Capital,* 108–10; Martin, *Behind the Scenes in Washington,* 190–91, 206; Townsend, *Events at the National Capital and the Campaign of 1876,* 113–14.

4. Thomas Speer to Benjamin Conley, March 24, 1872, Benjamin Conley Papers, Hargrett Rare Book and Manuscript Library, University of Georgia Libraries, Athens; Seip, *The South Returns to Congress,* 125–27, 132.

5. *Bainbridge Weekly Sun,* July 2, 1874.

6. House Select Committee on Reconstruction, "Petitions for the Removal of Legal and Political Disabilities Imposed by the Fourteenth Amendment," 40–41st Congress, Records of the U.S. House of Representatives, RG 233, NA; *Congressional Globe* (41st Congress, 3rd session), 2:186.

7. *Bainbridge Southern Sun,* March 23, 1871.

8. *Bainbridge Argus,* April 15, 1871.

9. Richard Whiteley to Rufus Bullock, February 25, 1871, file 2, Names, GDAH.

10. *Congressional Globe* (41st Congress, 3rd session), 3:1924–26; *Macon Weekly Telegraph and Journal and Messenger,* March 18, 1873; Tift Diary, February 15, February 17, 1871.

11. Blaine, *Twenty Years of Congress,* 2:448; *Congressional Globe* (42nd Congress, 1st session), 1:vii; *Weekly Columbus Enquirer,* April 25, 1871; Seip, *The South Returns to Congress,* 177–78; for Georgia delegation, see *Biographical Directory of the American Congress,* 591, 883, 1118–19, 1322, 1479, 1569, 1734, 1969; Shadgett, *Republican Party in Georgia,* 24.

12. Swinney,"Suppressing the Ku Klux Klan," 57–84, 138–75; *Congressional Globe* (42nd Congress, 1st session), 1:522.

13. Richard Whiteley to George Williams, November 15, 1872, reel 1, Letters Received by the Department of Justice from the State of Georgia 1871–84, RG 60, NA Branch, Eastpoint, Georgia; *Congressional Globe* (42nd Congress, 2nd session), 1:522; *Washington National Republican,* March 15, 1871.

14. *Congressional Globe* (42nd Congress, 1st session), 1:176; 42nd Congress, 2nd session), 5:3652; Seip, *The South Returns to Congress,* 184–97, 215, 268–69; Abbott, *History of the Republican Party and the South,* 215–16.

15. Martin, *Behind the Scenes in Washington,* 454–59; Shadgett, *Republican Party in Georgia,* 49–50; for an example of how patronage worked, see Franklin, *Autobiography of John Roy Lynch,* 171–73, and Orville Babcock to Wm. H. Smyth, March 31, 1873, Letterbooks and Telegram Book, 63, reel 3, ser. 2, Ulysses S. Grant Papers, microfilm, Hargrett Rare Book and Manuscript Library, University of Georgia Libraries, Athens.

16. Richard Whiteley to Clarke Swayze, January 19, 1871, Swayze Papers; Vol-

ney Spalding to William Chandler, July 23, 1872, book 25, 4896–97, Chandler Papers; Shadgett, *History of the Republican Party,* 49–50.

17. *Bainbridge Weekly Sun,* July 30, 1874.

18. Richard Whiteley to Clarke Swayze, March 8, 1871, Swayze Papers; *Macon American Union,* August 16, 1867; for Swayze, see Abbott, "Jason Clarke Swayze," 339–40, 360–61.

19. Thomas Speer to Clarke Swayze, March 18, February 28, 1871, Swayze Papers; Whiteley, Speer, Bigby to A. A. Plesanton, March 2, 1871, box 003, Applications for Positions as Internal Revenue, Revenue Collectors and Assessors, 1863–1910," RG 56, NA.

20. Thomas Speer to Clarke Swayze, March 29, 1871, Swayze Papers.

21. Richard Whiteley to George Boutwell, March 6, 1871, M. M. Hale to Ulysses Grant, August 14, 1871, box 050; A. D. Rockafellow to Ulysses Grant, December 20, 1871, box 051, Applications for Appointments as Customs Service Officers, 1833–1910, RG 56, NA.

22. Marriage Certificate of Thomas Morris and Catherine Cecilia Whiteley, family Bible of Thomas and Catherine Morris, and various genealogical materials, in possession of William M. McCoy Jr., King George, Virginia; telephone interview with William McCoy, December 20, 2002; District of Columbia Census 1870, roll 126, 494; *Quitman Reporter,* August 1, 1874; *Bainbridge Weekly Democrat,* September 3, 1874.

23. *Bainbridge Argus,* April 29, 1871; *Bainbridge Southern Sun,* November 17, April 27, 1871.

24. Gellatly to Secretary of the University, March 22, 1954, Alumni File, Princeton University; *Bainbridge Southern Sun,* May 25, June 27, 1871; "St. John's Church Records, Bainbridge, Ga.," 5, 9–13.

25. William H. Stark to Benjamin Conley, January 10, 1871, Benjamin Conley Papers, Atlanta History Center, Atlanta.

26. John Donalson to Burch and Wilson & Co., May 15, 1871, 411, John Donalson to C. Bonney, September 21, 1871, 412, Letterbook of Outgoing Correspondence (1865–72), John E. Donalson Papers, Bainbridge College Library, Bainbridge, Georgia; Trow, *Trow's New York City Directory,* 152; *Bainbridge Semi-Weekly Democrat,* January 23, 1872.

27. *Bainbridge Semi-Weekly Democrat,* January 9, 1872; Deed Book of Decatur County, Office of the Probate Judge, Bainbridge, Georgia, Q, 278, 670.

28. Lizzie Parsons to Erastus Craveth, March 1, January 2, 1871, December 11, 1870, reel 7, AMA Papers; *Bainbridge Argus,* April 8, 29, August 19, 1871; *Bainbridge Southern Sun,* November 17, 1870; December 7, 1871; Jones, *Soldiers of Light,* 142, 154; Litwack, *Been Too Long in the Storm,* 458–60.

29. Lizzie Parsons to Erastus Craveth, December 11, 1870, reel 7, AMA Papers; Jones, *Soldiers of Light and Love,* 95.

30. Lizzie Parsons to Erastus Craveth, May 1, 1871, reel 7, AMA Papers.

31. *Bainbridge Argus,* September 23, 1871.

32. Ibid., September 30, 1871; *Bainbridge Southern Sun,* September 21, 1871.

33. *Blakely Early County News,* October 6, 1871.

34. Richard Whiteley to Alvin B. Clark, August 31, 1871, J. W. Clift to Ulysses Grant, March 12, 1869, box 003, Applications for Positions as Internal Revenue Collectors and Assessors, 1863–1910, RG 56, NA.

35. John Bryant to Richard Whiteley, June 13, 1871, Bryant Papers; John Quarles to George Boutwell, March 5, 1871, box 003, Applications for Positions as Internal Revenue Collectors and Assessors, 1863–1910, RG 56, NA; Alvord, "Letters from the South, Relating to the Condition of Freedmen"; Currie-McDaniel, *Carpetbagger of Conscience,* 44–45, 90–100, 105, 108–9, 111, 122–23; Drago, *Black Politicians and Reconstruction in Georgia,* 58–62.

36. John Bryant to J. M. Edmunds, September 12, 1871, Bryant Papers; Duncan, *Entrepreneur for Equality,* 100–103, 107–8, 112–15; Currie-McDaniel, *Carpetbagger of Conscience,* 121–22.

37. Richard Whiteley to Henry Farrow, August 15, 1870, Farrow Papers; for one historian's summation of the Bullock administration, see Bartley, *The Creation of Modern Georgia,* 68–72.

38. John Bryant to J. M. Edmunds, September 12, 1871, Bryant Papers.

39. Richard Whiteley to Benjamin Conley, November 7, 1871, Conley Papers, University of Georgia; Henry Farrow to William Chandler, September 2, 1872, book 29, 5797–803, Chandler Papers; for Conley, see *Atlanta Daily New Era,* November 3, 1871; Shadgett, *History of the Republican Party in Georgia,* 26–32; Duncan, *Entrepreneur for Equality,* 135–36.

40. Poore, *Congressional Directory, Forty-second Congress, First Session,* 116; *Congressional Directory, Forty-second Congress, Third Session,* 1317; *Congressional Directory of the Forty-third Congress, Second Session,* 155; Boyd, *Boyd's Directory of the District of Columbia,* 310; Martin, *Behind the Scenes in Washington,* 62, 80.

41. Genealogical materials in possession of William McCoy Jr., King George, Virginia; telephone interview with William McCoy, December 20, 2002; *Bainbridge Weekly Democrat,* September 3, 1874; Martin, *Behind the Scenes in Washington,* 64–65; Green, *Washington Village and Capital,* 268, 313, 395–96; for a description by "Specks" of a typical day for a congressman, see *Atlanta Daily Herald,* April 10, 1874.

42. *Bainbridge Weekly Sun,* July 30, 1874; *Congressional Globe* (42nd Congress, 2nd session), 1:60; *Appendix to the Congressional Record* (43rd Congress, 1st session), 6:268–69.

43. *Congressional Globe* (42nd Congress, 2nd session), 1:470; *Bainbridge Semi-Weekly Democrat,* January 26, 1872.

44. *Congressional Globe* (42nd Congress, 2nd session), 2:1215–16; 1:196, 3:2439; 4:3383, 5:3744; *Weekly Columbus Enquirer,* March 12, 19, 1872; Dorris, *Pardon and Amnesty under Lincoln and Johnson,* 375–78.

45. *Congressional Globe* (42nd Congress, 2nd session), 1:470, 1879.

46. Richard Whiteley to Benjamin Conley, February 26, 1872, Conley Papers, University of Georgia; Issac Seeley to William Chandler, March 26, 1872, book 20, 3958–65, Chandler Papers, *Congressional Globe* (42nd Congress, 2nd session), 1:35–36, 196, 498; for poll tax in Georgia, see Nordhoff, *The Cotton States in the Spring and Summer of 1875,* 102–3; Shadgett, *The Republican Party in Georgia,* 44–45; Currie-McDaniel, *Carpetbagger of Conscience,* 130; Drago, *Black Politicians and Reconstruction in Georgia,* 148–49.

47. *Appendix to the Congressional Globe* (42nd Congress, 2nd session), 144–48.

48. *Congressional Globe* (42nd Congress, 2nd session), 2:1723, 1737, 1750; having a speech printed rather than delivered was common. Printed speeches circulated in the House and later were published in the appendix of the House proceedings. Martin, *Behind the Scenes,* 202–3.

49. Moses Hale to George Boutwell, January 9, 1872, box 052, Applications for Appointments as Customs Service Officers, 1833–1910, RG 56, NA; Richard Whiteley, Thomas Speer, and John Bigby to George Williams, February 22, 1872, box 27, Records Relating to the Appointment of Federal Judges, Marshals and Attorneys, 1853–1901 (Georgia, 1853–73), RG 60, NA; Thomas Speer to Benjamin Conley, April 7, 1872, Conley Papers, University of Georgia.

50. Richard Whiteley to George Boutwell, October 15, 1871, box 050, Applications for Appointments as Customs Service Officers, 1833–1910, RG 56, NA; *Savannah Morning News,* November 14, 1871.

51. Richard Whiteley to Benjamin Conley, February 26, 1872, Conley Papers, University of Georgia; *Macon American Union,* February 22, 1872.

52. *Congressional Globe* (42nd Congress, 2nd session), 3:2117; *Appendix to the Congressional Globe* (42nd Congress, 2nd session), 4:814–16.

53. *Congressional Globe* (42nd Congress, 2nd session), 2:1300.

54. *Bainbridge Weekly Sun,* July 30, 1874; March 16, 1872; *Albany News,* March 22, 1872; *Appendix to the Congressional Globe* (42nd Congress, 2nd session), 6:720.

55. *Appendix to the Congressional Globe* (42nd Congress, 2nd session), 6:144–48.

56. U.S. Congress, *Condition of Affairs in The Late Insurrectionary States, Georgia,* 6:523.

57. *Bainbridge Weekly Democrat,* June 20, September 12, 1872; *Bainbridge Search Light,* December 10, 1909.

58. *Bainbridge Weekly Sun,* September 7, 1872; *Bainbridge Weekly Democrat,* September 19, 1872.

Chapter 7: A Wily and Able Man

1. Van Deusen, *Horace Greeley,* 401–5; McFeely, *Grant,* 380–84.

2. *Weekly Columbus Enquirer,* January 2, 1872; *Atlanta Daily Herald,* December 2, 1872; *Atlanta Constitution,* July 6, August 22, 1872; *Athens Southern Watchman,* May 15, August 28, 1872; Van Deusen, *Horace Greeley,* 283–87, 380–83, 386, 409; Ross, "Horace Greeley and the South, 1865–1872," 324–31; Shadgett, *History of the Republican Party in Georgia,* 34, 42–43, 46, 49; Duncan, *Entrepreneur for Equality,* 137–38.

3. Richard Whiteley to George Boutwell, October 15, 1871, box 9050, Applications for Appointments As Customs Officers, 1833–1910, RG 56, NA.

4. Joel R. Griffin to Benjamin Conley, February 10, 1872, Conley Papers, University of Georgia; Abott, *For Free Press and Equal Rights,* 94.

5. M. A. Marshall and Benjamin F. Brimberry to Frederick Douglas, September 12, 1872, book 30, 6018–19, Chandler Papers, NA.

6. *Bainbridge Weekly Sun,* July 20, September 7, 1872; *Bainbridge Weekly*

Democrat, July 18, 1872; *Albany News,* August 16, 1872; Harris, *The Day of the Carpetbagger,* 94, 457; Drago, *Black Politicians and Reconstruction in Georgia,* 20–23; Rogers, *Black Belt Scalawag,* 29–30, 90–95.

7. *Bainbridge Weekly Democrat,* July 25, 1872; *Quitman Banner,* August 2, 1872; *Bainbridge Search Light,* December 10, 1909; U.S. Bureau of the Census, *Ninth Census, 1870, Population,* 20–22.

8. *Quitman Banner,* August 9, 1872; *Albany News,* July 5, September 6, 1872; *Cuthbert Weekly Appeal,* July 19, 1872; *Bainbridge Weekly Democrat,* July 25, 1872; *Dawson Weekly Journal,* July 18, 1872.

9. *Albany News,* September 6, 1872.

10. Ibid., July 16, 1874; *Dawson Weekly Journal,* October 3, 1872; Thronateeska Chapter, *History and Reminiscences of Dougherty County, Georgia,* 139–41; Georgia State Census 1870, Dougherty County, reel 147, 451; for election, see Rogers, "'Politics Absorbs Everything Else,'" 1–19.

11. *Albany News,* September 6, 1872.

12. *Cuthbert Weekly Appeal,* October 11, 1872.

13. *Dawson Weekly Journal,* October 3, 1872.

14. *Macon Journal and Messenger,* October 12, 1872; *Quitman Banner,* September 20, 1872.

15. *Albany News,* July 16, 1874; *Bainbridge Weekly Democrat,* September 12, 1872.

16. *Bainbridge Weekly Sun,* September 21, 1872; *Quitman Banner,* September 20, 1872.

17. *Macon Journal and Messenger,* October 12, 1872.

18. *Dawson Weekly Journal,* October 3, 1872; *Macon Journal and Messenger,* October 1, 12, 1872; *Bainbridge Weekly Sun,* September 21, 1872.

19. *Atlanta Constitution,* October 1, 1872; *Bainbridge Weekly Democrat,* September 7, 1872; U.S. Congress, *Condition of Affairs in the Late Insurrectionary States, Georgia,* 6:48.

20. *Atlanta Daily Herald,* August 20, 1874; *Quitman Banner,* August 16, 1872; *Albany News,* August 16, 1872; *Macon Telegraph and Messenger,* September 11, 1872; *Atlanta Constitution,* September 21, 1872.

21. *Macon Telegraph and Messenger,* September 12, 1872.

22. *Dawson Weekly Journal,* October 17, 1872.

23. *Blakely Early County News,* quoted in *Bainbridge Weekly Sun,* October 5, 1872.

24. *Macon Telegraph and Messenger,* September 12, 1872; *Dawson Weekly Journal,* August 27, 1874.

25. *Bainbridge Weekly Sun,* July 20, 1872.

26. Ibid., September 21, 7, 1872.

27. *Macon American Union,* September 5, 1872; *Bainbridge Weekly Democrat,* May 30, 1872; Abbott, "Jason Clarke Swayze," 351–52, 360, 366.

28. *Cuthbert Weekly Appeal,* October 11, 1872; *Atlanta Constitution,* October 16, 1872; Shadgett, *History of Republican Party in Georgia,* 43–44; Drago, *Black Politicians and Reconstruction in Georgia,* 48–49.

29. *Bainbridge Weekly Democrat,* August 29, 1872; *Dawson Weekly Journal,* October 10, 1872.

30. *Bainbridge Weekly Democrat,* August 20, 1874; U.S. Congress, *Condition of Affairs in the Late Insurrectionary States, Georgia,* 6:529.

31. *Dawson Weekly Journal,* August 15, 1872; *Macon Telegraph and Messenger,* September 12, 1872; *Atlanta Constitution,* August 21, 1872; *Savannah Daily Republican,* August 1, 1872.

32. *Albany News,* July 16, 1874; *Atlanta Constitution,* October 16, November 16, 1872; Henry Farrow to Postmaster General, July 22, 1874, Letterbook 1 (1874–77), Farrow Papers.

33. *Macon American Union,* September 5, 1872.

34. *Bainbridge Weekly Sun,* October 5, 1872.

35. Richardson, *A Compilation of the Messages and Papers of the Presidents,* 9:4153; Trelease, *White Terror,* 415.

36. *Atlanta Constitution,* October 11, November 1, 1872; *Macon Telegraph and Messenger,* October 31, 1872.

37. Richard Whiteley to George Williams, November 15, 1872, reel 1, Letters Received by the Department of Justice, RG 60, NA.

38. *Savannah Morning News,* January 16, 1873; *Washington National Republican,* February 13, 1872; *Bainbridge Weekly Democrat,* December 5, 1872. The "gay season" opened before the holidays and closed at Lent. Green, *Washington Village and Capital,* 151.

39. *Atlanta Daily Herald,* January 26, 1873; *Bainbridge Weekly Democrat,* December 5, 1873.

40. *Atlanta Daily Herald,* May 17, April 31, 1874.

41. *Georgia Weekly Telegraph and Journal and Messenger* (Macon), April 1, 8, 1873; *Savannah Morning News,* March 27, 1873; *Atlanta Daily Herald,* December 24, 1872, March 23, 1873.

42. Richard Whiteley to Commissioner of Internal Revenue, September 3, 1872, box 003, Applications For Positions as Internal Revenue Collectors and Assessors, 1863–1910; *Savannah Morning News,* March 10, 27, 1873.

43. *Georgia Weekly Telegraph and Journal and Messenger* (Macon), April 8, 1873; *Atlanta Daily Herald,* March 23, 1873.

44. *Savannah Daily Advertiser,* March 16, 1873; *Atlanta Daily Herald,* March 23, 11–12, 1873; *fugleman* was a term corresponding with *henchmen.*

45. Simon, *The Papers of Ulysses S. Grant,* vol. 24 (1873), 314; *Atlanta Daily Herald,* February 25, 1873.

46. *Congressional Globe* (42nd Congress, 3rd session), 2:1550–51; *Atlanta Constitution,* August 20, 1873.

47. *Atlanta Constitution,* March 19, 1873; *Atlanta Daily Herald,* March 23, April 3, 1873; *Georgia Weekly Telegraph and Journal and Messenger* (Macon), April 8, 1873; *Blakely Early County News,* March 28, 1873; Henry Farrow to Richard Whiteley, December 13, 1873, reel 1, Letters Received by the Department of Justice, RG 60, NA.

48. Richard Whiteley to Benjamin Conley, July 23, 1873, Conley Papers, Atlanta History Center; *Atlanta Daily Herald,* April 3, 1873.

49. *Macon Daily Enterprise,* June 9, 1873; *Atlanta Daily Herald,* April 3, 1873.

50. *Atlanta Daily Herald,* May 17, 1874; *Bainbridge Weekly Democrat,* April 3, 1873.

Chapter 8: The Prince Wire-Worker

1. *Bainbridge Weekly Sun,* June 21, 1873; *Bainbridge Weekly Democrat,* August 28, September 25, 1873; Gellatly to Secretary of the University, March 22, 1954, Alumni File, Princeton University.

2. *Bainbridge Weekly Democrat,* July 17, 1873; March 21, April 4, 1872; *Bainbridge Southern Sun,* January 13, 1872, May 3, 1873; *Savannah Republican,* February 16, 1872; "St. John's Church Records, Bainbridge, Ga.," 13.

3. *Bainbridge Weekly Democrat,* April 24, July 17, 1873; *Bainbridge Weekly Sun,* May 3, 1873; Freeman, "Some Aspects of Debtor Relief in Georgia during Reconstruction," 49–51; Nathans, *Losing the Peace,* 118.

4. *Bainbridge Weekly Democrat,* May 8, 1873.

5. Ibid., August 14, 1873; *Bainbridge Argus,* July 3, 1869.

6. Lizzie Parsons to Rev. M. C. Strichie, March 31, 1873, William Clark to Erastus Craveth, March 25, 1873; reel 8, AMA Papers; *Bainbridge Weekly Democrat,* June 5, August 7, 1873.

7. *Bainbridge Weekly Democrat* quoted in *Blakely Early County News,* August 29, 1873; *Bainbridge Southern Sun,* August 16, 1873; *Bainbridge Weekly Democrat,* August 14, 1873.

8. Benjamin Conley to Richard Whiteley, July 21, 1873, Conley Papers, Atlanta History Center.

9. Richard Whiteley to Benjamin Conley, July 23, 1873, Conley Papers, Atlanta History Center.

10. *Bainbridge Weekly Sun,* June 28, January 11, 18, 1873, March 30, 1872.

11. Ibid., September 6, January 11, 1873; *Bainbridge Weekly Democrat,* August 7, 1873.

12. Abbott, *For Free Press and Equal Rights,* 49, 3–4, 46, 49–50, 54, 93.

13. *Bainbridge Weekly Sun,* September 6, 1870, April 30, July 2, 1874.

14. *Bainbridge Weekly Sun,* July 2, 1874; November 9, 1871, January 18, 1873; Abbott, *For Free Press and Equal Rights,* 70–71.

15. *Bainbridge Weekly Sun,* September 6, 1873; Abbott, *For Free Press and Equal Rights,* 70–71; 103–04.

16. *Bainbridge Weekly Sun,* September 24, September 6, 1873; Abbott, *For Free Press and Equal Rights,* 103–4.

17. Richard Whiteley to Edward McPherson, Edward McPherson Papers, Library of Congress, Washington, D.C.; *Bainbridge Weekly Sun,* February 25, 1874; Abbott, *For Free Press and Equal Rights,* 58, 75–76, 131.

18. *Bainbridge Weekly Sun,* August 23, October 22, 1873.

19. Ibid., September 6, 1873.

20. *Bainbridge Weekly Democrat,* October 2, 1873, September 4, August 28, 1874; *Bainbridge Search Light,* December 10, 1909.

21. *Bainbridge Weekly Sun,* September 6, 1873; June 18, 1874; Abbott, *For Free Press and Equal Rights,* 182.

22. *Bainbridge Weekly Sun,* December 17, 1873.

23. *Quitman Banner* quoted in *Bainbridge Weekly Sun,* October 22, 1873.

24. *Bainbridge Weekly Democrat,* September 4, October 23, 1873.

25. *Bainbridge Weekly Sun,* September 6, August 6, 1873.

26. *Bainbridge Weekly Democrat,* July 17, 1873; *Bainbridge Weekly Sun,* August 23, September 6, 1873.

27. *Bainbridge Weekly Sun,* November 5, November 19, October 22, 1874; *Bainbridge Weekly Democrat,* October 30, 1874.

28. *Blakely Early County News,* December 5, 1873; *Atlanta Daily Herald,* December 5, 1873; *Bainbridge Weekly Democrat,* November 13, November 20, 1873; *Memoirs of Georgia,* 1:584; Rogers, "'Death Has Been Busily at Work.'"

29. Henry Farrow to Richard Whiteley, December 13, 1873, reel 1, Letters Received by the Department of Justice, 1871–84, RG 60, NA; *Atlanta Daily Herald,* January 22, 1874.

30. Richard Whiteley to George Williams, December 16, 1873, reel 1, Letters Received by the Department of Justice, 1871–84, RG 60, NA; *Atlanta Daily Herald,* January 22, 1874.

31. *Bainbridge Weekly Sun,* January 7, 1874; November 19, December 24, 1873.

32. *Atlanta Constitution,* December 10, 1873; *Congressional Record* (43rd Congress, 1st session), 1:369; Ellis, *Sights and Secrets of the National Capital,* 110.

33. *Index to the Congressional Record* (43rd Congress, 2nd session), ix; *Atlanta Daily Herald,* November 30, 1873; Seip, *The South Returns to Congress,* 27–18; Schott, *Alexander H. Stephens,* 498–99; Shadgett, *The Republican Party in Georgia,* 47; *Biographical Directory of the American Congress,* 970, 1706–7; Harris, *Day of the Carpetbagger,* 96; for John Lynch, see Lynch, *The Facts of Reconstruction.*

34. *Congressional Record* (43rd Congress, 1st session), 1:626; 3:3005; 4:3078; *Atlanta Daily Herald,* December 7, December 18, 1873; *Atlanta Constitution,* January 28–29, 1874; Seip, *The South Returns to Congress,* 224–38, 246–48; Schott, *Alexander H. Stephens,* 498–99.

35. *Atlanta Daily Herald,* March 20, April 4, 1874; *Savannah Morning News,* April 11, 1874; *Georgia Weekly Telegraph and Messenger* (Macon), January 21, 1873; *Savannah Daily Advertiser,* January 5, 1874; Henry Farrow to George F. Edmunds, January 16, 1874, Letterbook 1 (1874–77), Farrow Papers; *Congressional Record* (43rd Congress, 2nd session), 3:2207, 2511–12; Dorris, *Pardon and Amnesty,* 378, 380; Avery, *The History of the State of Georgia,* 425.

36. Henry Farrow to Richard Whiteley, January 18, 1874, Letterbook 1 (1874–77), Farrow Papers; *Bainbridge Weekly Sun,* February 14, April 1, 1874.

37. *Congressional Record* (43rd Congress, 2nd session), 3:2405, 2316–24, 2347, 2399–413, 2:1525; U.S. Congress, "Papers in the Case of Andrew Sloan vs. Morgan Rawls," 1–11; *Atlanta Daily Herald,* March 25, 1874; *Atlanta Constitution,* March 31, 1874.

38. *Bainbridge Weekly Sun,* June 18, 1874; Rogers, *Thomas County 1865–1900,* 184; Foner, *Reconstruction,* 531.

39. *Atlanta Daily Herald,* January 22, 7, February 11, 24, March 3, 1874; P. M. Sheibley to Benjamin Conley, April 14, 1874, Conley Papers, University of Georgia; Currie-McDaniel, *Carpetbagger of Conscience,* 130; Avery, *History of the State of Georgia,* 401; Smith, "The Republican Party in Georgia," 159–62, 177, 197.

40. *Atlanta Constitution,* February 8, 1874; *Weekly Sumter Republican* (Americus), January 30, March 20, 1874.

41. *Weekly Sumter Republican* (Americus), April 17, 1874; *Atlanta Constitution,* April 11, 1874.

42. *Atlanta Daily Herald,* April 17, 1847.

43. Benjamin Conley to Whiteley, April 20, 1874, Conley Papers, University of Georgia; *Blakely Early County News,* September 25, 1874; *Atlanta Daily Herald,* January 16, 1874; for attempts by Conley to gain office, see Shadgett, *History of the Republican Party in Georgia,* 50–52.

44. Richard Whiteley to Foster Blodgett, January 12, 1874, Conley Papers, University of Georgia.

45. *Atlanta Daily Herald* quoted in *Savannah Morning News,* April 10, 1874; *Atlanta Daily Herald,* April 3, 1873; March 18, 26, 1874; *Savannah Morning News,* March 26, 1874; *Savannah Advertiser and Register,* March 24, 1874.

46. Charles Whiteley to Benjamin Conley, March 19, 1874, Conley Papers, University of Georgia; *Biennal Register of Officiers and Agents,* 45–48; Gellatly to Secretary of the University, March 22, 1954, Alumni File, Princeton University.

47. David Porter to Benjamin Conley, April 22, 1874, Conley Papers, University of Georgia.

48. Richard Whiteley to Benjamin Conley, June 6, 1874, Conley Papers, University of Georgia; Benjamin Conley to Richard Whiteley, June 3, 1874, Conley Papers, Atlanta History Center.

49. *Atlanta Constitution,* April 15, 1874; *Atlanta Daily Herald,* January 25, 1874.

50. David Porter to Benjamin Conley, April 22, 1874, Conley Papers, University of Georgia; *Atlanta Daily Herald,* January 25, 1874.

51. Parker W. Perry to Richard Whiteley, February 5, 1872, in "Applications for Positions As Internal Revenue Collectors and Assessors, 1863–1910," box 003, RG 56, NA.

52. *Atlanta Daily Herald,* April 11, 1874.

53. *The Sun and Columbus Enquirer Weekly,* May 19, June 23, 1874; *Congressional Record* (43rd Congress, 2nd session), 1:452; Edward Anderson Diary, vol. 5, entries for April 9, April 10, 1874, 211–12, Southern Historical Association Collection, University of North Carolina, Chapel Hill; Seip, *The South Returns to Congress,* 207.

54. *Congressional Record and Appendix* (43rd Congress, 1st session), 6:268–69; *Atlanta Constitution,* June 13, 1874; *Bainbridge Weekly Sun,* June 18, 1874; *Sun and Columbus Enquirer Weekly,* May 19, 1874.

55. *Sun and Columbus Enquirer Weekly,* May 19, 1874.

56. *Atlanta Daily Herald,* May 17, 19, April 15, 1874.

57. *Congressional Record* (43rd Congress, 2nd session), 6: 5189; 4:4559; *Atlanta Daily Herald,* June 19, 1874; *Atlanta Constitution,* June 23–24, 1874.

58. Gillette, *Retreat from Reconstruction,* 188–207; Litwack, *Been in the Storm So Long,* 261–67.

59. *Atlanta Daily Herald,* May 31, 184; *Atlanta Constitution,* June 2, 14, 1874; *Congressional Record* (43rd Congress, 1st session), 5:42–43; Gillette, *Retreat from Reconstruction,* 205–6.

60. *Bainbridge Weekly Sun,* July 30, 1874; Drago, *Black Politicians and Reconstruction in Georgia,* 98–100.

61. *Congressional Record* (43rd Congress, lst session), 6:5113, 5112; *Atlanta Constitution,* June 21, 1874; *Dawson Weekly Journal,* June 25, 1874.

62. *Bainbridge Weekly Sun,* July 2, April 30, 1874.

63. Ibid., September 10, 1874.

64. *Bainbridge Weekly Democrat,* September 3, 1874.

Chapter 9: The Scalawag Whiteley Will Be Driven into Obscurity

1. *Cincinnati Commercial,* August 17, 19, September 3, 1874; *Early County News* (Blakely), September 25, 1874 Abbott, *Republican Party and the South,* 230; Gillette, *Retreat from Reconstruction,* 191–97, 217–24; Foner, *Reconstruction,* 340–41, 412–17.

2. Gillette, *Retreat From Reconstruction,* 228, 225–29; Tunnell, *Edge of the Sword,* 101–92.

3. *Bainbridge Weekly Democrat,* September 20, June 11, August 13, 1874; *Bainbridge Weekly Sun,* August 13, 1874.

4. *Early County News* (Blakely), August 28, 1874.

5. William Clark to Erastus Craveth, April 27, 1874, reel 9, AMA Papers; *Bainbridge Weekly Sun,* April 30, May 14, July 2, 1874.

6. *Bainbridge Weekly Sun,* July 2, April 30, June 18, 1874; *Albany News,* January 22, 1874; "Proceedings of the Republican Convention of the Tenth Senatorial District Held at Albany, Georgia, February 20, 1872," Broadside Collection, Hargrett Rare Book and Manuscript Library, University of Georgia Libraries, Athens.

7. *Albany News,* April 30, 1874; *Bainbridge Weekly Sun,* May 14, 1874; *Bainbridge Weekly Democrat,* October 29, 1876; "Proceedings of the Republican Convention!" Thronateeska Chapter, *History and Reminiscences of Dougherty County,* 171–72.

8. William Clark to Erastus Craveth, April 27, 1874, reel 9, AMA Papers; *Bainbridge Argus,* July 3, 1869; *Thomasville Times,* July 11, 1874.

9. *Bainbridge Weekly Sun,* May 7, 14, 1874.

10. Ibid., July 2, 1874.

11. William Clark to Erastus Craveth, June 26, 1874, reel 9, AMA Papers.

12. Ibid., June 30, 1874.

13. *Thomasville Times,* July 11, 1874.

14. *Albany News,* June 11, 1874.

15. William Clark to Erastus Craveth, June 26, 1874, reel 9, AMA Papers.

16. *Bainbridge Weekly Sun,* May 14, June 18, 1874.

17. Ibid., July 2, 1874.

18. *Early County News* (Blakely), July 10, 1874; *Dawson Weekly Journal,* July 16, 1874; *Bainbridge Weekly Sun,* July 2, 1874; *Albany News,* July 3, 1874.

19. *Bainbridge Weekly Sun,* July 2, 1874.

20. *Albany News,* July 9, 1874; *Bainbridge Weekly Sun,* July 23, 30, 1874.

21. *Thomasville Times,* July 18, 1874.

22. *Early County News* (Blakely), July 24, 1874.

23. *Bainbridge Weekly Sun,* July 23, August 6, 1874; *Cuthbert Weekly Appeal,* September 11, 1874.

24. *Bainbridge Weekly Sun,* August 6, July 23, 30, 1874; *Albany News,* July 23, 30, 1874.

25. *Albany News,* July 30, 1874.

26. *Cuthbert Weekly Appeal,* July 17, August 7, 1874.

27. *Dawson Weekly Journal,* July 2, 1874; *Savannah Morning News,* August 8, 1874.

28. *Albany News,* August 27, 1874.

29. *Thomasville Times,* August 22, 1874; *Albany News,* August 27, September 3, 1874; Thronasteeska Chapter, *History and Reminiscences of Dougherty County,* 142–44.

30. *Atlanta Daily Herald,* August 29, 1874.

31. *Early County News* (Blakely), September 24, 1874.

32. *Bainbridge Weekly Sun,* July 30, 1874; *Atlanta Constitution,* June 21, 1871; *Dawson Weekly Journal,* June 25, 1874.

33. Ibid., September 10, 1874.

34. Ibid., July 30, 1874; *Bainbridge Weekly Democrat,* October 15, 1874; *Dawson Weekly Journal,* August 20, 1874; *Early County News* (Blakely), October 16, 1874.

35. *Gallaher's Independent* (Quitman), September 19, October 3, 1874; *Savannah Morning News,* February 22, 1873; Huxford, *History of Brooks County,* 221–22.

36. *Dawson Weekly Journal,* October 8, 1874; *Quitman Reporter,* September 7, 1876; *Albany News,* September 10, 17, 1874; *Early County News* (Blakely), October 16, 1874.

37. *Thomasville Times,* August 29, 1874; *Albany News,* September 3, 1874; *Bainbridge Weekly Democrat,* August 13, 1874.

38. *Albany News* quoted in *Thomasville Times,* August 15, 1874.

39. *Albany News,* September 3, 1874.

40. *Cuthbert Weekly Appeal,* August 21, 1874.

41. *Bainbridge Weekly Democrat,* September 3, 1874.

42. *Quitman Reporter,* August 1, 1874; *Bainbridge Weekly Democrat,* September 3, 1874.

43. *Bainbridge Weekly Sun,* September 10, July 9, 23, 1874; *Gallaher's Independent* (Quitman), October 3, 1874; *Dawson Weekly Journal,* August 20, 1874; *Early County News* (Blakely), September 25, 1874.

44. *Bainbridge Weekly Sun,* September 10, 1874.

45. *Savannah Daily Advertiser,* September 20, 1874; *Thomasville Times,* September 26, 1874.

46. Savannah *Daily Advertiser,* September 22, 1874; *Thomasville Times,* July 15, August 1, 1874; *Early County News* (Blakely), October 1, 1874

47. Edward C. Wade to Henry Farrow, September 14, 1871, reel 2, Letters Received by the Department of Justice.

48. Louis Guild to George Williams, September 10, 1874, reel 2, Letters Received by the Department of Justice.

49. Solomon Parker to George Williams, September 10, 1874, reel 2, Letters Received by the Department of Justice; *Daily True Georgian* (Atlanta), July 2, 1870.

50. Benjamin Brimberry to Edward C. Wade, September 8, 1874, reel 2, Letters Received by the Department of Justice.

51. Edward Wade to George Williams, September 14, 1874, reel 2, Letters Received by the Department of Justice.

52. *Bainbridge Weekly Sun,* September 10, 1874.

53. Bixby et al., *History of Clear Creek and Boulder Valleys,* 697; *Bainbridge Weekly Sun,* December 17, 1873, August 6, September 24, 1874; *Early County News* (Blakely), September 25, 1874; *Bainbridge Weekly Democrat,* September 9, 1872; January 16, 1873; *Boulder Daily Camera,* December 4, 1922.

54. *Early County News* (Blakely), October 16, September 25, 1874; *Savannah Daily Advertiser,* October 9, 1874; *Albany News,* September 17, 1874.

55. *Early County News* (Blakely), October 9, 1874.

56. *Bainbridge Weekly Sun,* September 24, 1874; *Early County News* (Blakely), October 9, 1874.

57. *Dawson Weekly Journal,* August 20, 1874; *Bainbridge Weekly Democrat,* October 15, 1874.

58. *Bainbridge Weekly Democrat,* October 29, 1874; *Thomasville Times,* October 17, 1874; *Early County News* (Blakely), October 2, 1874.

59. *Thomasville Times,* October 24, 1874; *Dawson Weekly Journal,* August 27, 1874; *Early County News* (Blakely), November 13, 1874; *Gallaher's Independent* (Quitman), October 3, 1874.

60. *Savannah Daily Advertiser,* November 3, 1874; *Albany News,* November 26, 1874; *Atlanta Constitution,* November 10, 1874; *Early County News* (Blakely), October 23, November 13, 1874.

61. *Cuthbert Weekly Appeal,* November 6, 1874; Nordhoff, *The Cotton States in the Summer of 1875,* 110.

62. *Dawson Weekly Journal,* October 1, 1874.

63. *Bainbridge Weekly Democrat,* August 20, 1874.

64. *Bainbridge Sun,* July 30, 1874; *Albany News,* November 12, 1874.

Chapter 10: The Ablest and Strongest Radical in the District

1. Richard Whiteley to Ben Perley Poore, December 9, 1874, Georgia Political Leaders' Autographs 1782–1940, Special Collections, Robert D. Woodruff Library, Emory University, Atlanta; Gillette, *Retreat from Reconstruction,* 211–47; Foner, *Reconstruction,* 549–53; *Atlanta Daily Herald,* January 21, 26, 1875; Richardson, *Compilation of the Messages and Papers of the Presidents,* 9:4251–53; McKinney, *Southern Mountain Republicans,* 39–40, 43–44, 54–55.

2. *Bainbridge Weekly Sun,* July 30, 1874; *Atlanta Daily Herald,* February 6, 1875; *Congressional Record* (43rd Congress, 2nd session), 1:378; Accompanying Papers to Forty-third Congress, House of Representatives, box 16, "Petition of Trustees of African Methodist Church at Marietta," RG 233, NA.

3. *Bainbridge Weekly Sun,* September 17, 1874; *Atlanta Daily Herald,* February 6, 1875; *Washington National Republican,* December 22, 1874; *Congressional Record* (43rd Congress, 2nd session), 1:71, 169, 1:552.

4. *Atlanta Daily Herald,* January 16, 1875.

5. Alexander Allen to brother, January 6, 1875, Allen Papers.

6. *Atlanta Daily Herald,* January 16, 24, March 12, 1875.

7. *Savannah Morning News,* January 27, 1875; W. P. Pierce to Benjamin Conley, March 19, 1875, Conley Papers, University of Georgia.

8. *Atlanta Daily Herald,* March 11, 1875; *Congressional Record* (43rd Congress, 2nd session), 2:1101; Amos Akerman to Richard Whiteley, October 1, 1874, reel 2, 295; Amos Akerman Letterbooks, Special Collections, Alderman Library, University of Virginia, Charlottesville; Gillette, *Retreat from Reconstruction,* 259–73; Shadgett, *History of the Republican Party in Georgia,* 51.

9. *Louisville Courier-Journal,* February 13, 1875; *Cincinnati Daily Gazette,* February 13, 1875; *Washington National Republican,* December 21, 1874, January 11, 1875; *Cincinnati Commercial,* January 10, 15, 1875; *Congressional Record* (43rd Congress, 2nd session), 3:1935; Gillette, *Retreat from Reconstruction,* 280–91; Harris, *Day of the Carpetbagger,* 645–48.

10. Richard Whiteley to Benjamin Conley, April 2, 1875, Conley Papers, University of Georgia: W. P. Pierce to C. C. Adams, April 13, 1875, "Records Relating to Charges against Collectors of Internal Revenue, 1866–1881," box 1, RG 56, NA; *Atlanta Daily Herald,* March 14–15, March 20–21, April 7, 1875.

11. *Bainbridge Weekly Democrat,* July 22, January 7, January 14, January 21, 1875, September 24, 1874.

12. Ibid., January 7, April 8, 1875.

13. Ibid., December 10, December 24, 1875, January 14, 1876.

14. Richard Whiteley to Benjamin Conley, April 2, 1875, Conley Papers, University of Georgia.

15. Richard Whiteley to Henry Farrow, December 28, 1875, Farrow Papers.

16. *Bainbridge Weekly Democrat,* January 7, 1875.

17. Ibid., November 11, 1875; Gellatly to Secretary of the University, March 22, 1954, Alumni File, Princeton University.

18. *Bainbridge Weekly Democrat,* July 22, July 15, May 13, June 3, 1875.

19. Ibid., July 8, July 29, 1875.

20. Ibid., July 29, May 20, May 27, July 22, December 9, 1875; December 17, 1874.

21. Ibid., November 18, May 20, September 16, September 30, 1875; February 10, July 20, 1876; September 11, 1873; Nordhoff, *The Cotton States in the Spring and Summer of 1875,* 105; Harris, *Day of the Carpetbagger,* 577.

22. *Bainbridge Weekly Democrat,* November 18, July 8, 1875.

23. Ibid., February 3, 1876; Decatur County Superior Court, Minutes Book 1, 1875–80, 198, microfilm, GDAH.

24. *Bainbridge Weekly Democrat,* February 17, 1876.

25. Ibid., April 13, 1876, October 28, 1875.

26. Ibid., April 27, 1876.

27. Ibid., March 9, 1876.

28. Ibid., March 30, May 11, 1876.

29. Nordhoff, *The Cotton States in the Spring and Summer of 1875,* 110; John Bryant to Ulysses Grant, January 12, 1875, Records Relating to Charges against Collectors of Internal Revenue, 1866–81, box 2, RG 56, NA; *Atlanta Constitution,* May 4–5, 1876; *Bainbridge Weekly Democrat,* May 11, 1876.

30. *Bainbridge Weekly Democrat,* April 27, August 3, 1876.

31. *Thomasville Southern Enterprise,* August 16, 1876; *Dawson Weekly Journal,* August 17, 1876; *Bainbridge Weekly Democrat,* August 3, August 10, 1876.

32. *Early County News* (Blakely), August 18, 1876.

33. *Dawson Weekly Journal,* August 17, August 24, 1876.

34. *Quitman Reporter,* September 7, 1876; *Valdosta Times,* September 9, 1876; *Early County News* (Blakely), July 21, September 8, 1876.

35. *Valdosta Times,* September 16, 1876; *Dawson Weekly Journal,* September 21, 1876; *Quitman Reporter,* September 21, 1876.

36. *Bainbridge Weekly Democrat,* April 27, 1876; *Thomasville Southern Enterprise,* September 6, 1876.

37. Nordhoff, *The Cotton States in the Spring and Summer of 1875,* 112, 110; *Early County News* (Blakely), October 20, November 3, 1876.

38. *Bainbridge Weekly Democrat,* September 7, 1876; *Thomasville Southern Enterprise,* September 6, 1876.

39. *Thomasville Southern Enterprise,* August 30, September 16, 1876.

40. Ibid., August 30, 1876.

41. *Thomasville Times,* September 2, 1876.

42. *Dawson Weekly Journal,* September 28, 1876.

43. Ibid., October 26, 1876; *Valdosta Times,* September 16, 1876.

44. *Early County News* (Blakely), October 20, 1876.

45. *Dawson Weekly Journal,* November 2, 1886; *Valdosta Times,* September 16, 1876; *Early County News* (Blakely), November 10, 1876; Rogers, "'Death Has Been Busily at Work,'" 418.

46. *Cuthbert Weekly Appeal,* October 27, 1876; *Early County News* (Blakely), November 17, 1876.

47. *Thomasville Southern Enterprise,* August 30, 1876; *Bainbridge Democrat,* April 27, 1876.

48. *Cuthbert Weekly Appeal,* September 1, October 20, May 5, 1876; *Early County News* (Blakely), October 20, 1876; *Thomasville Times,* October 21, 1876; *Valdosta Times,* October 7, 1876.

49. *Cuthbert Weekly Appeal,* October 13, 1876.

50. *Thomasville Times,* October 21, 1876, *Early County News* (Blakely), October 20, 1876.

51. *Thomasville Southern Enterprise,* October 18, 1876; Shadgett, *History of the Republican Party,* 57–60.

52. *Early County News* (Blakely), October 20, 1876; *Cuthbert Weekly Appeal,* October 20, October 27, 1876; *Thomasville Southern Enterprise,* September 6, 1876.

53. *Dawson Weekly Journal,* October 26, 1876.

54. *Cuthbert Weekly Appeal,* September 15, 1876.

55. *Dawson Weekly Journal,* October 26, 1876.

56. *Early County News* (Blakely), October 27, 1876.

57. *Early County News* (Blakely), October 20, 1876; *Thomasville Southern Enterprise,* November 8, November 15, November 22, 1876; *Cuthbert Weekly Appeal,* November 10, 1876; *Atlanta Constitution,* November 16, 1876.

58. *Thomasville Southern Enterprise,* September 6, 1876.

59. *Thomasville Times,* September 2, 1876.

60. Amos Akerman to Richard Whiteley, November 8, 1876, Akerman Letterbooks, reel 1, 654.

61. John Bryant to Richard Whiteley, December 9, 1876, Bryant Papers; Currie-McDaniel, *Carpetbagger of Conscience,* 134–35.

62. William A. Pledger to Richard Whiteley, December 2, 1876, in William A. Pledger Letterbook, Bryant Papers; Currie-McDaniel, *Carpetbagger of Conscience,* 133.

63. *Bainbridge Sun,* July 30, 1874; *Bainbridge Weekly Democrat,* June 26, July 17, 1873; *Congressional Record* (43rd Congress, 1st session), 5:4692; Carl Abbot, *Colorado,* 51–60; Billington, *Westward Expansion,* 617–21.

64. Bixby et al., *History of Clear Creek and Boulder Valleys,* 697.

Chapter 11: Major Whiteley Will Make His Mark

1. John Hayes to Col. E. C. Wade, March 13, 1877, U.S. Courts, Southern District of Georgia, Savannah General Court, Correspondence and Clerks Papers (1868–1910) RG 621, NA Branch, Eastpoint, Georgia; *Denver Rocky Mountain News,* March 28, 1877; Fossett, *Colorado: Its Gold and Silver Mines, Farms and Stock Ranges, and Health and Pleasure Resorts,* 11, 17, 84.

2. *Boulder County Herald,* April 5, 1882; *Colorado Banner* (Boulder), January 2, 1879; *Boulder County News,* February 18, 1876, April 19, 1878, September 13, 1878; Bixby et al., *History of Clear Creek and Boulder Valleys,* 204, 401, 403; Fossett, *Colorado: Its Gold and Silver Mines,* 8–9, 252–54, 272–74, 281.

3. Fossett, *Colorado: Its Gold and Silver Mines,* 7.

4. *Boulder County News,* October 19, 1877.

5. *Colorado Banner* (Boulder), April 18, 1878.

6. *Boulder News and Courier,* January 3, 10, February 7, 1879; *Boulder County Courier,* October 18, 1878; *Boulder County News,* May 25, 1877; *Colorado Banner* (Boulder), June 7, 1877.

7. *Boulder County News,* February 18, November 26, 1876, January 5, May 18, October 19, 1877; *Colorado Banner* (Boulder), January 3, 1879; *Boulder County Herald,* March 15, 1882; Bixby et al., *History of Clear Creek and Boulder Valleys,* 119, 404, 407–11; Smith, *A Look at Boulder,* 64; Davis, *Glory Colorado,* 6–19.

8. *Boulder County News,* February 16, June 29, November 26, 1877; *Colorado Banner* (Boulder), July 19, 1877.

9. *Boulder County Herald,* May 12, 1880; *Boulder County News,* March 16, 1876.

10. *Boulder County News,* October 20, 1876; U.S. Bureau of the Census, *Tenth Census, 1880, Population,* [illegible].

11. *Bainbridge Search Light,* December 10, 1909; Margaret Whiteley to John Donalson, January 14, 1911, Donalson Papers; Gellatly to Secretary of the University, March 22, 1954, Alumni File, Princeton University; *Cuthbert Appeal,* March 23, 1877; *Dawson Journal,* March 22, 1877; *Boulder County News,* April 6, April 20, 1877; Deed Book of Boulder County, Office of the Probate Judge, Boulder, Colorado, book 41, 240, book 45, 466, book 69, 206; for the development

on Colorado towns on traditional lines, see Underwood, *Town Building on the Colorado Frontier,* 36, 107; Abbott, *A History of the Centennial State,* 69; for Blake, see Bixby et al., *History of Clear Creek and Boulder Valleys,* 613–14.

12. Margaret Whiteley to John Donalson, Donalson Papers.

13. *Colorado Banner* (Boulder), October 4, 1877.

14. *Boulder County News,* November 23, 1877, October 20, December 29, 1876; Deed Book of Boulder County, Office of the Probate Judge, Boulder, Colorado, book 42, 488, 495.

15. *Boulder County Herald,* March 10, 1880, September 30, 1885; *Boulder County News,* May 10, 1878; *Boulder News and Courier,* June 3, 1881; U.S. Bureau of the Census, *Tenth Census, Population, 1880,* 382; *Tenth Census, Agriculture, 1880,* 216–17; Bixby et al., *History of Clear Creek and Boulder Valleys,* 613–14, 688–89; Fossett, *Colorado: Its Gold and Silver Mines,* 14; Abbott, *A History of the Centennial State,* 157; Billington, *Westward Expansion,* 747–49.

16. *Boulder County News,* May 4, 1877, May 12, 1876; *Colorado Banner* (Boulder), June 7, 1877.

17. *Boulder County News,* April 27, 1877; *Colorado Banner* (Boulder), June 7, 1877; Appraisal of Estate of Richard H. Whiteley, Estate Records of Richard H. Whiteley, Boulder County Court, Colorado State Archives, Denver.

18. *Boulder County News,* June 28, February 8, March 1, March 8, 22, April 5, May 3, August 2, 1878; June 8, June 15, November 23, 1877; *Boulder County Herald,* May 26, July 7, 1880, August 3, June 15, 1881; Bixby et al., *History of Clear Creek and Boulder Valleys,* 118–19; Davis, *Glory Colorado,* 28; *Catalogue and Circular of the University of Colorado 1881–1882,* 26–27; Academic Records, book A, 7–8, University of Colorado Admissions and Records, Archives, University of Colorado at Boulder Libraries.

19. Parish Register, St. John's, Boulder, Col., Nos. 1 and 2, 216–19, 224–26, St. John's Episcopalian Church, Boulder, Colorado; *Boulder County News,* January 4, February 8, March 22, April 5, May 3, May 10, 1878; *Boulder News and Courier,* July 11, November 7, December 5, 1879; *Colorado Banner* (Boulder), April 4, 1878; for Wright, see Bixby et al., *History of Clear Creek and Boulder Valleys,* 413, 699–700; Smith, *A Look at Boulder,* 68.

20. *Boulder County News,* April 6, 1877; Billington, *Westward Expansion,* 622–23; Smith, *Rocky Mountain Mining Camps,* 78–82; West, *The Saloon on the Rocky Mountain Frontier,* 18–20; Perrigo, "Law and Order in Early Colorado Mining Camps," 41–62.

21. *Boulder County News,* February 22, 15, 1878; *Sunshine (Colo.) Courier,* November 17, 1877.

22. *Boulder County News,* February 15, 1878.

23. Ibid., March 29, 1878; October 12, 1877; Billington, *Westward Expansion,* 731–35.

24. *Boulder County News*, August 30, 1878; for politics in mining communities, see Smith, *Rocky Mountain Camps,* 155–58.

25. *Boulder County News,* August 23, 1878.

26. *Boulder County Courier,* August 23, 1878.

27. *Boulder County News,* September 6, 1878.

28. Ibid., September 13, 1878.

29. Ibid., September 27, 20, 1878.

30. *Boulder County Courier,* October 4, 1878.

31. *Boulder News and Courier,* April 4, May 9, 1879.

32. Ibid., October 31, 1879; *Boulder County Herald,* September 30, 1885.

33. *Boulder News and Courier,* February 14, 1879; Academic Records, Book A, University of Colorado.

34. *Boulder News and Courier,* June 27, 1879.

35. *Boulder County Herald,* February 23, 1881, April 28, 1880, September 29, 1880; *Boulder County News,* May 3, 1877.

36. *Boulder County News,* October 26, 1877.

37. *Colorado Banner* (Boulder), July 31, 1879; *Boulder County News,* January 4, 1878.

38. *Boulder County Herald,* March 10, 1880; *Boulder News and Courier,* December 19, 1879, January 9, 1880.

39. *Boulder News and Courier,* February 13, 1880.

40. *Boulder County Herald,* February 23, 1881.

41. Ibid., July 25, 1883.

42. Gellatly to Secretary of the University, March 22, 1954, Alumni File, Princeton University; *Boulder County Herald,* March 31, July 7, August 25, 1880; *Boulder County News and Courier,* August 13, 27, 1880; McFeely, *Grant,* 483–84.

43. *Boulder News and Courier,* July 30, 1880; *Boulder County Herald,* August 1, 1880.

44. *Boulder News and Courier,* October 1, 1880.

45. *Boulder County Herald,* September 28, 1881; *Boulder News and Courier,* September 30, 1881.

46. *Boulder County Herald,* March 30, October 26, 1881, July 5, 1882; *Boulder News and Courier,* August 20, 1880.

47. *Boulder County Herald,* March 16, 1881.

48. Ibid., March 30, 1881, July 5, 1882.

49. *Boulder News and Courier,* November 4, 1881; *Boulder County Herald,* July 5, 1881; *Longmont (Colo.) Ledger,* October 14, 1881; Charles Campbell, "To the Voters of Boulder County," folder 7, Charles Campbell Papers, Archives, University of Colorado, Boulder; for Wolff and Berkley, see Bixby et al., *History of Clear Creek and Boulder Valleys,* 608–9, 7045.

50. *Boulder County Herald,* November 2, 1881, June 13, 1883; *Boulder News and Courier,* July 15, 1881; Deed Book of Boulder County, Office of the Probate, Boulder, Colorado, book 42, 346; 41, 240, 461; 62, 449.

51. *Boulder County Herald,* October 27, 6, 1880, April 20, 1881, May 10, 1882, March 5, 1884; *Boulder News and Courier,* July 15, 1881; for Boulder Hose Co. No. 1, see Bixby et al., *History of Clear Creek and Boulder Valleys,* 415–16.

52. *Boulder County Herald,* February 23, 1881, January 18, April 26, 1882.

53. *Boulder News and Courier,* April 1, 1881.

54. *Boulder County Herald,* December 7, 1881.

55. Boulder City Council Proceedings, vol. 3 (June 9, 1879–April 14, 1882), 3–4, Carnegie Branch Library, Boulder, Colorado; *Boulder County Herald,* November 17, 1886.

56. *Boulder County News,* September 13, 1881; *Boulder County Herald,* November 17, 1886; Abbott, *A History of the Centennial State,* 114.

Chapter 12: Peace to His Ashes

1. Bixby et al., *History of Clear Creek and Boulder Valleys*, 696.

2. *Boulder News and Courier*, April 21, 1882; *Boulder County Herald*, December 7, 1881; January 18, 1872; Myres, *Westering Women and the Frontier Experience*, 224.

3. *Boulder County Herald*, April 26, July 12, November 29, 1882, July 4, July 11, September 5, 1883, February 18, 1885; *Boulder County News*, February 18, 1876, May 4, 1877, May 3, 1882; Smith, *A Look at Boulder*, 88; such problems were not unique to Boulder. See Underwood, *Town Building on the Colorado Frontier*, 52–73.

4. *Boulder News and Courier*, July 14, June 30, 1882.

5. *Boulder County Herald*, June 14, 1882; Davis, *Glory Colorado*, 40–41.

6. *Boulder News and Courier*, June 7, 1882; *Boulder County Herald*, June 14, 1882.

7. *Bainbridge Democrat*, February 1, 1883; *Boulder County Herald*, February 28, July 4, 1883; *Boulder* County *News and Courier*, September 22, November 10, 1882; *Boulder Weekly Herald*, November 15, 1882.

8. *Boulder County Herald*, May 10, 1882; *Boulder News*, October 2, 1890.

9. *Boulder County Herald*, May 17, 1882.

10. Ibid., May 24, 1882.

11. Ibid., August 2, November 1, 8, 1882; *Boulder News and Courier*, July 21, October 13, 1882.

12. *Boulder County Herald*, November 8, 1882.

13. Ibid., July 18, June 6, 1883, May 10, 1882; March 14, 1873; *Boulder News and Courier*, February 9, July 29, 1883.

14. *Boulder County Herald*, July 25, 1883.

15. Ibid., July 4, July 11, 1883.

16. *Boulder County Herald*, October 10, 1883.

17. *Boulder County Herald*, October 31, 1883.

18. Ibid., March 5, February 20, July 4, October 31, 1883; *Boulder News and Courier*, May 5, 1882; *Colorado Banner* (Boulder), November 21, 1878; West, *The Saloon on the Rocky Mountain Mining Frontier*, 110–29.

19. *Boulder County Herald*, March 12, 5, 1884.

20. Ibid., March 26, 12, 1884; prohibition battles were common. See Underwood's study of Grand Junction, *Town Building on the Colorado Frontier*, 52.

21. *Boulder County Herald*, April 2, 1884; for Maxwell, see Bixby et al., *History of Clear Creek and Boulder Valleys*, 652–54.

22. *Boulder County Herald*, July 2, 1884.

23. Ibid., August 6, June 11, July 2, 1884; for Berkley, see Bixby et al., *History of Clear Creek and Boulder Valleys*, 608–9.

24. Ibid., April 9, 1913; *Boulder News and Banner*, August 15, 1884; Colorado State Census 1880, Boulder County, 1718; Margaret E. Whiteley vs. Richard H. Whiteley, August 11, 1884; Divorce Decree, Boulder County Court, Colorado State Archives, Denver; Margaret Whiteley to John Donalson, October 8, 1890, Donalson Papers; *Denver News*, August 13, 1884; *Boulder Daily Camera*, October 29, 1893, October 28, 1936.

25. *Boulder News and Banner,* August 15, 1884; *Boulder County Herald,* August 13, 1884; *Denver News,* August 13, 1884; Margaret E. Whiteley vs. Richard H. Whiteley, August 11, 1884, County Court, Boulder County; Divorce Decree, Colorado State Archives, Denver.

26. *Boulder County Herald,* August 20, July 2, 1884.

27. Bixby et al., *History of Cross Creek and Boulder Valleys,* 696; *Boulder News and Banner,* August 15, 1884; *Boulder County Herald,* January 9, August 20, 1884, May 20, 1885, October 1, 1890; *Boulder News,* October 2, 1890; Margaret Whiteley to John Donalson, October 8, 1890, John Donalson to Margaret Whiteley, February 12, 1912, Donalson Papers.

28. *Boulder County News,* February 9, 1877; Deed Book of Boulder County, Office of the Probate Judge, Boulder, Colorado, book 92, 164.

29. *Boulder County Herald,* October 22, 15, 29, September 24, 1884.

30. Ibid., May 27, 20, March 25, April 1, 1885; for Brace, see Bixby et al., *History of Clear Creek and Boulder Valleys,* 611.

31. *Boulder County Herald,* April 8, 1884; for Develine, see Bixby et al., *History of Clear Creek and Boulder Valleys,* 630–31.

32. *Boulder County Herald,* April 1, 1885.

33. Ibid., March 25, April 8, 1885.

34. *Boulder Sentinel,* September 24, 1886.

35. Georgetown *Courier,* August 12, 1886; *Boulder County Herald,* June 3, 1885; Margaret Whiteley to John Donalson, October 8, 1890, Donalson Papers.

36. *Boulder County Herald,* June 2, July 7, 1886, May 4, 1887, September 5, November 14, 1888, April 3, 1889; *Portrait and Biographical Record of Denver and Vicinity,* 332.

37. *Boulder County Herald,* June 2, February 10, December 1, 1886; Margaret Whiteley to John Donalson, October 8, 1890, Donalson Papers.

38. Gellatly to Secretary of the University, March 22, 1954, Alumni File, Princeton University; *Boulder County Herald,* May 5, 26, December 22, 1886, January 5, 1887; *Boulder News and Banner,* May 22, 1888, *Boulder County Herald,* January 5, 1887; for Tyler family, see Bixby et al., *History of Clear Creek and Boulder Valleys,* 687–88; Davis, *Glory Colorado,* 54.

39. *Boulder County Herald,* February 8, 1888; *Boulder News and Banner,* February 7, 1888.

40. *Boulder County Herald,* February 6, 1889.

41. Margaret Whiteley to John Donalson, August 25, October 8, 1890, Donalson Papers.

42. Margaret Whiteley to John Donalson, October 8, 1890, Donalson Papers.

43. *Boulder County Herald,* October 1, 1890; *Boulder News,* October 2, 1890.

44. Margaret Whiteley to John Donalson, October 8, 1890, Donalson Papers.

45. *Boulder County Herald,* October 7, 1885.

46. *Boulder News,* October 18, 1888; *Boulder News and Banner,* August 3, 1886; *Boulder County Herald,* October 24, 1888, November 13, 1889; Appraisal of Estate of Richard H. Whiteley, Estate Records of Richard Whiteley, Boulder County Court, Colorado State Archives, Denver; Deed Book of Boulder County, Office of the Probate Judge, Boulder, Colorado, book 110, 298.

47. *Boulder News and Banner,* April 17, 1889; *Boulder County Herald,* February 6, 1889.

48. *Boulder County Herald,* February 13, February 6, 1889; *Boulder County News,* February 15, 1889.

49. *Boulder County Herald,* February 13, 1889; *Boulder News,* February 14, 1889.

50. *Boulder News,* February 14, 1889; *Boulder County Herald,* February 12, October 23, 1889, February 12, 1890; Margaret Whiteley to John Donalson, October 8, 1890, Donalson Papers.

51. Margaret Whiteley to John Donalson, October 8, 1890, Donalson Papers; *Boulder County Herald,* October 1, 1890; *Boulder News,* October 2, 1890.

52. *Boulder County News,* October 2, 1890.

53. Ibid.; *Boulder County Herald,* October 1, 1890.

54. *Boulder County Herald,* October 1, 1890.

Conclusion

1. U.S. Congress, *Condition of Affairs in the Late Insurrectionary States, Georgia,* 6:40.

2. U.S. Congress, "Affairs in Alabama," 507.

3. *Bainbridge Weekly Sun,* July 30, 1874.

4. *Congressional Globe* (42nd Congress, 3rd session), 2:1550.

5. *Bainbridge Weekly Sun,* July 30, 1874; *Blakely Early County News,* August 17, October 17, 1877; for migration of blacks to Kansas, see Painter, *Exodusters.*

6. *Congressional Globe* (42nd Congress, 3rd session), 2:1550.

7. Campbell, "George W. Whitemore," 17–24; Binning, "The Tennessee Republicans in Decline 1869–1876," 70–71; Harris, *Day of the Carpetbagger,* 94, 457, 64; Rogers, *Black Belt Scalawag.*

8. *Bainbridge Weekly Sun,* July 30, 1874; *Bainbridge Weekly Democrat,* July 18, 1872.

BIBLIOGRAPHY

Manuscripts

Atlanta History Center, Atlanta
- Benjamin Conley Papers

Bainbridge College Library, Bainbridge College, Bainbridge, Georgia
- John Donalson Papers

William R. Perkins Library, Duke University, Durham, North Carolina
- John E. Bryant Papers

Robert W. Woodruff Library, Emory University, Atlanta
- Georgia Political Leaders Autographs, 1782–1940 Papers

Robert Strozier Library, Florida State University, Tallahassee
- American Missionary Association Papers (microfilm)

Georgia Department of Archives and History, Atlanta
- Rufus Bullock Papers
- Executive Department, Correspondence
- File 2, Names
- Reconstruction File

Kansas State Historical Society, Topeka, Kansas
- J. Cameron Swayze Papers

Library of Congress, Washington, D.C.
- William E. Chandler Papers
- Edward M. McPherson Papers
- John Sherman Papers
- Thaddeus Stevens Papers

National Archives, Washington, D.C.
- Applications for Appointments as Customs Service Officers, 1833–1910, Georgia, Department of the Treasury, RG 56
- Applications for Positions as Internal Revenue Collectors and Assessors, 1863–1910, Department of the Treasury, RG 56
- Records of the Assistant Commissioner for the State of Georgia, Bureau of Refugees, Freedmen and Abandoned Lands, 1865–69, RG 105
- Records of the House of Representatives, Accompanying Papers to Forty-third Congress, "Petition of Trustees of Agrican Methodist Church at Marietta," RG 233
- Records of the House of Representatives, "Petitions for the Removal of Legal and Political Disabilities Imposed by the Fourteenth Amendment," RG 233

Records of the Office of the Judge Advocate General, Army Court Martial Case Files 1869–94, RG 69
Records of the United States Army Continental Commands, Third Military District, 1867–68, RG 393
Records Relating to the Appointment of Federal Judges, Marshals and Attorneys, 1853–1901, Georgia, Department of Justice, RG 60
Records Relating to Charges against Collectors of Internal Revenue, 1806–81, Department of the Treasury, RG 56
National Archives Branch, Eastpoint, Georgia
Letters Received by the Department of Justice from the State of Georgia, 1871–84, RG 60
Records of the Assistant Commissioner for the State of Georgia, Bureau of Refugees, Freedmen and Abandoned Lands, 1865–69, RG 105
Records of the Superintendent of Education for the State of Georgia, Bureau of Refugees, Freedmen, and Abandoned Lands, 1865–70, RG 105
U.S. Courts, Southern District of Georgia, Savannah General Court, Correspondence and Clerks Papers, 1868–1910, RG 621
University of Colorado, Boulder
Charles Campbell Papers
University of Georgia, Hargrett Rare Book and Manuscript Library, University of Georgia Libraries, Athens
Benjamin Conley Papers
Henry Farrow Papers
Ulysses S. Grant Papers (microfilm)
Nelson Tift Papers
University of North Carolina, Southern Historical Collection, Chapel Hill, North Carolina
George Washington Allen Papers
Edward Anderson Diary 7
Thomas Settle Papers
University of Virginia, Charlottesville, Virginia
Amos Akerman Letterbooks (microfilm)

Contemporary Articles, Books, Pamphlets, and Various Archival Sources

Academic Records. Book A. University of Colorado Admissions and Records, University of Colorado, Boulder.

Alvord, J. W. "Letters from the South, Relating to the Condition of Freedmen." Washington, D.C.: Howard University Press, 1870.

American Missionary Magazine (June 1868, May 1869).

Andrews, Sidney. *The South since the War, as Shown by Fourteen Weeks of Travel and Observation in Georgia and the Carolinas.* Boston: Ticknor and Fields, 1866.

Barnes, William H. *The History of the Congress of the United States.* New York: W. H. Barnes, 1871.

Biennal Register of Officiers and Agents, Civil, Military and Naval in the Services of the United States. Washington, D.C.: Government Printing Office, 1874.

Bixby, Amos, et al. *History of Clear Creek and Boulder Valleys, Colorado, Containing a Brief History of the State from Its Earliest Settlement to the Present Time, Embracing Its Geological, Physical and Climatic Features; Its Agricultural, Stockgrowing, Railroad and Mining Interests; An Account of the Ute Trouble; A History of Gilpin, Clear Creek, Boulder and Jefferson Counties, and Biographical Sketches.* Chicago: O. L. Baskin, 1880.

Blaine, James G. *Twenty Years of Congress, From Lincoln to Garfield.* Vol. 2. Norwich, Conn.: Henry Bill, 1886.

Boulder City Council Proceedings. Vol. 3 (June 9, 1879–April 14, 1882). Carnegie Branch Library, Boulder, Colorado.

Boyd, William H., comp. *Boyd's Directory of the District of Columbia Together with a Compendium of Its Governments, Institutions, and Trades.* Washington, D.C.: Philp and Solomons, 1874.

Buckingham, James Silk. *The Slave States of America.* London: Fisher, Son. 1842.

Catalogue and Circular of the University of Colorado 1881–1882. Boulder: Daily Herald Steam Print, 1882.

"Circular Grand Council Chamber, Union League Association in Georgia, February 5, 1868." Broadside Collection, Special Collections, Hargrett Rare Book and Manuscript Library, University of Georgia Libraries, Athens.

Clark, R. H., T. R. R. Cobb, and D. Irwin, *The Code of the State of Georgia.* Macon: J. W. Burke, 1873.

Diary of Nelson Tift, (1868–1871). In possession of Mr. C. S. Pritchett, Albany, Georgia.

Ellis, John B. *The Sights and Secrets of the National Capital: A Work Descriptive of Washington City in All Its Various Phases.* St. Louis: National, 1869.

Fossett, Frank. *Colorado: Its Gold and Silver Mines, Farms and Stock Ranges, and Health and Pleasure Resorts.* New York: C. G. Crawford, 1879.

Johnston, R. M., ed. *City of Bainbridge and County of Decatur, Georgia: Historical Sketches of the City and County; A Full Description of the Entire County, Its Resources, Soil, and Climate, Its Schools, Churches, Social Advantages, Healthfulness, Etc.* Atlanta: R. M. Johnston, 1877.

Letterbook of Outgoing Correspondence (1865–1872). John E. Donalson Papers, Bainbridge College Library, Bainbridge, Georgia.

Martin, Edward W. *Behind the Scenes in Washington: Being a Complete and Graphic Account of the Credit Mobilier Investigation, The Congressional Rings.* New York: Continental, 1873.

Masons Book, Orion Lodge No. 8, Free and Accepted Masons from May 26, 1855 to December 26, 1857. In possession of Benny Brooksip, Bainbridge, Georgia.

"Meeting of the State Central Committee of Union Republican Party of Georgia Held at Atlanta, Wednesday, November 24, 1869." Atlanta: New Era Job Office, 1869. Duke Pamphlet Collection, Perkins Library, Duke University, Durham, North Carolina.

Memoirs of Georgia Containing Historical Accounts of the State's Civil, Military, Industrial and Professional Interests, and Personal Sketches of Many of Its People. Vol. 1. Atlanta: Southern Historical Association, 1895.

Minutes of [Bainbridge] City Council, 1865–1868. City Hall, Bainbridge, Georgia.

Nordhoff, Charles. *The Cotton States in the Spring and Summer of 1875.* New York: Appleton, 1876.

Parish Register, St. John's, Boulder, Col., Nos. 1 and 2. St. John's Episcopalian Church, Boulder, Colorado.

Poore, Ben Perley, comp. *Congressional Directory, Forty-second Congress, First Session.* Washington: Government Printing Office, 1871.

———. *Congressional Directory, Forty-second Congress, Third Session.* Washington, D.C.: Government Printing Office, 1871.

———. *Congressional Directory of the Forty-third Congress, Second Session.* Washington, D.C.: Government Printing Office, 1875.

Portrait and Biographical Record of Denver and Vicinity, Colorado, Containing Portraits and Biographies of Many Well-Known Citizens of the Past and Present. Chicago: Chapman, 1898.

"Proceedings of the Republican Convention of the Tenth Senatorial District Held at Albany, Georgia, February 20, 1872." Broadside Collection, Rare Book and Manuscript Library, University of Georgia Libraries, University of Georgia, Athens.

Reconstruction Registration Oath Books. Vol. 42. Georgia Department of Archives and History, Atlanta.

Registers of First Garvagh Presbyterian Church. First Garvagh Presbyterian Church, Garvagh, Ireland, Co. Londonderry.

Returns of Qualified Voters under the Reconstruction Act, Vol. 25, Decatur County. Georgia Department of Archives and History, Atlanta.

Richardson, James D. *A Compilation of the Messages and Papers of the Presidents.* Vol. 9. New York: Bureau of National Literature, 1897.

Roll and Record Book of Session of First Presbyterian Church, Augusta, Ga., From November 1838 to April 1856." Augusta Genealogical Society Library, Augusta, Georgia.

Simon, John Y., ed. *The Papers of Ulysses S. Grant.* Vol. 24 (1873). Carbondale: Southern Illinois University Press, 2000.

"St. John's Church Records, Bainbridge Ga." St. John's Church, Bainbridge, Georgia.

Thomson, William. *A Tradesman's Travels, in the United States and Canada, in the Years 1840, 1841, and 1842.* Edinburgh: Oliver and Boyd, 1842.

Townsend, George A. *Events at the National Capital and the Campaign of 1876: A Complete History of the Foundation and Growth of Our Governing City.* Hartford, Conn.: Jas. Betts, 1876.

Trow, John F. *Trow's New York City Directory 1869–1870.* New York: John F. Trow, 1870.

White, George. *Statistics of Georgia.* Savannah: W. Thorne Williams, 1849.

Woodward, K., comp. *The Augusta Directory and City Advertiser for 1841.* Augusta: Browne and McCaffery, 1841.

Public Documents: Federal

Biographical Directory of the American Congress. Washington, D.C.: U.S. Government Printing Office, 1971.

Congressional Globe. 40th, 41st, 42nd Congress.

Congressional Record. 43rd, 44th Congress.

Index to the Congressional Record. 43rd Congress.

U.S. Bureau of the Census. *Eighth Census of the United States: 1860, Population.*
———. *Eighth Census of the United States: 1860, Agriculture.*
———. *Ninth Census of the United States: 1870, Population.*
———. *Tenth Census of the United States: 1880, Population.*
———. *Tenth Census of the United States: 1880, Agriculture.*
U.S. Congress. House Misc. Document 52, "Condition of Affairs in Georgia." 40th Congress, 3rd session.
———. *Testimony Taken by the Joint Select Committee to Inquire into the Condition of Affairs in the Late Insurrectionary States.* Vol 6. *Georgia.* Washington, D.C.: Government Printing Office, 1872.
———. House Misc. Document 68. "Documents in Connection with the Contested Election Case of Tift vs. Whiteley in the Second Congressional District of Georgia." 41st Congress, 3rd session.
———. "Report on Joint Committee on Reconstruction." 39th Congress, 1st session.
———. House Misc. Doc. 20. "Papers in the Case of Andrew Sloan vs. Morgan Rawls." 43rd Congress, lst session.
———. House Report No. 262. "Affairs in Alabama." 43rd Congress, 2nd session.
———. Senate Report 308. "The Committee on the Judiciary, to Whom Were Referred the Credentials of Joshua Hill, H. V. M. Miller, Henry P. Farrow, and Richard H. Whiteley, Claiming to Have Been Elected Senators from the State of Georgia." 41st Congress, 3rd session.
———. *War of the Rebellion: A Compilation of the Official Records of the Union and Confederate Armies.* Ser. 1, vols. 20, 30, 38.

Public Documents: State

Colorado State Census 1880.
Compiled Service Records of Confederate Soldiers Who Served in Organizations from the State of Georgia. (A–J, K–Z, St–Z.)
District of Columbia Census 1870.
Georgia State Census 1840, 1850, 1860, 1870.
Georgia State Census (Slave) 1860.
Journal of the Proceedings of the Constitutional Convention of the People of Georgia Held in the City of Atlanta in the Months of December, 1867, and January, February, and March, 1868. Augusta: E. H. Pughe, 1868.
Journal of the Senate of the State of Georgia (1870). Atlanta: Public Printer, 1870.

County Records

Boulder County Courthouse, Boulder, Colorado, Probate Judge Office
Deed Record Book 41, 42, 45, 62, 92, 110
Clarke County Courthouse, Athens, Georgia, Probate Judge Office
Tax Digests, 1852, 1853, 1854

Colorado State Archives, Denver
Estate Records of Richard H. Whiteley, Boulder County Court
Boulder County Court, Divorce Records
Decatur County Courthouse, Bainbridge, Georgia, Probate Judge Office
Deed Record Book, L, N, O, Q
Superior Court Pleadings File (1850–69)
Superior Court Old Interrogatories File (1854–74)
Superior Court Pleadings File (1851–71)
Superior Court Minutes Book F (1859–63)
Georgia Department of Archives and History, Atlanta
"Court of Ordinary Minutes," book C, Decatur County (1866–76)
Decatur County, Georgia, Court of Ordinary Book, 1860
Greene County Marriage Licenses (1849–53)
Reconstruction Registration Oath Books 42, roll 3–3057
Returns of Qualified Voters under the Reconstruction Act, vol. 25, Decatur County, roll 4–351
Superior Court Minutes, book 1, Decatur County (1875–80)
Tax Digests for Decatur County, 1856, 1875, 1860
Richmond County Courthouse, Augusta, Georgia, Probate Judge Office
Richmond County Marriage License Book (1839–55), book B

Newspapers

Albany News (1869–70, 1872, 1874)
Albany Tri-Weekly News (1867)
Albany Tri-Weekly Republican (1870)
Athens Southern Watchman (1868)
Atlanta Constitution (1868, 1870, 1872–74, 1876)
Atlanta Daily Herald (1872–75)
Atlanta Daily New Era (1867–68, 1870)
Augusta Daily Chronicle and Sentinel (1847)
Augusta Daily Constitutionalist (1847)
Augusta National Republican (1868)
Bainbridge Argus (1856, 1858, 1869–71)
Bainbridge Post Search-Light (1920)
Bainbridge Search Light (1909)
Bainbridge Semi-Weekly Democrat (1872)
Bainbridge Southern Georgian (1858–60, 1866)
Bainbridge Southern Sun (1869–71)
Bainbridge Weekly Democrat (1872–76, 1883)
Bainbridge Weekly Sun (1872–74)
Blakely Early County News (1871–77)
Boulder County Courier (1878–79)
Boulder County Herald (1880–90, 1913)
Boulder County News (1876–78, 1881, 1888, 1890)
Boulder Daily Camera (1893, 1922, 1936)
Boulder News and Banner (1884, 1888–89)

Boulder News and Courier (1879–83)
Boulder Sentinel (1886)
Boulder Weekly Herald
Cincinnati Commercial (1874)
Cincinnati Daily Gazette (1875)
Colorado Banner (1877–79)
Cuthbert Weekly Appeal (1868, 1870, 1872, 1874)
Dawson Weekly Journal (1868, 1870, 1872, 1874, 1876)
Denver News
Denver Rocky Mountain News (1877)
Gallaher's Independent (Quitman) (1874)
Georgetown Courier (1886)
Georgia Weekly Telegraph (Macon) (1868)
Longmont (Colo.) Ledger (1881)
Louisville Courier-Journal (1875)
Macon American Union (1870,1872)
Macon Daily Enterprise (1873)
Macon Journal and Messenger (1872)
Macon Telegraph and Journal and Messenger (1872–73)
Milledgeville Weekly Federal Union
New York Herald (1867)
New York Times (1867–68)
New York Tribune (1868)
Quitman Banner (1872)
Quitman Reporter (1874)
Savannah Advertiser and Republican (1874)
Savannah Daily Advertiser (1874)
Savannah Daily Republican (1868, 1871)
Savannah Morning News (1871, 1873–75)
Sun and Columbus Enquirer Weekly (1874)
Sunshine (Colo.) Courier (1877)
Thomasville Semi-Weekly Southern Enterprise (1867)
Thomasville Southern-Enterprise (1876)
Thomasville Times (1874)
Valdosta Times (1876)
Washington Evening Star (1870)
Washington National Republican (1871–72, 74)
Weekly Columbus Enquirer (1871–72)
Weekly Sumter Republican (Americus) (1870, 1874)

Secondary Sources

Abbot, Carl. *Colorado: A History of the Centennial State.* Boulder: Colorado Associated University Press, 1976.

Abbott, Richard H. *The Republican Party and the South, 1855–1877: The First Southern Strategy.* Chapel Hill: University of North Carolina Press, 1986.

———. *For Free Press and Equal Rights: Republican Newspapers in the Recon-*

struction South. Edited by John Quist. Athens: University of Georgia Press, 2004.

Avery, I. W. *The History of the State of Georgia from 1850 to 1881.* New York: Brown and Derby, 1881.

Baggett, James Alex. *The Scalawags: Southern Dissenters in the Civil War and Reconstruction.* Baton Rouge: Louisiana State University Press, 2003.

Bartley, Numan V. *The Creation of Modern Georgia.* Athens: University of Georgia Press, 1983.

Bentley, George R. *A History of the Freedmen's Bureau.* Philadelphia: University of Pennsylvania Press, 1955.

Billington, Ray Allen. *Westward Expansion: A History of the American Frontier.* New York: Macmillan, 1967.

Boatner, Mark M. *The Civil War Dictionary.* New York: David McKay, 1967.

Bryant, Jonathan M. *How Curious a Land: Conflict and Change in Greene County, Georgia, 1850–1885.* Chapel Hill: University of North Carolina Press, 1996.

Campbell, Randolph B. *Grass-Roots Reconstruction in Texas 1865–1880.* Baton Rouge: Louisiana State University Press, 1980.

Carey, Anthony Gene. *Practice, Slavery, and the Union in Antebellum Georgia.* Athens: University of Georgia Press, 1997.

Cashin, Edward J. *The Story of Augusta.* Augusta: Richmond County Board of Education, 1980.

Cimbala, Paul A. *Under the Guardianship of the Nation: The Freedmen's Bureau and the Reconstruction of Georgia, 1865–1870.* Athens: University of Georgia Press, 1997.

Connelly, Thomas L. *Army of the Heartland: The Army of Tennessee, 1861–1862.* Baton Rouge: Louisiana State University Press, 1967.

———. *Autumn of Glory: The Army of Tennessee 1862–1865.* Baton Rouge: Louisiana State University Press, 1971.

Conway, Alan. *The Reconstruction of Georgia.* Minneapolis: University of Minnesota Press, 1966.

Current, Richard N. *Those Terrible Carpetbaggers: A Reinterpretation.* New York: Oxford University Press, 1988.

Currie-McDaniel, Ruth. *Carpetbagger of Conscience: A Biography of John Emory Bryant.* Athens: University of Georgia Press, 1987.

Daniel, Larry J. *Soldiering in the Army of Tennessee: A Portrait of Life in a Confederate Army.* Chapel Hill: University of North Carolina Press, 1991.

Davis, William E. *Glory Colorado: A History of the University of Colorado.* Boulder: Pruett Press, 1965.

Decatur County Historical Society. *Decatur County, Georgia, Past and Present 1823–1991.* Roswell, Ga.: W. H. Wolfe, 1991.

Degler, Carl. *The Other South: Southern Dissenters in the Nineteenth Century.* New York: Harper and Row, 1974.

Dorris, Jonathan T. *Pardon and Amnesty under Lincoln and Johnson: The Restoration of the Confederates to Their Rights and Privileges, 1861–1898.* Chapel Hill: University of North Carolina Press, 1953.

Drago, Edmund L. *Black Politicians and Reconstruction in Georgia: A Splendid Failure.* Athens: University of Georgia, 1992.

Duncan, Russell. *Entrepreneur for Equality Governor Rufus Bullock, Commerce, and Race in Post–Civil War Georgia.* Athens: University of Georgia Press, 1994.

Dunning, William A. *Reconstruction, Political and Economic, 1865–1877.* New York: Harper, 1907.

Fleming, Walter L. *Civil War and Reconstruction in Alabama.* New York: Columbia University Press, 1905.

Fitzgerald, Michael W. *The Union League Movement in the Deep South: Politics and Agricultural Change during Reconstruction.* Baton Rouge: Louisiana State University Press, 1989.

Foner, Eric. *Reconstruction: America's Unfinished Revolution 1863–1877.* New York: Harper and Row, 1988.

Franklin, John Hope ed., *The Autobiography of John Roy Lynch.* Chicago: University of Chicago Press, 1970.

Garner, James W. *Reconstruction in Mississippi.* New York: Macmillan, 1901.

Gillette, William. *Retreat from Reconstruction 1869–1879.* Chapel Hill: University of North Carolina Press, 1984.

Green, Constance Mclaughlin. *Washington Village and Capital, 1800–1878.* Princeton, N.J.: Princeton University Press, 1962.

Grice, Warren. *The Georgia Bench and Bar: The Development of Georgia's Judicial System.* Macon, Ga.: J. W. Burke, 1931.

Harris, William C. *The Day of the Carpetbagger Republican Reconstruction in Mississippi.* Baton Rouge: Louisiana State University Press, 1979

Henderson, Lillian, comp. *Roster of the Confederate Soldiers of Georgia 1861–1865.* N.p., n.d.

Hill, Melvin B., Jr. *The Georgia State Constitution.* Westport, Conn.: Greenwood Press, 1994.

Huxford, Folks. *History of Brooks County, Georgia.* Quitman, Ga.: McGregor, 1949.

Johnson, Deloach Pharris, comp. *Under the Southern Cross: Soldier Life with Gordon Bradwell and the Army of Northern Virginia.* Macon: Mercer University Press, 1999.

Jones, Charles C., and Salem Dutcher. *Memorial History of Augusta, Georgia.* Spartanburg, S.C.: Reprint Company, 1980.

Jones, Frank S. *History of Decatur County.* Bainbridge, Georgia, 1971.

Jones, Jacqueline. *Soldiers of Light and Love: Northern Teachers and Georgia Blacks, 1865–1873.* Athens: Brown Thrasher Books, 1992.

Litwack, Leon F. *Been in the Storm So Long: The Aftermath of Slavery.* New York: Knopf, 1979.

Lynch, John R. *The Facts of Reconstruction.* New York: Neale, 1913.

McFeely, William S. *Grant: A Biography.* New York: Norton, 1981.

McKinney, Gordon B. *Southern Mountain Republicans 1865–1900: Politics and the Appalachian Community.* Chapel Hill: University of North Carolina Press, 1978.

McPherson, James M. *The Battle Cry of Freedom: The Civil War Era.* New York: Oxford University Press, 1998.

McWhinney, Grady. *Braxton Bragg and Confederate Defeat.* Vol. 1. *Field Command.* New York: Columbia University Press, 1969.

Myres, Sandra L. *Westering Women and the Frontier Experience, 1800–1915.* Albuquerque: University of New Mexico Press, 1982.

Nathans, Elizabeth S. *Losing the Peace: Georgia Republicans and Reconstruction 1865–1871.* Baton Rouge: Louisiana State University Press, 1968.

Olson, Otto H., ed. *Reconstruction and Redemption in the South.* Baton Rouge: Louisiana State University Press, 1980.

Painter, Nell Irvin. *Exodusters: Black Migration to Kansas after Reconstruction.* New York: Knopf, 1976.

Perman, Michael. *The Road to Redemption: Southern Politics, 1869–1879.* Chapel Hill: University of North Carolina Press, 1984.

Rable, George C. *But There Was No Peace: The Role of Violence in the Politics of Reconstruction.* Athens: University of Georgia Press, 1984.

Richardson, Joe M. *Christian Reconstruction: The American Missionary Association and Southern Blacks, 1861–1890.* Athens: University of Georgia Press, 1986.

Roark, James L. *Masters without Slaves: Southern Planters in the Civil War.* New York: Norton, 1977.

Robinson, William M., Jr. *Justice in Grey: A History of the Judicial System of the Confederate States of America.* Cambridge: Harvard University Press, 1941.

Rogers, William Warren. *Thomas County 1865–1900.* Tallahassee: Florida State University, 1973.

Rogers, William Warren, Jr. *Black Belt Scalawag: Charles Hays and the Southern Republicans in the Era of Reconstruction.* Athens: University of Georgia Press, 1993.

Schott, Thomas E. *Alexander H. Stephens of Georgia: A Biography.* Baton Rouge: Louisiana State University Press, 1988.

Sefton, James E. *The United States Army and Reconstruction 1865–1867.* Baton Rouge: Louisiana State University Press, 1967.

Seip, Terry L. *The South Returns to Congress: Men, Economic Measures, and Intersectional Relationships, 1868–1879.* Baton Rouge: Louisiana State University Press, 1983.

Shadgett, Oliver Hall. *The Republican Party in Georgia from Reconstruction through 1900.* Athens: University of Georgia Press, 1964.

Shofner, Jerrell H. *Nor Is It Over Yet: Florida in the Era of Reconstruction, 1863–1877.* Gainesville: University of Florida Press, 1977.

Smith, Duane A. *Rocky Mountain Mining Camps: The Urban Frontier.* Bloomington: Indiana University Press, 1967.

Smith, James Russell. *Atlanta 1847–1890: City Building in the Old South and New.* Baton Rouge: Louisiana State University Press, 1988.

Smith, Phyllis. *A Look at Boulder: From Settlement to City.* Boulder: Pruett, 1981.

Stampp, Kenneth M. *The Era of Reconstruction 1865–1877.* New York: Knopf, 1972.

Taylor, Joe Gray. *Louisiana Reconstructed 1863–1877.* Baton Rouge: Louisiana State University Press, 1974.

Thomas, Francis T. *A Portrait of Historic Athens and Clarke County.* Athens: University of Georgia Press, 1992.

Thompson, Mildred C. *Reconstruction in Georgia: Economic, Social, Political, 1865–1872.* New York: Columbia University Press, 1915.

Thronateeska Chapter, Daughters of the American Revolution, comp. *History and Reminiscences of Dougherty County, Georgia.* Spartenburg, S.C.: Reprint Company, 1978.

Trelease, Allen W. *White Terror: The Ku Klux Klan Conspiracy and Southern Reconstruction.* New York: Harper and Row, 1971.

Tunnell, Ted. *Crucible of Reconstruction: War, Radicalism and Race in Louisiana 1862–1877.* Baton Rouge: Louisiana State University Press, 1984.

———. *Edge of the Sword: The Ordeal of Carpetbagger Marshall H. Twitchell in the Civil War and Reconstruction.* Baton Rouge: Louisiana State University Press, 2001.

Underwood, Kathleen. *Town Building on the Colorado Frontier.* Albuquerque: University of New Mexico Press, 1987.

Van Deusen, Glyndon G. *Horace Greeley: Nineteenth-Century Crusader.* Philadelphia: University of Pennsylvania Press, 1953.

West, Elliot. *The Saloon on the Rocky Mountain Frontier.* Lincoln: University of Nebraska Press, 1979.

Wiggins, Sarah Woolfolk. *The Scalawag in Alabama Politics, 1865–1881.* Tuscaloosa: University of Alabama Press, 1977.

Williford, William B. *Americus through the Years: The Story of a Georgia Town and Its People, 1832–1975.* Atlanta: Cherokee, 1975.

Works Progress Administration, comp. *Historical Background of Dougherty County 1836–1940.* Atlanta: Cherokee, 1981.

Articles

Abbott, Richard H. "Jason Clarke Swayze, Republican Editor in Reconstruction Georgia, 1867–1873." *Georgia Historical Quarterly* 79 (summer 1995), 337–66.

Alexander, Thomas. "Persistent Whiggery in the Confederate South 1860–1877." *Journal of Southern History* 27 (August 1961), 305–29.

Binning, F. Wayne. "The Tennessee Republicans in Decline, 1869–1876." Pt. 2. *Tennessee Historical Quarterly* 40 (spring 1981), 68–84.

Campbell, Randolph B. "George W. Whitmore: East Texas Unionist." *East Texas Historical Journal* 28 (1990), 17–36.

Donald, David H. "The Scalawag in Mississippi Reconstruction." *Journal of Southern History* 10 (November 1944), 447–60.

Fair, John D. "Nelson Tift: A Connecticut Yankee in King Cotton's Court." *Georgia Historical Quarterly* 88 (fall 2004), 338–74.

Formwalt, Lee W. "The Camilla Massacre of 1868: Racial Violence as Political Propaganda." *Georgia Historical Quarterly* 71 (fall 1987), 399–426.

Griffin, Richard W. "The Origins of the Industrial Revolution in Georgia: Cotton Textiles, 1810–1865." *Georgia Historical Quarterly* 42 (December 1958), 355–75.

———. "The Textile Industry in Greene County, Georgia, before 1860." *Georgia Historical Quarterly* 48 (March 1964), 81–84.

Matthews, John M. "Jefferson Franklin Long: The Public Career of Georgia's First Black Congressman." *Phylon* 42 (June 1981), 145–56.

O'Donovan, Susan. "Philip Joiner: Southwest Georgia Black Republican." *Journal of Southwest Georgia History* 4 (fall 1986), 56–71.

———. "The Journal of Nelson Tift 1835–36." *Journal of Southwest Georgia History* 3 (fall 1985), 64–100.

Perrigo, Lynn I. "Law and Order in Early Colorado Mining Camps." *Mississippi Valley Historical Review* 28 (June 1941), 41–62.

Roberts, Lucien E. "The Political Career of Joshua Hill, Georgia Unionist." *Georgia Historical Quarterly* 21 (March 1937), 50–72.

Rogers, William Warren, Jr. "'Death Has Been Busily at Work': Yellow Fever at Bainbridge in 1874." *Georgia Historical Quarterly* 84 (fall 2000), 410–33.

———. "'Not Reconstructed by a Long Ways Yet': Southwest Georgia's Disputed Congressional Election of 1870." *Georgia Historical Quarterly* 82 (summer 1998), 257–82.

———. "'Politics Absorbs Everything Else': A Reconstruction Referendum in Georgia. " *Southern Studies* 7 (winter 1996), l-19.

Ross, Earle D. "Horace Greeley and the South, 1865–1872." *South Atlantic Quarterly* 16 (October 1917), 324–38.

Smith, Charles H. "Some Recollections of Law and Lawyers of Other Days." In *Report of the Tenth Annual Meeting of the Georgia Bar Association Held at Rome, Ga., July 5, 6, 1893*. Atlanta: Franklin Printing, 1893.

Trelease, Allen W. "Who Were the Scalawags?" *Journal of Southern History* 29 (November 1963), 445–68.

Wynne, Lewis Nicholas, and Milly St. Julien. "The Camilla Race Riot and the Failure of Reconstruction in Georgia," *Journal of Southwest Georgia History* 5 (fall 1987), 15–37.

Theses and Dissertations

Bloom, Charles G. "The Georgia Election of April, 1868: A Re-examination of the Reconstruction Amendments, 1870–1874." Ph.D. diss., University of Texas, 1966.

Freeman, Henri H. "Some Aspects of Debtor Relief in Georgia during Reconstruction." Master's thesis, Emory University, 1951.

Hume, Richard L. "The 'Black and Tan' Constitutional Conventions of 1867–1869 in Ten Former Confederate States: A Study of Their Membership." Ph.D. diss., University of Washington, 1969.

Smith, Allen Chandler. "The Republican Party in Georgia 1867–1871. Master's thesis, Duke University, 1937.

Swinney, Everette. "Suppressing the Ku Klux Klan: The Enforcement of the Reconstruction Amendments, 1870–1874." Ph.D. diss., University of Texas, 1966.

INDEX

WILLIAM WARREN ROGERS JR. is a professor of history at Gainesville State College in Gainesville, Georgia. He is the author of *Black Belt Scalawag: Charles Hays and the Southern Republicans in the Era of Reconstruction* and *Confederate Home Front: Montgomery during the Civil War.*

The University of Illinois Press is a founding member of the Association of American University Presses.

Composed in 9.5/12.5 Trump Mediaeval at the University of Illinois Press Manufactured by Thomson-Shore, Inc.

University of Illinois Press
1325 South Oak Street
Champaign, IL 61820-6903
www.press.uillinois.edu